Applied Strategic Marketing

This book, originally published in Dutch, provides a uniquely practical approach to strategic marketing planning. Combining a comprehensive overview of theory with practice, each chapter takes the reader step by step through the strategic marketing process. Beginning with identifying the value proposition, it moves on to the situational analysis that underpins the corporate strategy, and finally details the overall implementation and creation of a customer and brand values. *Applied Strategic Marketing* equips the reader with the necessary tools and techniques to develop and deliver a thorough and effective marketing strategy.

With a broad range of international case studies that bring the theory to life, this well-renowned and updated translation is vital reading for undergraduate and postgraduate students of marketing management and strategic marketing. It should also be of interest to marketing practitioners who want a clear overview to aid them in the planning process.

Karel Jan Alsem is Professor of Marketing at the Hanze University of Applied Sciences in Groningen, The Netherlands. In addition, he is Assistant Professor of Marketing at the Faculty of Economics and Business at the University of Groningen, The Netherlands. He is also consultant in branding and health care marketing. His main research interests concern strategic brand management, marketing communications, and marketing planning. Alongside a number of books, he has published papers in journals such as the *International Journal of Research in Marketing*, *Applied Economics*, and the *Journal of Market Focused Management*.

Applied Strategic Marketing

A Step by Step Approach

Karel Jan Alsem

Routledge
Taylor & Francis Group

LONDON AND NEW YORK

Published in Dutch by Noordhoff Publishers, 1993, 2017

This edition published in English by Routledge, 2019
by Routledge
2 Park Square, Milton Park, Abingdon, Oxon, OX14 4RN

and by Routledge
52 Vanderbilt Avenue, New York, NY 10017

Routledge is an imprint of the Taylor & Francis Group, an informa business

First edition published by Noordhoff Publishers, 1993

British Library Cataloguing-in-Publication Data
A catalogue record for this book is available from the British Library

Library of Congress Cataloging-in-Publication Data
Names: Alsem, K. J., author.
Title: Applied strategic marketing : a step by step approach / Karel Jan Alsem.
Other titles: Strategische marketingplanning. English
Description: Abingdon, Oxon ; New York, NY : Routledge, 2019. | "Published in Dutch by Noordhoff Publishers, 1993, 2017." | Includes bibliographical references and index. |
Identifiers: LCCN 2018043038 (print) | LCCN 2018044147 (ebook) | ISBN 9780429823374 (ebook) | ISBN 9781138331907 (hardback : alk. paper) | ISBN 9781138332089 (pbk.)
Subjects: LCSH: Marketing--Management.
Classification: LCC HF5415.13 (ebook) | LCC HF5415.13 .A435313 2019 (print) | DDC 658.8/02--dc23
LC record available at https://lccn.loc.gov/2018043038

ISBN: 978-1-138-33190-7 (hbk)
ISBN: 978-1-138-33208-9 (pbk)
ISBN: 978-0-4298-2337-4 (ebk)

Typeset in Times New Roman by
Servis Filmsetting Ltd, Stockport, Cheshire

Visit the eResources: www.routledge.com/9781138331907

Contents

Part III: Corporate decisions and marketing decisions

Part IV: Implementation

Preface

This book describes the current thinking on strategic marketing from a how-to perspective. The theory of strategic marketing is presented in steps. Those steps can be followed to arrive at a strategic marketing plan. This book features a combination of five attributes that make it different from other marketing strategy books. First, it deals only with *strategic marketing*. Therefore, there are no separate chapters devoted to consumer behaviour, market research, or marketing instruments (the four Ps are included in two chapters). The second attribute is the *process approach*. The third attribute relates to what the author feels is important in marketing: customers and brands. A *customer and brand orientation* is followed throughout the book: in the analysis, in choosing options, in developing marketing strategy, and in implementation. The fourth attribute is that in many places in the book *strategic guidelines* are given: what to do and what not to do in marketing practice. Finally, there is much attention focused on *tools and techniques* that may be helpful in the planning process. In summary, this book combines an academic and applied approach of strategic marketing planning.

The book is primarily targeted at students with a basic knowledge of marketing. Thus, the relevant target groups are undergraduates in the third or fourth year and some MBAs. The book may be used in, for example, courses in marketing strategy or marketing management. The book may also be used in executive teaching, and by marketing practitioners who are looking for academic support for their daily decision making.

The book consists of four parts comprising 14 chapters, with each chapter being a step in the strategic marketing planning process.

Part I Introduction and marketing planning

1. The essence of marketing
2. The strategic marketing planning process

Part II Situation analysis

3. Mission, value strategies, and market definition
4. Internal analysis
5. Customer analysis

6. Industry analysis
7. Competitor analysis
8. Analysis of distributors and suppliers
9. SWOT analysis

Part III Corporate decisions and marketing decisions

10. Corporate objectives and corporate strategies
11. Marketing objectives and marketing strategies

Part IV Implementation

12. Product, price, place
13. Marketing communication
14. Organization and implementation of marketing

Throughout the text many examples are included, most of them in separate boxes, enabling readers to concentrate on the theory or the examples, or both. Each chapter ends with a summary and an illustrative international case with questions.

This book tries to reduce the gap between strategic marketing theory and marketing practice. The main message is that you should ask yourself continuously what effect your company's behaviour has on potential customers. For example, you might ask: How does my amusing commercial score on brand recall? Or: Do more brand extensions reduce or increase customers' confusion? Things like this have to do with the attitude of the manager and also with the way the planning process is done. Both aspects receive attention in this book. The content of the book is the result of continuously wondering whether strategic marketing issues are and should be applicable in marketing practice. However, there is no 'truth'. Science by definition is a matter of 'asking questions', and a field as young as marketing science is only at the beginning of the process of finding the 'truth'. It is my hope that the ideas in this book not only lead to better marketing decision making but also lead to the asking of better marketing questions.

I would greatly appreciate it if you, as my customer, make me part of your ongoing needs and perceptions with regard to this book.

Karel Jan Alsem
Hanze University of Applied Sciences, Groningen
July 2018

Acknowledgements

This book is an updated and revised version of its Dutch counterpart, which is now in its seventh edition. First, I thank my Dutch publisher Noordhoff for permitting me to undertake this international version.

Second, I owe many thanks to Erik Kostelijk for preparing the cases and questions. He has been my 'case partner' for many years, and I hope this will continue in the future. I thank my publisher Routledge for publishing the book. Finally, I thank my main co-brand Cato, and my sub-brands Tom, Sophie, Anne, and Floor for being inspiring and down-to-earth sparring partners in this current dynamic life.

Part I

Introduction and marketing planning

1. The essence of marketing
2. The strategic marketing planning process

This book was written to bridge the gap between the theory and practice of strategic marketing. Current marketing theory describes how a company (or a brand) can implement the strategic marketing planning process, and how strategic marketing decisions can be based on an analysis of the brand and the environment. Therefore, we will focus on the *activities* that must be carried out by a company within the framework of strategic marketing. These activities may be categorized as evaluation/retrospective, analysis, planning (strategy development), and implementation (execution).

The book is divided into four parts. Part I describes the basic assumptions of the book and the marketing planning process. Then, each step of this process will be described. Part II is dedicated to evaluation and situation analysis. The basic assumption here is that without a thorough, systematic situation analysis, the success of a strategy is more a matter of luck than of skill. Part III deals with the development of the strategy, with particular attention paid to brand positioning decisions. Part IV concerns the translation (e.g. into communication) and execution (implementation) of strategic decisions. The three main parts result in three parts of a marketing plan:

- a marketing report (insights as a result of the analysis, Part II)
- a strategic marketing plan (long-term decisions, Part III)
- a tactical marketing plan (the marketing instruments for one year, Part IV).

All marketing activities should be carried out with a single objective: to create value for the customer through a recognizable brand image. This objective (customer and brand) provides the basis for the description of the activities as well as practical advice.

This book may be used for the development of a marketing plan and also as a guidebook for re-examining a company's marketing policy.

Part I begins with an overview. Chapter 1 describes the essence of marketing and the role of a sustainable competitive advantage of a brand. Chapter 2 provides an outline of the entire strategic marketing planning process that a company can follow to develop a marketing plan. This process is the common thread running through the book.

Chapter 1

The essence of marketing

Key points in this chapter

- Outline what marketing is and describe how marketing developed.
- Introduce marketing (customer and brand) as the key to developing customers' relationship with a brand.
- Describe aggregation levels in organizations.
- Stress the importance of a sustainable competitive advantage.

Introduction

This book covers the concept of strategic marketing from the customer and brand perspective. It is done step by step, leading to a marketing plan for a brand. Following the route, the reader will be confronted with different theories and models, each of them contributing to the marketing plan. There are no sideways (i.e. chapters with interesting theories not directly being a step in the marketing planning process, such as a sideway about 'consumer behaviour').

In this introductory chapter, we first deal with the content of marketing itself. A reason for this is that there are many definitions of marketing and even some image problems with marketing. Often, marketing is confused with communication or sales. In section 1.1 we start by describing a number of trends ('landscape'), leading to a growing importance of marketing. Then, in section 1.2, we outline the content of marketing as we see it. We pay attention to the hierarchy in the marketing concept, as well as to developments in marketing.

1.1 The changing landscape of marketing

As we will point out in section 1.2, the essence of marketing is to act in a customer-oriented way from a clear brand identity. Marketing is one business discipline, next to, for example, finance, human resource management, and information and communication technology (ICT). All these disciplines operate in a volatile landscape. In this section, we discuss a number of developments/trends in the marketing landscape. Some of them affect the importance of marketing. Some of them (for example, the rise of social media) affect the contents of the marketing plan: the planned marketing actions for a company. In our view, however, the current marketing theory in itself, which in this book is limited to the contents of marketing and the manner of how marketing decisions are reached, is barely affected by these trends. So, we disagree with statements like 'the SWOT-analysis does not work anymore'. Or that 'branding is dead'. The essence of marketing does not need to change, but we should be flexible in handling how to implement it.

We will now discuss some trends directly affecting the importance of marketing and also the way of how marketing should be done. We will separately go into another important, global trend: climate change.

The following factors affect the importance and implementation of marketing.

1. *There is a growing supply of products and services.* Companies and customers are faced with an increasing amount of new products and services. Also, products are marketed using new varieties and with different brand names. Innovation is realized at an increasing rate of speed. For customers, this looks great: more choice (offline and online), so more possibilities to meet one's own specific needs. However, a lot of choice also leads to more stress because of the need to choose. Schwartz (2004) talks about the 'paradox of choice': people grow tired of the need to always make choices, whether they buy jeans, coffee in the supermarket, or coffee in the restaurant; there is an enormous supply, and routine decisions are becoming more complex.

2. *Communication leads to more communication.* This is what we call the communication spiral. Brands are doing their best to come into consumers' minds. As so many brands are doing this, it is becoming increasingly difficult to realize this. A natural reaction is to increase communication activities, etc.

3. *There is more information about brands available through the internet.* Not only is information from companies themselves available 'with one click', but also and especially consumers' own evaluations may be found on the internet. A well-known example is booking.com, where many reviews may be found about almost all hotels, houses, etc. Scores are given, enabling consumers to choose from a ranking. In addition, qualitative information is available about a consumer's own experience. In some countries, rankings are regularly published for some categories, such as about hospitals and universities. For universities there are several rankings, enabling managers to focus in their communications on those rankings where performance is best.

4. *New forms of competition and distribution are developed through the internet.* The internet enables the introduction of new intermediate stakeholders between consumers and suppliers. One example has already been mentioned: booking.com. But airbnb.com and uber.com are further examples of new online competition. These organizations are only using data and the internet in a smart way without offering new products or services themselves.

5. *Social media enlarge consumers' power.* The rise of social media empowers consumers. This is because social media are an extremely fast way of spreading 'word of mouth': in a few minutes many people can be informed about anything about a company, such as a mistake, failure in service, etc. The 'viral' spread of information

will even act faster if famous people participate, or if a journalist is involved who might use other media as well to spread the news.

6. *Governments in many countries are striving to accommodate market forces and to stimulate competition.* Even traditionally non-commercial organizations and markets, such as postal services, energy, and health care, are placing more emphasis on listening to the customer.

7. *Consumers are becoming more critical.* Due to some of the previous developments, consumers are becoming more independent, are learning more, and are presumably placing a higher value on transparency and sustainability.

The conclusion is that marketing is important for all companies and other organizations. They should listen very carefully to their customers (target groups) and also ensure that their activities are planned in accordance with the brand identity.

Sustainability

Worldwide agreement exists about the need for more sustainable behaviour. In 2017 the World Economic Forum mentioned climate change as the most important threat to global stability. Since 'Paris 2015' sustainability has strongly grown in importance. The year 2018 was the first in which a large city comprising a million people (Cape Town) experienced the risk of lack of water. Climate change, of course, is not a marketing problem. It is a broad, complex problem where many disciplines are involved. Nevertheless, one could wonder whether the need for sustainability should be part of marketing theory. Some authors believe that this is the case. Kotler and Keller (2016) argue that marketing should better acknowledge that a broader, more integrated perspective is often necessary. Therefore, they introduced the *holistic marketing concept*, which consists of four dimensions: relationship marketing, integrated marketing, internal marketing, and socially responsible marketing. Socially responsible marketing is critical of excessive consumerism and environmental damage caused by corporations. It is based on the idea that market offerings must not be only profit-driven, but they must also reinforce social and ethical values for the benefit of citizens. Sometimes the phrase 'purposeful marketing' is used to indicate that companies should incorporate social goals beyond making a profit. This terminology is a little confusing, since any company will have a purpose. For example, the purpose of a coffee retailer may be to provide the best coffee experience, while a social purpose may be to only buy coffee from local suppliers in a socially responsible way for a good price. In our view, being responsible is important but it is not part of marketing theory. Although marketing theory in itself does not need to change, we do agree with Kumar (2018) and other authors in a special issue of *Journal of Marketing* that the foregoing technological, environmental and other trends are so important that marketing implementation will strongly change. Kumar introduces the term '*transformative marketing*' for this.

1.2 What is marketing?

Marketing is often associated with 'advertising' or 'sales'. This is not the essence of marketing as we see it. In this section, we first show that marketing exists on three

Case 1.1 Marketing relevant for all organizations

One marketer on the value of bringing an 'FMCG mindset' to health care and utilities

Soviet politics and Eastern European studies don't exactly ring marketing bells, but you only need to take one glance at Belinda Moore's CV to see she's not one to follow the conventional path to the top. Instead, her career has been a never-ending quest for 'a blank sheet of paper' – a fresh challenge. Once found, Moore likes to make her mark, only to continue her search for the next blank sheet. Moore's CV screams variety, creativity, adventure, and endurance, having worked across numerous sectors from fast-moving consumer goods (FMCG) and health care to travel, and most recently utilities as the director of marketing and communications at energy brand E.ON.

"I enjoy starting things from scratch, challenging the status quo and really bringing that ability to make things happen to businesses," she says. Moore studied Soviet politics and Eastern European studies at the University of Sussex and, despite the course having "nothing to do with marketing", she says it was a "big driver" in her career direction. After graduating she set her sights on a job abroad, as she says there weren't many opportunities for her in London unless she wanted to work in diplomatic services or become a teacher. "I didn't even know what marketing was, all I knew was that I was interested in people and how things worked," Moore says.

Source: *Marketing Week*, 5 June 2018

Case 1.2 The importance of sustainability

Unilever's sustainable brands grow best

The most sustainable brands of Unilever grow 46 per cent more than the rest of the company. They represent 70 per cent of the growth in turnover. This is in line with the mission of CEO Paul Polman, who wants to show that sustainability and growth in turnover can be combined. All Unilever brands should lower environmental pressure but the 26 sustainable living brands score best. The biggest of these brands are Dove, Lipton, Dirt is Good, Rexona, Hellmann's, and Knorr. More than 40,000 employees of Unilever are involved in making sustainable plans at Unilever.

Source: *Financial Daily* (Financieel Dagblad), 18 May 2018

levels within an organization (1.2.1). Next, we outline the developments in marketing up until the beginning of the twenty-first century (1.2.2). We then discuss developments in marketing after the year 2000: the role of brand identity (section 1.2.3) and certain other developments (1.2.4). Section 1.2.5 describes the activities relevant for marketing, which are the focus of this book.

1.2.1 Hierarchy in marketing

Marketing can be interpreted in different ways (Webster, 1992, 2005):

- As an *organizational culture* (the marketing concept or marketing paradigm): a set of values and beliefs that drives the organization to make a fundamental commitment to serving customers' needs as the path to sustained profitability. Later in this chapter, we argue that the brand identity should also be part of the marketing concept.
- As a *strategy*: defining target markets and positioning product offerings.

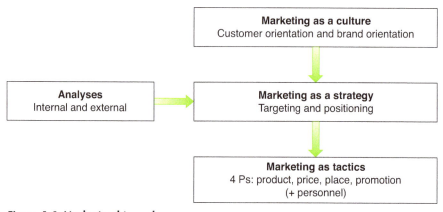

Figure 1.1 Marketing hierarchy

- As for *tactics*: the day-to-day activities of the four marketing instruments: product development, pricing, distribution, and communication. Sometimes, personnel is also added as a fifth P.

We realize that defining the 4 P's as 'tactics' (short term decisions for example for a year) is somewhat ambiguous. We agree with Varadarajan (2010) that many 4 P-decisions are also strategic in nature. For educational purposes we think Figure 1.1 is very helpful. The three meanings of marketing have been interpreted as a hierarchy in marketing theory. The top level (the marketing concept or marketing paradigm) defines the core content of market-ing. It stresses the main issues in marketing in general and provides a rough indication of what is important at the lower level: marketing strategy. The marketing strategy (targeting and positioning) is chosen using the results of an internal and external analysis. Marketing strategy should give a direction to the lowest level: marketing tactics (Figure 1.1).

Marketing strategy deals with segmenting, targeting, and brand positioning, raising the question of how to compete (Adcock, 2000). The issue of branding is discussed increasingly in the context of marketing strategy (Aaker, 1991, 1995; Keller, 2013), and also in wider-ranging marketing textbooks (Kotler and Keller, 2016). Clear choices about the target group and brand positioning impose boundaries on a company's choice of the appropriate marketing mix (relationship with the lowest level).

However, the relationship between the marketing concept and marketing strategy is somewhat ambiguous. The marketing concept focuses on the customer (the demand side), whereas marketing strategy mostly attempts to create a balance between the demand side (the customer) and the supply side (the brand identity) of the market. Therefore, the marketing concept should be updated by adding branding to the paradigm. Before describing our view of the marketing concept, we discuss developments in the marketing concept through the years.

1.2.2 Development of the marketing concept before 2000

In the first edition of his textbook, Kotler (1967) introduced the concept that companies must be both customer- and market-driven. In an influential paper, Day and Wensley

(1983) introduced the so-called *strategic marketing concept*. That concept is, in fact, an expansion of the 'classic' marketing concept, which indicates that a company should use the wishes and desires of its customers as the basis for its actions, otherwise known as a 'customer orientation'. The strategic marketing concept states that a company should pay attention to:

- Customers (as in the classic marketing concept).
- Competitors (not just to be better but also perhaps to collaborate).
- Long-term relationships (including developing products for which there is a latent need and thus a potential demand).
- Other interest groups inside and outside the organization (such as distributors, employees, suppliers, financiers). Recently, Hillebrand et al. (2015) introduced the name *stakeholder marketing* to stress the importance of multiple stakeholders.

These issues largely correspond to what is called 'market orientation' (Kohli and Jaworski, 1990). Market orientation consists of three components:

1. *A customer-oriented philosophy* (*customer orientation*) would focus on the following questions: Does the company make reasonable promises, and is it able to keep those promises? Are customers treated as individuals? Is market research used concretely to determine the wishes and opinions of the target audience? If so, does that lead to actionable objectives for the company?
2. *A competitor-oriented philosophy* (*competitor orientation*). Here a company asks: Do we have a lot of information about individual competitors? Is that information analysed systematically and distributed throughout the organization? Does the company know when it should respond to actions of competitors and how it can differentiate itself from competitors? What are sustainable competitive advantages given the marketplace?
3. *Interfunctional coordination* (*integrated decision making*). It is important to realize whether the information is shared within the company. Are the strategies for various functional areas integrated? Are joint decisions made? Is the whole organization truly interested in its customers?

Over the years, the critical elements of the strategic marketing concept have shifted. In the 1980s, strong emphasis was placed on a competitor orientation. In the 1990s, another component of the strategic marketing concept moved to centre stage: the development of long-term relationships, especially with customers. In this context, the focus is no longer on one-time transaction-oriented marketing but rather on relationship marketing (Gummesson, 1987, 1999; Webster, 1992). Relationship marketing focuses on obtaining and sustaining a structural, direct relationship between a supplier and the customer. In this context of relations, Morgan and Hunt (1994) theoretically and empirically show that *trust* is a key factor in relationship commitment. Due to the need to create direct (one-to-one) relationships, the use of databases increased. Therefore, relationship-based marketing is sometimes called *direct marketing* or *database marketing*.

In the 2000s the shift continued, with increased attention given to customer value and services. Customer value is the value that users derive from products. In theory, this is the user benefit derived from product attributes minus the price and the effort made to obtain a product. In practice, customer value is determined by measuring not only customers' perceptions of product attributes but also their benefits as well as the goals they hope to attain by using a product (Woodruff, 1997). The difference from the relationship philosophy of the 1990s is that at that time it was stated that companies should always strive for direct relationships as the way to provide customer value. Now the theory suggests that customers can receive customer value in various ways. In this context, Treacy and Wiersema (1993) name three value strategies that may be summarized as customer leadership (*customer intimacy*), *product leadership,* and leadership in terms of convenience or price (*operational excellence*). Providing customer value is an important but insufficient condition for achieving customer loyalty. In addition, bonding and familiarity are necessary.

Later, Vargo and Lusch (2004) argue that marketing is focused on services. In their view, marketers focus too much on products. Goods (tangible resources) are only distribution mechanisms for service provision. Put differently, companies should focus on value creation, on solving the 'problems' of their customers. In building relationships with customers, intangible assets such as knowledge about customers and customer-friendly methods of dealing with complaints are highly relevant as well. These intangible competencies are embedded in the people working in a company. Only if all the people in a company are really interested in customers can that company really build relationships (Gummesson, 1998). Thus, the service perspective of marketing is closely related to the relationship orientation (Ravald and Grönroos, 1996).

It could be argued that the focus on customer value in effect represents a revival of the classic marketing philosophy. After all, the point of departure for classic marketing is that customers' wishes must be satisfied. This is essentially no different from stating that value must be provided to customers. This line of reasoning may be 'not wrong'. The most important factor here is that although fulfilling customers' wishes has been a basic principle of marketing for a long time, actual marketing practice appears to have lost track of customer satisfaction. There are many examples of situations in which customers are annoyed (e.g. telephone sales whether or not done under the guise of research), dissatisfied (user-unfriendliness of personal computers and cameras), and unhappy with a bad settlement of complaints. Fournier and associates argue that it is important to avoid "the premature death of relationship marketing" (Fournier et al., 1998). A central assumption of marketing should be that it leads to win-win situations, both for the supplier and the customer. In essence, the emphasis on customer relationships may be translated into an increasing need to provide the customer with real 'value' (Webster, 1992). Suppliers should strive primarily for customer loyalty: maintaining their most profitable customers. By contrast, in classic marketing, suppliers focused more on attempting to recruit new customers (Reicheld, 1993, 1996). Figure 1.2 summarizes developments in the marketing history.

1.2.3 Developments in marketing after 2000: the role of brand identity

In summary, the marketing concept focuses on the demand side of the market: customers. But both from a practical as well as a theoretical perspective it may be argued that this focus is too narrow. In practice, for example, it is noticeable that consumers are often not able to come up with ideas for innovation, simply because they cannot imagine what new products can be made. So, ideas for innovation should often come from the company.

Period	Marketing	Emphasis on
Until circa 1980	Classic marketing	Customer needs
1980–1990	Strategic marketing	Customer needs Competitive advantages Long-term
1990–2000	Relationship marketing	Direct relationship with customers Customer value and customer loyalty Offering services

Figure 1.2 **Developments in the marketing concept up until 2000**

On the other hand, it might be that customers ask more than a company wants to deliver, because a company will also have its own ideas about their portfolio. This has to do with the brand identity of the company. The issue of branding is strongly related to the resource-based view of the firm (Wernerfelt, 1984) and to the focus on core competencies (Prahalad and Hamel, 1990). These approaches suggest that the source of superior performance is the possession and development of distinctive and hard-to-imitate resources. This corresponds to the competitive advantage approach by Porter (1980). The resource approach appears to be supply-oriented, whereas the marketing concept is by definition demand-oriented. The question is how these two can or should be combined. Some authors argue that being too market-oriented can be disastrous (Day, 1999) because customers may demand products or services that do not fit in with the core business of the firm. This is also true of branding: customers may demand benefits that do not match the brand identity. Hooley and colleagues (1998, 2004) suggest combining marketing and the resource-based view of the firm in what they refer to as resource-based marketing. In this approach, firms base their marketing strategies on an equal consideration of the requirements of the market and their ability to serve the market.

So, it is increasingly recognized that listening to the customer is not 'everything', but this realization does not seem to affect current thinking about the marketing concept. This is the theoretical part of our discussion about the contents of marketing. In terms of the hierarchical meanings of marketing, if nothing is said in the marketing concept, nothing about resources or branding, applying the marketing concept leads to the unbalanced guideline of strongly following customers' needs. Thus, the marketing concept can be augmented by stating that organizations should focus both on the customer and on *building a strong brand (or reputation)* (Figure 1.3): delivering customer value and building brand equity. Alsem and Kostelijk (2008) introduced this renewed marketing concept under the title 'identity-based marketing'; however, it should be viewed as 'normal' marketing.

A manager should find a balance between the customer approach and the brand approach when selecting the company's positioning. In practice, it may be noted that there are inadequacies on both sides of Figure 1.3. Because companies often reason too much on the basis of the supply perspective:

▪ Too little attention is paid to the customer: Does the customer really want this?
▪ Too little attention is paid to the brand personality: Are we making real choices and are we consistent in time? Without a choice, a brand will not be

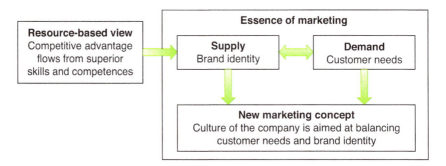

Figure 1.3 **Marketing as a balance between customer and brand**

recognized. Thus, the starting point of positioning should be a certain degree of specialization.

In the remainder of this book, both customer-oriented philosophy and brand-oriented philosophy will assume a central place.

The needs of the customer and the identity of the brand are not fixed constructs. They affect each other, so there are dynamics (Figure 1.4). First, the brand identity affects the needs of the customer, since consumers cannot always think of innovations themselves and have to learn from innovations created by companies. This is clearly visible with electronics: market research in the 1990s showed that there was no need for mobile phones. Now, a mobile phone is a basic need for everyone. On the other hand, companies can change their core competencies if they realize that the future requires this change. A company like Kodak seemed to adjust to new techniques too slowly. Philips adjusted much better by focusing on health care innovations and by selling even the product line from the start of Philips: lighting.

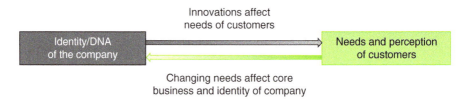

Figure 1.4 **Identity and needs**

1.2.4 Other developments in marketing

We now focus on some other developments in marketing:

- Big data and social media.
- The role of emotion
- Studies of Sharp.

Big data and social media

'Big data' means 'a lot of data'. This term has become very popular since the rise of social media. Because of the immense use of social media, a huge amount of data has become available, which is very interesting for marketers to analyse and for companies to use in their targeting. In fact, due to our own intensive online and social media behaviour, companies know a lot about our behaviour and are increasingly using these data to reach us with targeted messages. Since big data and social and other online media are becoming much more important for companies, there is a growing demand for people who can handle data for marketing purposes (for example, when dealing with social media and search engine optimization, i.e. optimizing a website in such a way that it will come higher up in Google results; see also Chapter 13).

Although handling data is very important in marketing, the marketing theory in itself will not change. The way research can be done will be affected by big data, as well as the way of, for example, targeting consumers online, which also leads to ethical questions in marketing.

The relevance of the unconsciousness and emotion

Economic science has had the central assumption for many years that people are rational. A consumer makes rational decisions, for example, by collecting information about alternatives, comparing them, making a choice and then buying. However, recent studies in psychology and economics show that a human being is actually more driven by emotion and unconscious decisions than by conscious, rational decision processes. In economics, a Nobel prize was even awarded to experts in 'behavioural economics', a stream within economic science dealing explicitly with the emotional consumer. Many psychological experiments show that people should, for example, not take too much time to make a decision, since the outcome can be worse. A famous experiment was one where people had to choose a large painting for a wall. One group had limited time, and the other group had much more time. One year later, the satisfaction of the first group was higher than that of the second group. For marketers, this means that brands should present themselves in a broad way and also that all signals should be consistent with brand identity.

Studies of Sharp

In a number of well-known publications, Byron Sharp of London Business School presents the results of a number of studies using large datasets about the buying behaviour of consumers (Sharp, 2010; Romaniuk and Sharp, 2015). The main conclusion from these studies is that the level of brand awareness is by far the most important factor determining the level of sales of a brand. Information about, for example, product quality and the brand's positioning more generally looks less important. Sharp shows, for example, that brands which in the view of customers are almost the same compete at a much lower level than expected. The size of the brand is much more important. Not only is the mental availability of a brand important, but also its physical availability.

An explanation of Sharp's findings could be that many consumers have a low involvement in buying products. They simply do not want to spend much time searching for the best brand. Consumers more or less choose the brand they know, or the brand they are just confronted with, in communication or in the shop. An example is Heineken. The awareness of this brand is probably up to 100 per cent in many countries. However, one could wonder how 'unique' Heineken's positioning is. The company ran a large number of different brand campaigns and perhaps many consumers do not have specific associations with the brand, other than 'beer'. But Heineken is a market leader. Should the taste be the reason for Heineken's success? Although Heineken would probably hope that it is, it is probably not the reason, simply because research shows that when doing a blind taste experiment with beer, consumers rarely point out their preferred brand as having the best taste. So it is about branding. Heineken is a very well-known brand, the brand gives a kind of good feeling, the taste is OK, and that is enough for a low-involved consumer making emotional, unconscious decisions to buy this brand.

This explanation also shows that emotional brand loyalty is probably low. That is indeed what Sharp shows. People have a kind of behavioural loyalty ('I normally buy Heineken'), but if another brand has an interesting discount 'I might also buy another brand'.

Although the findings of Sharp are in some sense logical, his results are the subject of an academic dispute. In a winning paper, Pauwels and Ewijk (2013) show that ('soft') attitudinal measures as well as ('hard') online behaviour tracking data are a good prediction of sales. So, brand image does matter. In addition, Hanssens (2015) shows that the mean advertising elasticity is only about 0.1, which does not suggest that strong media pressure affects sales.

Our conclusion from the 'relevance-of-image' debate is that both brand awareness and brand image are important.

1.2.5 Marketing as a set of activities

We introduced marketing as a concept, strategy, and tactics. Resulting from these three levels, a number of activities are required. To make strategic marketing as applied as possible it is helpful to categorize what these activities enhance. Following Kotler and Keller (2016), marketing activities can be divided into four parts: analysis, planning, implementation, and control. Examples of these activities are market research (analysis), decisions regarding positioning and communication (planning), execution of a campaign (implementation), and evaluation of results (control). We will focus in more detail on the activities of strategic marketing, employing the four-part division for this purpose.

Analysis within the framework of strategic marketing refers to analysing potential customers (e.g. through market research), competitors, distribution structures and the suppliers, the industry structure and the macro environment (e.g. demographic developments), and internal factors as the company and the company's brand (see also Varadarajan, 2010).

We interpret *planning activities* within the framework of strategic marketing as all decisions that are made as well as the documentation of those decisions in plans. In conducting planning activities, a company should be able to answer the following questions (Adcock, 2000):

1. *Where (and when) to compete?* This refers to the choice of markets, positions, and periods.
2. *How to compete?* This refers to the choice of a sustainable competitive advantage, including positioning, target audience definition and segmentation, and determination of the objectives regarding the use of marketing mix elements.

For example, the strategic marketing of a furniture manufacturer should focus on the following questions:

1. Where to compete?
   - In which markets do we want to be active in the future (cupboards, couches, tables, or for final customers, offices, other companies, etc.)?
   - Which positions do we want to achieve in those markets within how many years?
   - How much money should we invest in the various markets?
2. How to compete?
   - Which competitive advantages should we strive to achieve (quality, cheapness, etc.)?
   - To which segments should we orient ourselves?
   - What are we striving for with the use of marketing mix elements?

These decisions show that strategic *marketing* planning is a very important component of strategic management. The choice of *markets* in which to be active is an extremely important decision for a company and therefore is at the heart of the corporate strategy. Proposals for and information ('analysis') about these decisions are provided by the functional area of marketing. In addition, it is clear that the components of strategic marketing mentioned above have implications for other functional areas. The sphere of activity of strategic marketing, therefore, cannot be separated from that of other functional areas. On the contrary: developments in society (described in section 1.1) are so complex that increasingly interdisciplinary cooperation is needed to tackle the challenges we face. Figure 1.5 shows the main relations between marketing and other functional areas ('disciplines') in an organization.

The relation between marketing and R&D is innovation. R&D (including information and communication technology (ICT)) is an important source for new ideas and new

Figure 1.5 **Marketing and other functions in an organization**

products. Customers are not always able to think of new products, so the starting point of innovations may be the company itself. An inspiration for innovation can come from marketing, for example, by sharing results of market research focusing on problems consumers encounter in using products.

The relation between marketing and human resource management is, of course, the P of personnel. Two related issues are important. Internal branding means that all employees should behave in the line of the positioning of the organization (Foster et al., 2010). The concept of 'part-time marketers' is introduced by Gummesson (1991) and entails all employees being customer-oriented. Thus, a customer that comes into contact with the organization will have an optimal experience throughout the whole 'journey'.

One relation between marketing and finance/accounting is that marketing should be able to show its results: How accountable is marketing? In marketing science, much attention is devoted to developing methods to show the results of marketing. There are also journals focusing on these relations, such as the *Journal of Accounting and Marketing*. Van Helden and Alsem (2016) recommend that marketing performance is measured using multiple metrics beyond financial measures.

There is a logical relation between the three interdisciplinary issues: innovation is a logical start of many marketing plans; in the implementation it is important to involve the employees; and finally, the effects of marketing should be measured. The conclusion is that at different stages of the marketing planning process, different relations between marketing and other functional areas are relevant.

Examples of activities relating to the *implementation* (execution) of these strategic marketing decisions are negotiating with top management about budgets (although this often takes place during the planning phase), motivating and managing the company's personnel, and involving and briefing the advertising agency.

In the framework of strategic marketing, *control* refers to items such as an analysis of the sales data and financial data, an evaluation of the results against objectives, and a check of the implementation of the decisions that were made.

All these activities are part of the strategic marketing planning process.

Summarizing, we can define marketing as a set of activities as follows: *marketing is choosing – based on an analysis of the market and the own organization – a distinctive offer of products and services that offer value to chosen target groups/ stakeholders, and to sell the products/services by means of brand-related choices of price, channels, and communication, supported by a brand-related behaviour of the employees.*

Summary

Several global developments make marketing increasingly important for organizations. The essence of marketing is to link customer needs to the brands' identity. Marketers should first conduct a thorough analysis of the market and the company, and then come to focused targeting and positioning decisions. In line with marketing strategy, the four Ps are implemented: product/service, price, place, and promotion. In addition, the P of personnel is strongly related to marketing: all employees should be customer-oriented and strengthen the brands' identity. Marketing is not only related to human resource management. Innovations may be developed together with R&D

and ICT. Marketing should also be financially driven in realizing measurable results. Recent developments such as online communication and social media, as well as global challenge number one, climate change and sustainability, strongly affect the marketing decisions which companies make. The essence of marketing theory itself has barely changed.

Case Fender: will the engine of rock continue to rock?

For decades, the style and the sound of the Fender Stratocaster had a strong influence on rock 'n' roll. But the American guitar company is facing an uncertain future. Because of the developments in music, electronics are increasingly replacing the guitar.

In 1948, radio repairman Leo Fender took a piece of wood, screwed another piece of wood to it and added an electric system. You have heard the rest of the story, even if you do not know it. You've heard it in the guitar riffs of Buddy Holly, Jimi Hendrix, George Harrison, Keith Richards, Eric Clapton, Pete Townsend, Bruce Springsteen, Mark Knopfler, Kurt Cobain, and so on. It is the sound of the electric Fender guitar.

The Fender company, in full, Fender Musical Instruments, is the world's largest manufacturer of guitars. The Stratocaster, which came on the market in 1954, is still one of the most-sold guitars. The cutting sound of the Strat stands for everything that is rock 'n' roll. But in 2018 the heart of rock is no longer beating as it once did.

A Stratocaster is expensive; it is just not one of the first necessities of life for most people. But Fender suffers from more than its price alone. The company is also plagued by the powerful guys that make the money move on Wall Street. In 2012, almost half of Fender was in the hands of the venture capitalist Weston Presidio, who wanted to sell his share for a nice price. The economy was in bad shape, and he hoped to get some of his investment back. However, the initial public offering (IPO) went no further: investors were not convinced by the possibilities that the Fender brand could offer. After the withdrawal of the public offering,

Weston Presidio sold its stock to the private equity arm of Hawaiian automotive retailer Servco Pacific, which in turn sold a portion of its stake to San Francisco's TPG Growth. With all these changes in ownership, the company experienced a rough ride and is trying to look for some stability now.

In the past years, Fender has made some ballsy moves. First, Fender made the move to let customers order direct from their website. In 2015, Fender launched a division called Fender Digital to focus on apps, websites, platforms, and tools. The company debuted Mod Shop, an online customization site where customers can design their own colourful guitar or bass. While the digital move is currently only limited to 'custom-configurable' guitars, it probably still left a bad taste in the mouths of many of the company's dealers. Then, in 2016, the company released Fender Tune, a free app that helps players tune their guitars. It is the first in what is to be a line of teaching devices which the company plans to launch over the next years, according to CEO Andy Mooney.

But even now, with the currently booming economy, uncertainty about the future is what makes life hard for Fender. Times have changed. In the 1950s, 1960s, and 1970s, guitars were the engine behind all developments in pop and rock music. And the real rock 'n' roll enthusiast still wants this. However, these enthusiasts are fewer and fewer. For most musicians, even the average enthusiast, the guitars of that time have been replaced by electric turntables, drum computers, and synthesizers. Hip-hoppers and rappers do not need a guitar to hit the charts.

The guitars that are still sold are those from the lower segment. The instruments are made in China and cost a fraction of the more than €1,200 that you will quickly spend on a Fender 'Eric Clapton' Stratocaster. But with such a cheap guitar you can also 'make a nice piece of music'. Fender has already outsourced part of its production to low-wage countries and, like many other guitar builders, is building simple guitars. But the profit margins on those instruments are much lower than on the show-pieces of the past.

The American Guitar Center, the largest musical instrument store in the world, is also experiencing difficult times. According to analysts, the Guitar Center is crucial for Fender. No fewer than one-sixth of the guitars that Fender sells is purchased at that instrument store.

One of the big problems that Fender has to deal with, ironically enough, is Fender itself. When Fender first released its classic Stratocaster and Telecaster guitars in the 1950s, it became one of the first electric guitar manufacturers in the United States. Since then, the company has developed a reputation for high quality among professional musicians. The guitars that were produced in the 1960s and 1970s are much more beloved than the instruments that the company produces nowadays. Whether it is true or not, musicians have the idea that the classic Fenders have a different, more beautiful sound and are qualitatively better than the guitars that are produced nowadays. Modern techniques might make the sound of new instruments more perfect than ever, but it is the imperfections that create the classic sounds so much loved by real musicians.

Take Rick Barrio Dill. He is the bassist for the soul and rock band Vintage Trouble and went crazy when his specially made Fender Reissue Precision bass guitar was stolen while he was on tour with the Cranberries. "I felt like someone had just died; I was a complete wreck", says Dill. He reported the theft via Twitter. Before he knew it he got a message from Gibson Guitars, the big rival of Fender. The company offered him a new guitar. Dill rejected the offer. But he grabbed with both hands a similar bid that Fender made him shortly after. "Fender is flowing through my veins", says Dill. The guitarist also collects vintage Fenders. In 1999 he bought a Tobacco Sunburst Fender Jazz Bass from 1969 for €900. Four years later he sold the instrument for €2,000. "Now I try to find one again and I have to pay at least €5,000 for it."

How to proceed is the big question for Fender. One of the shareholders of the company said: "I love Fender. It is the most beautiful company in the world. We are in it for the long term and we will do what is right for Fender." But whether the right thing is the old-fashioned guitar, the internet, or even guitar education, is a question that still remains unanswered.

Questions

1. Which trends affect the Fender brand?
2. The book discusses a hierarchy in marketing. Illustrate this marketing hierarchy for Fender.
3. Discuss whether the strategic marketing concept can be used by Fender.
4. Illustrate the resource-based view by using the information about Fender in this case.
5. Identity marketing tries to find a balance between customer needs on the one hand and brand identity on the other. Show how this 'tension' between supply and demand is relevant for Fender.
6. Give some strategic marketing advice for Fender, based on the information in this case.

Chapter 2

The strategic marketing planning process

Key points in this chapter:

- To know different levels in a company and the content of strategy at these levels.
- To know the essence of the marketing strategy.
- To know the different steps in the marketing planning process.

Introduction

As was explained in the previous chapter, marketing is important for every organization. We also argued that marketing is a strategic discipline where the marketing strategy, targeting, and positioning are the most crucial decisions. But how can an organization do their marketing? In this chapter we will outline the different steps that should be taken. The remainder of the book goes through each of these steps.

2.1 Levels within a company

There are companies that limit their activities to a single market; for example, a car manufacturer that produces small cars for one target audience. Many smaller or startup companies also focus on a single market. However, many companies are active in *more than one market*. For example, Sara Lee/DE is active in various consumer markets, such as food and luxury foods, and personal care items. However, even a small company such as a local restaurant can serve several markets, for example, room rental, catering, and local dinners. To achieve clarity in the marketing planning process about what should be analysed and what should be decided upon, it is important to understand the levels within a company. Three levels may be distinguished (see Figure 2.1):

1. The company (or corporate) level.
2. The division and strategic business unit (SBU) level.
3. The product and marketing mix instrument level.

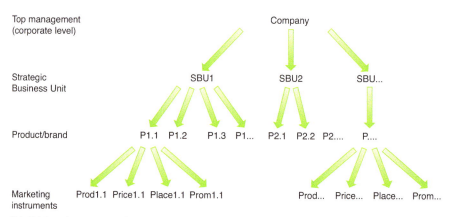

Note: This figure does not represent the way marketing should be organized within a company; see also Chapter 14

Figure 2.1 Aggregation levels in a company

2.1.1 The company level

The company level is the 'top' level. This level relates to the company as a whole. All the different products which a company puts out on the various markets are collectively designated as the *product mix* or the *assortment*. For example, the product mix of Sara Lee/DE includes coffee, tea, beverage systems (warm and cold drinks for industrial customers), food, and rolling tobacco and pipe tobacco as well as items for the household and for personal care.

2.1.2 The division level and strategic business unit level

A division is a somewhat autonomously operating unit within a company. A division may include several *product groups*. A product group (also called a product line, a product category, or simply a category) contains a group of related products. Examples of product groups are appetizers, internal transport, consultancy, foot care products, and men's clothing. In practice, a product group is often used for market definition; for example, the market for health insurance. Although the product group is only one of three dimensions in a market definition (the other two are customer groups and functions; see Chapter 3), product groups often correspond to markets. This book therefore makes this connection regularly.

A strategic business unit (also called a strategic product group) is concentrated on a single product group (and therefore usually on one market). Many companies employ SBUs. AKZO is one example. In that company all activities are classified into various business units to which sufficient authority has been delegated to allow for a fast and decisive response to market developments. At AKZO the various business units are grouped into five divisions. Another company where divisions and SBUs do not coincide is Sara Lee/DE. This company consists of two divisions, namely food and luxury foods, as well as household and personal care products. The division for food and luxury foods includes activities in the following markets: coffee, tea, beverage systems, nuts and snacks, rice, rolling tobacco, and pipe tobacco. Although there is often a difference between the division level and the SBU level, in the remainder of this book we do not distinguish between these levels because a division level may be regarded as a company level but one step lower. In practice, divisions are often smaller companies within a large company. Therefore, everything that is stated below about company objectives and strategies may be applied to division objectives and strategies. For example, company strategy often determines which financial resources are available for SBUs. If a division level exists between the company level and the SBU level, the division strategy determines the resource allocation for the SBUs.

For a company active in just one market, the company level and the SBU level coincide and the assortment is restricted to one product group.

2.1.3 The product level and marketing mix level

A product is an item (good or service) offered in a market. A product may be aimed at different target audiences. A combination of a product and a target audience is usually called a *product–market combination*. Sometimes different *varieties* of a product are presented in a market; for example, there may be differences in sizes or packets and flavours. A company often brings individual products into the market and supports them through the use of marketing mix elements. Typically, four categories of marketing mix elements are distinguished: product (composition, packaging), price, distribution (place), and sales promotion (e.g. advertising). Because marketing mix elements are applied to products, the marketing mix level corresponds to the product level.

2.1.4 The position of the brand

A brand is a word, name, symbol, letter, or picture (or a combination of these elements) used by a company to distinguish its products from those of the competition. The brand is the bearer of a reputation or image. From the perspective of the provider, a brand is also the manifest identity the product must embody.

At which levels do brands play a role? The most obvious is the product level. A product is almost always offered under a brand name. Examples of products are Pampers diapers, ABN/AMRO student bank accounts, and Nespresso coffee makers. The brand designation has been associated with products for many years. Brand names at the product level are most visible in the consumable goods market: every product has its own brand name. However, this is an understatement of the importance of brands. Brand names play a role not only at the product level but also at all three levels in the company. Indeed, large conglomerates such as Procter & Gamble rarely promote the name of the company to the consumer, but P&G is still a brand in the labour and financial markets. Brands are also found at the intermediary division level. The manufacturers Van den Bergh Nederland and Iglo/Ola are also brands.

Sometimes brand names in the service and durable consumer goods markets are the same as company names (e.g. Philips, Ford). We will take a closer look at brands and brand levels in Chapter 11.

2.2 The core of marketing strategy

It is important to make a distinction here between:

- The corporate (or company) strategy (section 2.2.1).
- The marketing strategy (section 2.2.2).

2.2.1 Corporate strategy: direction of growth and value strategy

At each of the levels mentioned above, decisions are made and strategies outlined. The content of the decisions is different at the different levels. Thus, the chairperson of the board of directors (corporate or company level) does not spend time on advertising decisions (product level). Similarly, a product manager of a brand of margarine (product level) does not spend time deciding to invest more in diaper sales; that is a concern of upper management (company level).

A clear connection can be made between the strategic marketing mentioned in Chapter 1 and the levels described in section 2.1. This connection is summarized in Figure 2.2.

The two main questions that must be answered at each level are:

- *Where are we going to compete? In which markets, with which products, when, and to what extent?*
- *How are we going to compete? How are we different from competitors, what is our competitive edge?*

The elaboration of both questions depends on the level.

At the company level, the question "Where will the company compete?" entails the following. The management of the company or division spends time on the establishment of the desired positions (such as desired growth) of product groups and brands. This must be done in such a way that the desired company targets (such as a certain amount of growth in turnover) can be attained with all products collectively. Growth can be achieved:

- With existing products and brands or with new ones.
- With existing customers and target groups or with new ones.

Level	Where to compete	How to compete (choice of competitive edge)	Other
Company strategy	Determine composition and desired positions of product groups and brands (directions of growth)	Choice of value strategy	Choice of partners (with whom)
Marketing strategy	Specify target groups	Brand positioning	
Market instrument strategies		Elaboration of positioning	

Figure 2.2 **Types of strategies and levels**

The deadlines for reaching the targets are also a matter with which upper management is concerned. Upper management must also determine the available resources in terms of the desired targets for the various brands. Ambitious plans take a lot of money.

In practice, the selection of targets and investments is not a one-sided top-down affair. Target projections and budgets at lower levels result from negotiations between upper management and lower management. Product or brand managers must try to sell their ambitious plans to upper management. A convincing plan attracts more money.

At the company level, the question 'How will we compete?' is related to the choice of a value strategy. Does the company want to promote itself to customers on the basis of leadership in quality and innovations, efficiency and low prices, or the building of a relationship?

The company strategy also determines whether the company wants to grow on its own or with the help of others ('with whom?': cooperation, acquisition, merger).

2.2.2 Marketing strategy: target group and positioning

A distinction can be made between the *where* and the *how* at the level of the marketing strategy as well. The *where* question involves a more detailed description of the target group. The *how* question involves the distinguishing power or the competitive edge. What reason would a customer have to purchase this company's brand instead of another brand? Ideally, that competitive edge should be defendable as well.

The concept of a *sustainable competitive advantage* has become a central tenet in the literature on competitor analysis and competitive strategies since the start of the 1980s (see e.g. Porter, 1980). Simply put, sustainable competitive advantage means that a company:

- Is good at something (has a strength).
- Has something that its competitors do not have and that would be difficult for them to acquire (sustainable).
- And that strength is important to customers.

So, three stakeholders (three Cs) are most important in realizing a sustainable competitive advantage:

- The company: the company or the brand.
- The customers.
- The competitors.

Companies which have that kind of an advantage are able to achieve the best financial results in the industry. The efforts of each company should therefore be focused on achieving a sustainable competitive advantage with its products.

This definition shows that there is an important difference between a company's strength and a sustainable competitive advantage. Not all strengths lead to a sustainable competitive advantage. This happens only when two conditions have been met (see Figure 2.3):

1. The competitors do not have that particular strength: it is therefore a *relative* strength.
2. The strength is relevant: it is important to customers.

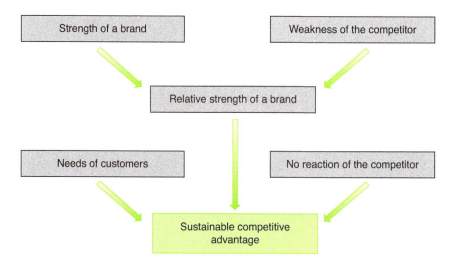

Figure 2.3 **Sustainable competitive advantage**

Therefore, a company may be good at something, but if it is not relevant to the company's customers that the company has this strength or if the competitors have the same strength, this does not yield any benefits. An example is the safety of airline companies. Because almost every airline company is safe (this is an absolute necessity), safety is not a sustainable competitive advantage. Thus, if a company has a particular strength, it is imperative to check whether its competitors have the same strength (this is determined in the competitor analysis), and subsequently the strength should be converted to an advantage for customers, for example, through better quality or a lower price. In addition, this advantage needs to be communicated (e.g. through advertising) to customers. An example of this is the quality of safety for cars. In the car industry safety can be a sustainable competitive advantage because not all cars are equally safe. There are clear differences which, not surprisingly, are emphasized by companies such as Volvo (Case 2.1).

A company should consider whether a competitive advantage is sustainable over the longer term. A company with, for example, a technological lead that can easily be imitated will probably lose that advantage relatively quickly. If the competition is able to employ an even better technology (*leap-frogging*), the original advantage can even turn into a disadvantage. In practice, the sustainability of competitive advantages is the biggest challenge. Almost every advantage can be and is quickly imitated. Research also shows that followers can sometimes achieve larger market shares than innovators (Kerin et al., 1992; Bowman and Gatignon, 1996). Pioneers should therefore take a flexible position and also attempt to learn from the experiences of followers (Christen, 2000). To gain insight into the sustainability of its competitive advantage, a company may attempt to predict what the competition will do in the future. This is one of the objectives of competitor analysis.

The idea of a defendable competitive edge is closely linked to the concept of positioning. Positioning means determining the position of a brand in relation to the products of the competition in the minds of consumers: What image or associations does a company

Case 2.1 Sustainable competitive advantage

Volvo is safety

Although all cars are pretty safe, there are differences. Since its start in 1927, the whole company of Volvo has focused on safety. In 1959 Volvo invented the three-point belt and nowadays every car is equipped with this feature. Many other safety inventions also come from Volvo, such as airbags. This example shows that it is difficult to sustain an advantage. Through continuous focus on innovation in safety Volvo continues as the safest car brand.

want to attach to the brand? Ries and Trout (1981) describe positioning as the battle for the customer's mind. Positioning entails selecting the brand associations that:

- Are relevant to buyers.
- Are unique to the brand.

If a brand successfully communicates the desired associations in such a way that the brand associations:

- are strongly anchored with the target group,

the three most important requirements for a successful brand have been met (Keller, 2013): strong, relevant, and unique. In addition, a brand should have a high awareness (Figure 2.4).

In Figure 2.4 we make a distinction between *'mind share'* and *'heart share'*. This is a reflection of the fact that brands have both a functional/informative part as well as a more emotional part in that a brand also has a personality and may meet people's values. This means that brands appeal to the minds as well as to the hearts of customers. The

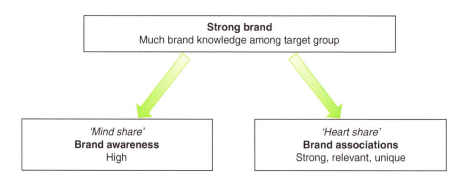

Figure 2.4 **Strong brand**

awareness of a brand is especially related to the minds of customers, since this is about 'having heard of the brand'. The associations people have with the brand may lead to a more emotional bond with the brand.

Good positioning requires profound knowledge of the psychology of the customer. Another important requirement for positioning is the willingness to choose foci for goal-oriented positioning. A broad choice is no choice at all, as is often said. The search process often comes down to choosing a single word with which a brand can distinguish itself. The choice of that word is difficult, essential, and subtle. It is difficult because general attributes such as quality, young, dynamic, and reliable typically do not distinguish a brand. A lot of brands want to be these things. It is also difficult because companies are often unwilling to choose; after all, if you have a single central message, "so many other good things are left unsaid". It is essential because this is the central choice in brand identity; that identity will be the basis of everything else. It is subtle because it requires a lot of creativity and empathy for the consumer and other parties in the environment to come up with the 'right' word.

The concept of positioning is sometimes applied only with respect to communication. In this case, it's mainly about the slogan or "what interesting things we're going to say in the campaign this year". But brand positioning is a lot more than that. It is the focal point of all the activities related to the brand: production, personnel, purchasing, all marketing instruments, and so on. After all, positioning is a promise to the client, and promises must be kept. This can be done only if everything has been set up to ensure its success. It starts with the people who pick up the telephone, and it ends with the customer's level of satisfaction with the product. Thus, brand positioning serves not only an external function (a promise to the customer) but also an internal function (for the employees). The communication of the brand positioning to internal target groups is called *internal branding* (see also Chapter 14).

The concept of positioning is not significantly different from concepts such as desired reputation, identity, vision, and competitive edge. Since brands exist at different levels within a company, positioning also exists at different levels: at the company and product levels. At the company level, this concerns the reputation of the company, or 'corporate identity', also known as 'reputation'. Philips' brand name is the same as that of most of its product names, and so the company identity is the same as that of all Philips products.

2.3 The strategic marketing planning process

2.3.1 The importance of an environmental analysis

If a manager has a problem, there are two ways to arrive at a solution (see Figure 2.5): to provide a little support quickly or to provide proper support more slowly. The first method is sometimes quite successful; a manager does not have to be an analyst to achieve success. In this book, however, we operate under the assumption that the probability for success is greater with better support. This 'better support' lies in making use of a good system and good tools based on marketing theory and more and better knowledge, because all the parties in the environment of the company are analysed. The explicit formulation of alternatives is also a part of the better (more scientific) approach to practical management problems.

A more scientific approach to a marketing problem does not mean that the result will be less practical. A more holistic approach is needed for the final choice of a solution; this includes creativity, innovation, and a feel for the market. The 'input' for this comes from doing one's homework. The way in which a company should go about doing its homework and subsequently translating it into targets and strategies makes up the content of the strategic marketing planning process. We will describe the overall setup of the process and then go into further detail about the parts of the process.

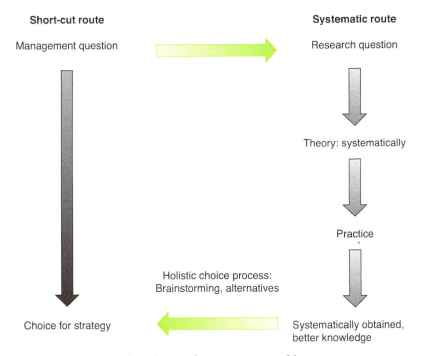

Figure 2.5 Approaches to the solution of management problems

Case 2.2 Evidence-based marketing

We need evidence-based marketing to save us from the fads and fashions

Medicine is all about being 'evidence based'. Doctors will base their decisions on evidence-based knowledge and on a thorough analysis of the patient. And that is normal. Now try this exercise: replace the word 'medicine' with the word 'marketing' and 'doctors' with 'marketers', and you have an uncanny reflection of what is happening in our industry today.

The sad fact is that even we marketers, the supposed experts in positioning, branding, and communication, have become suckers for the sales patter of Google, Facebook, and various industry 'gurus'. Instead of spotting hucksterism for what it is, our bias towards the new and the novel stymies us. In fact, we love new and exciting things even when they are vastly inferior to old ideas. Snapchat strategies versus television campaigns, anyone? I am not alone. Only in the past few weeks, I met representatives of an international airline who believed that their core customer base was millennials, whereas the analysis showed that few people under the age of 40 flew with them. So, what to do? Let's start with some simple basics: don't fall into the traps that various vendors and slick agencies tell us. Stop the nonsense such as 'Facebook marketing', 'inbound marketing', 'content marketing' – these are fake names invented to brand something that has been around for years.

Remember: it is essential to adopt the practices and mindset of evidence-based marketing. Why? So then we can see the forest, the trees, and everything in between. Let's make it even easier and have this as our mantra: tools change, tactics occasionally change, strategies can change, but marketing principles never change.

Source: Colin Lewis, *Marketing Week*, 9 May 2018

2.3.2 Overview of the process

In marketing literature, various authors (e.g. Kerin et al., 1990; Ferrell and Hartline, 2010; Aaker, 2013) outline the different steps a company may take to arrive at a strategy. Different authors use different ways to develop this process. Figure 2.6 indicates the steps that in our opinion a company should take in the planning process. We will now clarify Figure 2.6, first globally and then in more detail. The various steps will be elaborated further in the following chapters.

The global organization of the process is as follows: a combination of an *external analysis* (analysis of the environment) and an *internal analysis* (analysis of the company and the brand) forms the basis for the formulation of objectives and strategies. The goal of the external analysis is to provide insight into the *opportunities* and *threats* that may be expected. The most important goal of the internal analysis is to determine the company's *strengths* and *weaknesses*. The combination of strengths, weaknesses, opportunities, and threats (SWOT) forms the input for the phase in which a strategy is chosen.

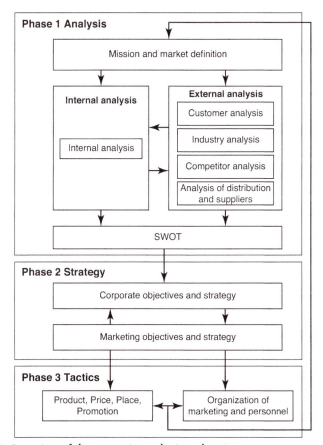

Figure 2.6 Overview of the strategic marketing planning process

Situation analysis (Part II)

The situation analysis starts with a definition of the market and the current activities, including the company's vision and mission, and an evaluation of the results achieved so far. This first step usually provides a reasonable impression of potential problems (problem identification). The next step is to follow the various phases from the external analysis (predominantly at the SBU level and the product level) and the internal analysis (at all levels). These two components together form the *situation analysis*. Various authors prefer different sequences of phases in the situation analysis. We start with the internal analysis because we can ascribe the evaluation of the results to it. We basically consider the strengths and weaknesses of the company and the brand as preconditions for the development of the strategy. After all, financial attributes, management culture, company mission, and so on cannot be changed overnight. This is also the case for the competition and organizational analysis in the external analysis. These factors must also be regarded as preconditions.

This does not apply to the most important target group: the customer. Marketing serves as an excellent method for 'learning' target groups. In principle, the customer can be easily influenced. Since in both theory and practice a lot of attention is paid to achieving value for the customer, the external analysis should start with an analysis of the customer. Insight into the wishes, satisfaction, and perceptions of customers and non-customers (individual or otherwise) must be obtained continuously. This customer analysis is the source of a variety of information during other phases of the analysis. Subsequently, the other components of the external analysis are dealt with: an overview of the whole industry, followed by specific analyses of the competitors, distributors (or other intermediaries), and suppliers. Finally, a separate phase SWOT occurs in which the results from the internal and external analyses are linked to one another. The first blocks are the analytical component of the planning process.

Strategy: decisions at the company level and the marketing level (Part III)

After the analytical component, company objectives and strategies are chosen; these elements primarily answer questions dealing with where and when the company will compete. Because the analyses are often performed for SBUs (markets) and a company is often active in several markets, various situation analyses will form the basis for the company strategy.

If a new market is chosen, a new analysis should be performed. Subsequently, the marketing objectives and marketing strategies are chosen; the focus in this case is on sales goals as well as decisions about target audiences and brands. These decisions mainly determine 'how the company will compete'.

Tactics and implementation (Part IV)

The marketing strategy determines the choice of marketing mix elements. This is the marketing tactic, and it may be considered the marketing implementation.

Once the decisions have been documented in a marketing plan, the implementation is carried out. At this point, the organization of marketing and communication is also relevant. A manager should also pay sufficient attention to the employees. Without proper internal management, a good implementation is impossible.

2.3.3 Description of the phases

Strategic marketing and marketing plan (this chapter)

The marketing plan reflects the results of the strategic marketing planning process (analyses and decisions) and documents all the action steps for the coming year. This plan can serve later as a guideline for the evaluation of the results. It also fulfils a communicative role: everyone in the company can read in the plan the direction the company wants to take and how it intends to achieve its chosen objectives. At the end of this chapter we include a layout of a marketing plan.

After the implementation of the strategies, an evaluation should take place: Have the objectives been achieved, and if not, what are the causes of this failure? This evaluation marks a new phase in the planning process. Therefore, in Figure 2.6 a feedback loop has been included from the last planning step back to the first steps (market definition and evaluation of results). The process outlined above should not just be completed only periodically (e.g. once a year); instead, there should be a continuous internal and external analysis as well as an evaluation of objectives and strategies. The dynamic nature of the environment makes it too risky to treat planning as a merely periodic activity.

This book describes the different phases of the strategic marketing planning process. In doing so, we attempt to depict an ideal version of that process. The framework outlined here is in principle applicable to any company that is active in a particular market and is faced with competitors and customers. Such companies include producers of non-durable consumer goods (e.g. producers of food products) and service providers (e.g. banks). The framework may also be used by companies that are active in industrial markets (e.g. engineering offices); in that case, the customers consist of other companies. In addition, components of the process may be applicable to non-profit organizations (e.g. Greenpeace, hospitals).

However, it would be an illusion to think that each company could or even should follow this process. Organizations and markets differ so substantially that some of the steps in the planning process may be less important for certain companies or may be followed in a different sequence.

Mission, value strategies, and market definition (Chapter 3)

There can be no situation analysis of a brand and a market until we form a picture of what the situation is: What are the market boundaries? For example, without an identification of market boundaries the market share cannot be calculated. Is Coca-Cola active in the soft drink market or the cola market? This will have a strong influence on the size of the market share as well as the amount of competition. To determine this, we must examine the mission of the company. Typically, this is what statements on the market are based on. This should be considered a precondition for the development of a marketing strategy.

From the positioning perspective (the core of the marketing strategy), it is also important to know which value strategy the company is following. The brand positioning should not be in conflict with that strategy.

Finally, the current product–market combinations are brought into view and the market boundaries are specifically defined in terms of customer needs. At this point it is a matter of defining the current market: the market we are active in at the moment. (What business are we in?)

Internal analysis (Chapter 4)

The internal analysis starts with the question 'What have the results been thus far?' This is the 'control': an evaluation of the results achieved. The desired results must be analysed. These are the targets. Chapter 4 begins with a brief explanation of targets. The results of the strategy (and targets) may be measured as profit, sales, market share, and so forth; the choice of the unit of measurement depends on the way in which the targets were formulated. In addition to financial criteria, we look at customer-oriented standards such as customer satisfaction (the concept of the balanced scorecard will be discussed). This step provides an initial impression of where problems may lie. This analysis is carried out in as much detail as possible; that is, not only on the product and instrument levels but also within those levels where possible, according to regions, customer groups (segments), varieties, and retailers. Then internal factors that are important for developing a new strategy are examined. For this purpose, the strengths and weaknesses of the company, the SBU, the product, and the marketing mix elements are determined. In this process, the perspective of the target audience is assumed as much as possible. The strengths and weaknesses are compared with those of competitors. If the strengths can be translated into added value of the products for customers, they provide a clue to sustainable competitive advantages (see Figure 2.3). If they threaten to create strategic problems, the weakness should be improved. This can be accomplished through internal improvement or through collaboration with competitors.

Chapters 5 to 8 discuss the external analysis.

Customer analysis (Chapter 5)

The central assumption of this book is that the policy of a company should focus on creating optimal value for the customer. Maintaining a continuous 'feeling' for the target audience is therefore essential. A good customer analysis (which includes potential customers) will provide that connection. More specific objectives for the customer analysis are to obtain insight into customers' attributes (Who are the customers? Can we distinguish separate segments? Which customers are the most profitable?), needs (the importance of concrete and abstract product attributes), and perceptions (How do they perceive the company's product and its competitors?). As already mentioned, big data make a lot of information available. The customer analysis is implemented for an entire market (SBU level) as well as for individual segments and products (product level). The customer analysis also serves as a source of data for other phases in the situation analysis, and because of that it is the core of the situation analysis. Therefore, there are straight lines to the competitor analysis (identification of competitors and determinants of success as well as the strengths and weaknesses of competitors), the distribution analysis (the brand's position at the retailer), the industry analysis (expected market growth), and the internal analysis (strengths and weaknesses of the brand).

Industry analysis (Chapter 6)

After the customer analysis, the focus moves from 'macro' to 'micro': first an analysis of the whole industry and then a closer look at several interest groups within it, including competitors, distributors, and suppliers. A goal of the industry analysis is to identify potential opportunities and threats, especially from the macro environment. Another goal is to obtain an understanding of the attractiveness of the market. For that purpose, items such as the industry structure are analysed. The attractiveness of the market has a strong impact on the objectives and investments that are determined for each SBU.

Three categories of factors are analysed in the industry analysis:

1. Macro environment factors, such as social-cultural and political developments.
2. Aggregated market factors, for example, market size and market growth.
3. Factors relating to industry structure, such as the intensity of the competition and the power of distributors.

Because it is especially important to gain insight into the *future* attractiveness of the market, this should include attempts at *forecasting*. In light of the uncertainty in the external environment of a company, it is advisable to define *scenarios* in this step, for example, scenarios regarding factors in the macro environment such as the economic situation. The analysis of industry structure takes place primarily at the SBU level, and it is done for the whole market. In addition, a company may research the attractiveness of specific segments.

Competitor analysis (Chapter 7)

The goal of *competitor analysis* is to obtain insight into the likely future behaviour as well as the strengths and weaknesses of the most important competitors of the company. The future behaviour of competitors provides an understanding of potential opportunities and threats. A company should be familiar with the strengths and weaknesses of its competitors so that it can identify its own *relative* strengths and weaknesses (see Figure 2.3). A competitor analysis can be performed at all levels. At the product level, the most important competitors are the suppliers that focus on the same target audience as the company. The competitor analysis receives input at several points from the customer analysis (identification of competitors and their strengths and weaknesses).

Analysis of distribution and suppliers (Chapter 8)

After an analysis of the customers and competitors, the other parties (interest groups) in the industry are critically analysed. As was indicated earlier in the discussion of the strategic marketing concept, because of their growing power, distributors constitute an increasingly important interest group for manufacturers. It is becoming increasingly important to enter into partnerships with distributors, whether or not they are supported by systems such as *category management* (joint 'management' of product groups).

A distribution analysis takes place at three levels. At the macro level, the focus is on the distribution structure; at the meso level, on the distribution of power within a single group of distributors, such as retailers; and at the micro level, on the behaviour of individual distributors. At this stage, information from the customer analysis about purchasing behaviour at and satisfaction with retailers may be integrated.

Suppliers are a final interest group that merit further analysis. A good relationship with suppliers means that purchasing can occur more efficiently and effectively.

SWOT analysis (Chapter 9)

The SWOT analysis is the link between various analyses and the strategy phases. First, it is important to consider the different possibilities for the value strategy. Next, we brainstorm ideas for the marketing strategy on the basis of a selection of strengths, weaknesses, opportunities, and threats. In this process, 'facts' are creatively translated into 'ideas'. The SWOT analysis eventually produces a few different directions (options). Finally, the product manager comes to a decision about the desired strategy by dealing with the options with a number of selection criteria and preconditions. It is important to realize that, from this phase on, creativity and innovation are important. A strategy cannot be 'computed' or 'derived' from the insights in the SWOT analysis. So, in this book we will not introduce 'weighting systems' or other 'objective' methods to arrive at a strategic choice. The SWOT is the base and forms an inspiration for strategy development.

Corporate objectives and corporate strategies (Chapter 10)

A first step in this analysis is a re-evaluation of the company mission: Should the business of the company be modified? Subsequently, the objectives of the company are determined. The methodology of the portfolio analysis also provides a connection between the internal and external environments. A portfolio analysis compares the expected incoming and outgoing cash flows of different SBUs or brands. The results of this comparison are used to decide which SBUs or brands to invest more in and which to invest less in. The third step is choosing the corporate strategy. The corporate strategy embraces the choice and position of business units and brands. The fourth component is the competitive growth strategy: Does the company want to achieve growth:

- Through its own development; that is, a *position-strengthening strategy*? and/or
- Through a *competition-decreasing strategy*: through collaboration with competitors, takeover or merger with competitors (horizontal integration), or integration with suppliers or distributors (vertical integration)?

All three components of the company strategy commit both resources and people for a longer term and are therefore typically not changed significantly from year to year. Generally, these changes will be a matter of modification. We also emphasize here the interaction with marketing plans: the company decisions will receive input from the direction of the SBUs. Therefore, a feedback loop is included from the next planning step in the planning process (Figure 2.6).

Marketing objectives and strategies (Chapter 11)

After the formulation of company decisions, the objectives and strategies are chosen for marketing. The marketing objective is deduced from the SBU strategy. Marketing objectives are formulated per product; for example, growth of the market share of product Y to 34 per cent in one year.

The marketing strategy includes the choice of the target audience (including segmentation) and the desired positioning of the brand. The marketing strategy forms the link between the company strategy and the decisions regarding marketing mix elements; therefore, this strategy is crucial. Without an explicit formulation of the marketing strategy, the use of the various elements of the marketing mix is aimless. The positioning of a brand is part of the value strategy of the SBU. The specific choice of the brand identity is a multi-year process that needs to be carried out on a long-term and consistent basis.

Objectives and strategies for marketing mix elements (Chapters 12 and 13)

Subsequently, the marketing strategy is translated into marketing tactics: decisions relating to the elements of the marketing mix (the four Ps): product, price, place (distribution), and promotion (marketing communication). However, in the case of the marketing mix element 'product', an important part of the strategic decisions has already been determined through the development of both the company strategy and the marketing strategy (such as brand decisions). In light of the great importance of promotion in brand positioning, a relatively large amount of attention is paid to the communication planning process.

Implementation and human resource management (Chapter 14)

Finally, plans have to be converted into actions: the implementation. In many companies it is precisely in the implementation that things go wrong. It is important for the organization to adapt to the customer: to bring the customer in-house by using customer managers. All communication should be geared towards identity and preferably directed by a 'reputation manager'. During implementation, it is important to provide support and guidance to the employees. Some useful tools are leadership, a clear vision, and employee incentives based on customer targets. There are a few planning tips at the end of the book.

2.3.4 Characteristics of the planning process

In the previous section the contents of the marketing planning process are described. We will now deal with two characteristics of this process:

- The importance of analytics and creativity.
- The breadth of the process.

Analytics and creativity

Analytical thinking is mostly convergent in its nature. The homework has to lead to solutions. Creativity will require divergent thinking: thinking outside of the box. Looking at the planning process, the first part is clearly analytical, but subsequently the SWOT creativity is more important. First, in coming to a positioning that fits the brand, and later also in the tactical part where especially communication (both offline and online) demands creative solutions to beat competition. Actually throughout the whole planning process the marketer should look for the 'good news' and the 'pearls', since these should be used especially in communication.

Breadth of the process

Regarding the breadth of the process, it is important in the analytical part not to be too focused, since all internal and external issues can be important. Of course one has to limit the analysis to a specific market and brand; otherwise any analysis will be impossible. But in this analysis, one has to take into account also issues outside the current market, in order to have inspiration for new activities. But after the SWOT a different mindset is required. First, the SWOT should be reduced to a limited number of relevant issues. Next, the core brand values and the positioning have to be chosen. For this decision, focusing is very important. A clear message is a focused message. Trying to tell everything about the brand is telling nothing. Distinctiveness can only be realized with a focused proposition.

After this, the planning process will widen, since the chosen message should be communicated strongly within and outside the company. Actually, some kind of 'exaggeration' is needed to reach the customer's mind. The need for a strong mental but also physical availability of a brand is supported by the research of Sharp (2010).

This leads to an hourglass way of depicting the marketing planning process (Figure 2.7).

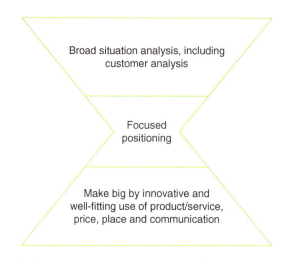

Figure 2.7 **The marketing planning process as an hourglass**

2.4 Structure of a marketing plan

Figure 2.8 contains an overview of the components of a marketing plan. The various components largely parallel the structure of the strategic marketing planning process. It should be noted that the development of a marketing plan does not include company objectives or company strategies. A marketing plan is essentially developed for a single brand.

Component	Number of pages
1. Executive summary	1–2
2. Introduction and background	2–3

- Company mission, company objectives, and SBU objectives
- Market definition and product or brand background
- Evaluation of results and conclusion about problem

3. Situation analysis	6–10

- Internal analysis
- Customer analysis
- Industry analysis
- Competitor analysis
- Distribution analysis

4. SWOT analysis	2–3

- Key issues (SWOTS), vision on environment, core problem
- Value strategy
- Marketing strategy options with choice of option

5. Marketing objectives/expected results	1
6. Marketing strategy	2–4

- Target audiences
- Brand or product positioning
- Brand architecture and design

7. Decisions regarding marketing mix elements ('marketing programmes')	6–10

- Communication plan
- Other marketing mix elements

8. Financial indicators and budgets	1–2
9. Evaluation criteria	1
10. Attachments	10+

- Any further market data and information about past marketing activities
- Any clarifications for the situation analysis
- Scenario analysis and 'contingency plans'
- Timetable and schedule of activities
- References

Figure 2.8 **Contents of a marketing plan for a product or brand**

Source: Based on Dibb et al. (2003).

1 Executive summary

The summary enables top management to review the core points of the plan quickly. The summary includes the most important conclusions from the SWOT analysis, the goals included in the plan, the chosen strategies, and financial expectations. In the summary the *arguments* supporting the chosen strategy are very important. The summary should be short and relatively succinct.

2 Introduction and background

This part serves as general introduction to the marketing plan and a framework for decision making. The following components are included.

The first item is a description of the company mission and the company objectives as well as SBU objectives. It may be assumed that these objectives are considered an established fact for the product or brand. Subsequently, the market that is specifically applicable to the particular product is defined according to the dimensions discussed in Chapter 3. Without this definition it is not clear what the plan refers to. At this point it is also an option to describe the results of the identification of the competition (the first step in competitor analysis). The advantage of doing this is that it provides an idea of the market at the beginning of the marketing plan. Some background information about the product or brand is also included. After all, not every reader of the marketing plan will be familiar to the situation to which the marketing plan refers. Finally, a summary conclusion regarding the basic problem is provided. This forms the starting point for the plan. Therefore, it is included at the beginning. In the actual planning process, the conclusion regarding the basic problem is dealt with at a later stage (see section 9.4).

Any available time series of various relevant variables (such as market shares and advertising expenses) may be attached as a 'product fact book'.

3 Situation analysis

The situation analysis is reviewed extensively in this book. Forecasts and/or planning assumptions for variables for the various components may also be included. This involves prognoses of variables such as macro-environmental factors, market data, and competitor behaviour. For variables for which no prognoses were made, the assumptions about future development should be provided. These assumptions (like the objectives) should be defined as specifically as possible. For example: the assumptions for the next year are:

- Economic growth of 2 per cent.
- Inflation of 4 per cent.
- No reaction from competitor G will follow.
- No increase in excise duty will occur.
- Costs of raw materials will remain constant.
- Market demand will grow 5 per cent.

The explicit description of assumptions is very important for the process of choosing objectives and for the later evaluation of the results (in the internal analysis). If the predicted results are not achieved, this may have been caused by an assumption that was not met; for example, a competitor showed a reaction while it was expected that he would not react. In such a case an alternative strategy should be chosen (this is described in part 10 of the marketing plan).

In practice, the competitor analysis and the industry analysis are often described together.

4 SWOT analysis

The SWOT analysis forms a summarizing description of the situation analysis and provides a starting point for strategies.

5 Marketing objectives/expected results

The results that need to be achieved in terms of sales, turnover, and market share are an important reason why a particular strategy is chosen. Objectives are often formulated for several years; for example, for a three-year period.

6 Marketing strategy

A brief indication of the marketing strategy is not sufficient here. Elements such as target audience personality, brand personality, and type of positioning should be described in detail. The line of reasoning that supports the choice of a particular strategy should also be described.

7 Decisions regarding marketing instruments

The plans should be translated in detail into *concrete programmes of action for the upcoming year* (*year plans*). In this context, four questions should be answered: *What* exactly is going to happen? *When* will it happen? *Who* will do it? *How much* will it cost? A detailed development and assignment of responsibilities is important for a successful implementation.

8 Financial indicators and budgets

Financial understanding is a very important component of the marketing plan. In this part the following financial indicators are described:

- The required budgets: budgets for sales promotion, sales expenses, research, product development, and so forth.
- The predicted expenses, revenues, cash flow, and profit; these predictions have been used at an earlier stage during the analysis of shareholder value.

This part is very important for top management, providing it with insight into the required investments and the extent to which the plan will contribute to the financial objectives of the company. The financial part therefore becomes the starting point for the negotiations between the manager who submits the plan and top management. To gain a perspective on the *risks*, top management will always judge the 'financial picture' in relation to the assumptions. Although an expected high profit is attractive, if there is great uncertainty about this assumption, it becomes an important minus. Top management will also attempt to estimate the pay-off time, which is determined by issues such as the point when a profit will start to be made. If this point is too far in the future, the plan will not be considered very attractive.

9 Evaluation criteria

To allow an evaluation of whether the plan will be able to meet its targeted goals during the course of a year, two subjects should be elaborated in this part. First, the objectives and budgets must be translated (differentiated) into regions, varieties, distribution channels, and periods within the year (for example, for each month or for each quarter). Next, the information that is needed for progress control should be indicated. In other words, the company needs to know which criteria will be used for the control and how they will be measured. These criteria depend on the objectives. Suppose the company wants to gain a market share of 5 per cent in one year with the introduction of new brand X (marketing objective). This objective is translated as follows. On 1 April a share of 2 per cent needs to have been achieved; on 1 July, 3 per cent; on 1 October, 4 per cent; and on 31 December, the full 5 per cent. Progress control occurs through Nielsen data.

10 Attachments

Especially in a strongly dynamic environment, it is advisable to have alternative strategies in case something unexpected (a contingency) occurs, such as the introduction of a competing product. These unexpected events may already have been analysed in the scenario analysis. A 'contingency plan' may be based on a strategy that was considered earlier but dropped. An attachment could describe which option should be chosen in which scenario. In addition, it should be indicated as specifically as possible *when* a particular scenario becomes relevant; for example, "when sales are more than 10 per cent below the objectives" or "when the weighted distribution does not exceed 70 per cent".

For easy reference and for monitoring afterwards, it is important to include in the attachment time schedules with planned activities. For convenience, this could involve the use of a time frame.

Summary

Three levels play a role within a company: the entire company (upper management), strategic business units (product groups), and products. Brands play a role at every level. In addition to customer satisfaction, brand reputation is important in achieving customer loyalty. The brand positioning (desired brand associations) should be a balance between customer desires and the unique strengths of the brand. It is important to be willing to make a choice. Basically, the essence of marketing is that choices for customer values are made both at the company level (value strategy) and at the brand level (positioning), a kind of specialization. To make the most effective marketing decisions it is best to use a systematic approach to knowledge acquisition. This book discusses the strategic marketing planning process. Starting from the chosen market definition, a situation analysis is performed: an internal analysis, including the evaluation of results and an external analysis (customers, industry, competitors, distributors, and suppliers). The results are summarized in a SWOT analysis, after which objectives, strategies, and a marketing plan are formulated. Finally, the plan needs to be implemented. Monitoring the implementation and the results occurs through interim measurements. The evaluation results provide the input for a new planning process.

Marketing planning starts broad (situation analysis), then focuses (brand positioning), and then gets broad again (enlarge your message). A marketer should have analytical as well as creative skills.

Case experience: Disneyland Resort Paris

Disneyland Resort Paris is part of The Walt Disney Company. The park opened in 1992. Since then the park has become the largest theme park in Europe. During the record year of 2012, 16 million people visited the famous amusement park. In that year, Disneyland Paris celebrated its twentieth anniversary. This twentieth anniversary, with new attractions and major renovations of the parks and hotels, and close media attention, contributed to the high number of visitors. This proved difficult to surpass the following year. In the years after 2012, partly due to the poor economic situation, the number of visitors gradually decreased. However, this decline seems to have halted: the number of visitors increased by 600,000 people in 2015 to a total of 14.8 million people.

Eurodisney is becoming less and less dependent on French visitors alone. According to Disney, the company's new pricing policy – fewer promotions, discounts, and last-minutes – is the reason that the number of French visitors has fallen in recent years.

Partly due to the increase in the number of visitors, the company's turnover increased by 7 per cent in 2015 to €1.37 billion. However, this increase was also caused by visitors spending more money during their visit to Eurodisney: the average guest spending in parks has been increasing in recent years. According to Eurodisney, this increase is caused by continuous investments in 'customer experience'. These investments fit in well with the mission of The Walt Disney Company:

> The mission of The Walt Disney Company is to be one of the world's leading producers and providers of entertainment and information. Using our portfolio

of brands to differentiate our content, services and consumer products, we seek to develop the most creative, innovative and profitable entertainment experiences and related products in the world.

The Walt Disney Company is an international company that specializes in family entertainment. The company consists of five elements:

- Parks and Resorts. In addition to Eurodisney, these include the Disneyland Resorts in Los Angeles, Florida, Tokyo, and Shanghai.
- The Walt Disney Studios, responsible for the production of the Disney films.
- Disney Consumer Products markets the Disney Experience in the form of toys, books, and countless other articles.
- Media Networks: the television channels of the Disney Television Group.
- Disney Interactive, with a focus on high-quality entertainment through games, social media, and other digital platforms.

The Eurodisney Group consists of two parts. On the one hand there are the theme parks of the resort: Disneyland Park (including Fantasyland, Frontier Land, and Main Street USA) and the more television and film-oriented Walt Disney Studios Park. These parks host well-known attractions such as Big Thunder Mountain and Pirates of the Caribbean. The revenues in these parks are driven by two factors: the number of visitors and the spending per visitor (on food and drinks, admission prices and merchandise). Next to the parks there is the Hotels and Disney Village. Visitors to Disneyland can stay overnight here, but the hotels are also used for the organization of events and conferences.

Eurodisney aims to increase sales and profitability in the future through increasing visitor numbers and increasing average spending per visitor. To achieve this, the company continues to invest in the 'experience' that Disney offers its visitors. After all, if expectations of the visitors are exceeded, this leads to repeat visits and positive word-of-mouth advertising. Continued investment is also necessary: the competition in the market is constantly growing, and the competitors are not sitting still either.

An interview with 'Président' Tom Wolber, adapted from the annual report of Eurodisney in 2015, illustrates the confidence with which Eurodisney faces the future:

How do you see the 2015 fiscal year?

Throughout the year we increased our efforts to enhance the guest experience and to make our resort something truly special. We launched an ambitious programme to renovate ten of our iconic attractions, including the emblematic Space Mountain: Mission 2, and Mystères de Nautilus. These major innovations are starting to bear fruit. Revenue was up 7.3 per cent, thanks to increases in theme park attendance, hotel occupancy rates, and average spending per guest. Disneyland Paris welcomed 600,000 additional guests this year, and average spending reached a record level of €53.8 per guest – an increase of 6 per cent.

How do these results reflect your strategy?

These results demonstrate the positive impact of our long-term strategy to improve the quality of the guest experience and to increase guest satisfaction. This strategy is part of our constant drive for excellence, which is vital because our future lies in providing the very best quality. Continuous investments are necessary if we want to stay ahead of the competition and secure the future of Disneyland Paris. We operate in an increasingly competitive environment, as the leisure sector in Europe offers an ever-widening range of products and alternatives. We need to stand out to maintain our position as the sector leader.

What is the key to the success of Disneyland Paris?

Over the years, Disneyland Paris has strengthened its position as Europe's leading tourist attraction. Our success

is first and foremost the result of the commitment of our employees. Their talent, creativity, and enthusiasm bring the Disney magic to life every day for millions of guests. We are increasing our creative efforts to enchant our guests, drawing on the heritage of the Disney brand. Our brand represents the values of sincerity and excellence, as well as the importance of dreams, and is one of the pillars of our success.

What are your priorities for the coming years?

We continue our renovation efforts in our parks and hotels, and we continue to offer new experiences to our guests. This work is part of our constant drive for excellence, and is also part of the build-up to our twenty-fifth anniversary in 2017. For this symbolic date, we want our resort to be even more attractive, more magical, and more welcoming than ever. As Europe's leading tourist destination, we should continue to do everything in our power to set an example in all areas, not only in our efforts to offer an experience but also in our HR policy or in our social and environmental responsibilities.

Providing a family experience is what made Disney great. Visitors come mainly to meet the Disney characters in person. Disney offers a unique opportunity to get a cuddle from Mickey Mouse or to take a photo together with Donald Duck. These are memories and experiences that people really remember, that lead to a second or third visit, and that cost relatively little money in terms of investment. Celebrations accompanied by parades, festivities, and more shows to permanently enrich the Disney feeling will continue to play a major role in the parks.

Questions

1. Three levels can be distinguished in a company. Illustrate these three levels for The Walt Disney Company.

2. Does Disneyland Resort Paris have a sustainable competitive advantage? If yes, which one? Please explain your answer.

3. Define the objective for Disneyland Resort Paris, based on the information in the case.

4. Define the company strategy, the marketing strategy, and the market instrument strategies for Disneyland Resort Paris. Use information from the case where possible.

5. a) In the external analysis, several specific analyses have to be performed. Which analyses are these?

   b) For each of these analyses, give an example of information that is of interest to Eurodisney. Use information from the case where possible.

Part II

Situation analysis

In Part II the different parts of the situation analysis are presented. A thorough situation analysis based on qualitative as well as quantitative data should lead to relevant insights that form the base for strategies. We start by defining the current market, which should be within the mission of a company (Chapter 3). The first real analysis phase is the internal analysis (Chapter 4), including a check of the results thus far (control). The external analysis starts with the most important one: the customer (Chapter 5). Next, an overview is given of the industry, including the macro-environmental factors (Chapter 6). We then focus on some specific stakeholder groups. Chapter 7 is devoted to competitor analysis where individual competitors (or potential partners) are analysed. In Chapter 8 we look at distributors (channels) and suppliers. In Chapter 9 the SWOT analysis is presented as the bridge between the analysis and strategic decisions

Chapter 3

Mission, value strategies, and market definition

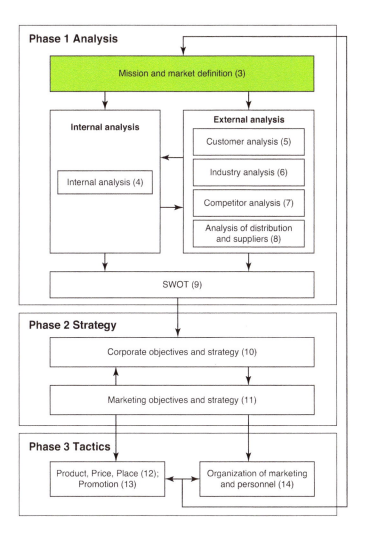

Phase 1 Analysis

Mission and market definition (3)

Internal analysis

Internal analysis (4)

External analysis

Customer analysis (5)

Industry analysis (6)

Competitor analysis (7)

Analysis of distribution and suppliers (8)

SWOT (9)

Phase 2 Strategy

Corporate objectives and strategy (10)

Marketing objectives and strategy (11)

Phase 3 Tactics

Product, Price, Place (12); Promotion (13)

Organization of marketing and personnel (14)

Key points in this chapter

- ◾ Know the function and components of a mission and a vision.
- ◾ Be able to formulate a vision and a value strategy.
- ◾ Know how to define a market: components and guidelines.

Introduction

The first step in creating a marketing plan is to define the market. Without market definition, no analyses can be performed. A market definition for a brand should always be contained in the mission of a company. Therefore, the mission should be clear. This chapter starts with a section about the mission and the vision (section 3.1). Within the vision the value discipline is important: Which customer needs does the company want to serve? We deal with value strategies in section 3.2. After that, in section 3.3 we discuss ways to define markets. Market definition is relevant at different levels in the organization.

3.1 Developing a customer-oriented vision

3.1.1 Mission and vision

Many organizations have a *mission statement*. However, mission statements can be quite varied in their objective. On the basis of research on 59 large companies in Great Britain, Klemm et al. (1991) classify missions into four different types:

1. *The pure mission.* This is a representation of the company's long-term objectives, based on the philosophies of top management. Here is an example from a publisher: "We want to make an increasing contribution to the information supply and the formation of public opinion in the UK."
2. *Strategic objectives.* This is a global representation of the company's desired direction and positions. Here is an example: "We want to become the market leader in the magazine industry."
3. *Quantified planning objectives.* These are the concrete objectives for a specific period. Here is an example: "Next year we want a profit 10 per cent higher than this year's profit."
4. *Definition of the market (business definition).* This is a definition of the scope and activities of a company. Here is an example: "We publish newspapers and magazines."

This list shows that the missions formulated by companies can vary from very broad to very narrow. By way of an example, we provide here Shell's mission:

The objectives of Shell companies are to engage efficiently, responsibly and profitably in the oil, gas, chemicals, coal, steel and other appropriate businesses, and to participate in the search for, and development of other sources of energy. Shell companies seek a high standard of performance and aim to maintain a long-term position in their respective competitive environments.

The goal of a mission is threefold:

1. *Market definition*. The process of formulating a mission forces a company to reflect on its activities (asking: What business are we in?). Thus, a mission statement is an important component of the strategic planning process.
2. *Employee motivation*. The second function of a mission statement is that it serves as an internal purpose of motivating employees. A mission should therefore lay out actionable objectives to help guide employees in their work.
3. *External image*. The third function is to create an outward image that allows the public to have a clear understanding of what you do. For that purpose, the identity of a company may be included in the mission, as well as, for example, its social objectives.

According to Klemm et al. (1991), the internal function of a mission statement is especially important, as it is meant to sell the philosophies and values of top management to the employees. An example of a very brief but also very motivating mission comes from a Japanese car manufacturer that for some time had the mission "beat Mercedes Benz". Research has also shown that companies are more likely to change their mission statement as a result of a change in management than as a result of a change in 'market circumstances'. Research has also shown that it is necessary to distinguish 'mission' from 'vision' (Hooley et al., 1992). Formulating a brief, motivating vision that states what the organization aims to achieve in the future is called a company's 'strategic intent' (Hamel and Prahalad, 1989).

Based on this analysis, it may therefore be argued that a mission has a real function only when it acts as a motivating force. Because in reality this is often not the case, it has been argued that companies should formulate *ambition statements* rather than *mission statements*. In this regard a distinction should be made between a vision and a mission. A mission is what a company is and does now, whereas a vision is what a company wants to achieve in the future. That vision acts as a motivating force. Figure 3.1 indicates which choices should be used as the basis for a strategic business plan. We let the mission be defined first so that it may be used to indicate what the company wants to achieve in the future (vision). We now discuss in more detail each of the components in Figure 3.1.

The mission: What are we doing now?
- Definition of activities
- Social mission (external and internal) and other dimensions of corporate image

The vision/ambition: What do we want to achieve in the future?
- Beliefs: explanation of what is important to the company
- Indentity and positioning of the organization: value strategy
- Long-term goals

Figure 3.1 **Mission and vision of an organization**

3.1.2 Mission

In this section we first discuss the mission component 'market definition', and then the component 'corporate identity'.

The first mission component refers to the definition of current activities: What business are we in? Using the dimensions introduced by Abell (1980), a market definition may contain the following dimensions:

- Products ('customer technologies'; we design systems that link client needs with the supply of information).
- Customer groups (segments; our target audiences are private individuals and companies in Vietnam).
- Customer functions (needs; we help our customers search for information more effectively and efficiently on the internet).

The most obvious method is to define markets on the basis of the *products*. A market in that case consists of all the companies that bring a certain product onto the market. For example, companies may be active in the beer market, the car market, the coffee market, the market for air travel, the market for personal computers, and so on. A disadvantage of defining markets on the basis of products is that this relates only to the supply side; it does not indicate for whom the products are intended, or who demands the product. As such, a market definition should include the *customers* as well. For example, beer may be manufactured for home use or for use in the catering industry, or both. Personal computers may be intended for individuals, schools, or companies. A company can also differentiate its customers based on geography. Does the company serve only the national market or also the international market, and if it serves the latter, which countries? In short, a market definition should describe the products as well as the customer.

Another disadvantage of using products to define a market is that it does not focus on the underlying *needs* of the customer for whom the product is intended. The danger in this case is that a company will overlook competitors that serve the same function for the customers (i.e., respond to the same needs) but with very different products (Levitt, 1960). For example, a gasoline company may use the product-oriented market definition "we sell gasoline" or the customer-oriented definition "we supply energy". In the second scenario, the company keeps the option to supply other products that meet the same need, such as natural gas. Thus, a market definition should be formulated not only in terms of products but also in terms of functions for customers (Abell, 1980; Abell and Hammond, 1979). A classic example of a product-oriented mission is provided by Swiss watch manufacturers, which for many years focused their market definition on manually produced precision clocks. The arrival of chip technology meant that they were surpassed by foreign manufacturers that could supply the same quality for significantly lower prices (digital watches). Only when sales of Swiss watches dropped dramatically did Swiss companies redefine the market on the basis of consumers' need "to know what time it is". Subsequently, those companies also started using new production methods and producing cheaper watches (Swatch).

Case 3.1 Relevance of customer-oriented mission

Digital photo technology and mobile phones radically shift market shares

From 2000 onward digital photography made huge strides. For consumers, digital photography is much more convenient than 'classical' photography. One can immediately see the result, there is no need to print everything, and it is easy to handle photos on the computer. In the beginning, with 2- and 3-megapixel cameras, the quality was not comparable with that of classical photos. However, since the introduction of affordable 4-megapixel cameras, the quality has become sufficiently good. Since that time, classical photography has disappeared from the consumer market. Famous film producers Agfa and Kodak were not able to define new markets and dramatically lost share. In addition, some retailers that changed too late to digital photography disappeared from the market. In the camera market, market shares changed enormously in favour of, for example, Canon, which positioned itself as a leader in consumer photography. Since mobile phones are now equipped with good cameras, competition in the photo industry has radically changed.

The other component of the mission is the social mission. The need for a company to act socially has grown strongly since 2000. Acting socially has to do with the well-known *three Ps: people, planet, profit*, the first two Ps being the components of being social beyond making profit. The 'people issue' relates to several stakeholders. First, the company's own employees, thus being employee-friendly; for example, by affirmative action and by providing maternity leave; but also by being responsible to suppliers and preventing the suppression of suppliers, such as not buying cheap clothes in countries where the social circumstances of workers are bad. A third stakeholder group important in social behaviour is the whole society. The bad examples are bank managers who were responsible for the economic crisis in the early 2000s due to their criminal way of dealing with customers' money.

A second dimension of acting socially is related to the planet and deals with preventing climate change, and thus to do business in an environmentally friendly way.

Both P issues (people and planet) are often summarized using the term 'sustainability', where this is not limited to climate issues but also to sustainable behaviour in relation to people.

3.1.3 Vision and ambition

The vision is the 'dream of the entrepreneur'. It is the top management's view of a company and the role it plays in the marketplace. The vision originates to a large extent from the existing core competencies: What are we best at?

Visions may relate to three components (Figure 3.2):

1. Opinions about where the company believes the market is going (for example, "we believe that due to tempestuous communication technology developments, over the next five years consumers will develop a strong need for products that help them navigate the abundance of information online").
2. The identity of the company ("our goal is to become the most innovative and best supplier of such products within five years"); this will often be based on the core competencies of the company (see, for example, Case 3.2).
3. The long-term goals of the company ("we want to become the largest supplier of such navigation products").

An important issue here is that the vision should contain a clear and motivating *ambition* with which the entire workforce can identify. A vision should not be handed down to the staff as a straitjacket, but rather it is important that the company's leaders generate internal support for the vision. The ability to formulate a clear and challeng-

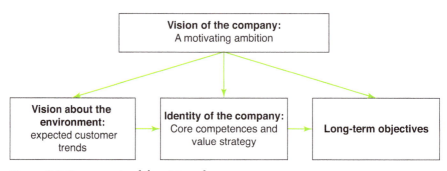

Figure 3.2 Components of the vision of a company

ing ambition is an important requirement for a leader. This principle is well known in politics: world leaders excel in conveying what they want. The same thing applies to organizations. A clear ambition is a strong tool for creating teams. However, in practice many organizations lack a challenging vision. We will return to this issue in Chapter 14.

3.2 Value strategies

It was indicated in Chapter 1 that having a competitive advantage is essential. For the choice of such an advantage, the theory of Treacy and Wiersema (1993) in regard to what they call 'value disciplines' can be used, with excellent results. First, in section 3.2.1 we will present this theory, and then we will compare it with the theory of Porter (1980) (section 3.2.2); we will conclude in section 3.2.3 with our own adaptation of the value disciplines (or value strategies).

3.2.1 Value strategies of Treacy and Wiersema

In their frequently quoted article "Customer Intimacy and Other Value Disciplines", Treacy and Wiersema (TW) present three potential value strategies (Figure 3.3). The value strategies are:

1. *Product leadership*. The development of innovative, value-added products; this strategy is employed, for example, by Procter & Gamble, which uses the basic assumption for all markets in which it is active that Procter brands will have the

Figure 3.3 **Value strategies**

highest quality in their category and will be the best at fulfilling the customer need for which a product was made. Other companies that seem to choose product leadership are technologically strong companies such as Apple, Microsoft, Sony, and Philips.

2. *Operational excellence* (leader in low costs for the customer). This literally means to excel in the correct and efficient implementation of all corporate processes. This encompasses the idea that an 'excellent production process' leads to the fact that the client has to minimize expenditure; thus, a low price is the most obvious way to comply with customer demands. Although this is not necessarily the case, 'costs' can also be non-financial, such as the effort expended to buy the product (convenience). 'Always delivering on time' can also be part of the strategy. With regard to this value strategy, standardization is important for a company, along with the achievement of economies of scale. This value strategy is chosen, for example, by the airline EasyJet, which saves costs in as many areas as possible (including the 'service' en route: food is charged for), and can therefore compete at very low prices. Other companies that excel in operational excellence are McDonald's, Dell Computers (direct delivery through the internet), Aldi, Ikea, and Walmart. This value strategy deals explicitly with excelling in efficiency. In principle every company tries to keep its costs as low as possible and make the internal processes run as smoothly as possible (Philips, KLM, etc.); this does not mean, however, that these companies excel in creating low cost for the customer.

3. *Customer intimacy* (individual customer approach: 'client leadership', or the best in relationship marketing). 'Intimate' relations with the customer are achieved by supplying customized products and/or through a policy that is totally focused on attention to the individual customer and customer loyalty. Some companies follow this discipline; for example, internet service providers such as Amazon.com and Bol. com, which know the preferences of individual customers and make appropriate offers (of books, compact discs, etc.) on the basis of those preferences. In business markets customer intimacy is normal as well: personal contacts and products and services that are adjusted to individual customers (companies) are common in industrial markets. In small and medium-size enterprises an individual customer strategy seems to be applicable as well. Similarly, in service markets for consumers, there are possibilities for the implementation of customer intimacy. However, in the practice of marketing, many firms deal with sales instead of building relationships. In other sectors there are few providers that excel in this strategy, although some companies pay attention to individual customer care; for example, KLM with its frequent flyer programme, through which loyal customers are rewarded with relevant offers. This does not mean, however, that the company excels in this area. Therefore, customer intimacy seems to be capable of offering a competitive edge in many sectors in the future.

Treacy and Wiersema suggest that every company has to make a basic choice to excel in one of these three disciplines: Which value does the company primarily want to support? This choice is decisive for the entire company management: production, staff, marketing, and so on. Furthermore, the other two value disciplines should be at an acceptable level. This condition is often omitted in the description by Treacy and Wiersema. However, it is very important, because these authors suggest that a company can excel in only one of the three disciplines once a minimum quality level of internal processes (operational 'excellence') has been achieved. In fact, at first all three should be at an acceptable level; only thereafter can a company excel in one of them. A company should therefore have 'its things in order' in the fields of innovation, efficiency, and customer orientation before it tries to excel in one of them. Furthermore, these authors suggest that expectations from customers should not only be met but also exceeded. This can be done, for example, by offering an unsolicited service. Vargo and Lusch (2004) even posit that the core marketing concept should be focused on services.

3.2.2 Comparison with Porter

Treacy and Wiersema's arrangement has similarities to the well-known generic competitive strategies of Porter (1980). Porter mentions three ways in which a company can differentiate:

1. *Differentiate*: be different from the competition.
2. *Cost leadership*: try to achieve the lowest costs in the industry.
3. *Focus*: focus on a specific customer group or 'niche'.

Porter also mentions a fourth strategy: *'stuck in the middle'*. So, no clear choice. This leads to low profitability according to Porter. Also TW recommend that companies make choices: every company should excel in something.

TW's product leadership strongly corresponds to Porter's strategy of differentiation. Operational excellence appears to be similar to cost leadership but is actually substantially different. Cost leadership is an internal strategy that includes an emphasis on cost reduction, whereas operational excellence starts from the perspective of a customer who wants convenience or a low price. The third strategy is the focus strategy. The strategy of customer intimacy may be interpreted as a farther-reaching form of segmentation: the company does not necessarily orient itself towards a small segment but instead towards individual customers. Porter's recommendations correspond relatively well to those of Treacy and Wiersema: a company should focus on one of the three options. Treacy and Wiersema also state that focusing is important, but they add that an adequate level in the other two disciplines is also required. Since their framework is really customer-oriented, it is strongly preferred to that of Porter.

Both in the systems of Porter and of Treacy and Wiersema, it is justifiable to ask whether they apply to the whole company. Can different value strategies be chosen within one company? Hendry (1990) suggests in his paper "The Problem with Porter's Generic Strategies" that Porter's concept should be applied at the level of SBUs. When we extend this to the system of Treacy and Wiersema, we conclude that within an SBU one value strategy should be chosen, but that different value strategies between SBUs are possible. The clearest way to do this is to choose one value strategy for a complete company, but if there are more or less autonomously operating divisions or SBUs within a company, differences in value strategies are imaginable.

3.2.3 The Brand Benefiting Model

Although the model of TW is very useful, some methodological comments can be added to the theory of Treacy and Wiersema:

1. *The brand image is not explicitly included.* In the model of Treacy and Wiersema no clear space has been created for companies or products that distinguish themselves on the basis of brand image. For example, in the market for soft drinks and beer, the difference based on brand image is demonstrably the most important. In our opinion, this could be interpreted as a type of product leadership in which the image excels, and the company should in fact excel by using the means of communication. In this way a company such as Coca-Cola is also a product leader. Although it has been proved during taste tests that Pepsi and Coca-Cola are appreciated more or less equally, the market share of Coca-Cola is remarkably greater. Coca-Cola is apparently very good at image building.
2. Although TW should reflect the customers' perspective, the value strategy 'operational excellence' does not sound like this. It looks to deal with lowering costs, an internal issue.
3. Another problem with the operational excellence strategy is that when taking the customer perspective, it is about two totally different needs of customers: convenience and a low price. These two needs do not necessarily combine successfully.

Figure 3.4 shows our own model of strategies. It is focused on brand promises and is indicated as the Brand Benefiting Model.

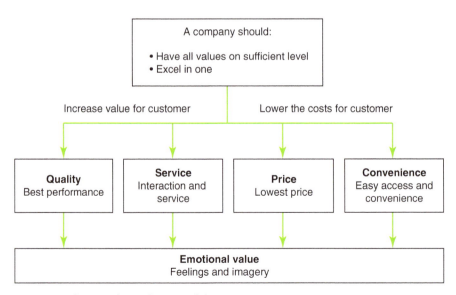

Figure 3.4 **The Brand Benefiting Model**

The Brand Benefiting Model suggests that there are two ways of improving customer value:

- increase the benefits;
- lower the costs (in a broad sense).

Increasing the benefits may be done through:

1. Increasing the core quality, so be the best in 'objective' performance. Innovation is important.
2. Increasing service and customer orientation. This is about really paying attention to individual customers; for example, providing good after-sales service, dealing with complaints, etc.

A company may also choose to focus on lowering sacrifices for customers:

3. Lowering price.
4. Lowering other sacrifices: easy access and high convenience, so no waiting times, easy to find, fast delivery, etc. (see Case 3.2).

If a company has all values at a sufficient level, the next step is to try to excel in one value.

Values 1 to 4 may be seen as real, functional benefits. Once having chosen the most important one, the final step is to form a link to the feelings of the customer:

5. Adding emotional values.

In our view the combination of instrumental and emotional values offers the opportunity for a brand to appeal to the mind as well as the heart of a customer.

3.3 Market definition

3.3.1 Market definition at the SBU level

For convenience, in Chapter 2 an SBU was defined around a specific market or product category; for example, the SBU salad dressing, children's clothing, student accounts, or travel insurance. This definition implies that an SBU is not always concretely visible as an organizational unit within a company.

A market definition at the SBU level occurs in a similar manner as it does with the mission: according to the dimensions of products, target audiences, and needs. However, there are two differences between the company level and the SBU level. First, because marketing plans are determined at the SBU level, the market definition at that level needs to be as concrete as possible, whereas vaguer terms may be used for the mission. Second, the market for an SBU by definition is smaller than that of a company; the 'sum' of all market definitions of the SBU will in theory correspond to the market definition of the entire company.

The definition of customer need has a direct impact on the range of the competition. After all, a competitor is by definition a supplier that can satisfy the same customer need.

Case 3.2 Brand benefit convenience

Ofo: offering convenience

Using a bicycle in China is made extremely simple due to several brands offering bikes all over the city. An example is Ofo, a Beijing-based bicycle-sharing company founded in 2014. As of 2017 it operated over 10 million yellow bicycles in 250 cities and 20 countries. The dockless Ofo system uses its smartphone app to unlock and locate nearby bicycles, charging an hourly rate for use. As of 2017 the company was valued at $3 billion and had over 62.7 million monthly active users. The system also works very well for tourists. Ofo strongly focuses on convenience: the bikes are available randomly in the cities, so are not limited to certain locations. Simply find one on your phone, unlock by scanning the QR code, and go. Once finished just park the bike somewhere and lock it.

Therefore, the manner in which that need is defined determines the competition. In that regard, not only are the concrete needs important but also associated product characteristics, such as prestige and status. These values may also be used for market definition.

We illustrate the use of the dimensions at the SBU level through an example (Figure 3.5). The SBU 'jam' of a manufacturer researches the possibilities for the three different dimensions. The need that is addressed is defined concretely in this example; it is the need for sandwich fillings. Alternative needs are cake filling and components for desserts. Potential customer groups are home users, the catering industry, the health care industry, and company cafeterias. Alternative customer technologies (associated with the need for sandwich fillings) are jam, peanut butter, sandwich spread, cheese spread, cheese, and sliced meat. Within these dimensions the following market definition is chosen: "We provide for the need of home users to have sandwich fillings by making jam." In Figure 3.5 it should be noted that in principle the definition is constructed for the level of the final customers (consumers).

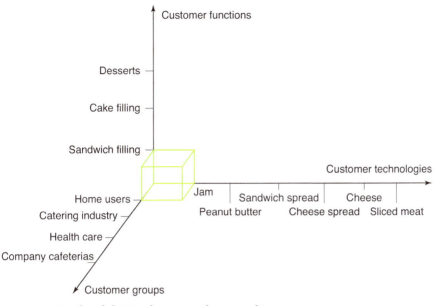

Figure 3.5 **Market definition for a manufacturer of jam**

The use of these three dimensions is not only important for defining the current market, it also allows for a structural approach to considering potential growth directions during the process of company decision making. The four well-known growth strategies as defined by Ansoff (1957) (see section 10.3.2) can be linked directly to the axes in Figure 3.5. The relationships between the dimensions of the market definition and Ansoff's growth strategies are shown in Figure 3.6.

Growth along dimensions				
Customer function (needs)	Customer groups (segments)	Customer technology (products)	Growth strategy according to Ansoff	Example of jam producer
–	–	–	Market penetration	Price reduction of jam
X	–	–	Market penetration	Emphasize another application: jam as cake filling
–	X	–	Market development	Sell jam to catering industry or abroad
–	–	X	Product development	Produce peanut butter for consumers
–	X	X	Related diversification	Sell peanut butter abroad
X	X	X	Unrelated diversification	Produce fruit juices or ready-made pizzas

– = "no change"; X = "change."

Figure 3.6 **Market dimensions and growth strategies**

Case 3.3 Offering several markets

Market dimensions in sport markets

Organizations in sports markets (clubs, associations, stadiums, etc.) have to deal with two target groups: spectators and viewers, and advertisers (sponsors). The 'product' sport is 'a battle'. The special aspect of this product is that it is not stable. The course and outcome are always unsure. There are two kinds of sports marketing: marketing of sports and marketing through sports (sponsoring). Organizations that deal with the marketing of the 'battle' (sports) might best apply the planning concepts described in this book. In that case it is important to sell the company's own product as well as possible to viewers and advertisers, and to build up relationships with those target groups. In the case of marketing 'through sports', the main issue is communication. Sponsors can use the 'medium' sports to realize brand targets (brand name, image) and to build up their own relationships (for example, invite customers to sky boxes).

Figure 3.6 shows which growth strategy is applicable for a certain combination of changes in market dimensions. For instance, if the goal is to grow within the existing three dimensions, it is a matter of market penetration. The same applies if only the customer function is changed. Growth that occurs exclusively in the dimension of customer groups implies market development, whereas growth that exclusively involves expansion of the product dimension (that is, for the same needs and customers) is called product development.

Change in the dimensions of customer groups and products means diversification. In the case of related products that cover the same needs, this is called related diversification.

If other needs are also addressed, it is called unrelated diversification. Figure 3.6 may serve as a checklist for generating growth options. The process of creating options is addressed in Chapter 9 on SWOT analysis. Final decisions about growth directions are made after the situation analysis during the process of creating a company strategy. Therefore, in Chapters 10 and 11, we return to growth strategies.

3.3.2 Market definition at the product or brand level

Aside from a market definition at the SBU level, a more detailed definition can be helpful for brands during further analyses. Concretely, this may involve a segmentation of two of the three previously mentioned dimensions: target audiences, and products and services. For this purpose, all products are listed. This should be a relatively quick procedure for companies that produce goods, but for suppliers of services it is more challenging: What are the products of a bank, for example? A second step is the description of the different target audiences (customers) of the organization. An obvious distinction is between private customers (final customers) and companies (business markets). However, it is also possible to segment further within those groups on the basis of various segmentation criteria ranging from general background characteristics (age, type of business, store chain, etc.) to more product-specific variables such as heavy versus light 'users' or price buyers versus quality seekers. Third, it should be indicated which combinations of products and target audiences are currently relevant for the organization.

Figure 3.7 contains a worksheet that may be used. An advantage of overviews such as the one shown in Figure 3.7 is that they may be used as the basis for subsequent analyses. Case 3.3 illustrates the importance of defining products and audiences.

Description of products (and varieties)

Product 1

Product 2

Product 3

Product 4

Product ...

Description of target audiences

Target audience 1

Target audience 2

Target audience 3

Target audience 4

Target audience ...

Matrix of product–target audience combinations

	Target audience 1	Target audience 2	Target audience 3	Target audience 4	Target audience ...
Product 1					
Product 2					
Product 3					
Product 4					
Product ...					

Mark each section with a "x" if that combination exists for the organization.

Figure 3.7 Worksheets for defining product–market combinations

3.3.3 Market definition and new activities

Defining the market (at the levels of the company, the SBU, and the product) before doing the situation analysis seems to imply that this definition is not influenced by the results of the situation analysis, but this is not the case. For example, if there are very negative developments in the market for newspapers and magazines in which a publisher is active, that could be a reason to revise the publisher's mission (e.g. being active in the consumer market of the media) and to become active in the supply of information for companies. In that case, the question What should our business be?" (supply of information for companies) is answered differently than is the question "What business are we in?" (consumer market of the media). This clarifies the relationship with the vision once again: the vision is the difference between the current market and the desired market.

However, if there is a difference between the current field of activities and the intended activities, this means that the new field (in the example, supplying news via the internet) also should be analysed to determine whether the new markets are attractive.

Finally, it may be asked whether ideas for new activities will even appear on the radar screen if the company analyses only the existing markets from the perspective of the existing SBUs. In this regard, both during the SWOT analysis and during the reconsideration of the mission, the company needs to pay explicit attention to signals that indicate opportunities outside the scope of current activities (Figure 3.8).

In summarizing the material above, the following steps can be taken in the process of market definition and mission formulation:

1. Start with a definition of the market in which the company is currently active.
2. Complete an external analysis of the environment. This should include an analysis of the opportunities and threats outside the existing market.
3. On the basis of the external (and internal) analysis, determine whether there is a reason to become active outside the existing market; in other words, define the desired market.
4. If this is the case, complete a new external analysis with the changed market definition. This is necessary because a different market definition also involves a different competitive situation and different market growth. With a broader market definition, the number of competitors will be higher.

Component of situation analysis	Signal
Internal analysis	Core competencies: possibilities for extensions
Customer analysis	Unfulfilled customer needs to be determined from problems with existing products
Industry analysis	Substitute products and expected developments in macro environment
Competitor analysis	Competitor activities outside the 'own' existing market
Distributor and supplier analysis	Distributor experiences in other categories

Figure 3.8 **Signals for new activities**

Case 3.4 Changing your market

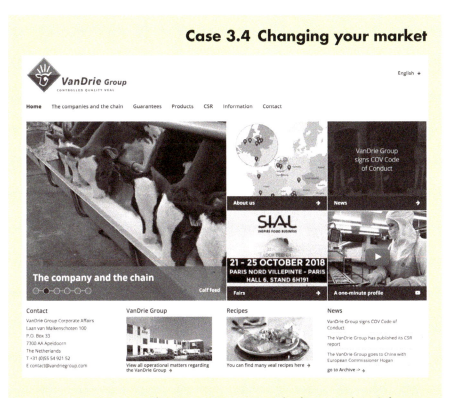

Vandrie Group step outside their market definition

The Vandrie Group is one of world's largest companies in veal (calf meat). Until 2018 they dealt solely in veal and not in other meat, as Vion does, a large, broader-oriented meat company. In 2018 the Vandrie Group acquired a cattle slaughterhouse from Ameco. So, now the Vandrie Group also deliver beef to their customers. In terms of market definition they broadened their market from veal to veal and beef, which may seem a small step but may be a large step for a focused company such as the Vandrie Group.

Source: *Financial Daily* (Financieel Dagblad), 31 March 2018

After the external analysis has been performed again, the company should determine whether the chosen market is still considered attractive. If it is, the planning process will be continued.

This process is summarized in Figure 3.9.

In short, the phases 'definition of the (current) market', 'external analysis', and 'formulation of company decisions: definition of the desired market' are completed until the company perceives no further reason to change the market definition. In practice these steps are usually completed only once or at most twice: first for the current market and then for a more broadly defined market.

Here is an example that will clarify Figure 3.9.

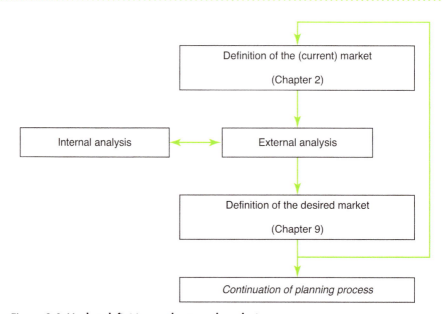

Figure 3.9 **Market definition and external analysis**

Suppose a manufacturer uses the production of toy trains for a current market definition and mission. An analysis of the toy train market indicates that sales are decreasing. An important cause of this situation appears to be the growth of computer games. An important reason for the growth in the market for computer games is strong technological developments that have made it possible to bring these games onto the market for relatively low prices. Based on this assessment, the manufacturer must make an important choice: either leave the mission unchanged and attempt to maintain the sales level of toy trains through marketing efforts, or adapt the mission and decide to enter the market for computer games. The choice of whether to adapt the mission depends, among other things, on the situation in the market for computer games. Therefore, the manufacturer completes an additional external analysis specific to the market for computer games. This analysis shows that there is very strong competition in this market. Therefore, the manufacturer decides not to alter the mission but attempt to restore the company's sales of toy trains by focusing more on the target audience of fathers.

In reality, the situation analysis is often repeated when a company is considering whether to become active abroad. In that case, in the second round the foreign market should be analysed.

3.3.4 The importance of a market definition

In the article "Marketing Myopia", Levitt (1960) warned against a market definition that is too supply-oriented. In relation to the mission, section 3.1.2 discussed the example of an overly narrowly defined, product-oriented market definition among producers of Swiss watches. It is of vital importance how broadly or narrowly a manager defines the market. With a broad definition, there will be many competitors. If a company restricts its business to a niche (narrow market definition), the number of competitors will be low. Thus, there is a direct relationship between the market definition and the number of competitors: setting the boundaries of a market is actually the same as defining the competitive set (Lehmann and Winer, 2008). This also implies a direct relationship with the concept of market share. Since the market share is calculated over the designated market, a limited market definition (e.g. the market for health yoghurt) implies a higher market share than does a broader market definition (the market for all yoghurts). In practice, shares are often calculated on the basis of market segments rather than on that of entire markets.

In this regard, Lehmann and Winer (2008) describe four levels related to competition:

1. *Product form competition.* This is competition between brands that are aimed at the same market segment, for example, Diet Pepsi versus Diet Coke.
2. *Product category competition.* This is competition between products with comparable characteristics, such as various soft drinks.
3. *Generic competition.* These are products that address the same consumer needs, such as drinks.
4. *Budget competition.* This is competition for the money of the consumer, as in food and entertainment.

The market definitions used in the context of annual marketing planning are usually based on product form competition or product category competition. Chapter 7 will discuss these forms of competition in the context of the identification of competitors.

Summary

To be able to perform a situation analysis and make strategic decisions, it should be known in what market the company operates and which value strategy the company pursues. The marketing strategy is developed within these constraints. The market definition is related to the mission, and the value strategy is related to the vision. Organizations can best be directed if there is a clear mission and a common vision. A vision pertains to the future: What does top management consider important? Which identity should the organization have? And what are other long-term goals? The corporate identity may be formulated in terms of a value strategy: product or brand leadership, operational excellence, or customer intimacy. A company should be sufficiently good in all these areas and should try to excel in one. A clear and differentiating vision is necessary to motivate personnel, and to attract and retain customers. The market for the organization is defined in the mission. At the SBU level a further market definition occurs, based on the dimensions of products, needs, and target audiences. The market definition chosen at that level forms the starting point for the situation analysis. At the level of the product or brand, the dimension of target audiences may be further disaggregated to obtain a more precise definition of product–market combinations. A market definition should be demand-oriented and not too small in order to avoid overlooking important competitors and new market developments.

Case Starbucks: coffee is experience

Laurie comes straight from university where she has been working on a statistics exam; girlfriend Alice comes straight from home. They sit together in a local Costa Coffee in Leeds, their favourite coffee shop. "We love coffee," says Laurie. She likes to drink a cappuccino or a latte caramel; Alice prefers a latte vanilla.

Why do they like to come here? "It's homely," says Alice. "The interior belongs in some way to coffee drinking. And they do their best for your cup of coffee. As if you were a bit special."

Laurie and Alice are real fans of Costa Coffee, where the counter is deliberately kept low and the barista puts a milk froth in your coffee before your eyes. They are the ideal customers: young, with plenty of time, and coffee lovers. With them, a coffee company builds a relation for a lifetime. But they are also the exception to the rule. For coffee companies they belong to the target group that forms a 'challenge', according to the marketing manager of Costa Coffee. The brand is doing everything to stay relevant. Costa Coffee is hunting for the youthful target group: young people who prefer to drink their coffee from a cardboard cup downtown. The coffee café fits perfectly with the current 'out-of-home' culture.

Youngsters no longer drink much coffee, but they easily find their way to coffee shops such as Costa Coffee, Caffe Nero, and of course Starbucks. All these concepts are similar: they all have internet, newspapers, literature, and a happy, carefree appearance. The coffee shop, with its cardboard coffee cups to take away, not only has a cosmopolitan allure and atmosphere, it also has Frappuccino, Chai Latte, and Vanilla Cream.

Coffee companies do well with their coffee café among the youngsters. But this should of course not be at the expense of the dedication of the oldest category of coffee drinkers, also the heaviest users of coffee. "I did not really know that there were these kinds of cafés," says Anne Wright (78). "It's the first time I've been here." Accompanied by her grandson's girlfriend, she drinks coffee on the terrace of Starbucks in London.

Costa Coffee is the largest and fastest-growing coffee shop chain in the United Kingdom. But the company is experiencing a lot of competition from Starbucks. Starbucks has become a real status symbol in Europe. For example, in airports you will see that people, once they have drunk their coffee, will continue to walk with their Starbucks cup in their hand for a long time. The most important thing for Starbucks is that the customer does not feel like a customer, but a kind of family friend. When you place your order, you will first be asked for your name. Then they will call something like "one café latte for Bob". And then it is "Bob, your latte is ready". And when you leave, they say "Bye Bob". It gives the customer the feeling that "they know me here, they like me". The homely feeling is enhanced by the relaxed chairs, and the tables dotted with newspapers, comic books, and opinion magazines. The free WiFi makes the coffee shop the perfect place to work or meet one's friends in a homely atmosphere.

Starbucks is a strong brand, but something else is going on as well. "For us, the memory of America is very relevant," said a communication adviser. "When you step inside Starbucks, you imagine yourself in New York. Anyone who has been in America knows how he went to Starbucks there and, to his great joy, got some coffee. This memory makes Starbucks an experience. You feel like a cosmopolitan, and at the same time it feels familiar."

---

www.starbucks.com profiles the mission statement of Starbucks

The Starbucks Mission: to inspire and nurture the human spirit – one person, one cup and one neighbourhood at a time.

Here are the principles of how we live that every day.

Our coffee
It has always been, and will always be, about quality. We're passionate about ethically sourcing the finest coffee beans, roasting them with great care, and improving the lives of people who grow them. We care deeply about all of this; our work is never done.

Our partners
We're called partners, because it's not just a job, it's our passion. Together, we embrace diversity to create a place where each of us can be ourselves. We always treat each other with respect and dignity. And we hold each other to that standard.

Our customers
When we are fully engaged, we connect with, laugh with, and uplift the lives of our customers – even if just for a few moments. Sure, it starts with the promise

of a perfectly made beverage, but our work goes far beyond that. It's really about human connection.

Our stores
When our customers feel this sense of belonging, our stores become a haven, a break from the worries outside, a place where you can meet with friends. It's about enjoyment at the speed of life – sometimes slow and savoured, sometimes faster. Always full of humanity.

Our neighbourhood
Every store is part of a community, and we take our responsibility to be good neighbours seriously. We want to be invited in wherever we do business. We can be a force for positive action – bringing together our partners, customers, and the community to contribute every day. Now we see that our responsibility – and our potential for good – is even larger. The world is looking to Starbucks to set the new standard, yet again. We will lead.

Our shareholders
We know that as we deliver in each of these areas, we enjoy the kind of success that rewards our shareholders. We are fully accountable to get each of these elements right so that Starbucks – and everyone it touches – can endure and thrive.

Questions

1. Treacy and Wiersema distinguish three value disciplines.
   - Which value discipline was chosen by Costa Coffee? Please explain your answer.
   - Explain also why you think the TW model is not entirely applicable to Costa Coffee.
2. Create the 'three-dimensional' representation of the market definition for Costa Coffee at consumer level.
3. Lehmann and Winer distinguish four levels of competition.
   - Identify potential competitors of Costa Coffee for each of these levels.
   - Identify potential competitors of Nescafé instant coffee for each of these levels.
4. Assess the mission statement of Starbucks. To what extent does this mission statement fit in with the components and objectives of a mission as defined in the book?
5. Starbucks offers a variety of 'trendy' coffee, tea, and chocolate products, in combination with sweet snacks for a quick breakfast or lunch, or for 'on the go'. For each of the four growth strategies of Ansoff, create a product that could be marketed by Starbucks.

Chapter 4

Internal analysis

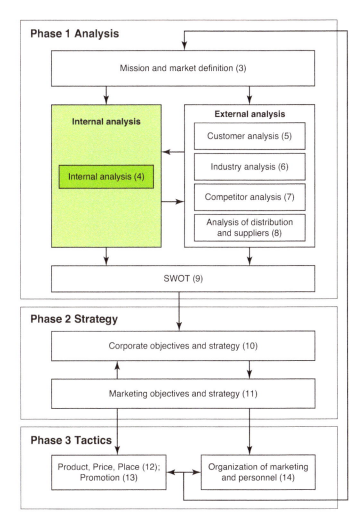

Phase 1 Analysis

Mission and market definition (3)

Internal analysis

Internal analysis (4)

External analysis

Customer analysis (5)

Industry analysis (6)

Competitor analysis (7)

Analysis of distribution and suppliers (8)

SWOT (9)

Phase 2 Strategy

Corporate objectives and strategy (10)

Marketing objectives and strategy (11)

Phase 3 Tactics

Product, Price, Place (12); Promotion (13)

Organization of marketing and personnel (14)

> ## Key points in this chapter
>
> - ■ Know how to define objectives for a company.
> - ■ Recognize the importance of applying customer-oriented objectives.
> - ■ Be capable of analysing a brand's performance.
> - ■ Apply appropriate frameworks for a strengths–weaknesses analysis.
> - ■ Know how to assess a company's marketing effectiveness.

Introduction

In Chapter 3 the market was defined and a company's value strategy and other ambitions were reviewed. In this chapter, a company's strengths and weaknesses are analysed in an internal analysis. When these elements are compared with those of competitors, insight is developed into the company's relative strengths and weaknesses – relative in relation to the competition. In Chapter 9 these relative strengths and weaknesses are contrasted with the corresponding opportunities and threats. However, before going into the strengths–weaknesses analysis it is important to get a feel for how the brand is performing. Thus, a detailed analysis of the brand's performance with respect to its objectives is needed. This is the 'control' phase of the planning process, which is the starting point.

This chapter is organized as follows. Section 4.1 starts by describing how objectives should be formulated and which objectives can be chosen (the balanced scorecard). At this stage it is not yet possible to formulate objectives; what is needed is a review of the current objectives. Section 4.2 presents a framework for a performance analysis. Section 4.3 underlines the importance of denominating the DNA of the brand, which is part of the internal analysis. Sections 4.4 and 4.5 are devoted to the core part of the internal analysis: the strengths–weaknesses analysis on corporate level (4.4) and brand level (4.5).

4.1 Objectives

4.1.1 Requirements for objectives

Formulating an objective has a number of functions. First, within the company it serves as a guideline for what the company wants to achieve; thus it has, among other functions, a communicative or motivating function: namely everyone knows what is being pursued. A second function of an objective is that it is a tool for the planning process: an objective is a standard for determining whether a strategy has succeeded. If the objective has been achieved, the company can be satisfied and perhaps continue in the same vein, but if the objective has not been achieved, the strategy should probably be altered.

In light of these functions, an objective should meet five requirements, summarized by the acronym SMART (originally introduced by Doran, 1981):

1. *S*pecific
2. *M*easurable
3. *A*mbitious

4. *R*ealistic
5. *T*imed

Specific relates to being precise about what the company is going to achieve.

Measurability means that it is possible to document whether the objective was achieved. The objective should therefore be expressed in measurable variables and preferably be quantitative – expressed in numbers. In practice, objectives are often used that are not quantitative, such as "achieving a high market share", "a reasonable profit", "continuously being able to offer good quality products", and "a good work atmosphere". Although it is not objectionable per se for a company to have qualitative objectives, the company should realize that such objectives cannot play a role in the planning process. At most they serve a motivating function, but even in that role the question remains whether management has achieved the objectives: for example, how does a company know that "a good work atmosphere" exists?

Ambitious means that the objectives should not be set too low. If the level of aspirations is set too low, it will lead to a reduction in the motivation to perform.

However, the objective should be *realistic*. It should be reasonably possible to achieve it. An objective such as doubling the market share in one year may be challenging and ambitious but is typically not feasible. This leads to the unnecessary situation in which every strategy will in effect 'fail'. The need to be realistic also has to do with relevance for the person or department for which the objective is defined. That person or department should be able to influence the chosen objective.

Finally, an objective should be defined for a specific *time period*. If this does not happen, it is difficult to determine the moment when it is possible to check whether the objective was achieved. If the planning horizon is longer than one year (e.g. three years), it is prudent to indicate a timeline so that interim evaluations are possible. For example, the objective might be: We want to achieve the following market share development with new product X over the next three years: year 1, 10 per cent; year 2, 12 per cent; year 3, 14 per cent.

The acronym SMART is well known and often differently described. For example, the *A* is also used for 'achievable' (resembling realistic), 'assignable', 'acceptable' or 'agreed upon'. In addition, other conditions are mentioned: for example, clear, challenging, and customer-focused. We return to the issue of choosing customer-oriented objectives in Section 4.2 and in Chapter 12.

In summary, an objective should be quantified, include a time frame, and be ambitious but realistic.

4.1.2 The balanced scorecard

In making both decisions (prioritization and value definition), the method of the balanced scorecard (BSC) as developed by Kaplan and Norton (1992, 1993) may be helpful. This method means that in joint deliberations involving lower management, middle management, and top management, measurable objectives are developed for four fields: customer satisfaction, efficiency, innovation, and finances.

Financial goals

Nearly every company sets financial goals. Those goals may be defined in terms of profit, gross margin, cash flow, share price, and so on. Some financial measures may be stated in absolute or relative terms: for example, in relation to sales (profit margin) or to invested capital (return on investment (ROI)). Ultimately, financial measures are the main criteria for judging a marketing plan. For this reason, every marketing plan should be accompanied by a forecast of revenues and profit. We will provide an example of this in Chapter 14.

Setting financial goals, however, is one-sided. Kaplan and Norton state that it is also important to develop goals in relation to the building blocks of, for example, profit. Those building blocks include costs and revenues. Revenues in turn are influenced by customer perceptions of the quality and the degree of innovation of the company. Kaplan and Norton argue that formulating goals related to costs, customer-oriented measures, and innovation will provide a more balanced interpretation of the objectives.

Customer-oriented goals

Aside from financial goals, customer-oriented goals may be developed. Such goals are also called marketing objectives. They may include the following:

- 'Hard' goals such as sales, turnover, and market share.
- More underlying ('softer') goals such as:
  - Customer satisfaction.
  - Customer loyalty or brand loyalty, which is measured on the basis of interviews and/or analyses of data regarding purchasing patterns.
  - Perceived quality or other image aspects of the brand: "How does the customer perceive the company's brand and that of competing products?"
  - Number and content of complaints.

Customer satisfaction and customer loyalty are strongly related but are not identical (Oliver, 1999). The pursuit of customer satisfaction and customer loyalty is receiving a lot of attention; this can be explained by the increased focus on value management. Customer loyalty has two dimensions: a behavioural dimension (this could be measured as the share of the brand or the company in the category purchases of the customer: the 'market share' of the customer) and an emotional dimension (the attitude of the customer towards the brand, which is measured through questionnaires).

Internal goals

This dimension relates to functioning effectively and efficiently in the internal environment. The goals in this context relate to efficiency and the employees. Measures for efficiency include the following:

- Turnover in relation to investments.
- Turnover rate.

- Accounts receivable.
- Liquidity.
- Overhead costs.

Measures for employee satisfaction include the following:

- Work atmosphere and morale.
- Personal development.
- Staff turnover.
- Use of sick leave.
- Turnover per employee.

Setting goals for employees is becoming more important in practice. This is related to the insight that customer satisfaction can be achieved only when everyone in the organization, especially the direct-contact staff, operates in a customer-friendly fashion.

Innovation goals

According to Kaplan and Norton, innovation is the basis for success. Only companies that introduce new products regularly are relatively successful. In this regard, the extent to which a company learns from prior experiences also plays a role. Measures in this regard could be the percentage of successful product introductions, the turnover from new products, and the number of concrete new product plans that are being developed.

Figure 4.1 shows an elaboration of the BSC. In the vision, long-term goals for financial growth, customer satisfaction, costs, and innovation are formulated. If top management finds stimulating customer orientation and brand building important and realizes that this may bring in additional investments, the financial goals can be placed somewhat lower and the customer-oriented goals higher. Subsequently, the long-term goals are made more specific for the short term. Thus, "elevating customer satisfaction" is translated into "enhancement of brand image", "elevation of frequency", and "elevation of customer satisfaction". Then, with all of these factors, it is indicated how they should be measured. In this way the enhancement of the brand image is measured by the percentage of people from the target group who associate the brand with the identity characteristic 'bold'. Finally, the numerical goals are indicated. This is done after consultation between top management and middle management, during which the goals are assigned to certain managers.

The advantages of the BSC are that there is a balanced planning and control process and the motivation of the managers to achieve their goals is increased. In addition, the formulation of common measurable goals strengthens team spirit. The balanced scorecard is therefore an important instrument for the implementation of strategies. A problem lies in the implementation of the method: it requires a long and detailed information and control system. Each criterion has to be quantified, and for this purpose many detailed data have to be collected (internally and externally). Another problem involves flexibility: if certain goals (for example, sales) are not going to be met and this is accepted by the management, the criteria should be changed.

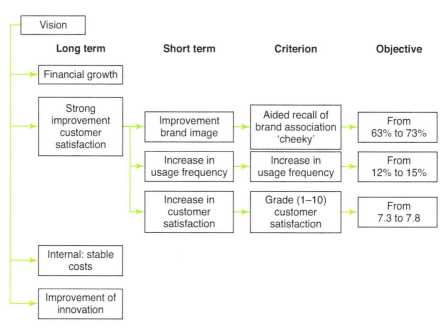

Figure 4.1 **Example of balanced scorecard with elaboration of customer part**

The importance placed on the different areas and the interpretation of that placement will depend on the chosen *value strategy*. With operational excellence, more emphasis will be put on the costs and customer-oriented criteria will be important, though not in detailed form; instead, an aggregated form will be used. With product leadership, innovation is very important, and with customer intimacy, certain client criteria will be very important: for example, how long customers want to remain customers of the company (brand loyalty). Figure 4.2 shows some relationships between value strategy and the four areas of the BSC.

	Financial objectives	Customer objectives	Efficiency objectives	Innovation objectives
Operational excellence	Very relevant in short and long term	Especially total measurements	High importance	Less importance
Product leadership	Of importance	Of high importance, attitude, measurements of the perception of innovations	Less important, especially in the long term	Most important
Customer intimacy	Of importance	Of high importance, deaggregated (individual) measurements, lifetime value, etc.	Less important, especially in the long term	Of importance

Figure 4.2 **Relationships between value strategy and relevance of objectives**

4.2 Evaluation of the results

In this section we focus on the analysis of quantitative data. As mentioned before, the amount of available data is increasing. First we will describe the goal of measuring all kinds of variables. We then go deeper into measuring customer-oriented data.

4.2.1 Why measure variables?

Measuring results is only useful if the information it provides is used. Verhoef et al. (2016) state that an analysis of (big) data should lead to better ways to deliver value to the customer and in the end also value to the firm. Measuring and evaluating data is part of the so-called PDCA cycle: Plan, Do, Check, Act (Figure 4.3).

'Plan' means making plans with measurable goals: for example, a marketing plan. 'Do' is the implementation of the plan. 'Check' is in essence the evaluation of results: Did we meet our goals? 'Act' is doing anything to reach the goals.

The continuous measurement of a number of metrics is part of 'marketing intelligence'. Marketing intelligence is the collection and analysis of all data relevant for marketing decisions. In marketing science there is much attention paid to developing the best metrics. Some companies do a lot of data collection and analysis, such as manufacturers of fast-moving consumer goods like Unilever and Procter & Gamble. But also large retailers such as Walmart have many data available, and companies with a strong online presence also have 'big data'. On the other hand, many small and medium-sized companies pay little attention to measuring and analysing data.

The first step with marketing intelligence is to look at what data are present in the company: for example, the outcomes of customer satisfaction surveys, or online data about sales. The second step is to decide whether additional data are needed: for example, about competition, or about the image of the brand. The third step is to transform data into information by means of analysing the data. A distinction can be made between

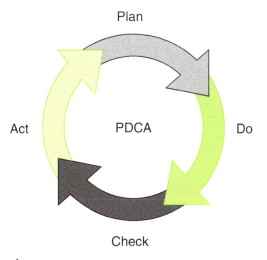

Figure 4.3 PDCA cycle

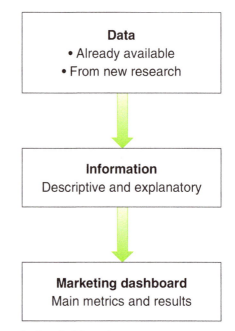

Figure 4.4 **Developing a marketing dashboard**

descriptive methods and explanatory methods. Descriptive methods simply summarize the main findings: for example, the level of satisfaction and the changes in this variable. Explanatory methods show relations between variables: for example, differences in satisfaction between younger and older customers, or the relation between brand image and brand loyalty. The main results of the analysis of the data may be summarized in a *marketing dashboard*: an overview of the main metrics in combination with the interpretation (information) (Figure 4.4).

4.2.2 Detailed analysis of customer-oriented variables

A distinction can be made between two categories of customer-oriented variables:

- Data collected by the company: for example, by means of questionnaires or registration of sales by the company or by market research agencies.
- Data about online behaviour of customers, such as information-seeking behaviour (sites visited, click behaviour, etc.), but also buying behaviour and 'after-sales' behaviour, such as experiences expressed online.

We now focus on the first category: data collected by the company. Online data are dealt with in Chapter 5.

Every company will measure sales and turnover. These are examples of customer-oriented variables. In many cases the analysis of these data can go deeper. The level of detail for the analysis of customer data depends on the availability of data. A large number of data are available for the market for food products (store panel data of Nielsen, IRI, and GfK: see Chapter 5). We first discuss analyses that may be performed with these data and then conclude this section with several remarks about branches other than those of daily-use goods (fast-moving consumer goods).

For markets for food products, the following sales developments may be analysed:

1. Market developments: sales developments for the entire market and for market segments (varieties).
2. Analysis of the manufacturer's brands:
   - Developments for each brand total and for packaging units.
   - Regional differences in brand developments.
3. Competitor analysis:
   - Identification of the largest competitors.
   - Sales developments of competing manufacturers.
4. Position of manufacturer brands and competitor brands at the various retail organizations as well as developments over time (analysis of sales and distribution).
5. Sales developments at retailers with and without promotions (provide insight into effects of promotions).

If data from household panels or sales figures for customers from the company's own database are available, additional sales analyses may take place that are disaggregated by target audiences.

These detailed analyses are required because it is difficult to assign causes on the basis of aggregated data. For example, a slight growth in sales may appear not to be an unfavourable result, but it may in reality be a combination of strong growth in region A and stabilization or even a decline in region B. This would lead to the conclusion that there are problems in region B, such as disappointing distribution.

A careful analysis of the market share may also give indications of problems (Hulbert and Toy, 1977). Is it a case of a decrease or an increase? For a market share analysis, the market definition is crucial (see section 2.2). With a smaller market, the market share automatically becomes 'larger'.

A useful tool for market share analysis is the *Parfitt–Collins analysis* (Parfitt and Collins, 1968). This type of analysis divides the market share of a brand into the product of three components:

1. *Degree of penetration.* This is the percentage of households that have ever bought the product.
2. *The percentage of repeat purchases.* This is the degree to which, after the purchase of a brand, the same brand is purchased again.
3. *The usage intensity index.* This is the degree to which buyers of the brand use more or less of the relevant product group.

For example, if these three components assume values of 10 per cent (penetration), 40 per cent (repeat purchases), and 1.5 per cent (usage intensity), the market share will be 6 per cent. The development of these separate components provides better insight into potential problems than does the progress of the market share as a whole.

The Parfitt–Collins analysis is often used in combination with awareness measurements. The following indicators are then relevant:

1. *Awareness* (spontaneous or aided): percentage of people who know the brand.
2. *Consideration set:* percentage of people who are considering the brand.
3. *Trial*: percentage of trial purchases.
4. *Repeat*: percentage of repeat purchases.

The size of the various percentages and especially the differences between them form an important starting point for the formulation of objectives for the elements of the marketing mix. For example, a low awareness and a relatively high *trial* lead to the conclusion that the communication should be intensified. A low *trial* may be related to a price that is too high or distribution that is too limited. A low *repeat* is more closely related to the performance of the product itself.

Although less detailed, careful analyses are possible in other areas. The most important data limitation outside the markets for fast-moving consumer goods (FMCGs) is that the data typically are not collected centrally and therefore no solid competitor sales data are available. However, each company may document its own sales in detail and may also perform customer research through research agencies. It is important to ensure that data collection is long-lasting and consistent. As long as a company's own sales data or measures of customer satisfaction are used instead of market share, many organizations are able to measure and analyse results in detail.

4.3 Goal of the internal analysis: finding the DNA

Sections 4.1 and 4.2 deal with the 'control': analysis of results. The more strategic, second function of an internal analysis is to find out what the 'DNA' of the brand is. The reason why this is important is that marketing is by definition relating customer needs to the identity of the brand: thus not only listening to customers, but also to 'go your own way'. But what is this 'own way'? The internal analysis has to find out the strengths and weaknesses of the brand/company and, in addition, the DNA of the brand.

How difficult is it for a company to find and identify its DNA? Very difficult, for two reasons. First, the company is perhaps not really having a competitive advantage, thus being 'stuck in the middle'. But we assume that most companies will have some edge. The other reason why it may be difficult to define your own core, unique strength is that you as a manager can no longer see it. Because you are too close and too strongly involved. You may need someone else to help you.

The problem with defining your own strategy is that many companies do not make or follow written strategic plans. They just do their job based on feelings. When the company started up many years ago there was some kind of an idea, and some years later we arrived at a certain point we had never expected at the beginning. Looking back, all kinds of rationalizations can be made about the 'strategic choices' and the 'resulting success'. What is happening, then, is in fact seeking patterns and naming it strategy. Sometimes strategy is defined as such: "giving a name to a set of coherent actions performed for many years in the past".

Doing business based on gut feeling is not wrong. It is probably how many entre-preneurs operate, such as Steve Jobs of Apple. One way of defining a company's DNA is by defining brand values that best fit the company and sticking to them. Also in this respect Steve Jobs is a wonderful example, since in a legendary interview he explained why it is so important for Apple to always stick to the core values of the company (see Case 4.1).

Case 4.1 Relevance of core values

Steve Jobs: Apple's core value

Steve Jobs gives an inspiring talk about the core values of Apple, and more importantly, himself. Steve Jobs was discussing a new campaign "Think Different" and talked about how Apple needs to change its marketing strategy to one which emphasizes its core values. He went on to talk about how Apple's core value was to honour people who believe they can change the world with their passion.

Apple's core value is not the Think Different campaign. Its core value is to make the best products in the market and focus on selected products so that they can develop and innovate. These core values are the reason that Apple products have been so consistently excellent, and they are the reason that you can walk into any Apple store across the world and get the same experience. From sales associates to top executives, Apple is united by a common culture. It is that culture which ensures that Apple customers enjoy the experience that they have come to expect whenever they interact with Apple.

Source: www.thinkmarketingmagazine.com

In section 4.4 we propose a number of methods that can help in finding the strengths and weaknesses of a company and brand, including how to 'find' the core values of the company.

4.4 Internal analysis at the company level

Figure 4.5 contains a number of methods that can be used for the analysis of strengths and weaknesses. First we go into the methods for the company level. Then we go into those for the brand level.

Method	Source of data	Result
Company level		
Value strategies	Management judgement	Main direction of competive advantage
Checklist functional areas	Management	Judgement for each function
Marketing audit	Management	Marketing orientation
Brand level		
Perceptual research customers	Customers	Judgements from customers
Four or five P's	Customers	Judgement of functional brand performance
Checklist brand values and brand personality	Management or customers	Scores on brand values of personality treats

Figure 4.5 Methods for the internal analysis

4.4.1 Value strategies

In Chapter 3 we presented some models to define a company's value strategies. We will not repeat them here, but they may be used for an internal analysis in group discussions in the management team by letting managers give a grade for the level of each of the values. Figure 4.6 shows an example using the Brand Benefiting Model.

Brand benefit	Current score	Desired score
Quality	6	7
Service	7	8
Price	6	6
Convenience	7	7
Emotion	7	8

Figure 4.6 Possible outcome management discussion brand benefits

4.4.2 Management judgement of functional areas

At the company level, strengths relate especially to functional areas. The core skills of a company are often referred to in this context as *core competencies* (Prahalad and Hamel, 1990). We devoted attention to the core competencies of a company in section 2.1. To analyse the strengths and weaknesses at the level of the company, a checklist may be used (see Figure 4.7, from Aaker (2013), who presents this list for the competitor analysis). This list relates to potential strengths and weaknesses of the various functional areas within a company:

- Innovation: technological skills, research and development (R&D), expenditures, patents, and so on.
- Production: added value, capacity, and so on.
- Financing possibilities: in the short term, in the long term, possibility for financing through the parent company, and so on.
- Management and organization: quality of top management, organization structure, company culture, and so on.
- Personnel: motivation, customer orientation.
- Marketing: customer orientation of top management and staff, product quality, width of the product line, strength of the advertising agency, and so on.

The strengths and weaknesses mentioned in Figure 4.7 are not independent of one another. For example, the attitude and motivation of the staff strongly depend on the quality of top management and the organization structure, and that motivation also has an influence on the creativity and the innovative capacity of the company, and so on.

We end this section by discussing the following aspects of the measurement of strengths and weaknesses: the analysis of financial strengths, the marketing audit, and the issue of constraints in developing strategies.

Analysis of financial strengths

In relation to the analysis of the financial position of the product and the company, the well-known financial ratios may be calculated and analysed in relation to the following:

- *The liquidity*. This is the extent to which a company can meet its ongoing financial obligations; it is measured, for example, through the current ratio (current assets/ current liabilities).
- *The financial structure (solvency)*. This is measured, for example, through the debt ratio (debt capital/total invested capital).
- *The activities*. These activities include the turnover rate of the inventory (sales/ inventory) and the average credit term of creditors (average amount receivable/sales per 365 days).
- *The profitability.* This is measured, for example, through the gross or net profit margin or the profitability of the net assets (net profit/net assets).

Innovation
Technical product superiority
New product possibilities
Research and development
Technologies
Patents

Production
Cost structure
Flexibility in production
Means of production (machines, etc.)
Access to raw materials
Vertical integration
Production capacity

Finances and access to capital
From the operational activities
From resources available in the short term
Possibilities for attracting net assets and debt capital
Willingness of 'parent company' to finance

Management and organization
Quality of top and middle management
Knowledge of the market
Company culture
Organization structure
Strategic objectives and plans
Company qualities
Planning system
Staff turnover
Quality of strategic decision making

Marketing
Customer orientation
Product quality
Width of the product line
Segmentation
Distribution
Relationship with distributors
Quality of the communication (including online)
Representatives
Service

Staff
Attitude and motivation of staff
Customer orientation

Figure 4.7 **Potential strengths and weaknesses (sources of advantages) at the company level**
Source: Adapted from Aaker (2013).

Case 4.2 Defining the strength of a company

Starbucks' deal with Nestlé shows the brand knows where its core competencies lie

Starbucks has partnered with Nestlé to help it sell coffee. At first sight, that sentence appears a little odd. Like selling coals to Newcastle or ice to Eskimos, why on earth would Starbucks need any help with selling coffee?

To understand why Starbucks needs Nestlé you have to grasp two of the more established theories of management thinking: core competency and competitive strategy.

In Starbucks' case, its core strategic strengths are an ability to market premium products on an international scale and to retail them through an on-premise retail model. It sells the majority of its coffee through its own channels and into its own cafés. That means it has very little experience of selling through wholesalers and, ultimately, into big retail chains. Only about 10 per cent of the coffee company's revenues come from retail sales, so it's clear why Starbucks needs Nestlé. The Swiss giant is a master at mass marketing and sells most of its brands through wholesale channels into big retailers. Nestlé gets the Starbucks brand to complement its own growing coffee business and also gains a brand with significantly more heft in the USA where it has traditionally struggled with its existing coffee portfolio.

Source: *Marketing Week*, 8 May 2018

4.4.3 Marketing audit

Measuring the quality of the marketing department is the subject of a marketing audit: an independent 'investigation' of all marketing activities in the company or the SBU. Put differently, the question is whether the company is truly customer-oriented. This involves an evaluation of the following:

- The extent to which a company is operating in a market-oriented fashion: Do clearly formulated objectives and strategies exist? Do the objectives and strategies explicitly take environmental factors into account? Do the strategies actually relate to environmental factors? How do customers perceive the company and its products?
- The knowledge that the company has of the environment: What does the company know about developments in the macro environment, about factors related to industry structure, about competitors, and about customers?

Customer philosophy
1. Does management recognize the importance of designing the company to serve the needs and wants of the chosen markets?
2. Does management develop different offerings and marketing plans for different segments of the market?
3. Does management take a whole marketing system view?

Integrated marketing organization
4. Is there high-level marketing integration and control of the major marketing functions?
5. Does marketing management work well with management in research, manufacturing, purchasing, logistics, ICT, and finance?
6. How well organized is the new product development process?

Adequate marketing information
7. When were the latest market research studies of customers, buying influences, channels, and competitors conducted?
8. How well does management know the sales potential and profitability of different market segments, customers, territories, products, channels (offline and online), and order sizes?
9. What effort is expended to measure and improve the cost-effectiveness of different marketing expenditures?

Strategic orientation
10. What is the extent of formal marketing planning?
11. How clear and innovative is the current marketing strategy?
12. What is the extent of contingency thinking and planning?

Operational efficiency
13. How well is the marketing strategy communicated and implemented?
14. Is management doing an effective job with its marketing resources?
15. Does management show a good capacity to react quickly and effectively to on-the-spot developments?

Figure 4.8 **Marketing effectiveness review instrument**

Source: Kotler (1977, pp. 67–75).

■   The analysis the company has made of the environment: Is market research being performed? Are predictions being made? Is there a regular strategy evaluation? Is there a marketing information system?

To perform a marketing audit, a checklist may be used. Figure 4.8 shows the marketing effectiveness review instrument developed by Kotler (Kotler and Keller, 2016). For each question a maximum of two points can be scored; the total score provides an indication of the level of marketing effectiveness.

Financial and management strengths may not only present a source of advantage but also serve as constraints within which strategies have to be developed. For example, strategies should be financially feasible and fit within the 'culture' of the company. There is little use in recommending a strongly innovative strategy if the company is not ready for such a strategy from an organizational perspective. We will discuss preconditions during strategy selection in section 9.7.

4.5 Strengths and weaknesses at the brand level

4.5.1 Using checklists

The methods described above provide insights at the company level. It is also essential to judge the strengths and weaknesses at the brand level. This will largely be done through a customer analysis. Performing customer analyses will be discussed in Chapter 5.

Part of the insights that are relevant in customer research is how customers perceive the brand. Brand perceptions or brand associations form the brand image. And as already mentioned in Chapter 1, the brand associations should be unique, strong, and favourable. So, analysing the associations gives insights into how customers judge the brand. This is the 'image' of the brand.

Several checklists may be used to measure brand associations. First, we mention the Brand Benefitting Model, presented in Chapter 3. Another simple model is to measure the performance of brands along the five P dimensions (Figure 4.9).

The five P model emphasizes the functional attributes of a brand. However, a brand also has emotional meanings. A distinction can be made between two kinds of emotional meanings

■   Personality dimensions, such as 'masculine', 'tough', 'young', etc.
■   End values, such as 'freedom', 'intimacy', 'honesty'.

Marketing instrument	Metric
Product	Quality
Price	Price perception, 'value'
Place (channels, location)	Availability
Communication	Communication style, clarity
Personnel	Customer orientation, service, expertise

Figure 4.9 **Measuring the strength of the Ps of a brand**

These dimensions are part of the 'means–end chain', a model described in Chapter 11. For measuring personality dimensions, the brand personality scale of Aaker may be used (Chapter 5), and for measuring end values, we introduce the Value Compass in Chapter 11.

4.5.2 Coming to conclusions from the internal analysis

Important goals of the internal analysis are to come to insights into the strengths and weaknesses and about the DNA of the brand.

The term 'strengths and weaknesses' assumes that a judgement may be given in the sense of 'good or bad'. This means that there should be a kind of standard. The standard is what the manager thinks is important. In fact this is about image and identity. Image is how customers perceive the brand. Identity is how a brand wants to be seen. Chapter 5 (customer analysis) provides insight into, among others, the image of the brand. The decision about identity is part of marketing strategy: targeting and positioning (Chapter 11). In the internal analysis a manager can already take one of the checklists and make his (preliminary) choices about the desired level. For example, from the Brand Benefiting Model it may appear that customers judge the price on a 10-point scale from very cheap to very expensive as a 6, which is an intermediate felt price level. The manager may decide that this level is too low, since the brand may be a high-quality brand of which the 'felt price' may score an 8. Using the Value Compass it may be that customers score the brand with a 6 on the dimension 'excitement', while the brand manager wants it to be seen as highly exciting, scoring at least an 8.

All results from the internal and customer analysis together should lead to a conclusion about the DNA of the brand. What can be done to come to this insight is to organize a session with several employees from the organization, and let all of them fill in the desired associations. This can be the starting point for a discussion about the 'essence' of the brand. Another way is to go back to the birth of the brand. What was the original idea of the brand? Especially if the founder of a company is no longer alive, the risk is that the company will 'forget' its core values.

The conclusion about the DNA of the brand should be that some functional and emotional values are unique to the brand. Often, companies end up with conclusions like "we are competent, deliver the best quality, are reliable, offer good service and a good price". One way to check whether this is really unique is to see if the conclusion also fits with a competitor. If this is the case, find something else. Finding the unique DNA is difficult. Chapter 11 will elaborate on this point.

Summary

The goals of an internal analysis are to provide insight into the performance and the company's strengths and weaknesses, including the core values. During the evaluation an inventory is made of which goals are achievable for the different levels and whether the goals that were set have been achieved. The principle of the balanced scorecard states that besides financial goals, other, underlying goals should be measured: criteria on innovation, efficiency, and customer satisfaction. Subsequently, customer-oriented criteria are subjected to a detailed analysis to obtain insight into possible problem areas.

Subsequently, an analysis of strengths and weaknesses is performed. At the organization level, strengths or weaknesses may be identified through evaluation of the strengths and weaknesses in the various functional areas (completing a marketing audit). At the brand level, input should be used from customer analyses. Checklists such as the five Ps, or, for emotional values, the Value Compass, may be used to compare the perceptions of customers about the brand (image) with the desired brand associations (identity).

Case how Walmart found its footing in the Amazon Era

This is not a story about rebranding. Walmart US Chief Marketing Officer Tony Rogers is clear about that. Although the country's largest retailer has evolved its marketing, product mix, private label offerings, agency and vendor relationships, strategy, and more, Rogers is adamant that there's no fundamental change in how Walmart operates. "As business and technology advance and customer habits continue to change, it requires any brand to pause and refresh or redefine as necessary," he says.

That adaptability has helped Walmart reverse the streak of same-store sales declines that marked 2013 and 2014. Today it boasts 12 straight quarters of same-store sales growth at gradually accelerating rates.

To survive the retail carnage that pushed Sears and Kmart towards irrelevance and dragged down success stories like Target and Kroger, the $485 billion giant remade itself as a unified online-offline proposition. It has rolled out drive-thru pickup of grocery orders to 1,000 of its more than 4,000 US stores and has installed automated kiosks at about 100 stores where people can collect orders inside. It's using technology more smartly to maximize checkout orders at Walmart.com.

For customers who shop in person, the chain has improved its quality with revamped produce sections and higher end exclusive or private label apparel, food, and nonfood items.

But through all of this, Walmart hasn't lost sight of its signature low-price proposition. Although the old slogan "everyday low prices" has been transformed into "We don't just save you money, we allow you to live better", the slogan is the fundamental tenet of a cult masquerading as a company. Over the years, Walmart has relentlessly wrung tens of billions of dollars in cost efficiencies out of the retail supply chain, passing the larger part of the savings along to shoppers as bargain prices. In the USA, wherever Walmart competes, average grocery prices are 14 per cent lower than elsewhere.

Needless to say, parts of these savings have also been realized by continuous pressure on the already low wages for the Walmart sales clerks. Walmart's huge advantages in buying power and efficiency force many rivals to close. For every Walmart supercentre that opens, two other supermarkets will close. As the number of supermarkets shrinks, more shoppers will have to travel farther from home. Meanwhile, the failure of hundreds of stores will cost their owners dearly and put thousands out of work, only some of whom will find jobs at Walmart. Most likely at lower pay: Walmart is blamed sometimes for the sorry state of retail wages in America. On average, Walmart sales clerks –'associates' in Walmart terminology – earned an average of around $9.00 an hour, or around $18,000 a year. As a comparison, the federal poverty line for a family of three in 2017 was $20,420.

Walmart enterprise strategy

Price, access, assortment and experience drive a customer's choice of retailer. Historically, Walmart led on price and assortment. Retail environments are more competitive today, especially with e-commerce. To win, Walmart will lead on price, invest to differentiate on access, be competitive on assortment, and deliver a great experience.

We understand not only what our customers want and need, but also where they want it and how they want to experience it.

Figure 4.10 Walmart customer proposition

The low-cost strategy is obvious, but what might most separate it from Sears is that Walmart knows change is expensive, and sometimes you have to lose money to make it. Walmart management recognizes that the big retailers of the past made decisions to preserve the models they created. Walmart has decided it wants to be a retailer for the long haul, even if that means being a little suboptimal in its returns.

Walmart is [also] willing to invest in a new business model, even one that it's kind of bad at and will take them a while to get good at.

The price/convenience equation

Walmart's vaunted lower prices have made life harder for such rivals as Target, Kroger, and Dollar General, even if the primary intended targets were Amazon and hard discounters like Aldi and Lidl. In a presentation to corporate officers in May, Rogers outlined Walmart's marketing strategy, but emphasized this point: "None of this matters unless we have price leadership. We're always maniacal about not letting people get distracted from price."

But price is a game no retailer wins all the time. Avoiding the fate of failed retailers rests at least as heavily on delivering the second half of Walmart's slogan, "Save Money. Live Better", with a bigger focus on convenience and quality.

'Clean, fast and friendly'

Rogers' biggest surprise when he came back to the USA last year from a two-year stint as CMO for Walmart in China was "how much convenience had been elevated as a driver for consumer behaviour," he says. That's partially based on expectations raised by online shopping and other digital services. But Rogers says the demand for more shopping convenience also stems from sobering factors specific to the USA: both parents working in 60 per cent of two-parent households, people working an average of five hours longer a month than a few years ago, and people tethered to work via smartphones, which put them in contact with their jobs on average 13.5 hours a day, or, as Rogers puts it, "nearly all their waking hours".

Walmart reaches every demographic in the USA, says Rogers, but to win on convenience, the retailer is focusing more on a segment it calls 'busy families'. They're "the most intense combination of being busy and money-challenged," he says. "They have the highest bar in terms of delivering on price, quality and convenience. If you can deliver on this subset, you can probably deliver on everybody."

This group is "a little higher income than we've defined our customer in the past," Rogers adds. But that doesn't mean Walmart is going upscale as much as it's targeting a segment that's more suburban and multicultural than its prior core.

"They've found the right balance between promotion and everyday low price," says Don Stuart, managing partner of Cadent Consulting Group. The company has removed some of the clutter of bargain-bin store-floor displays, for example, but hasn't done away with them entirely. Most shoppers give Walmart credit for having the lowest prices most of the time, Stuart says – or at least being close enough that it's not worth the effort to shop around.

Walmart US CEO Greg Foran, an Australian who joined McMillon's team early on, was accustomed to operating in a duopoly market down under, with less price competition and more significance to the store experience, says Fletcher, of Bernstein Research. So Foran is focused on making sure checkout lines aren't longer than three deep and generally keeping the store experience 'clean, fast and friendly'. Walmart has improved customer satisfaction as a result, according to its own measures and external sources such as the American Customer Satisfaction Index, which tracked a major lift this year.

Add to clean-fast-friendly the three-legged stool of price-convenience-quality. Winning on those last three is key for Walmart to succeed across the biggest customer base in America, as Rogers sees it.

Just based on trading area, Walmart skews a lot more Middle American or red state than its more coastal, blue state competitors Amazon and Costco. But Rogers is convinced that Walmart's demos look pretty much the same as America's. He identifies three very different groups of shoppers who are particularly interested in Walmart's defining proposition of saving money:

- people living from pay cheque to pay cheque;
- people scrimping on basics to pay for high-end purchases such as iPhones;
- well-off consumers who got that way in part by frugality.

Linking online and offline

Though Amazon is on track to pass Walmart as the biggest US retailer sometime in the next decade, Walmart's e-commerce growth rate is outpacing Amazon's. Walmart also recently inked a deal with Google to provide products for its online shopping mall Google Express, escalating its Amazon counterattack.

Winning in e-commerce is crucial for all segments of shoppers, who all want convenience. To try to buttress an online presence still dwarfed by Amazon, Walmart has enlisted its huge portfolio of stores. As of this year, Walmart finally appears to be breaking through in making 'bricks and clicks' work together in a way that meaningfully affects online sales growth. Free two-day delivery on millions of items without an Amazon Prime-like annual fee was one key to sparking a surge in e-commerce sales, up 63 per cent in the first quarter and 60 per cent in the second quarter of 2017. Amazon's e-commerce growth, meanwhile, hovered in the 20 per cent range. Discounts for store delivery on nearly a million items are also helping. And the chain put advertising weight usually reserved for the brick-and-mortar stores behind the efforts, according to Rogers.

It wasn't easy to convince executives to put the bulk of Walmart's advertising this winter behind a dot-com initiative, but it happened in part because of an effort to unify Walmart's e-commerce and general marketing teams last year. In a similar vein, Walmart is uniting tech teams in its Bentonville, Arkansas, headquarters; San Bruno, California; Hoboken, New Jersey; and India under the @WalmartLabs banner and expanding staffing not just in Silicon Valley but also in lower cost outposts.

Walmart is also using tech to tweak its pricing strategy. Under Walmart e-commerce chief Marc Lore, who was CEO of online retailer Jet.com before

Walmart acquired it in September 2016, the retailer is experimenting with bringing Jet's more complex pricing model, which bestows steeper discounts on larger orders. Shoppers might get a lower price on Walmart.com, for example, by adding baby wipes to a basket that includes diapers.

The whole variety of inducements looks to be working. TABS Analytics, which calculates market share based upon online tracking surveys of 2,000 consumers, suggests Walmart has doubled its online share of vitamins to 9.1 per cent between April 2016 and April 2017. And it gained ground in baby care, where it has been weak relative to its market share in other categories. Walmart's online market share in the diaper category rose 0.9 percentage points to 5.1 per cent, for example. Amazon's share fell 0.1 point to 7.1 per cent. Target also did well, up 1.1 points to 4.3 per cent. However, Walmart also gained in offline diaper share, rising 0.5 points to 18.1 per cent, while Target fell 1.1 points offline to 11.9 per cent, giving up its online gains.

Mixing up the product mix

With rivals like Aldi, Lidl, and Costco competing largely based on their private label programmes, Walmart is putting more resources into its own brands, too, and not just the lowest cost tiers but also higher end products.

Consequently, Walmart sells private label products aimed not just at the biggest mass brands, but also emerging players such as L'Oréal USA's Matrix salon brand. "Aspirational products at disruptive prices" was how Scott McCall, senior VP of home and seasonal, described Walmart's product development effort. This includes some Walmart 'exclusives', such as a Keurig K-Cup coffee maker hitting stores now priced at $59–$30 or more below prices elsewhere – and Yankee Candles priced around $10 less than they sell for elsewhere.

Walmart has significantly staffed up development for its own baby-care brands in the past 18 months, executives said, focusing on everything from pouch meals to baby wipes and strollers, with products priced 25 per cent to 50 per cent below branded rivals. Winning in packaged goods is key to winning online and offline with those "busy families", says Rogers. And families with newborns are among the most prized, not to mention the busiest. They eat at home more and buy more of just about everything as they establish households. "Walmart.com was built on big-ticket purchases like TVs," says Rogers. "What's happening now is a much more balanced approach where consumables play a much bigger role in customer acquisition."

Everyday low supplier pricing?

While Walmart has seldom hesitated to throw its weight around to get better prices, it's starting to use its power in new ways. One example was in what appears to be a first for the retail industry: Walmart recently conducted a review to streamline the army of third-party field merchandisers that help place displays and products in its stores, culling the firms involved to 5 from more than 30. It was an audacious move because outside marketers, such as P&G and Unilever, pay the firms for their efforts, not Walmart. But Walmart was able to engineer a roster that made the process more efficient in its stores, a spokesman says. It also ensured that each supplier had an in-store marketing force dedicated specifically to the chain. The expectation is that the resulting supply-chain savings get passed back to Walmart.

But it also meant forcing big suppliers like Unilever to switch vendors. "Right now they're in a fairly enviable position in that they're indispensable for shoppers and suppliers," according to Walmart. "Suppliers may not be happy with how they do business in every case, but they can't walk away."

Walmart acknowledges that the efforts to get more efficient may mean some added tension with suppliers. Then again, suppliers have plenty of grumbles about other retailers.

Walmart as startup

Even as Walmart wields its bigness in new ways, it's playing with small flanker brands in e-commerce. Counting Jet.com, it has acquired six small e-commerce players whose customers often weren't big on Walmart, including Hayneedle, Shoebuy, ModCloth, Moosejaw, and Bonobos.

Perhaps one true sign of a shift is that Walmart says it's not imposing itself on these brands. Rogers describes Walmart's approach to the newly acquired online retailers this way: "Imagine if you get purchased by the world's largest company and you have access to those resources, and yet they aren't really going to change you. All they want is for you to be better versions of yourselves."

Walmart has learned from startups that Wall Street will let you be 'suboptimal' on profit as long as you grow. Righting the ship on store operations has also bought Walmart permission to make big and so far money-losing bets on e-commerce, where even Amazon is at best thinly profitable.

Amazon eked out a 2.3 per cent operating margin in North America in the first half. But take away cloud computing and Amazon remains a roughly $150 billion-a-year startup losing money quarter after quarter. Walmart remains more than three times Amazon's size by global sales. And Walmart's $13.6 billion in after-tax profit last year stacks up nicely against Amazon's $1 billion in pre-tax profit on retail.

Whatever you call it – reinvention or something else – Walmart is "not going down the path of generational decline like Sears and Kmart," Rogers says. But he still isn't convinced that Walmart has the bricks part of the bricks-and-clicks equation completely figured out – that the work is done. "That doesn't mean there aren't still too many stores," he says, "and that the stores themselves aren't still too big for where we see America's shopping patterns headed."

Source: *Ad Age*, 27 September 2017

Questions

1. Which value discipline (Treacy and Wiersema) has been chosen by Walmart? Give reasons for your answer with the information in the text box 'Walmart Enterprise Strategy'.

2. "The second-worst thing a manufacturer can do is sign a contract with Walmart. The worst? Not sign one." Explain this expression.

3. a. Use the information in the case to identify strengths and weaknesses for Walmart.

    b. Use your analysis of strengths and weaknesses to determine the DNA of Walmart.

4. Illustrate with an example how Walmart could use big data to fine-tune its operations.

5. Create a means–end chain for Walmart by using the information in the case.

6. What is the relation between key success factors and the competitive advantage of an organization? Illustrate this relation for Walmart.

7. Define objectives for Walmart. Use the balanced scorecard. Use the information from the case, but make your own assumptions wherever necessary.

8. According to marketing theory, a strategy can only be developed after an extensive situation analysis. But some organizations seem to focus initially on their own core competencies, without adapting the strategy to the (external) environment. Which choice did Walmart make here? Explain briefly.

Chapter 5

Customer analysis

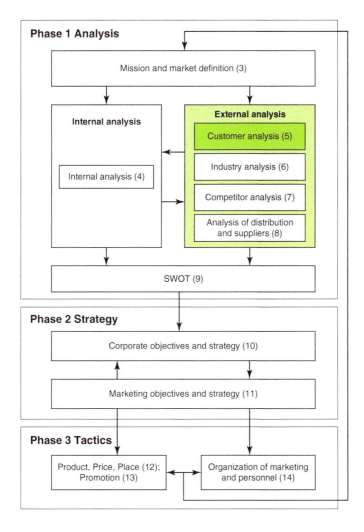

Phase 1 Analysis

Mission and market definition (3)

Internal analysis

Internal analysis (4)

External analysis

Customer analysis (5)

Industry analysis (6)

Competitor analysis (7)

Analysis of distribution and suppliers (8)

SWOT (9)

Phase 2 Strategy

Corporate objectives and strategy (10)

Marketing objectives and strategy (11)

Phase 3 Tactics

Product, Price, Place (12); Promotion (13)

Organization of marketing and personnel (14)

Introduction

Recent developments in the marketing concept have placed greater emphasis on the idea that the creation of customer value should be a company's central focus. That is the reason the external analysis starts with an analysis of the target audience. With analysing 'customers' we also mean potential customers. It is about an analysis of 'demand', sometimes referred to as 'market research'. Market research can be quantitative as well as qualitative. Many books are devoted to market research. In this chapter we focus on 'what to research' and not so much on how to do this (methodology, statistical techniques, etc.).

This chapter is structured as follows. In section 5.1 the goals of a customer analysis are outlined. Section 5.2 is dedicated to segmentation. Sections 5.3 and 5.4 deal with the analysis of customer perceptions. First, several helpful models are described (section 5.3), and then a framework for analysing customer perceptions is outlined. Section 5.5 is about mesuring brand strenght, while section 5.6 briefly reviews individual customer data. Section 5.7 provides some guidelines for primary research, discussing both qualitative and quantitative research.

5.1 Phases in the customer analysis

An important theme in this book is that there should be a greater focus on customer satisfaction and customer loyalty, and on bringing together brand identity and customer needs. The issue thus becomes how a brand can achieve this aim. To discover how to do this, it is essential to 'talk' with those customers. What do they want, and how do they see 'you'?

This chapter provides a structure for conducting a customer analysis.

A customer analysis ('market research') is not the only source for insight into customers' wishes. The largest problem in market research is that it is difficult for people to indicate what they might like in the future. People typically underestimate their future needs. Data from a customer analysis should therefore not be used as a direct guideline for action, but should be interpreted and subsequently combined with other sources. With that in mind, we now consider what may be called the most important phase of the situation analysis.

Customer research may be used for different purposes. A distinction is often based on the type of research (Malhotra et al., 2017):

- *Exploratory*: qualitative research.
- *Descriptive*: quantitative research (surveys and observation).
- *Causal*: experiments.

This distinction is clear but does not indicate what kind of data are required.

Another way to subdivide the customer analysis is by the kind of information sought: for example, the six Ws (Ferrell and Hartline, 2010):

1. Who are our current and potential customers?
2. What do our customers do with our products (use situations)?
3. Where do our customers purchase our products?
4. When do our customers purchase our products?
5. Why and how do our customers choose our products (e.g. perception of brands and products and needs)?
6. Why do potential customers not purchase our products?

This division is very useful, but it is limited by the fact that no distinction is made between the different strategic goals of the customer analysis. A customer analysis has various potential usage situations, and each situation requires that different information be collected.

There are four usage situations or goals of the customer analysis:

1. Use for segmentation and choice of the target market (Chapter 11).
2. Use as a basis for strengths and weaknesses research (Chapter 4), and positioning decisions (Chapter 11).
3. Use to check achieved results (Chapter 4) and to measure the effects of marketing mix elements (Chapter 13).
4. Use to identify competitors (Chapter 7).

Each of these goals requires specific information (the division by questions) and a specific research approach (the division by research method). Figure 5.1 summarizes this.

The first three of these goals are discussed in detail in this chapter.

Goal of customer analysis is information for	Required data from primary research	Type of research	Research discussed in
1. Segmentation and choice of target market	Who, what, where, when, why	Quantitative	Section 5.2
2. Positioning and strengths and weaknesses	Value hierarchy and customer satisfaction: why, why not?	Qualitative and quantitative	Sections 5.3
3. Analysis of results (control) and research on effects	Why, why not, e.g. brand awareness, brand associations, customer satisfaction	Quantitative	Sections 5.3 and 13.10
4. Competitor analysis and competitors	Who, what, why, why not: chosen brand	Quantitative	Section 7.2

Figure 5.1 **Goals of the customer analysis**

5.2 Segmentation research

5.2.1 Conditions for segmentation

Segmentation is dividing the group of potential customers into subgroups. The reason for doing this is that it is assumed that different groups can have different needs. So, maybe making one product for all customers is not a good idea. It may be better to give different groups their own product. Segmentation is part of the analysis phases of strategic marketing. The next step is targeting, which is part of marketing strategy. The third step is positioning. Often the abbreviation *STP* is used: segmenting, targeting, positioning.

So, a segment is a group of potential customers. A group of customers may be considered a segment if the following four conditions are met:

1. *Homogeneity/heterogeneity.* Within a segment the response to a marketing activity should be as homogeneous as possible, and between segments it should be as heterogeneous as possible.
2. *Sufficient size.* Segments that are so small that profitable exploitation is impossible are not meaningful.
3. *Measurable/identifiable.* The customers in segments should be identified in one way or another so that results and strategies can be linked to concretely described segments. In addition, without identification it is difficult to estimate the size of a segment.
4. *Accessible.* To use the elements of the marketing mix, especially distribution and promotion, it is essential that the segment be accessible.

Only quantitative research can provide insight into these conditions. This type of research involves collecting a large quantity of data from a large number of people and then attempting to identify groups of consumers that meet these requirements (segments).

5.2.2 Steps and methods

A segmentation analysis is divided into three phases.

1. Collection of the data

First, tools such as in-depth interviews and group discussions with customers are used to obtain as much insight as possible into the motivations, attitudes, and behaviour of the customers. With this knowledge, a questionnaire is created that is administered to a large group of customers. For consumer markets, this process has to include data collection about three categories of segmentation variables: personal (geographic, demographic, psychographic), product behaviour, and brand attitude (Figure 5.2). Figure 5.3 includes an overview of segmentation variables for business markets (industrial markets). The data mentioned in Figures 5.2 and 5.3 may be considered the minimum background data collected from customers.

Category	Sub-category	Variables
A. Personal (general)	1. Geographic data	• Region • Province, municipality • Degree of urbanization
	2. Demographic data/ socio-economic data	• Age • Gender • Family size • Family phase • Religion • Race • Income • Profession • Education • Social status
	3. Psychographic data	• Lifestyle (Activities, Interests, Opinions) • Personality • General values
B. Product (category)	1. Benefits	• Benefits sought = product-specific values • Importance of product characteristics (price, quality, taste, etc.)
	2. Purchasing behaviour	• Role in decision-making process (Initiator, Influencer, Decision maker) • Buying process • Buying/shopping behaviour
	3. Usage behaviour	• User status • Usage situations • Values in usage situations • Usage amount (light, medium, heavy users)

C. Brand	1. Brand awareness and attitude	• Towards own brand
		  – stage in purchasing process (awareness, attitude, intention, purchase)
		• Towards competitive brands
		  – consideration set

	2. Brand associations (perceptions)	• Own brand
		  – strength
		  – relevance
		  – uniqueness
		• Competitors' brands

	3. Brand loyalty	• Behaviour
		  – customer share (share of wallet)
		  – switching behaviour
		• Emotional
		  – recommendation: ambassador, fan

Figure 5.2 **Most important segmentation variables for consumer markets**

Category	Variables
Demographic	Industry sector Company size Location
Usage variables	Technology (required technology at the customer level) Usage status (heavy user, light user, none) Customer capacities (need for service)
Purchasing approach	Purchasing organization (centralized, decentralized) Power structure (technically oriented, financial, etc.) Types of relationships (strong, weak) Purchasing policy (leasing, service, systems, etc.) Purchasing criteria (quality, service, price, etc.)
Situation-related factors	Urgency of delivery Applications of delivered product Size of order
Personal characteristics	Degree of similarity to supplier Risk attitude Supplier loyalty

Figure 5.3 **Segmentation variables for business markets**

Source: Bonoma and Shapiro (1983).

2. Analysis of the data

Based on the collected data, segments should be deduced. This process can occur in principle in two ways (Figure 5.4):

■ *Forward segmentation* (*a priori segmentation*). Customers are classified on the basis of personal characteristics (for consumer markets, the first three categories of variables mentioned in Figure 5.2); subsequently, differences between groups in terms of product and brand (behavioural) characteristics are examined.
■ *Backward segmentation* (*segmentation based on behavioural differences*). This process starts with groups of customers that demonstrate different behaviour in

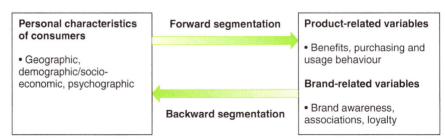

Figure 5.4 **Segmentation approaches**

relation to the product or brand variables: for example, by having different preferences (benefits); subsequently, a search is made for general (personal) characteristics that may be used to describe the groups.

The behaviour analysis is often based on differences in the importance customers attach to certain product attributes (benefits). This form of segmentation is therefore called *benefit segmentation.* The major advantage of benefit segmentation is that if segments are discovered, at a minimum the condition of homogeneity/heterogeneity has been met: there is a direct relationship to purchasing behaviour. This means that different products and varieties can be developed for the different benefit segments. Because of this, benefit segmentation is increasingly used in practice.

Typically, two analysis techniques are used for benefit segmentation: *factor analysis* to reduce the dataset to a smaller number of factors, and then *cluster analysis* to create segments that are as differentiated from one another as possible. In doing this, the researcher should indicate the 'behaviour' variables on which the search for a cluster should be based.

3. Description of the segments

Subsequently, a profile ('persona') is created for each discovered segment, based on the scores for the examined variables. The focus is on identifying the most distinguishing characteristics of the segments and, for identification purposes, each segment is given a name. Since markets change, the segmentation phases should be repeated regularly. Once target markets have been defined, media are used to reach a certain target market.

There are several market research agencies having their own segmentation models. The assumption is that the segments they found will show different needs for all categories (and definitely for the categories the customers of the market research agency are in). Clearly, this is not necessarily the case. For example, differences in age may lead to differences in preferred beer brands but not in differences in car brands. Another disadvantage of using 'ready to serve' segments it that the agencies responsible for these services do not provide information about how they developed their segments or the statistical power of their model. So, it is a kind of 'black box'.

Thus it is preferred to make one's own segmentation.

5.2.3 Guidelines for segmentation

Segmentation is an important subject in marketing literature, not only because of its strategic importance but also because it is a quantitative subject on which a lot of empirical methodical research may be carried out. At this stage we will not elaborate on the statistical methods of segmentation, but these methods are becoming more 'flexible' all the time. Using these methods, it can be taken into account that one person ends up not in one but in two segments. This links up with the fact that people can have different preferences at different moments. Also, there are more methods becoming available all the time that enable segmentation in spite of missing data: for example, when people do not fill out a questionnaire completely.

A general finding appears to be that segmenting from product-connected variables produces better results than does segmenting from the background characteristics of people, such as age. The reasons for this include the following:

- People's behaviour is becoming less 'predictable'.
- In each user situation, the preferences of people can differ strongly.
- Within households, individual members can have very different preferences.

The backward segmentation method should be given preference. In all cases it is necessary to collect data on behavioural and background characteristics of a large number of potential customers.

5.3 Models of customer perceptions

Before a setup for research on customer wishes can be established, it is important to have an idea of what customer wishes in fact are. Three models are suitable here: the multi-attribute attitude model, the means–end chain of meanings, and, for service markets, the SERVQUAL model. These three simple models should be viewed as 'conceptual models' that can be the basis for a research method. A comprehensive model does not exist. Each manager has to choose for him- or herself which aspects he or she finds important to research.

5.3.1 Multi-attribute attitude model: needs and perceptions

The first model we review is the so-called multi-attribute attitude model (Figure 5.5).

The name of this model makes it seem more complex than it actually is: the model just shows that the value (the 'use') a customer extracts from a product is determined by the importance that customer attaches to certain product characteristics (for example, he or she attaches a lot of value to the price) and the score of a brand on those characteristics (a high price therefore leads to little 'use'). The name of the model means that a combination of *many characteristics* leads to a total judgement (*attitude*). Viewed 'mathematically', it may be said that if the importance of all characteristics is combined (multiplied) with the scores on all those characteristics, some sort of total use can be

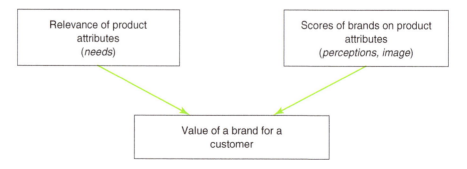

Figure 5.5 The multi-attribute attitude model

Case 5.1 Importance of customer research

The marketing insights of the top beer brands from YouGov research

YouGov conducted an in-depth study of beer and cider drinkers in the UK, and they investigated both the importance of product attribute as well as the perceptions of consumers about brands. Here's what it uncovered.

Usage situations and relevance of attributes

More than half of exclusive pub drinkers are over the age of 55, and the majority of them are male, while home drinkers over-index among women aged 35 to 44. Pub drinkers are defined as those who drink at the pub once a week or more and rarely or never drink at home, while home drinkers do the opposite. The former group also worry less about money than average, while the latter tend to have less disposable income.

Perceptions of brands

Peroni is beating its premium lager rival Stella Artois on perceptions of quality. Peroni, sold off to Asahi when AB InBev acquired SAB Miller in 2016, gets a quality score of 25 in YouGov's research, versus 19 for Stella Artois, which AB InBev hung onto. The gap has been widening since 2014, when their scores were just 1 point apart.

Kopparberg, Peroni, and Brewdog have top female appeal

Women are most likely to choose a flavoured cider or premium lager when buying beer or cider, with Kopparberg, Peroni, and Brewdog being the three they are most likely to buy in the next 30 days, according to YouGov. The results indicate the route to attracting more women drinkers is to place the marketing focus on these categories, rather than launching beers aimed at women. Ales and lower end lagers don't feature among their favourites, however.

Source: *Marketing Week*, 11 May 2018

Characteristic	Importance (%)	Score for shop A ('image')	Importance × score
Price level	40	7	2.8
Variety of selection	20	8	1.6
Friendliness of staff	20	5	1.0
Freshness of products	10	6	0.6
Cleanliness of shop	10	7	0.7
Total	100		6.7

Figure 5.6 Calculation example with the multi-attribute attitude model

obtained. Figure 5.6 shows a calculation example. The total mark ('use') shop A receives from the customer is 6.7.

The multi-attribute attitude model assumes that a product can be classified into separate characteristics and that it is possible to name those characteristics. In practice this is not always easy. Emotional ('brand') characteristics are especially difficult to group in the model. Furthermore, the importance people give to characteristics is strongly linked with their deeper motives and with the user situation. When buying daily consumer goods, for example, a customer may find the price more important than he or she does when doing Christmas shopping.

Nevertheless, it is important to realize that the question "Why does a customer buy our product?" (one of the 'six Ws' presented earlier in this chapter) is a combination of two totally different variables: needs (in the category) and perceptions (of brands). This means that a brand with a low preference (low score) should analyse the cause of this and act accordingly (e.g. communicating the importance of an attribute, or stressing the performance of the brand on an attribute).

5.3.2 Means–end chain

Both limitations are taken into account in the model of the product characteristics shown in Figure 5.7. The model is a combination of two other models that have a lot in common: the goal–means chain of meanings (means–end chain) and the customer value model. Both names for the model (shown in Figure 5.7) may be used.

The essence of the model is that it is important to know the motivation of people to buy products. For instance, people buy a yoghurt dessert because of its low fat content (attribute); they find that important because it keeps them slim (consequence); in turn, that is important because it makes them feel appreciated in their environment (value or motivation). The same dessert may be bought in the summer because of its fresh taste. In that case there is a difference in motivation, depending on the season. The higher values are often the basis for adding emotional characteristics to the brand by means of communication. The customer value model is hierarchical. 'Lower' benefits serve to satisfy 'higher' goals. The relations between the levels may differ depending on the usage situation. For example, drinking beer at home will probably be based on other values than drinking outdoors.

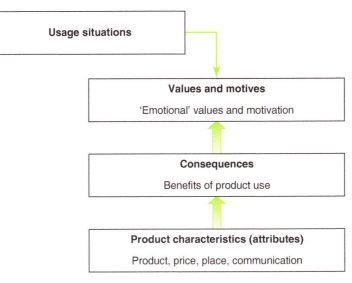

Figure 5.7 Model of customer value, or means–end chain

5.3.3 SERVQUAL model

When measured in terms of product value, in many countries services represent a larger category than do physical products. The model discussed above may also be used in services contexts. Nonetheless, a well-known model of *service quality* (Parasuraman et al., 1985), especially for service situations, has been developed. The SERVQUAL (service quality) model is shown in Figure 5.8.

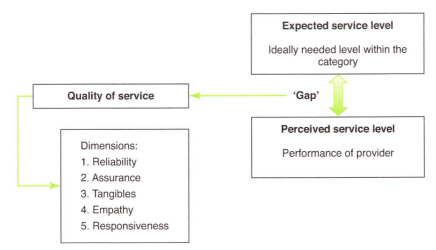

Figure 5.8 Model of service quality: SERVQUAL

Source: Parasuraman et al. (1985).

The central issue in using this model is that the quality of service is defined as the difference between the expected service and the realized service. When there is a gap between the two, there is not optimum quality. The idea of this model is to give customers what they want. When there is a gap, the gap can be for different reasons. The model explores this by showing a number of other gaps (not shown in Figure 5.8), such as the difference between what management thinks the customer wants and what the customer really wants.

Empirical research conducted with the aid of the SERVQUAL model has identified a number of dimensions of service quality:

1. *Reliability*: the extent to which the provider keeps his or her promises.
2. *Security*: how sure a customer can be that his or her expectations are being met (trust in the provider).
3. *Tangibility*: all tangible items of a service, such as leaflets and the atmosphere in a bank.
4. *Empathy*: the degree to which the provider puts itself in the position of the customer.
5. *Response*: willingness of the provider to listen to the customer and to do what the customer wants.

The measurement of service quality may be done by measuring the expectations of the customer as well as their realization. This is done per dimension. Per dimension, different sub-aspects can be questioned. Expectation is measured as what the customer would ideally want in the category, so not related to the specific provider: for example, a customer attaches great value to the fact that a provider of financial services shows that it knows the customer (aspect of empathy).

Both components – expectation and performance – show that the model originates from the multi-attribute attitude model, in that a demand (importance in general in the category) and a score (of the specific brand) are identified.

Finally, one must take into consideration the fact that the demands people have of brands and the performance of those brands are not separated. The more customers have frequent and long-term good experiences, the more their demands increase. This is a difficult issue because it means that the wishes of customers are never stable and customers constantly have to be 'taught' what they can and cannot expect. This also highlights the importance of innovation. At a certain moment people get used to something new, and then something else that is new has to be presented to them.

5.4 Research into customer values

5.4.1 Introduction

The classic way to do a needs assessment is to ask customers the following:

■   What they consider important: the importance of product characteristics.
■   How well the various brands meet those needs: how they score on the desired characteristics.

Phases	Components
1. Determination of target audiences (see also section 5.2)	
2. Determination of possible values per target audience (qualitative research)	◼ Usage situations: Where and when is the product category used? ◼ General values per usage situation: What is important in that situation, and why are you in that situation? ◼ Product-specific values per usage situation: What is important in those cases in the product category?
3. Determination of importance of values (qualitative research)	◼ Importance of general values (general needs): How important is … ? ◼ Importance of product-specific values (product-specific needs): How important is … ?
4. Performance of brands regarding values (consequences, benefits) and distinctiveness (qualitative and quantitative)	◼ Satisfaction: perceptions of brand performances, reasons why or why not ◼ Scores and distinctiveness regarding general values: To what extent is brand X a brand that possesses the abstract characteristic … ? To what extent is that a distinguishing feature? ◼ Scores and distinctiveness regarding product-specific values: To what extent is brand X a brand that possesses the tangible characteristic … ? To what extent is that a distinguishing feature?

Figure 5.9 **Structure for research on customer values**

Such research, which is often done quantitatively, is implicitly based on the multi-attribute attitude model described above. In this section we use Woodruff and Gardial (1996), and outline an action plan to achieve insight into customer values while taking into account the shortcomings mentioned above. Figure 5.9 represents the phases of this plan.

The analysis of target audiences was discussed in section 5.2. The other three phases will be discussed in sections 5.4.2 to 5.4.4.

5.4.2 Possible customer values per segment

This phase serves to uncover as many relevant values as possible. The research in this phase is explorative (drawing up an inventory), and is therefore done in a qualitative manner. Three steps may be distinguished.

1. First, the most important usage situations in the product category should be determined. This may include different locations (at home, recreational, at work), different points in time during a day, different periods during the year (holidays, vacation), differences in social environment (alone, with family, with

Case 5.2 Needs of a specific target market

The fashion industry pays attention to plus-size women

A good fit is everything, stylists often counsel, but in assessing its market America's fashion business appears to have mislaid the measuring tape. A frequently cited study done a few years ago by Plunkett Research, a market-research firm, found that 67 per cent of American women were 'plus-size', meaning size 14 or larger. That figure will not have changed much, but in 2016, only 18 per cent of clothing sold was plus-size, according to NPD Group, another research firm.

Designers and retailers have long thought of the plus-size segment as high risk. Predicting what these customers will buy can be difficult, as they tend to be more cautious about styles. Making larger clothes is more expensive; higher costs for fabric cannot always be passed on to consumers. In turn, plus-size women shopped less because the industry was not serving them well. "We have money but nowhere to spend it," says Kristine Thompson, who runs a blog called Trendy Curvy and has nearly 150,000 followers on Instagram, a social media site.

At last, that is changing. Fast-fashion brands, including Forever 21 and a fashion line sold in partnership with Target, a giant retailer, have expanded their plus-size collections. Lane Bryant, a plus-size retailer, and Prabal Garung, a designer, have done the same. In March [2017] Nike extended its 'X-sized' sportswear range.

Revenue in the plus-size category increased by 14 per cent between 2013 and 2016, compared with growth of 7 per cent for all apparel. Takings were $21.3 billion last year. Social media has played an important role in changing attitudes in the fashion business, says Madeline Jones, editor and co-founder of *PLUS Model Magazine*.

Source: *The Economist*, 13 July 2017

visitors), and so on. The following phases are performed separately for each of the most important usage situations. For example, beer is consumed at home and in bars.

2. The second step is to gain insight into what people find important in a general sense in the usage situation: the general values. For example, one might ask: "What do you consider important when going out or in a café? Quietness, chatting with friends (no noise, disco)?"

3. The third step involves looking for the consumers' product-specific values; in other words, which product characteristics consumers consider important (see Case 5.2).

The steps may be completed by using separate questions, but it is also possible to start from product-specific values to gain insight into general values. In doing this, a company attempts to determine the entire customer value hierarchy ('ladder') at once. A well-known technique that may be used for this purpose is *laddering*. This is a technique that completes the value hierarchy from the bottom to the top by continually asking the customer for the meaning of what he or she considers important: Why do you find that important, and so on? To discover as many 'ladders' as possible, it is advisable to review different usage situations explicitly with the customer (*grand tour technique*).

The only issue that is not clarified with qualitative research is the extent to which various phenomena play a role. For this purpose the following phases should be completed.

5.4.3 Importance of customer values and conjoint analysis

The importance a customer attaches to a certain value makes a statement about that customer's needs. What does he or she want? This question is directly relevant to identifying a sustainable competitive advantage. A competitive advantage can be obtained from a characteristic that customers consider important. A characteristic that is perceived to be important may be a factor that determines success in a market.

To determine the importance of values, it is necessary to distinguish between general values and product-specific values. Product-specific values are related to desired consequences (*benefits*) of product characteristics. For example, one might ask: How important is peace and quiet to you when you are going out (general value)? and How important is it that the café you visit uses your preferred brand (product-specific value)?

Direct methods

One way to research the importance of dimensions is to ask directly about that importance (with or without a scale technique; e.g. a 4-point scale ranging from very important to unimportant). However, a direct method of asking about importance has two disadvantages. One is that customers often indicate that they consider everything important and that they are not forced to take the interaction between product characteristics into account (e.g. quality and price). The second disadvantage is that customers have a tendency to think concretely. Tangible product characteristics are often mentioned as being important, whereas in reality abstract image aspects are often decisive. Therefore, it is better to use indirect methods such as conjoint analysis.

Conjoint analysis

Conjunct analysis is a method used to define the importance of product characteristics. This does not take place by asking for it but by deducing it from the choices consumers make in a simply designed experiment. Figure 5.10 shows how this process works. The basis is that a product consists of a bundle of characteristics. For example, the value (the 'use') of a cake for a person is defined by five characteristics (step 1). From each of those characteristics possible levels, which are realistic in practice, are defined for the experiment (step 2): for example, the taste (nice, neutral), the price ($1 or $2), the colour (yellow or brown), the freshness (fresh or not fresh), and the brand name (Hostess or Twinkies). Through conjunct measuring a manager tries to find out how important these characteristics are. Then new characteristics may be included. When the analyses have covered a large number of people, the differences between groups of consumers may be viewed (benefit segmentation).

Subsequently, a number of so-called products are defined, and every product is defined as a combination of characteristics (step 3: 'profiles'). For example, it may be determined that cake 1 has a nice taste, has a high price, is brown, is not fresh, and is from Hostess, whereas cake 2 is medium tasty, has a low price, is yellow, is fresh, and is from Twinkies. This is done until a certain number (e.g. 18 cakes) has been categorized. It is not necessary to use all possible combinations (in the example, these could amount to 32), but with the help of schemes developed especially for this purpose, a selection can be made. This concerns so-called fractional designs: overviews of combinations of profiles with a given number of attributes and levels per attribute.

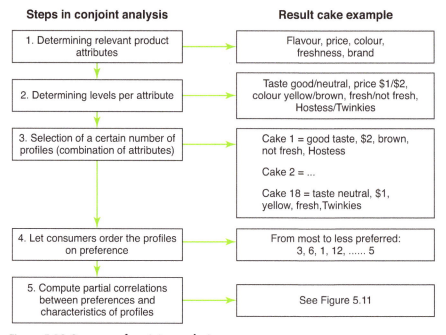

Figure 5.10 Structure of conjoint analysis

	Taste		Price		Colour		Freshness		Brand name	
	Level	Score	Level	Score	Level	Score	Level	Score	Level	Score
	Good	60*	$1	40	Yellow	10	Fresh	25	Hostess	30
	Neutral	10	$2	10	Brown	5	Not fresh	15	Twinkies	15
Difference between highest and lowest scores		50		30		5		10		15
Importance		45%†		27%		5%		9%		14%

*Means that level 'tastes good' of attribute 'taste' delivers a score of 60. The measurement scale is not of vital importance; what counts are the relative differences between levels.

†Computed as 50 divided by the sum of all differences (110).

Figure 5.11 **Possible result of conjoint analysis, example cake for one respondent**

The only thing the consumer has to do is sort the cakes according to his or her preference (step 4). For this purpose it may be useful to place a card on every product, with or without a suitable image. The consumer can then sort the cards. Using statistical software (e.g. SPSS Statistical Package for the Social Sciences), the preferences of respondents are statistically explained by the structure of the profiles. Per respondent (or group of respondents), it is then calculated how important the consumer found each of the characteristics (e.g. taste 35 per cent, price 20 per cent, colour 5 per cent, freshness 10 per cent, brand 30 per cent) (for a possible outcome, see Figure 5.11). Data for larger groups of consumers may be used for segmentation, product decisions, and price decisions.

The advantages of conjoint analysis are the simple questions (the choice process of customers is imitated) and the fact that the interaction among characteristics is included (respondents have to consider implicitly which characteristics they consider the most important). Conjoint analysis is used extensively in both marketing theory and practice, with a wide range of applications (Cattin and Wittink, 1989).

The results of either the conjoint analysis or the direct needs assessment are appropriate for segmentation. After all, this phase creates insight into what customers consider important, and that is an excellent basis for segmentation (see section 5.2).

In choosing respondents, the question is whether only existing customers should be researched or whether potential ones should be included. An argument can be made for either choice. Researching only the preferences of existing customers fits with the pursuit of customer relations. However, a brand cannot ignore the fact that new customers need to be attracted on an ongoing basis, and so research into potential customers is also important.

Researching existing customers has the advantage that customer preferences can be integrated into a client information system. When a client has been a client for a while, the importance of values may be deduced from the purchasing behaviour of users. Online purchase data offer good opportunities for this.

5.4.4 Brand perceptions and multidimensional scaling

How well or how badly do we provide the desired customer values? This question may be researched in a qualitative manner but also in a quantitative manner: How do we score and how does the competition score on characteristics and benefits? In effect this involves measuring brand perceptions. Here a comparison is appropriate with the measurement of what Keller calls 'brand equity'. According to Keller (1993), brand awareness and brand associations are the sources of brand equity. These sources should lead to results such as satisfaction, brand loyalty, and market. To know whether a brand is successful and why, it is therefore important to measure the sources and results of brand equity. The measurement of brand associations may be done through qualitative or quantitative methods.

Qualitative methods are:

- *The direct association method*: With what do you associate brand A?
- *Projective techniques*: indirect methods such as indicating matching photographs or describing the brand as a person with a character. This method is suitable for measuring the psychosocial (abstract) characteristics of a brand and offers important information for the purpose of choosing brand positioning.

Another goal of qualitative analysis is to gain insight into the satisfaction of consumers and especially into the underlying causes of the extent of that satisfaction. Talking with consumers about what they think of the brand, and why, is often an eye-opener for managers. As will be explained in section 5.7, qualitative research does not require a great number of respondents to obtain a relatively complete picture of the thoughts and feelings of customers (and non-customers). In cases where a company decides to not perform quantitative research, qualitative research becomes even more useful and may be used separately for making strategic decisions.

Quantitative methods may also be divided into direct and indirect methods. Direct methods use, for example, statements for which a respondent is asked to indicate on a ranking scale the extent to which he or she agrees. Ranking scales such as 5-point scales ranging from completely disagree through completely agree that force the respondent to choose a position are called Likert scales.

Indirect quantitative methods for measuring brand perceptions are used for *perceptual mapping.* Perceptual maps are, especially in the case of positioning and communication decisions, important and easily understood research methods. In this technique, brands are placed in a coordinate system in which the axes represent, for example, conservative/ dynamic, tough/feminine, or other brand personality characteristics (see the overview of brand values in section 11.4). Sometimes groups of consumers (segments) are placed in such maps. We discuss two methods:

- Multidimensional scaling.
- Semantic differential.

Multidimensional scaling

A valid method for obtaining such perceptual maps is the technique of multidimensional scaling (MDS). In MDS, brands, characteristics, and ideal points (wishes) of users are conveniently arranged in one figure through the use of a statistical method that employs simple questions for respondents to answer. Figure 5.12 includes an example of a 'joint

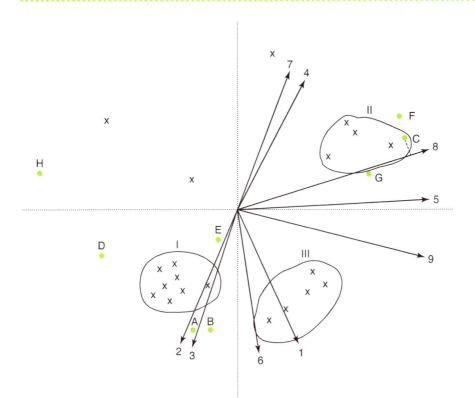

Explanation: A to H are the brands, 1 to 9 are the attributes,
X is the ideal point of a consumer, I, II and III are segments.

Attributes: 1 = pleasant, 2 = for young people, 3 = for women, 4 = bitter, 5 = tar,
6 = smells good, 7 = difficult to get used to, 8 = dark, 9 = smells strong.

Figure 5.12 **Example of multidimensional scaling: joint space with attributes, tobacco brands**

space' for the market for rolling tobacco. The figure demonstrates that tobacco brands C and F score the highest on the characteristic of femininity, whereas brand A has a young and feminine image. The image of brand A is quite similar to that of brand B. If brand A wants to grow at the expense of brand B, it should position itself differently: for example, more 'cosy' (in the direction of characteristic 1). An advantage of this strategy is that there is a segment of smokers that desires a brand that is strong and cosy (segment III), but no such brand exists.

MDS has several important advantages as a research method.

1. First, the results of MDS (graphic representations of the positions of brands) are easily understood, making it an excellent communication tool for positioning decisions.
2. Second, MDS makes it possible to use more than two dimensions. The dimensions on which people judge a brand are placed in the figure as vectors.

3. Third, the positions of the brands in the coordinate system space are 'hard'; that is, they have been calculated according to a quantitative method. This differentiates MDS from many of the other qualitative methods used to place brands in spaces.

4. Fourth, the method of data collection in MDS is true to life. Respondents are asked to compare brands as a whole with each other just as they would in a shop, and only afterwards are the characteristics placed in the figure. This means that MDS is an indirect method in which the respondents do not have to indicate what they consider important, yet this can be determined afterwards by the researcher on the basis of the results. Reliable MDS results may be obtained even with a small number of respondents, and the results are also suitable for segmentation into, for example, usage versus non-usage.

Semantic differential

A simple tool that represents both tangible and abstract brand characteristics in a conveniently arranged manner is the semantic differential: a graphic representation of brand scores on various characteristics. With the data collected in the research described earlier, such a figure is easy to construct. Figure 5.13 shows an example. Another way to show scores is to use a 'spider diagram' where, for example, eight attributes are arranged in a circle.

Conducting measurements such as those shown in Figures 5.12 and 5.13 creates insight into the strengths and weaknesses of a brand. At this point it is very important to distinguish between customers and potential customers. Potential customers (i.e. non-customers) often perceive a brand differently from customers (see Case 5.3).

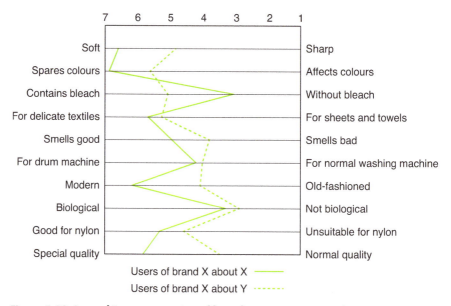

Figure 5.13 **A graphic representation of brand scores on various characteristics**

Case 5.3 Difference in perception between customers and non-customers

Will New Zealand remain a green and pleasant land?

"100 per cent pure New Zealand", Tourism New Zealand's catchphrase already used since 1999. Why mess with a good thing? The notion of a country blessed with pristine land, water, and air appeals not only to visitors. It goes to the core of what the country means to New Zealanders themselves. So the slogan has the 'authenticity' such gatherings always call for.

But there is a problem. New Zealanders are growing unsure about their country's 100 per cent pure image. One issue comes from the sheer numbers of tourists themselves. Another comes from the back end of a cow. Some of the most popular tourist places are getting 'hammered'. Another problem is fragile landscapes ravaged to make way for cows, such as in the Mackenzie district, a dry upland rich in endemic plant and animal species that has been completely changed by irrigation. Conservationists are appalled that a rare ecology has been destroyed. Indeed, water gets to the heart of New Zealanders' concerns. Dairy cattle need a lot of it, and produce copious excrement and urine in return. This pollutes watercourses and fills lakes with algal blooms, despite new requirements to fence streams off from livestock. Some rivers have become too polluted to swim in.

With images like that, it can't be long before visitors notice there's a problem in this pure, unsullied land.

Source: *The Economist*, 21 September 2017

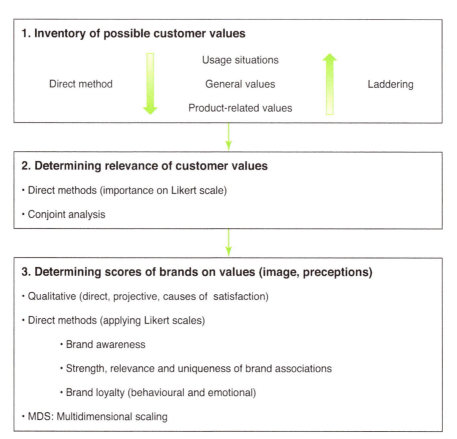

Figure 5.14 **Summary of main customer research phases**

An answer to the question "Why don't potential customers purchase our product?" is important for attracting new customers.

Figure 5.14 summarizes the main phases in customer research.

5.4.5 Future customer values

Research into customer values is valuable but does not generate direct insight into what customers will consider important in the future. However, that is more important than knowing the current situation. To arrive at prognoses for customer values, the following steps may be taken:

1. Aside from customer research, consult sources about trends in customer wishes such as sellers, researchers, consultants, and other experts.
2. Analyse the tracking data and attempt to link any changes in customer values to factors such as economic fluctuations and social-cultural developments.
3. Discuss the data from the customer analysis, the other sources, and the company's self-analysis in brainstorming sessions to arrive at prognoses collectively.

Finally, research into customer values can easily be connected to the value strategies of Treacy and Wiersema (discussed in earlier chapters). Those value strategies are in effect three ways to provide customer value. Research among customers must indicate which value or combination of values (innovative products, cheap products or convenience, direct relationships with customers) will have to be chosen in the future.

5.5 Measuring brand strength

5.5.1 Brand strength and brand value

A brand is an important asset for a company. Simply the fact that people know your brand and have some associations with your brand is valuable, also in monetary terms. There are several reasons why a company would want to know the value of their brand:

1. For marketing purposes.
2. Because of mergers or acquisitions.
3. Because of the need of a financial valuation.

The way of measuring brand value depends on the motives. For the latter two reasons (mergers, financial) a company wants to know the 'real financial brand value'. For marketing purposes, however, one value is quite useless to know because that does not provide any insights into the strengths and weaknesses of the brand. Keller (2013) makes a comparison with an aeroplane: a pilot needs a lot of meters to control the aeroplane.

We make a distinction between:

■ *Brand strength*: this is the power of the brand to attract customers.
■ *Brand value*: the financial value of the brand.

There is a logical relation between these two elements: more brand strength will lead to more brand value (Figure 5.15).

In this book we focus on brand strength. Following Keller, who introduced the term 'Customer Based Brand Equity', we propose brand strength to be measured from the customers' perspective. Measuring (financial) brand value is a difficult task. It is mostly

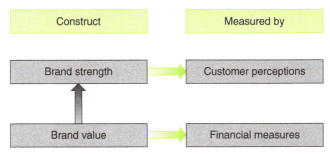

Figure 5.15 **Brand strength and brand value**

done by agencies, such as Interbrand. Interbrand makes an estimation of future cash flow and multiplies this with a factor depending on the brand strength. The way of choosing this factor is subjective and secret. For more information about methods to assess the financial value of a brand, we refer to accounting literature.

First, in section 5.5.2 we present a basic model about brand strength (model of Keller). Then, in section 5.5.3 we present our own model to measure brand strength, using the customers' perspective (BSS Brand Strength Scale). Finally, we show how the BSS can be used to derive the needs of customers.

5.5.2 Brand equity pyramid

Keller (2013) presents in his book the so-called brand equity pyramid (Figure 5.16 shows an adapted version). In his model the bottom is brand salience, which is in essence the level of awareness of a brand. It assumes that a brand should have a salient position in customers' minds. The second level ('identity') is about the performance of the brand (attributes, service, price, etc.) and the more emotional characteristics, such as the profile of the target group and the brand's personality. The third level ('image') is about the customer: How does he react? On the rational level this is about the perceived quality and the level of consideration. The feelings are about the felt excitement, warmth, etc. The highest, fourth level is about brand resonance and deals with the level of loyalty customers have with the brand: not only behavioural loyalty, but also emotional loyalty or even ambassadorship. The left-hand side of the pyramid deals with the 'functional' part of a brand, the right-hand side with the 'emotional' part.

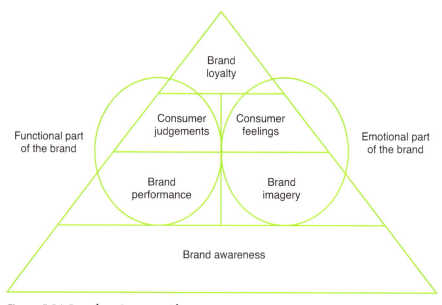

***Figure 5.16* Brand equity pyramid**

Source: Based on and adapted from Keller (2013).

5.5.3 Brand Strength Scale (BSS)

For marketing purposes, monitoring brand strength should be done with a multidimensional instrument. Using the pyramid of Keller and adding some specific items, we propose an instrument with the following dimensions:

1. Product usage.
2. Brand awareness.
3. Functional associations:
   - Importance of attributes
   - Brand scores on attributes.
4. Emotional associations.
5. Level of uniqueness.
6. Brand preference and loyalty.
7. Customer characteristics.

The main differences with the Keller pyramid are a different way of combining variables and separately adding category involvement and customer characteristics. Figure 5.17 shows an example of a questionnaire that may be used. It contains some items from the scale by Yoo and Donthu (2001). For 'emotional associations' several models may be used, such as the Value Compass and the Brand Personality Scale, both presented in Chapter 11. In Figure 5.17 we choose to use some emotional associations which we assume the brand would want them to communicate (assumed identity).

The outcomes of the Brand Strength Scale in itself are hard to judge, unless the scores can be compared with certain benchmarks. There are several ways to interpret the outcomes of the scale.

Category involvement
- How often do you buy deodorant?
- How important is buying deodorant for you?

Brand awareness
- I am familiar with Axe
- I can easily recognize Axe among other brands
- I can easily imagine some characteristics of Axe

Relevance of attributes
Could you indicate for the following attributes of deodorant how important they are for you?

- Price
- Scent
- Durability
- Easy to use
- Design

Figure 5.17 **Example of questionnaire to measure brand strength (Brand Strength Scale (BSS)) (*to be continued*)**

- Feeling on skin
- Socially responsible
- Quality

Functional performance brand ('functional image')

The next questions are about brand Axe. Indicate for each item the level of agreement.

- Axe is cheap
- Axe smell good
- Axe works a long time
- Axe is easy to use
- Axe gives me a good feeling on the skin
- Axe is socially responsible
- Axe has a good quality

Emotional performance brand ('emotional image')

Indicate how good the next associations fit with brand Axe.

- Young
- Pleasure
- Excitement
- Masculine
- Reliable
- Seduction

Competition and differentiation
- If Axe would not be available, which brand would then be your choice?
- How different is Axe from other deodorant brands?

Brand usage
- Do you have Axe at home right now?
- How often do you buy Axe?

Brand preference

How strongly do you agree with the following statements?

- Axe is my first choice in deodorant
- I would recommend Axe to my family and friends (brand ambassadorship)
- If another brand would be as good as Axe, I would buy Axe

Characteristics customer
- Gender
- Age
- Education
- Income

Figure 5.17 **Example of questionnaire to measure brand strength (Brand Strength Scale (BSS))** (*Continued*)

Comparing with scores in a previous period: monitoring

In general it is recommended to repeat measuring brand strength: for example, once a year. This is called 'monitoring', or 'tracking'. An obvious advantage is that it may be seen how the different dimensions of the BSS change over time, which provides useful insights for marketing. It makes a lot of difference if, for example, awareness is declining, or preference.

Comparing with competition and the NPS

The BSS may also be applied to a competitive brand. Comparing the outcomes with the own brand provides insight into the relative position *vis-à-vis* the main competitor. When making a comparison with competition, parts of the BSS may also be used: for example, the preference items. In particular the 'recommendation' question is very popular in market research. It is derived from what is called the 'Net Promoter Score' (NPS), a metric developed by Reicheld (2003). The only question posed to respondents is to indicate on an 11-point scale (0 to 10) how likely it is that they would recommend the brand to family and friends ('brand ambassadorship'). In a next step the respondents can be divided into three groups: Promoters (scores 9 to 10), Passives (scores 7 to 8), and Detractors (scores 6 and lower) (Figure 5.18).

The percentage of Detractors is then subtracted from the percentage of Promoters. The 'theory' behind this way of calculating is that only very high scores (9 and higher) lead to ambassadors of your brand: telling the news to others. Customers who score a 7 or 8 are probably quite satisfied but will not spontaneously be an ambassador of your brand. An NPS can also be negative. This does not necessarily mean that the brand is not performing well. In some categories, such as banking and insurance, NPS scores are generally low, simply because category involvement is low. The level of the NPS will also vary among countries due to cultural differences. US customers will probably tend to give higher ratings than in a more conservative country, such as Germany.

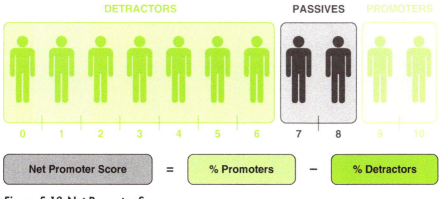

Figure 5.18 Net Promoter Score

Comparing image and identity

It is also very useful for managers to complete part of the BSS. In particular the image part (functional and emotional performance) is interesting if management point out which associations they want the brand to communicate ('identity'). The mean score of the managers may be compared with the mean score of the customers, providing insights into positioning issues.

Comparing between customer groups

Different customers may have different needs. This is the basic reason for segmentation, dealt with earlier in this chapter. For example, it is interesting to compare differences in the relevance of attributes between groups of customers (segments).

5.5.4 Measuring needs with the BSS

In section 5.3.1 we stressed the distinction between the relevance of product attributes ('needs of customers') and the score of brands on these attributes ('image'). In section 5.4.3 we mentioned that directly measuring needs (as we incorporated in the BSS), might not always provide useful answers, since customers might indicate that they find everything important. So, we proposed an indirect way of measuring needs: conjoint analysis.

The BSS also provides a relatively simple way of indirectly deriving the importance of attributes; namely to relate two metrics to each other:

■ the scores on the functional and emotional attributes;
■ a performance variable: for example, brand ambassadorship.

Performing a multiple regression analysis, explaining brand ambassadorship by the different performance scores, will logically provide the importance of each attribute (Figure 5.19). This is because if there is a statistical relation between, for example, the judgement of price and the level of recommendation, this means that price (partly) determines ambassadorship and thus that price is important for customers.

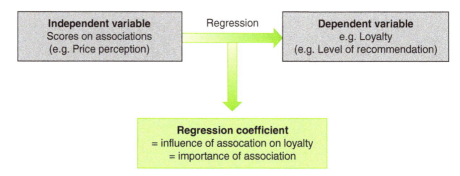

Figure 5.19 Estimating the relevance of attributes from performance scores

5.6 Individual customer data

In this section, we will focus first on the possibilities of individual customer data, especially online data, and then on the process of selecting customers.

5.6.1 Possibilities of online data

As was indicated in Chapter 1, the concept of creating direct relationships with customers (*customer intimacy*) has received a lot of attention since the 1990s. This value strategy implies and requires that a company has insight into customer preferences at the individual level and then to respond to those preferences. In section 5.2 we stated that, ideally, four types of client characteristics should be measured: geographic, demographic (and socioeconomic), psychographic, and behavioural. Before the 1990s it was a challenge to get individual buying behaviour data. For supermarkets and other retailers, it was and is relatively easy by using customer cards. For manufacturers, getting individual customer data was a big challenge. However, with the growth of online shopping, obtaining customer data is much easier nowadays. This is related to the issue of big data mentioned earlier.

So, 'data enough', one could assume. But how true is this? Ideally, a marketer would like to know for individual customers ('single source'): who these customers are (demographic variables), where they live (geographical), what their habits and lifestyle are (psychographic), and what they prefer and buy (behavioural). If all of these variables are available, a rich scala of segmentation and targeting methods can be used. Is this realized with big data? Partly.

Online data are about online behaviour. Online behaviour consists of:

1. *Communicating behaviour*: What do customers post on social media?
2. *Searching behaviour*: How (for example, using what terms?) are customers searching on the internet?
3. *Clicking behaviour*: Which (parts of) the website receive most clicks?
4. *Buying behaviour*: What do customers order online?

These are all behavioural data and are thus very relevant because they are about real behaviour. So, marketers have far more opportunities to analyse customer behaviour than they had in the past. Data from social media are a free source of customers' opinions about the category and sometimes the brand. A challenge is to properly analyse these data.

There are limitations for all four kinds of online data. First, online data are not collected from a representative sample of customers, since active online customers are a specific group with their own characteristics. Second, demographic and psychographic data about online customers are not directly available for brands, unless of course a brand has its own database with customers who gave permission for this.

The final question then is: How serious is the limitation of not having background data about online customers? This is likely not a big problem, because targeting customers online may be done without background data. If behavioural data can be linked (for example, with 'cookies') to where on the internet customers are, targeting may be done in a strongly focused way. For Google this is quite easy: based on keywords used in mailing ('I went to the dentist'), a customer can receive an ad about toothpaste immediately. Another way of targeting is sending targeted messages when people are at specific locations, spotted by a company using mobile data. This is an example of *mobile marketing*, which is a marketing technique focused on reaching a specific target audience on their smartphones (or other mobile devices) by means of social media, email, etc. The essence is that GPS enables a company to know where a customer is and when, making it possible to send time- and location-specific messages.

So, individual targeting is easier to implement with online data. It should be noted, however, that online sales in many categories are still a small part of total sales. So, the more classical ways of collecting customer data (for example, with loyalty cards) can still be useful.

A challenge in using individual client data is *privacy*. In many countries there is resistance to the use of individual personal details and household details. In practice, there are two systems for protecting individual client data: opt-in and opt-out. *Opt-in* means choosing to participate and includes the fact that people have to give explicit permission for the use of data (e.g. active agreement with a customer card); *opt-out* means choosing to 'leave' and implies a tacit assumption that personal data may be used unless objections are made (a passive agreement: for example, reacting to a coupon action). In practice, opt-out occurs more often than opt-in. As a result of the privacy problems mentioned above, it is argued that customers need to be asked for explicit permission. In this context the term *permission marketing* is used. You can start a direct relationship with the customer only if he or she has explicitly given his or her permission (therefore, this is a type of opt-in). When they sign up for such a card, customers have the option of revealing their names and giving permission for their individual data to be used for other purposes. The willingness of customers to participate in one-on-one programmes can be increased by, for example, providing a discount in exchange, a win-win situation).

5.6.2 Customer selection

For companies that are able to obtain customer-level data regarding purchasing behaviour, several tools are available to analyse those data. We will discuss two: the customer pyramid (Figure 5.20) and customer portfolio analysis.

Customer pyramid

The customer pyramid is a framework that places potential customers in a certain order. This arrangement may be based on annual sales per customer. It is likely that for customers a similar 80 to 20 rule exists as it does for products. Twenty per cent of customers may be responsible for 80 per cent of sales.

Of course, this is a fairly arbitrary rule of thumb and it is equally likely that another proportion applies, but the meaning is clear: a small number of customers are responsible for a large amount of sales. Further down the pyramid we find medium-sized and small customers, former customers, not or never customers, and finally a non-target audience. When customers are arranged in order, the next issue is the characteristics which the various groups possess. Why is a large customer large and a small customer small? Why have some customers left? Why are some members of the target audience not customers at all? Figure 5.20 can act as a tool for choosing the target audience and the value strategy. In theory, the best strategy would be one that involves as strong a

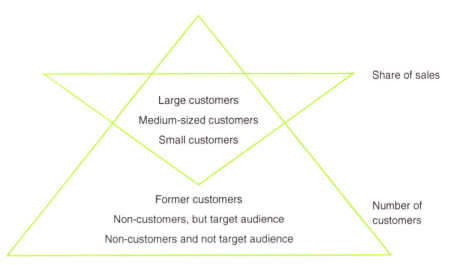

Share of sales

Large customers

Medium-sized customers

Small customers

Former customers

Non-customers, but target audience

Non-customers and not target audience

Number of customers

Figure 5.20 **Customer pyramid**

flow-through as possible from the bottom towards the top, but there are three different possibilities:

1.   Turning a non-customer into a customer.
2.   Maintaining customers.
3.   Increasing sales to customers.

Each of these strategies requires a different approach. In the context of relationship marketing it is often stated that maintaining customers is four times cheaper than attracting new customers. However, it is unwise to ignore new customers. Without growth the client base will decrease.

Customer portfolio analysis

Another tool that may be useful in this context is customer portfolio analysis. Each customer is classified on the basis of two characteristics:

1.   The extent to which the customer is a 'heavy user' in the product category: the potential size of the customer.
2.   The share of the brand sales in the customer's category purchases; in other words, the market share at the customer level (share of customer, or 'share of wallet').

The first criterion addresses the potential and/or expected attractiveness of the customer; the second addresses the customer's current attractiveness. A related variable used in this context is *customer lifetime value*: the financial value of a customer for a company, computed for the whole lifetime of a customer, including the recommendations the customer is giving to others. This variable shows that customer loyalty is essential for a company, since a customer turning into a non-customer can lead to the loss of a large amount of future sales. Marketing science increasingly offers methods to estimate customer lifetime value (Gupta et al., 2006; Borle et al., 2008; Blattberg et al., 2009).

5.7 Primary research

Primary data are data that the organization collects by itself through fieldwork (market research). For an extensive discussion of market research, refer to the literature (Malhotra et al., 2017; Cooper and Schindler, 2014). Here we pay attention to several points. In doing market research, the following choices have to be made:

1. *Choice of the target audience* (*who?*). For which target audience or audiences should the research be performed? This question largely determines the remainder of the structure.
2. *Desired information and choice of quantitative or qualitative research* (*what?*). We will focus on this in section 5.7.1.
3. *Structure* (*how?*) (sections 5.7.2 and 5.7.3).
   - data collection;
   - sampling;
   - method of questioning.

5.7.1 Qualitative or quantitative research

As is always the case in market research, there are in principle two possible ways to do research: quantitative and qualitative.

Quantitative research

By definition, quantitative research is performed on a larger number of people. The large-scale approach allows the drawing of 'harder' conclusions than is the case with qualitative research; after all, the results are stated in percentages. Another advantage is that differences among subgroups in the target audience (segments) can be made visible: for example, differences in satisfaction between youths and older people or among different types of companies (an 'explanatory' goal). Because the type of fieldwork done for quantitative research (written, by telephone, or on the internet) requires a structured approach, such research is most appropriate for 'factual' research; that is, descriptive research. It is not the primary goal of quantitative research to provide insight into the 'why' of certain results.

Qualitative research

Qualitative research consists of personal (face-to-face) interviews with individuals ('in-depth interviews') or groups (group discussions, focus groups). Qualitative research may be used as an independent source or may be performed before quantitative research as a source of inspiration and/or a pretest of a questionnaire.

The decision to do quantitative versus qualitative research should not be based primarily on the idea that quantitative research may by definition be more reliable than qualitative research. More important is the question of what type of information a company wants to obtain. If the organization, as part of its customer satisfaction research, wishes to obtain insight into the percentage of people from the target audience who are or are not satisfied with the product as well as the relationship with the composition and backgrounds of the target audience, a quantitative approach is required. However, a company should realize that such research will not provide information about the causes of any dissatisfaction. Information about those causes may typically best be obtained by checking the written comments of respondents (e.g. at the end of a questionnaire). In that way, the most important complaints become clear. However, that involves an incidental inventory of problems, which is in effect qualitative in nature. If a company wants to know why dissatisfaction exists and how the company can address it, a qualitative approach is appropriate.

Figure 5.21 contains the ideal choice in this regard: first qualitative, then potentially quantitative, and again qualitative. Customer research always starts with qualitative research, in which a first inventory of potential problems is obtained and information is collected for structuring the quantitative research. Such research may be followed by quantitative research to gain insight into whether goals were achieved, the extent to which certain problems exist, and differences among groups. Subsequently, a deeper qualitative analysis may be performed for target audiences to determine the cause or

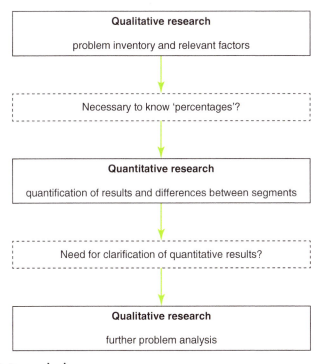

Figure 5.21 **Research phases**

causes of any problems and perhaps to propose potential solutions to respondents. Of course this is possible only if sufficient resources are available. If resources are limited, at a minimum some qualitative research will be required, because even a small number of discussions with customers provides insight into problems and potential solutions. The following are two examples.

By talking with just a few customers, a large telecommunications business discovered that customers did not consider the various subscription options to be as simple as the managers had expected. A bank allowed some customers to try out its technically clever website. It turned out that the customers failed to understand many of the options: the website had been created far too much from the perspective of the business and not sufficiently from the perspective of the customer.

Once it has been decided which type of research is the most appropriate, decisions should be made regarding the further structure as well as the size and composition of the sample. We will flesh out these subjects first for qualitative and then for quantitative research.

5.7.2 Structure of qualitative research

We will focus on some specific issues (see the reference section for an extensive discussion). In qualitative research, a choice should be made between individual discussions or interviews and group interviews. Generally, it may be said that if a company is interested in people's personal, individual behaviour (such as choice processes and usage behaviour), *individual discussions* are preferable. However, if the researcher primarily wants to discover how people think about the organization and its products, a *group discussion* is a good choice. A group discussion has the advantage that the interaction within the group brings more issues and ideas to the surface.

Subsequently, the sample size and composition must be determined. The composition is the most crucial component: the respondents should be selected carefully according to the relative composition of the entire target audience. If, for example, 30 per cent of the target audience consists of women over the age of 60, a research group comprising 20 people should have 6 women older than age 60. Using the 'correct' method of selecting respondents guarantees that the qualitative research will be sufficiently representative.

A related point is the *sample size*. An important criticism about qualitative research is that research among 'a few people' is sometimes used as the basis for an organization's strategic decisions. However, this may be countered with the fact that research shows that after approximately 15 to 20 respondents from a group have been questioned, hardly any other new issues come to the surface. Thus, after about 20 discussions, the researcher has a relatively good idea of the situation. In fact, at that point the researcher typically also has a reasonable impression of the extent to which issues are important to the target audience.

The normal recommendation for group discussions is to interview relatively homogeneous groups. These might include several customer groups as well as one or more groups of non-customers (potential customers) and perhaps some former customers. A frequently occurring problem in market research is that only existing customers are questioned. However, the results of such research are by definition not representative for the entire potential target audience because existing customers typically view the organization in a more positive light than do customers who use its competitor. Assuming that every organization does not exist only for the benefit of its customers but is also interested in potential customers, this means that non-customers should also be questioned. In terms of the size of groups for group discussions, six to eight people per group is considered appropriate in most cases.

The number 15 to 25 respondents applies to each of the groups to be researched about which the researcher wants to make statements. If the researcher wants to examine the differences among, for example, male customers, female customers, and non-customers, the numerical guideline should be applied three times. If the minimum of approximately 15 people per group is used and a choice is made to hold group discussions involving around 8 people per discussion, in this example at least 6 group discussions have to be organized.

In terms of the method of data collection, open questions are used in which the interviewer needs to ensure that all subjects will be discussed. One cannot ignore the danger of interviewer bias: contaminated answers that result from the influence of the interviewer. To obtain information that is as pure as possible, face-to-face research requires expert questioning. Thus, the power of qualitative research lies in 'creative listening'.

5.7.3 Customer journey mapping and neuromarketing

In this section we deal with two specific qualitative research tools: customer journey mapping and neuromarketing.

Customer journey mapping

A popular tool in qualitative research is *customer journey mapping*. This entails that a researcher investigates for individual customers their experiences with touch points with the organization from the very first contact to the last contacts and everything in between. For example, a hospital may want to know patients' feelings about all contacts, from the first phone call to the contact with the nurse when going home after a treatment: not only the customer journey but also the related issue of the customer experience receives considerable attention in marketing science literature. Lemon and Verhoef (2016) provide a useful state-of-the-art paper about the relationship between the journey and customer experiences.

Figure 5.22 shows a template that may be used:

1. A company has to define the relevant stages first.
2. Then, for each stage, customer satisfaction should be measured. Since customers would be asked to provide a lot of information at each stage, a simple measurement should be used, for example, by letting them choose a 'facial expression' describing their feelings at that particular stage.
3. When a quantitative picture is realized, a deeper analysis is needed, making use of customers' input, acquired by additional qualitative research. Quotes from customers may be helpful for illustration.
4. Finally, the results should form the material for internal discussions to make improvements.

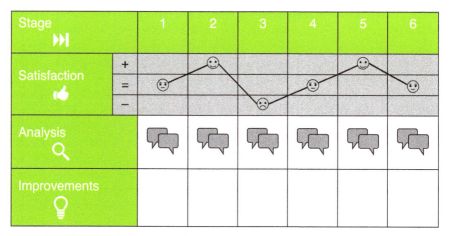

Figure 5.22 **Template for customer journey**

Neuromarketing

As mentioned in Chapter 1, about 90 per cent of customers' choices are led by unconscious motives. Knowing this, it is logical that researchers will want to know more about this 'unconsciousness'. So, marketers borrowed techniques from medical sciences such as fMRI and put customers in scanners to see what happened in customers' brains when showing, for example, a commercial for a brand. There are, however, two other points to be made. The first is a little semantic but still relevant: the name 'neuromarketing' is strange, since it literally would imply that there is specific marketing aimed at 'the neuro' (or brain). Perhaps this is the reason why some authors judge this kind of research to be 'unethical' because the purpose would be to search for the 'button to buy' in customers' brains, leading to unethical tactics. In itself, we do not believe this research to be unethical. The name, however, could better be focused on the research goal, so it could simply be called neuroscience of neuroresearch (for marketing). The second point is that as some other authors also argue, the link between the results of neuroresearch (parts of the brain activated by marketing stimuli) and marketing implications is difficult to make because results are difficult to aggregate over customers, and the link with behaviour is difficult to make.

Instead of looking into people's brains, we recommend to do the opposite: to focus on measuring behaviour, including experimental research.

5.7.4 Structure of quantitative research

Two types of data collection are in principle possible for quantitative research: by telephone and in writing (by mail or email). The advantages of research by telephone include a faster, higher response rate and the possibility of clarification of answers. A disadvantage is the limited length of the questionnaire. The advantages of a written questionnaire are the possibility of using a longer questionnaire and the relative ease with which a large number of people can be reached. However, the response rate is often very low

Case 5.4 The use of quantitative data for segmentation

The myths of marketing to mums

Brands are failing to connect with mothers, since marketing communications see them as mums first rather than women with children, a tactic that does not resonate with them. There are five myths of marketing to mums (detailed below) that marketers must wake up to and overcome if they are to reach this group effectively.

Research from Saatchi & Saatchi, seen by *Marketing Week*, surveyed 865 mothers across the UK. It found that only 23 per cent are happy with anyone other than their families calling them 'mum', and three out of ten agree they are 'me first and then a mum'.

ITV director of commercial marketing and research Sarah Speake says: "As a rule, mums tend to be lumped together as one homogeneous group, which inevitably doesn't resonate with us all. Whether a stay-at-home mum, single mum, working mum, married mum, mum of younger or older children, we all have fundamentally different requirements to make our lives easier and enable a connection or relationship. Brands that acknowledge these differences resonate better – where both the commonality of adoration of our children and our differences as individuals are recognized."

Source: *Marketing Week*, 10 April 2014

(for consumer research, often no more than 15 per cent). Both research by telephone and research by letter involve a completely prestructured multiple-choice questionnaire. Because a mistake or vagueness in a questionnaire that has been mailed cannot be rectified, it is essential to ensure that the questionnaire has been extensively tested beforehand until test persons no longer indicate any confusing items (after they have been explicitly asked about confusing items).

In terms of the sample size, the statistical reliability of the results increases to the extent that the sample size increases, but this is not a direct relationship. Without going more deeply into the formulas that can be used to calculate the margins of error for responses, it may be stated as a rule of thumb that a minimum of 100 respondents must be obtained for each target audience to be researched. Assuming an expected response rate of 20 per cent, this means that for a written research project, a minimum of 500 questionnaires should be sent out per group.

More important than sample size is sample composition. If the composition of the group of people who have participated does not resemble the target audience in terms of characteristics relevant for the research project (the composition is not representative), the results are unreliable. Therefore, it is very important to check afterwards whether the requirement of representation has been met. If the response group deviates from the target audience, additional respondents should be obtained or so-called reweighing applied during the analysis.

It should be noted that representativity is not related to sample size. Sometimes it is stated that "a research was very representative, since a large number of respondents participated". Obviously, this is a wrong statement.

Summary

Customer analysis comprises primary research (market research) and secondary research (existing sources).

Primary customer analysis has four goals. The first goal is to provide a foundation for segmentation. Identification of segments takes place through the analysis, based on large-scale quantitative research, of which groups of consumers or customers demonstrate similar preferences or similar usage behaviour and subsequently a description of those groups on the basis of the characteristics that are the most distinctive. The discovered segments form the basis for decisions that will later be made regarding the target audience (*targeting*).

The second goal of customer analysis is to provide the information required for making positioning decisions. For this purpose, insight has to be gained into the value hierarchy of customers: What are the goals for which customers use the products (usage situations)? What do they generally consider important in those situations (general values)? What do they consider important in products (product-specific values)? What are the achievements of our brand on those general values (abstract brand characteristics) and on the product-specific values (desired product characteristics, *benefits*)? And: To what extent are those achievements distinctive? This component provides insight into the strengths and weaknesses of a brand. Aside from insight into the value hierarchy, a manager needs to know the extent of customer satisfaction. One measure in that regard is brand loyalty. Brand loyalty has a behavioural component (market share at the customer level, or *customer share*) and an emotional component ('real brand loyalty', which can be measured through statements such as "I recommend brand X to my friends"). In these research phases, qualitative methods such as *laddering* are used and quantitative research also takes place. Both types of research are performed for customers and non-customers.

The third goal of customer analysis is to provide information for the testing of client-oriented objectives. For this purpose a number of measures, such as customer satisfaction and brand achievements, should be repeated regularly (*tracking*).

The fourth goal of customer analysis is to gain insight into how customers perceive the competition. Customer research does not address customers' future values directly. For that purpose, other sources have to be consulted.

Online data ('big data') provide many opportunities for market research. The big advantage is that online data pertain to real behaviour, which is a huge difference from 'classical' questionnaires. A limitation of (open) online data is the lack of representativity.

Case Kia: from 'budget' to premium

Kia certainly doesn't pull any punches when it comes to describing how British consumers might see the brand. 'Low value', 'budget', and 'small' are just some of the words that Kia's marketing director David Hilbert singles out. But that could all be about to change if the South Korean manufacturer can pull off its ambitious plan to go premium, a strategy it will be accelerating this year.

The car marque has been in the UK for 26 years, so Hilbert claims it is still "quite a new brand", which is one of the reasons why people on the street who know Kia but don't own one "still have the perception that we do low-value or budget cars". In recent years, however, Kia has set out to change perceptions by releasing more premium cars, such as its Sportage and Sorento models. Its latest endeavour, and soon to be the crown jewel in its line-up, is the Stinger. It is the result of nearly 10 years' worth of design and engineering, and a move Hilbert, who joined the brand nearly 18 months ago to drive the transformation, argues will redefine Kia as a 'luxury performance' brand.

"The launch of the Stinger is a way to challenge those perceptions of the Kia brand. Over the past few years you can see how we've developed our product range to really move away from that initial small car status we had in the UK," he says. "The Sportage is becoming a key model in our line-up. It's quite polarizing in its design, and that makes it stand out from the crowd."

Despite Kia's struggle to shake off its cheap car image among the UK public, it claims half of its volume sales are now driven by its Sportage and Sorento models, retailing for around £18,000 and £28,000 respectively. Kia finished last year with a 3.7 per cent market share. And while UK car sales fell 5.6 per cent in 2017, the brand managed to increase sales by 4.3 per cent – selling over 93,000 vehicles. Parent company Hyundai Motor and the global Kia brand, however, missed their 2017 sales targets for a third straight year.

As Kia has become a top 10 seller in the UK over the years, it no longer sees itself as a challenger brand but as a mainstream competitor, going up against brands such as Nissan, Hyundai, Renault, and Peugeot. Moving upmarket, however, does mean it will have to face off against a new set of brands. Hilbert believes its focus on tech, including safety features like a heads-up display, will set it apart from rivals. Features such as this will be added to its other models in future.

"With the Stinger, you don't have direct competitors, it's mainly premium ranges of mainstream brands, like Vauxhall's Insignia series or the high-end Ford Mondeos. But we also touch on competing with premium brands, such as the Audi A5 and A4 series," he explains. "With those premium marques you have to pay for the extras and added spec. But you get that as standard with the Kia Stinger. From a branding point of view, you could argue manufacturers like Audi are more premium than mainstream, but ultimately people buy cars on the exterior styling, and we believe we have a great-looking car that will turn heads."

Shift in marketing

The move to attract a more premium audience has also led to a change of approach in marketing. With its target audience – mostly men who are 'successful in their careers' – being hard to reach and time-poor, the brand decided to have multiple strands to the Stinger's launch campaign.

Launching this month, the campaign will involve a 'hero' TV ad and digital activity. A major part of the campaign will also include an out-of-home takeover at Waterloo Station in London where passersby can see, touch, and feel the car. "The best way to shift perceptions is by people seeing and physically touching the car, and to see how far we've come in terms of quality and design," Hilbert adds.

All media buying will be focused around the Six Nations Championship over two major rugby weekends, when the English team takes on Wales and Scotland. The brand doesn't sponsor the tournament but it wants to be associated with sporting events such as this. Sport has always been a 'crucial ingredient' of Kia's marketing strategy. It has previously rolled out global sponsorship deals around football and invested heavily in cricket on a local level. "Sports helps us build Kia's personality. As we are a relatively new brand we need to develop a personality and sports provides a good way of doing so," he says.

Yet the brand's head of communications Jane Fenn insists it isn't looking to become an official sponsor of rugby events just yet. "Obviously we have associations with football and cricket already, and rugby isn't something that we've sponsored. At the moment that's not our intention, it's around trying to best reach our audience and knowing that the audience's passion points are around sports," she says.

The challenge of turning a brand around

Kia is undoubtedly keen to attract a new demographic, as well as keep its appeal among its existing customer base. When asked if there is a risk of alienating consumers by trying to appeal to too many different audience segments, Fenn quickly refutes this claim. "The fact we've got such a diverse product portfolio means the future for us is very much around being a brand that sticks at every single life stage. It's about making sure we have models that fit into what people are looking for at any stage. I don't see it being an issue," she says.

The car marque also claims to be realistic about turning its image around, and is taking a 'long-term approach'. Hilbert says the UK car industry is "arguably one of the most competitive environments in the world", due to the nation's historic affection for cars. But a regional design office in Germany helps the Korean brand create new products for European tastes.

He concludes: "If you think about where we were about 18 years ago compared to where we are now, we've gone from selling 10,000 cars a year to 93,000. This is phenomenal growth and proves we are changing people's perceptions. The Stinger is the latest model to inject even more passion into that and push the boundaries."

Source: Marketingweek.com, 5 February 2018

Questions

1. *"Kia is undoubtedly keen to attract a new demographic".* Do you agree that demographics are the most relevant segmentation variable for Kia? Explain your answer.
2. Use the multi-attribute attitude model to determine how Kia is perceived, as compared to two competing brands: Toyota and Ford. You decide the characteristics based on which you compare the brands, and investigate by talking to at least five (potential) car owners.
3. Create a means–end chain for a premium car brand such as the Kia Stinger.
4. Use laddering to define customer values with respect to cars:
    I. Invite a car owner for an interview.
    II. During the interview, define the usage situation on which you wish to focus.
    III. Identify the general values with respect to that usage situation.
    IV. Finally, define the product-specific values for this car owner.
5. Kia focuses its promotion around two rugby events. On which dimension(s) of brand equity do you expect this promotion to focus: awareness, identity, image, or resonance? Explain your answer.

6. Do you personally feel that the image associated with rugby matches the brand image desired by Kia? Explain briefly.

7. Suppose Kia would like to measure whether rugby matches the brand image of Kia.
   - Would you advise qualitative or quantitative research? Or a combination? Explain your answer.
   - Create an appropriate research design.

8. Suppose Kia would like to use MDS to determine its position in the market. Which steps should be executed to do this analysis?

Chapter 6

Industry analysis

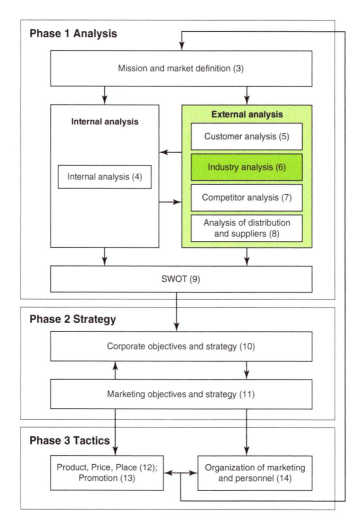

Phase 1 Analysis

Mission and market definition (3)

Internal analysis

Internal analysis (4)

External analysis

Customer analysis (5)

Industry analysis (6)

Competitor analysis (7)

Analysis of distribution and suppliers (8)

SWOT (9)

Phase 2 Strategy

Corporate objectives and strategy (10)

Marketing objectives and strategy (11)

Phase 3 Tactics

Product, Price, Place (12); Promotion (13)

Organization of marketing and personnel (14)

Key points in this chapter

- Know the differences between and the goals of an industry analysis and a competitor analysis.
- Know the components of an industry analysis.
- Realize that a Porter analysis is only part of an industry analysis, which in turn is part of an external analysis.
- Be able to perform a macro-environmental analysis for a company.
- Know how to assess the attractiveness of a market.

Introduction

This chapter will review the industry analysis. The most important goal of this type of analysis is to gain insight into opportunities and threats from the perspective of the industry and the macro environment as well as insight into the attractiveness of the market in which the organization operates. Insight into the attractiveness of the market is important with regard to issues such as determining the investment level. Section 6.1 discusses the concept of industry analysis in relation to the concept of competitor analysis; these two concepts are strongly related. In section 6.2 the goal and structure of an industry analysis are outlined. We then review the various phases of the industry analysis. Section 6.3 focuses on the analysis of the macro environment. The so-called aggregated market factors (including the product life cycle) are reviewed in section 6.4. In section 6.5 the factors related to industry structure (including the five competitive forces identified by Porter) receive attention. Finally, section 6.6 explains how the results of the entire industry analysis may be summarized into conclusions about market attractiveness.

Because an industry analysis reviews not only the existing suppliers but also potential ones as well as parties that are not operating in the market directly, this chapter uses the term *industry analysis*. In this regard we are giving a broader meaning to that concept than is done in daily usage, where it typically refers to a group of businesses that produce or trade strongly related products, such as the house construction industry, the garment industry, and the shoe industry.

6.1 Competitive analysis: industry and competitors

The question "What is competition?" seems redundant. After all, everyone knows the answer. However, we need to focus briefly on this concept, since in the literature there has been a tendency to classify more issues and parties under the designations *competition* and *competitor analysis*.

The concept of competition can have two meanings:

1. The extent of competition (rivalry, competitive struggle in a market: How strong is the battle in a market for the favour of the customers? In other words, how intense is the competition?).
2. The individual competitors: the collective name for all the competitors of a company.

Because of these two different meanings of the concept of competition, a competition analysis consists of two components (Alsem, 1991):

1. An analysis of the intensity of the competition in a market; this component of the analysis is included with the *industry analysis*.
2. An analysis of the behaviour of individual competitors: this is known as *competitor analysis*.

The most important difference between the two components is that a competitor analysis examines individual competitors, whereas in an industry analysis the competition as a whole is analysed (Figure 6.1). In other words, the industry analysis is a competition analysis on the macro level, and the competitor analysis may be seen as a competition analysis on the (meso and) micro level.

Another difference between the competitor analysis and the industry analysis is that completely different aspects of the competition are examined. In competitor analysis, the focus is on analysing and predicting the behaviour and reactions of competitor A, competitor B, and so on. For that purpose, the strengths and weaknesses of the competitors are portrayed. In industry analysis, the focus is on the competitive forces in a market: for example, the division of power among sellers or the negotiation power of suppliers. In this regard, Porter's model of five competitive forces is often used (Porter, 1980). This chapter on industry analysis, while chapter 7 is about competitor analysis.

6.2 Goal and structure of the industry analysis

6.2.1 Goal

One of the components of the industry analysis is an examination of the market structure: How large are the various suppliers? Is there a strong power concentration? Are

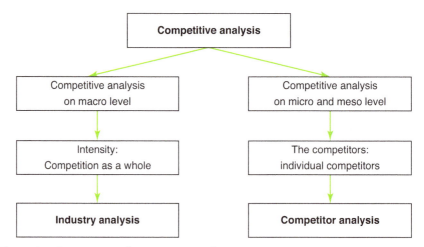

Figure 6.1 Components of competitive analysis

the products similar to each other, or does the customer perceive significant differences? Although these kinds of questions are interesting in and of themselves, a company needs to consider beforehand what should be done with the answers. If no clear goal for the analysis is formulated up front, many issues may be examined in great detail without a clear link to strategy formation. This would mean that the 'homework' was done to no avail.

In terms of the industry analysis, there are two explicit goals. We want to gain insight into the following:

1. The attractiveness of the market.
2. Opportunities and threats from the perspective of the industry (e.g. from macro-environmental factors).

The conclusions with regard to market attractiveness are especially important for the formulation of growth strategies and marketing objectives for the market being analysed. For example, a finding that the market is relatively attractive (e.g. due to expected growth) is more likely to lead to a decision to invest and to the formulation of ambitious growth objectives than is the case if the market is found not to be attractive (e.g. saturated). This demonstrates that the industry analysis has a strong relationship with the portfolio analysis. After all, the portfolio analysis is also done to determine the investments for each product–market combination. Obtaining insight into potential opportunities and threats is a logical component of the strengths, weaknesses, opportunities, and threats (SWOT) analysis. The opportunities and threats will be juxtaposed in a later phase with the strengths and weaknesses to arrive at potential strategies.

6.2.2 Structure

An industry analysis examines all factors that may influence market attractiveness. These factors may be divided into three groups:

1. *Macro-environmental factors.* These are factors over which the various suppliers in a market have little or no influence, such as government decisions.
2. *Aggregated market factors.* These are factors that are related to market demand and directly determine the attractiveness of a market, such as market growth.
3. *Industry structure factors.* These are factors that determine the intensity of competition in a market; for example, the distribution of the 'power' in a market: the concentration.

These factors are summarized in Figure 6.2.

The combination of the three categories in Figure 6.2 determines the attractiveness of a market. In the analysis, the main issue is to observe changes over time and ideally to make a prognosis.

6.3 Macro-environmental factors

We include in macro-environmental variables those variables that a company and other suppliers in the market cannot control or can control only to a limited extent. Figure 6.2

Macro-environmental factors
Demographic
Economic
Social-cultural
Technological
Ecological
Political-legal (government)

Market factors
Market size
Market and submarket growth and phase in product life cycle
Sensitivity to economic and seasonal trends

Industry structure factors
Profitability
Threat of new entrants
Bargaining power of customers
Bargaining power of suppliers
Intensity of competition
Threat of substitute products

Figure 6.2 **Components of the industry analysis**

shows the categories of such factors that can be distinguished (DESTEP factors): demo-graphic, economic, social-cultural, technological, ecological, and political-legal. In the context of the industry analysis, these factors are important because:

- In most cases they influence all the businesses in an industry.
- They directly influence market size and therefore market attractiveness.
- They may influence other functional areas in a company, such as personnel and production.

In this classification of macro-environmental factors, a process of mutual influence may exist among the different categories of factors. For example, political decisions regarding income distribution may lead to changes in economic factors. A social-cultural development such as increasing environmental awareness is linked with a more strict environmental policy and with technological developments that lead to products that are more environmentally friendly.

For each factor, the first step should be to determine the influence it had in the past. For factors that are quantifiable, such as economic and demographic develop-ments, causal models may be used (see section 13.10). Subsequently, the manager should indicate how much influence is expected in the future, but to be able to do this, the macro-environmental factor itself should first be predicted. For this purpose, a number of forecasting methods may be used (see section 9.1). For each category, discussed below, we will review the content, the data sources, and the predictability. We conclude with several general points about the macro-environmental analysis.

6.3.1 Demographic factors

The literal meaning of *demography* is 'description of the people'. Therefore, it relates to characteristics of the population. Demographic factors include the following:

- The size of the population in an area.
- The age distribution of the population.
- The number and size of households.
- The degree of urbanization of the population in an area.
- The composition of the population.

A well-known example of a demographic development in many modern countries is the ageing of the population: an increase in the percentage of elderly people (see Case 6.1). This has negative consequences for companies that bring products onto the market for babies, such as diapers. However, a positive consequence exists for markets for the elderly, such as trips for older people and magazines aimed at the elderly.

Other demographic developments in some countries include a decrease in population growth and decreasing household size. In most countries there are central statistical agencies that maintain detailed data, which are accessible on the internet, regarding both past and predicted demographic developments.

Although demographic developments are important issues for marketing, their effects appear gradually and in the long term.

6.3.2 Economic factors

Economic factors are important for many companies because these variables influence the extent to which consumers are likely to purchase certain products. Examples of these variables include the following:

- The economic situation, measured via:
  - Volume of world trade;
  - Gross national product;
  - Economic index;
  - Consumer confidence index.
- The purchasing power of consumers, measured via:
  - Paid wages and salaries;
  - Consumer expenditures;
  - Consumer credit;
  - Size of social security payments.
- Other variables, such as:
  - Price level of family consumption;
  - Unemployment;
  - Exports;
  - Energy prices.

Case 6.1 Relevance of ageing

The grey market

In 1965 Diana Vreeland, the editor-in-chief of *Vogue*, coined a phrase 'youth-quake' to describe how baby-boomers were shaking up popular culture. Today the developed world is in the early stages of a 'grey-quake'. Those over 60 constitute the fastest-growing group in the populations of rich countries, with their number set to increase by more than a third by 2030, from 164m to 222m. Older consumers are also the richest thanks to house-price inflation and generous pensions. The over-60s currently spend some $4 trillion a year and that number will only grow.

Yet companies have been relatively slow to focus on this expanding market – certainly slower than they were to attend to the youth-quake. The Boston Consulting Group (BCG) calculates that less than 15 per cent of firms have developed a business strategy focused on the elderly. The Economist Intelligence Unit, a sister organization to *The Economist*, found that only 31 per cent of firms it polled did take into account increased longevity when making plans for sales and marketing. One reason for this tardiness is that young people dominate marketing departments and think that the best place for the old is out of sight and mind.

Source: *Marketing Week*, 7 April 2016

The influence of these variables on market demand varies with the market. In general, because of their luxury nature, durable consumer goods are more sensitive to changes in economic developments than are fast-moving consumer goods. Economic developments typically do not have an important influence on the market demand for fast-moving consumer goods, but there may be a shift in demand. For example, an economic recession will have a positive influence on cheaper brands, such as a store's own brands.

Data about past economic developments are available in detail at national agencies that collect statistical data. In contrast to government-related factors, economic factors can be predicted with reasonable accuracy for the not too distant future. This is the case because economic factors typically involve long-term trends that do not change drastically at any single point in time. However, in the longer term (more than a year ahead) economic variables (especially economic cycles) are difficult to predict.

An advantage of predicting economic variables is the fact that a company does not have to do it on its own. Annually, various general economic businesses, both national and international, publish prognoses for various macro-economic variables. Since economic trends are strongly influenced by political developments, economic expectations can change drastically. However, as was indicated above, this typically is not the case and developments occur in accordance with trend lines.

6.3.3 Social-cultural factors

Social-cultural factors relate to issues such as people's way of life, opinions, and standards in a society. They include a large number of divergent developments, such as the following:

- Increasing environmental awareness and attention to nature.
- Increasing attention to health (eating habits, sports). (see case 6.2)
- Social changes within the family household, such as:
  - Marrying at a later age;
  - The increasing role of women in the labour process;
  - An increase of the role of men in the household;
  - Delayed childbearing;
  - Changes in the upbringing of children.
- The increase and revaluation of leisure time.
- Growth of subcultures.
- Changes in media use (increase in online and social media).

These factors may have important implications for marketing. For example, new and/or growing markets have come into being for leisure products, fast meals, 'healthy' eating, environmentally friendly products, and so forth. Social-cultural trends are relevant not only for product development but also for communications.

Partly as a result of several of these social-cultural and demographic developments, two trends have been noticeable over the past few years. First there is the so-called individualization trend. This means that an increasing number of people are creating their own worlds in which they pay as little attention as possible to other people.

A strategic implication of this trend is that within a single family different people make their own purchasing decisions, and so it is possible to find in one family several versions of a durable consumer product such as audio equipment.

Case 6.2 Social-cultural development

Growth of sustainable food will not stop

Biological food has become a large market worldwide. Products such as quinoa or avocados are very popular and so the prices of these products increase. Eating avocados is said to be good for health. And also other food, if grown under sustainable conditions is getting more popular. In 2016 the market for packaged biological food grew worldwide with 6 per cent to $32 billion, says Euromonitor. This is a strong growth although the market share of packaged biological food still is small (1.6 per cent).

Source: *Financial Daily* (Financieel Dagblad), 27 July 2017

A second trend is a decreased ability to observe a link between consumers' characteristics and their purchasing behaviour. For example, items such as a winter sports holiday, holidays by air, and a second car are no longer accessible only to consumers with high incomes. A related development is that the purchasing behaviour of many consumers appears to be increasingly capricious. One moment the consumer is driving an expensive car, and the next he or she is buying a cheap pair of jeans or eating junk food.

The implication of all this is that it will not always be easy for a company to convert a specific social-cultural development into a concrete opportunity.

Some national agencies maintain information about past and future social-cultural factors. In addition, newspapers and magazines often observe social-cultural trends at an early stage. A number of market research agencies also explicitly collect information on the various ways of life.

6.3.4 Technological factors

Technological developments can have far-reaching consequences. The development of cars, computers, personal computers, video games, microwave ovens, fax machines, the internet, and mobile telephones has led to important shifts in living patterns and consumption patterns. However, less sweeping developments such as the introduction of instant soup, instant coffee, and compact laundry detergent can present important opportunities or threats. Technological developments are important not only from the marketing perspective but also for other functional areas in the company, such as production, logistics, and information processing. In the context of marketing applications, it is often is stated that a new technological finding (technological push) is interesting only if it is accompanied by sufficient interest in the market (market pull).

The rate of technological development has increased over the past few years. Partly as a result of that, product life cycles are becoming shorter: the time until a new, better product is developed is getting shorter. Since basic technological research is typically very expensive, it is becoming increasingly important for companies to be the first in the market with a product. Only in that case will there be sufficient time and market potential for the company to be able to recover the development costs of a product. If a competitor is earlier, part of the market has already been supplied and the company no longer has the important image of being 'the first'.

In contrast to other macro-environmental factors, a company can partially influence technological developments by itself: for example, through a strong research and development programme. Influencing other macro-environmental factors is generally not possible.

Information sources about technological developments include specialized magazines.

6.3.5 Ecological factors

This category of factors has become extremely important, since almost all over the world countries realize that climate change is a serious threat and that fossil sources should be replaced. A related factor involves energy prices, which we have included under economic factors.

The spread of diseases may also be included under ecological issues. For example, animal-related diseases (such as avian flu) obviously have a direct impact on people's consumption habits, but indirectly they also lead to increased attention to health issues.

6.3.6 Political-legal factors (government)

Factors such as political developments, environmental policy, media policy, subsidy schemes, employment policy, and monetary policy may present, either directly or indirectly, threats to or opportunities for a company. This influence may be limited, but it may also represent a 'trend break' in the development of a market. An example of a 'sudden' political development is the election of Trump as President having led to (more) instability in the world. 'Brexit' is also a break. Not only globally, but also within countries, governments may strongly affect a company's environment. The influence of government regulation on the companies in a market depends to a large extent on the specific market and a company's ability to respond to the regulation (see also Case 6.3). For example, the many environmental regulations that have been enacted represent threats to environmentally unfriendly products such as diesel fuel but are opportunities for environmentally friendly products such as electric cars.

The internet and newspapers are an obvious source of information about government decisions. Many journalists keep a close watch on political issues. In terms of the possibility of *predicting* government decisions, the results of political deliberations are typically difficult to foresee. However, political decisions are often made as a reaction to other developments in the environment (such as environmental policy decisions), and this provides a point of departure for predictions.

Case 6.3 Influence of the government

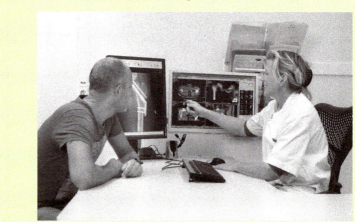

Health care markets strongly affected by political choices

Health care systems worldwide are strongly affected by governmental policies and political choices. In the USA the influence of the governmental rules is relatively low, leading to large numbers of people who are not insured and can thus not pay for medical treatments. In many European countries there is a mixed system of compulsory social insurance for basic health care and free choices of additional health care. In addition, rules for competition in health care markets differ among countries, a trend being that competition is slowly increasing in order to stimulate effective and efficient health care. Due to increasing competition, marketing in health care markets is of vital importance.

It is useful to follow politics closely to the extent that it is relevant to the company and to keep one's ear to the ground by networking in the hope of becoming aware at an early stage of any potentially important government decision.

In the USA, many companies consider the government so important that specific officers have been appointed to 'spot' the behaviour of the government and use it for deducing potential opportunities and threats. As of 2018 the 'government' in the USA looks very unpredictable.

6.3.7 Points of interest for the macro-environmental analysis

In the analysis of all these macro-environmental factors, three points of interest should have a central focus.

Opportunity or threat

The influence of an environmental factor on a company depends on the ability of that company to respond to the development; that is, on the company's relative strengths and weaknesses. Therefore, it is impossible to state a priori whether a specific development is an opportunity or a threat. For one company it may be an opportunity; for another it may be a threat. If it is a threat, a company may still attempt to turn that threat into an opportunity by applying as many resources as possible so that it can respond to the development.

We return to this issue in the discussion of SWOT analysis in Chapter 9. In the attempt to make a distinction between opportunities and threats, it is helpful to define an opportunity as a development that has a positive influence on a company's performance *if the company does not change its strategy.* Applying this condition enables one to classify environmental issues in terms of opportunities and threats.

Continuous analysis

As a result of the importance of making a timely response to developments in the macro environment and, where possible, being the first responder, a company should take care to be open to signals from the environment that indicate the start of a new trend. In this context the term *environmental scanning* has been used: the continuous scanning of the environment. Especially for larger companies, it may be advisable to assign someone to this task.

Environmental scanning should be limited to potentially relevant factors. A complete macro-environmental analysis is impossible and unnecessary. Instead, it can be focused on the most important factors in the external environment, about which a company should collect data continuously. These factors should be designated not only for the macro-environmental analysis (e.g. demographic trend A, economic trend B, government factor C) but also for the customer analysis (e.g. segments A and B) and the competitor analysis (e.g. competitor A and potential competitor B).

Forecasting and scenarios

Many developments in the macro environment are very difficult to predict. In reality, many predictions do not prove to be true or do so many years later (or earlier). Specialized agencies also produce new prognoses regularly. To be able to cope with this uncertainty during the planning process, it is advisable to define *scenarios* for the most important factors. A scenario is a description of a potential environmental situation: for example, a disappointing economic climate or, for a drinks manufacturer, a total prohibition on advertising for alcoholic drinks. A scenario may also be defined in relation to the competition; for example, the competitor reacts or does not react (see also Chapter 7).

In practice, typically no more than two scenarios are defined: a pessimistic one and a most probable one. In addition to a pessimistic variation, an optimistic scenario could be defined. After all, events may turn out to be disappointing but may also be better than expected. If events turn out better than expected, perhaps the planned strategy needs to be modified. However, in reality, the optimistic scenarios are often omitted because of cautiousness.

Defining a scenario is meaningful only if it also includes guidelines for how the company should react in that situation. For this purpose, the marketing plan may include an attachment that describes an alternative plan to be used for the pessimistic scenario. Such an alternative plan is also called a *contingency plan* and is accompanied by 'standards' (limiting values of variables) that indicate when the plan becomes current. The most likely scenario then becomes the basis for the marketing plan.

All scenarios should be realistic. A pessimistic scenario is not the same as the assumption that *everything* will go wrong. For example, it is extremely unlikely that simultaneously with disappointing economic growth, a competitor will introduce new, better products while energy prices rise and the government enforces important limitations on advertising.

As was indicated above, macro-environmental factors may have a direct impact on total market demand. In the next section we discuss aggregated market factors.

6.4 Aggregated market factors

In the previous section we reviewed the various categories of macro-environmental factors: demographic, economic, social-cultural, technological, ecological, and political-legal variables (DESTEP factors). As was indicated, each organization should attempt to stay informed about developments in these variables. Each potential change or trend may present an opportunity or a threat. In the context of macro-environmental analysis it is sometimes argued that threats do not exist. Each potential threat can be turned into an opportunity if the organization makes an effort to respond to that specific development. For example, a publisher of youth magazines does not have to consider the reduction in the number of youths and the increase in the number of elderly people as a threat if it is able to bring a magazine for older people onto the market.

A macro-environmental analysis is also very important in terms of an industry analysis, since developments in the macro environment may have an important influence on the attractiveness of a market. This influence works largely through total market demand. For example, in the case of the publisher of youth magazines, the reduction in the number of youths will have a negative impact on the market size (readers of youth magazines), whereas the ageing trend will have the reverse effect on the markets for products and services for elderly people. In this way we arrive at an analysis of aggregated market factors.

Aggregated market factors are variables that are defined in terms of the total market demand (the primary demand or the size of the market). This involves the following variables:

- The potential market size.
- The expected market growth and the phase in the product life cycle.
- Sensitivity to economic and seasonal trends.

6.4.1 Market size

The size of the market is important because larger markets are more *attractive* than smaller markets. After all, large markets have more sales possibilities, making it easier to recover the costs of investments. In addition, a larger market offers more opportunities for segmentation, such as searching for niches. Larger markets also attract more competitors, and that has a negative influence on the attractiveness of a market.

Another reason for determining market size is that it may be used to indicate the *meaning* of a certain market share. For example, a market share of 1 per cent in the market for laundry detergent will lead to many more sales than will the same market share in the market for liquid detergents. This implies that it is important to define a market clearly. Without precise *market definition,* it is unclear to what the various analyses in the strategic marketing planning process are referring. In this context, the manager can choose a broad or a narrow market definition. With a broad definition, the market share will be relatively low and the number of competitors will be large. With a narrow definition, the reverse applies. This may give the impression that a manager can easily 'manipulate' the company's market share by choosing another market definition, but that is not the case. The market definition is based on strategic choices: Which customer groups does the company serve, and who are the most important competitors?

In the analysis of the size of the market, a distinction must be made between the served market and the potential market. The served market is the current market; the potential market is the maximum of what would be feasible; for example, with a 100 per cent distribution of the product and a strong sales promotion. Determining the potential market requires the application of forecasting methods. Data about total market demand for food products are collected by agencies such as Nielsen, GfK and IRI. For other markets, data from trade associations should be used.

6.4.2 Market and submarket growth and product life cycle

Market growth is also an important criterion for the attractiveness of a market. In addition, growth in submarkets should be identified, as Aaker (2013) proposes in his industry analysis. Strong market or submarket growth implies that even with a stable market share, increasing sales may be expected. However, even if the aggregate market size declines, there may be opportunities:

- If market sales decline, competitors may leave the market and the firm may become dominant.
- If aggregate market sales decline, there may be submarkets that grow, and so a disaggregated market analysis is needed.

Market growth is so important that this factor has been included as *the* market characteristic in the portfolio analysis of the Boston Consulting Group (see section 8.3). Aside from current market growth, *expected* market growth is important. Therefore, predictions of market growth need to be made. In making prognoses, the concept of the product life cycle may be used because the phase in the life cycle in which the product happens to be helps determine the expected future development.

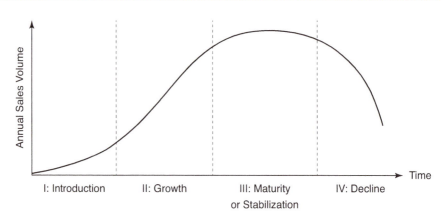

Figure 6.3 **Example of a product life cycle curve**

Many products have a life cycle. After the introduction and sales growth come stabilization and then decline. An important reason for this cycle is that as time goes by, other, better products come onto the market, after which sales of the 'old' product start to decline. The life cycle of a product is typically depicted with a graph that shows the course of sales over time. It is often assumed that this curve is S-shaped and that four phases may be distinguished (Figure 6.3).

In the introductory phase, sales are growing slowly: there are only a few consumers who know or use the product, and distribution is limited. In the growth phase, sales are increasing at an ever more rapid pace: The product catches on, distribution increases, and a growing number of consumers are buying the product. In the mature phase, sales are still increasing but the rate of growth is starting to slow down. There are no longer many 'new' consumers and later on sales start to decline slowly, after which, in this phase, sales drop sharply. In these later phases the function of the product is taken over by other products.

The concept of the product life cycle may be applied to product groups, brands, and varieties. At this point we are discussing the life cycle of a product group; for example, personal computers. Therefore, the focus is on the market as a whole. In that case, the implementation of the elements of the marketing mix will differ by phase. For example, brands in the growth phase of a market can grow by focusing on the market potential, whereas in the stabilization phase growth should be pursued by taking sales away from competitors (increasing market share) or through innovation. Brands and varieties can also have a life cycle, as in the case of Colgate toothpaste and Ariel Liquid laundry detergent. It has been argued that in the introductory phase of a brand, the brand values to be communicated should be mostly tangible, whereas in later phases the emphasis can be more on emotional characteristics.

However, the strategic implications of the life cycle concept are not always clear. A market in the growth phase appears attractive but also draws competitors. Often in growth markets, the number of suppliers becomes too large in relation to the final market size. This leads irrevocably to the downfall of a number of the suppliers. A product in the mature or saturation phase appears less attractive, but in these phases there may be segments that are still experiencing growth. If the most appropriate segmentation strategy is chosen, sales growth of the company's own brand is still possible. This shows that the life cycle of a product or brand should not be taken as a *given* because a company can influence and even lengthen this cycle. Through the choice of a good marketing strategy, a product or brand in the saturation phase can still offer many possibilities for remaining profitable or becoming profitable again.

6.4.3 Sensitivity to economic and seasonal trends

Markets in which sales are very sensitive to economic or seasonal trends are less attractive than markets in which this is not the case. After all, more uncertainty regarding sales and/or larger fluctuations means that a company needs to have a great deal of flexibility. Sensitivity to economic trends occurs especially with luxury goods (see case 6.4), which are often durable consumer goods. Sales fluctuations within a year that result from sensitivity to seasonal influences may occur with many products, such as drinks, travel, and sports products. A company that is active in several markets may attempt to reduce uncertainty regarding total sales through a careful choice of product–market combinations (a portfolio decision).

Case 6.4 Economic sensitivity

Travelling sensitive for economy and news

The better economic developments in recent years increased the intention for consumers to travel. The travel sector, however, stays very sensitive for bad news in countries. Also, consumers try to seek the cheapest ways, which is easier with the many online platforms for booking. At the same time, consumers want to have unique, personalized experiences. All these trends lead to increasing competition and a shift from traditional travel agencies to new, disruptive online suppliers.

Source: Rabobank, Numbers and Trends, 2015/2016

6.5 Factors related to industry structure

Factors related to industry structure determine the intensity of the competition in a market. An analysis of the intensity of the competition is important because a market is less attractive to the extent that the competition is more intense. Strong competition leads to increased marketing activity (promotional campaigns, intense advertising efforts), which increases costs; therefore, the average profitability of these companies is relatively low.

Since the profitability of companies is in the end a central point in the industry structure analysis, an attempt should be made to obtain more insight into profitability (section 6.5.1). Subsequently, factors that have an impact on average profitability should be examined. For this purpose, the industry model by Porter (1980) may be used (section 6.5.2).

6.5.1 Profitability

There may be significant differences among the profitability of various brands in a specific market. In addition, there are typically large differences in profitability among markets. Factors that determine profitability include the manufacturing process, the cost structure, and the competition. In an industry structure analysis, the task is to gain as much insight as possible into profitability. In addition, the *variability* of profitability is important: the extent to which profitability fluctuates over time. This represents an indication of the risks in a specific market. In markets with relatively high fixed costs, a decline in demand will lead to a stronger decline in profit than is the case in markets with relatively low fixed costs.

In practice, it is not easy to gain insight into the average profitability in a market. Although companies publish data about expenditures and revenues in their annual reports, these data are never broken down by products and/or markets. In The Netherlands, such data are considered extremely strategic and confidential. The average profitability in a market must therefore typically be estimated on the basis of impressions.

6.5.2 Industry structure according to Porter

In *Competitive Strategy*, Porter (1980) creates a link between the industry structure and competitive strategies. He argues that five factors (competitive forces) play a role in an industry (Figure 6.4). In Porter's model, the central industry factor is the intensity of competition among existing suppliers in a market.

External factors

The intensity of the competition is determined by external and internal factors. Figure 6.4 shows the *external* factors. This relates to the threat of new competitors (potential suppliers and substitute products) and the negotiating power of suppliers and buyers (distributors and final customers). If these 'threats' are strong, the intensity of the competition will be relatively strong and the average rate of return of companies will be relatively low.

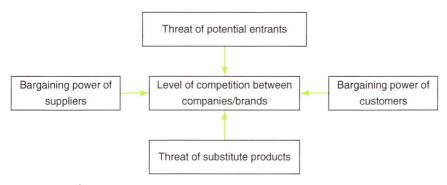

Figure 6.4 **Industry structure**
Source: Porter (1980)

The threat exerted by each of these four factors depends on a number of underlying factors. The *threat of new suppliers* is strong when:

- Entrance barriers are low because of:
  - The absence of economies of scale;
  - Limited communication intensity.
- There is little product differentiation.
- There is easy access to distribution channels.

In many markets for consumer goods there is little physical product differentiation, but because of that situation there are intense communication efforts. A new product or a new brand can be successful only if an appropriate corresponding communications budget is available. This also increases access to the distribution channels. Distributors prefer brands for which the manufacturer is engaged in intensive sales promotion.

The *threat of substitute products* depends on the broadness of the market definition on which the analysis is based. If a narrow market definition is assumed, there are a relatively large number of substitute products.

The *power of suppliers and/or buyers* (*distributors*) is strong when:

- Their power is strongly concentrated.
- They are not very price-sensitive.
- There is little product differentiation (presence of alternatives).

In the food industry in some countries, buyers (distributors) have strong power because of their concentration. As a result of various fusions and mergers (see also Case 6.5), only a few purchasing combinations are responsible for a large share of sales in the food industry. In other countries, that power is much smaller. Especially in the less developed grocery markets (for example, in Southern Europe), there are many smaller distributors and therefore these buyers have less power.

Case 6.5 Increasing power in the food market

Merger Sainsbury's and Asda radically changes power distribution

British Sainsbury's plan to merge with Asda will make this combination even bigger than the biggest FMCG-retailer in Great Britain, Tesco. Their combined market share would be around 31 per cent where Tesco has a market share of about 27 per cent (2018). The reason for the merger is quite clear. The margins of British supermarkets are declining, due to severe competition from the low-priced Aldi and Lidl, and also due to the growth of Amazon. More power makes them stronger in negotiation with suppliers. Sainsbury's promised to lower prices by 10 per cent after the merger.

Source: *Financial Daily* (Financieel Dagblad), 1 May 2018

It is clear that for manufacturers, the power of buyers is an important factor. The increased concentration in some countries has led to the development of the account management system by manufacturers and a greater emphasis on collaboration with distributors.

This demonstrates that in the context of Porter's model, it is important to analyse the *distribution structure*. The market structure of the distribution chain determines the power of the distributor and consequently determines the influence of this factor on market attractiveness.

Aside from the power of distributors, the power of final customers (consumers) is increasing because of the internet. As mentioned earlier (page 4), social media can function as an extremely fast 'word-of-mouth' communication. One complaint about an organization may result in a severe reputation problem, which will be accelerated if a journalist is also involved.

Internal factors: the supply structure

Aside from the factors mentioned above, the intensity of the competition between existing suppliers in a market is determined by a number of underlying *internal* factors. These are factors that directly determine the *supply structure* of a market. These factors are not shown in Figure 6.4 but will be discussed below. First, we discuss four elements that determine the supply structure: the number of suppliers, the degree of product differentiation (together these two dimensions determine the market form), concentration, and collaboration.

The market form determines the number of suppliers and the extent to which suppliers and products differ from one another.

1. *The number of suppliers.* A larger number of suppliers in principle leads to a larger degree of competition.
2. *The degree of product differentiation.* This is the extent to which suppliers and products differ from one another. In terms of the degree of product differentiation, if consumers perceive few differences among the offered products, the competition is more intense. As a result of the ever-increasing rate of technological development, in many markets products appear increasingly similar to one another.
3. *The degree of concentration of suppliers.* With a strong concentration, it is easier to make market agreements and the competition is typically less intensive; this is also the case if the number of competitors decreases. This relationship does not always apply. If a company merges with a competitor (which increases the concentration), the larger company can apply more resources to the competition battle. The relationship between concentration and competition is therefore not unequivocal and depends on the company conducting the analysis. For example, with a merger the competition for the merging partners will decrease by definition, whereas for the remaining suppliers the competition may increase.

   The degree of concentration can be measured by graphing the collective market share (concentration ratio) of the largest two (CR2) or four companies (CR4) and analysing it over time. An increasing concentration ratio indicates a more one-sided distribution of power in the market. Partly as a result of the importance of internationalization, the concentration in various markets has been increasing, for example, in sectors such as banking, insurance, and the airline industry.
4. *Collaboration within a market*. The existence of market agreements or other forms of collaboration between competitors has an influence on the organization of the market and therefore on the degree of competition.

Figure 6.5 provides an overview of the possible market forms.

	Number of suppliers		
	Many	**Few**	**One**
Homogeneity of the products			
Homogeneous	Full competition	Homogeneous oligopoly	Monopoly
Heterogeneous	Monopolistic competition	Heterogeneous oligopoly	Monopoly

Figure 6.5 **Market forms**

The dimensions mentioned above constitute the supply structure of the market. In addition, several other elements have an influence on the competitive behaviour of suppliers:

- *The development of the primary demand (market size).* In a shrinking market, sales growth can be achieved only at the expense of the competitors. Many markets are saturated, and so this factor generally leads to strong competition.
- *The proportion of fixed and variable costs.* If the fixed costs in the industry are relatively high, a company will have to fight harder to recover those costs.
- *The minimum scale required for capacity expansion.* In industries in which the production capacity can be expanded only in large leaps because of the optimal scale of the production unit, competition will be fiercer.
- *The surplus capacity.* The larger the surplus capacity, the fiercer the competition.
- *The strategic effort of companies.* If a company conducts its main activity in a certain industry, it will be more dedicated to the competitive battle than will a company that only has a sideline in that industry.
- *Uncertainty in regard to the production technology.* If the production technology is new or is still being developed, the competition will be more intense.
- *Exit barriers.* This refers to all the factors that make it difficult for a company to end loss-making business activities. The higher the exit barriers, the longer companies will continue with activities that lose money and the stronger the competition will be. Exit barriers may include the following:
  - ☐ Social factors: The legally required procedures regarding mass layoffs and the resistance of employees who are in danger of losing their jobs present very important exit barriers.
  - ☐ Strongly specialized assets: The liquidation value of a strongly specialized machine is often significantly lower than the utility value.
  - ☐ The connection of a certain product to other products, for example, through the collective use of fixed means of production (buildings, machines, etc.) or because of the desire to carry a full assortment or as a result of the image of the company (removing a product from the market will have a negative impact on the share price).
  - ☐ Emotional factors, such as attachment to a certain product.
  - ☐ Government support: Government support for companies in trouble may present an exit barrier.

Factor	Weight	Assessment	Score	Value
Aggregated market factors				
Market size	0.15	Large	5	0.75
Market growth/phase in product life cycle	0.20	Saturated	2	0.40
Sensitivity to economic and seasonal trends	0.05	Limited	4	0.20
Industry structure factors				
Profit margin	0.15	Fairly high	4	0.60
Threat of new entrants	0.05	Limited	5	0.25
Negotiation power of customers	0.10	Strong	2	0.20
Negotiation power of suppliers	0.05	Limited	4	0.20
Intensity of competition	0.20	Very heavy	1	0.20
Threat of substitute products	0.05	Fairly strong	3	0.15
Total	1.0			2.95

Figure 6.6 The calculation of the attractiveness score of the market for candy bars (1 = unattractive; 5 = very attractive)

For a company considering entering a market, one of these factors deserves special attention: *entrance barriers.* An analysis of entrance barriers is important not only to be able to determine the threat of potential suppliers but also to be able to determine which barriers the company has to overcome to enter the market. For a company that is considering entering a market, high entrance barriers obviously count as negative factors. In contrast, for companies that are already active in a market, high entrance barriers are a positive factor because they limit the threat of new entrants.

6.6 Determining market attractiveness

Completing an industry analysis serves two goals:

1. Obtaining insight into opportunities and threats from the perspective of the industry.
2. Obtaining insight into the attractiveness of the market.

To summarize an industry analysis, first, the observed opportunities and threats are listed.

Once a company has researched the attractiveness of a market by means of the factors listed in Figure 6.1, trying to arrive at summarizing conclusions may present a problem. After all, what should the conclusion be if some factors are interpreted positively and others are interpreted negatively? This problem can be solved through the assumption that a high score on one factor can compensate for a low score on another factor. With this assumption, it is possible to calculate a summarizing 'score' that is based on a weighted factor scoring method.

Suppose a manufacturer of ice cream is considering the production of candy bars. To research the attractiveness of the market for candy bars, the manufacturer examines the factors listed in Figure 6.6. The management rates each factor with a score on a scale ranging from 1 (very unattractive) to 5 (very attractive). In this example, a large market exists. This leads to a score of 5 for the factor market size. However, there is also intense competition. Therefore, that factor receives a score of 1. Subsequently, each factor receives a weight based on the importance (as assessed by management) of that factor for the attractiveness of the specific market. Because in different markets there are different determinants of success, these weights may differ by market. In addition, in the weighting process it matters how important management considers a factor to be. For example, one company may consider growth important, whereas for another profitability is the most important factor. In the example, the factor of market growth is considered the most important (weight 0.20). When all the factors have been multiplied by their weights and summed, we arrive at an attractiveness score of 2.95.

The next issue is how this score should be interpreted. Is 2.95 high or low? The interpretation depends, among other things, on whether the company that is doing the analysis is already active in that market. A company that is already active in the market could compare the results with those from a previous period. That would provide an answer to whether the market is becoming more or less attractive and why.

A potential entrant, as in the example, could compare the results with another market; for example, the market for sandwich fillings. The market with the higher score is the most attractive for entrance. In addition, the potential entrant needs to balance the score against the height of the entrance barriers: What problems need to be overcome to enter the market? A different market with a lower attractiveness score but with lower entrance barriers may be preferable. After all, the entrance barriers may be interpreted as the 'price' that has to be paid to enter a market.

Obviously, the factor scoring method described here is subjective. The biggest challenge is determining the appropriate weights for the individual factors. In addition, it is assumed that a low score on one factor may be compensated for by a high score on another factor. However, it is not unthinkable that a company requires minimum values for certain factors, for example, minimum required market growth.

An important advantage of the use of the factor scoring method in the industry analysis is that it provides a well-organized summary of the results of the entire analysis. A systematically implemented and well-organized depiction of the industry analysis is very important not just for the company's analyses but also for internal communication within the company.

In Figure 6.6 the macro-environmental factors shown in Figure 6.1 have not been included specifically. The reason for this is that these macro factors are included in the interpretation of the attractiveness of the market through their impact on market size and market growth.

The method of summarizing the industry analysis in Figure 6.6 allows a direct link with the portfolio analyses, in which several factors are considered (see section 10.2). The fact is that in the context of such 'multifactor portfolio analyses', the kind of analysis shown in Figure 6.6 is very common.

Summary

The goal of the industry analysis is to obtain an impression of future opportunities and threats from the perspective of the industry as well as changes in the attractiveness of the market in which a company is active. The attractiveness or expected profitability of a market is determined by the intensity of competition: the more intense the battle, the less attractive the market. The degree of competition is in turn determined by three categories of factors: developments in the macro environment (such as demographic, social-cultural, and ecological trends), aggregated market factors (such as the phase in the product life cycle), and factors related to the industry structure (such as the intensity of competition). The analysis of the macro environment is an important source of opportunities. If a company is able to respond quickly to a social-cultural development, it may achieve a competitive advantage. The attractiveness of a market and its submarkets should be determined by evaluating all these underlying factors and, based on this evaluation, determining an attractiveness score. By assigning weights to each of the examined factors and summing the various values, a company will arrive at an attractiveness score that may be compared with the scores for other markets or with the score for a previous period. Since trends in the industry may include high degrees of uncertainty with major consequences, a manager can define scenarios with respect to the main trends.

The information from an industry analysis regarding the attractiveness of a market is important in determining both objectives and the appropriate investment level of the organization in that specific market (corporate strategy; see Chapter 10). The information about possible opportunities and threats may be used in determining the marketing strategy.

Case price fighters amaze friend and foe

Flying has become so cheap that it has changed our daily lives. Five days of work on a job in Poland, a bachelor party in Riga, or monthly up and down to the second house in Spain for a family from London: it's all possible. Yet the future doesn't look that bright for many airlines. The low oil price is still supportive for many companies, but the ongoing threat of terrorism and the killing competition with other airlines will almost certainly offset the savings on fuel costs in the coming period.

For example, Air France-KLM announced in mid-2016 that the results will deteriorate during the second quarter. The company is concerned about the impact of terrorist attacks on the behaviour of the traveller. The company already experienced that Japanese travellers are less inclined to travel to France because of the terror. The economic and geopolitical uncertainty, such as Brexit and the failed coup in Turkey, also makes Air France-KLM somewhat pessimistic about the future. Air France-KLM is not the only airline that suffers from these uncertainties. Ryanair and Easyjet are also worried. For example, according to Ryanair's 2015 annual report, "Terrorism in the United Kingdom or elsewhere in Europe could have a material detrimental effect on the company."

Sales and margins are therefore under pressure in the airline industry. Air France-KLM saw a drop in sales of 5.2 per cent to 6.2 billion euros in the second quarter of 2015. Due to the low oil price, the airline company still managed to realize a profit of 41 million euros. A year earlier Air France-KLM made a loss of 79 million euros in the second quarter. These figures contrast with the results of Ryanair. Ryanair, the European market leader for cheap flights, achieved a profit of 866 million euros in 2015, 66 per cent more than in the previous year. The number of Ryanair passengers increased by 11 per cent to more than 90 million.

Low-cost carriers

Low-cost carriers such as Ryanair are also referred to as no-frills airlines. In Europe, they have emerged since the liberalization of the European aviation sector in the 1990s. Since 1 April 1997, airlines have been allowed to operate flights to and from any airport in Europe, regardless of the country in which they are established. The Irish Ryanair, the first low-cost carrier in Europe (founded in 1988), has grown since that date from 3 million passengers to 117 million in 2016. The low-cost model was replicated all over the world. The strategy is aimed at removing as many frills from a flight as possible. Regional airports, with much lower take-off and landing rights, are their base. There are no free drinks or meals, and an extra charge must be paid for luggage. National airlines can only survive by merging or even turning themselves into a price fighter. Meanwhile, an increasing share of the European aviation market is in the hands of price fighters. Ryanair is again the largest of these.

The efficiency of low-cost carriers is apparent from the overview in Table 6.1, which shows the number of passengers per employee (total number of passengers divided by the total number of employees of the company).

Table 6.1 **Number of passengers per employee (based on annual reports from the airlines)**

Ryanair	9,451
Easyjet	6,772
British Airways	735
Air France-KLM	715
Lufthansa	624

The consumer

While the prices of airline tickets have been falling for many years, the number of airline passengers worldwide doubled between 2000 and 2010 to a total of 2.5 billion per year in 2010. The growth in the number of passengers has levelled off in recent years; in 2015, for example, there was still a growth of around 3 per cent in Europe. There is a clear shift from 'traditional' airlines to low-cost airlines.

The increase in the number of passengers is caused by a number of factors. Due to the low cost of a ticket, people now fly to a holiday destination, while in the past they would have taken the car or train. However, the increase is not exclusively based on choosing another means of transport; low-cost carriers also expand the market. Bachelor parties in Latvia, a weekend in Mallorca, or shopping in Barcelona: without the low-cost carrier it would simply never have existed. Flying has become a commodity, and mobility is part of our lifestyle. We also seem to accept the fact that flying is very polluting. Although everyone may now consider sustainability important, we do not (yet) apply it to our flight behaviour.

The question is to what extent we accept that flying may become a luxury product again. Finally, globalization, the emerging economies in Asia and South

America, and European unification also contribute to increased mobility. Not only is the tourist looking further and further afield, but the business traveller also has more and more international contacts.

What about internationalization in European higher education? Student exchanges lead to international friendships, and in order to maintain those contacts, people have to travel. The rise of social networking reinforces this: all those international friends on Facebook should also be really visited, if only to be tagged in more photos.

The market and expectations

The question is of course whether mobility will continue to increase in the future. Consumer confidence may be rising in many countries due to the positive economic outlook, but this also implies that pilots, air stewards, and other airline personnel desire a higher salary. Brexit also has an influence. Since 2016, many more Britons turned out to celebrate their holidays in their own country. It is of course questionable whether a possible Brexit will lead to less traffic between Great Britain and the Continent in the future, but uncertainty is never good for the market. Ryanair also recognizes the risks:

> The Airline Industry is particularly sensitive to changes in economic conditions. A continued recessionary environment would have a negative impact on Ryanair's result of operations. Ryanair's operations and the airline industry in general are sensitive to changes in economic conditions. Unfavourable economic conditions such as government austerity measures, the uncertainty relating to the Eurozone, high unemployment rates, constrained credit markets, and increased business operating costs could lead to reduced spending by both leisure and business passengers. Unfavourable economic conditions, such as the conditions persisting as of the date hereof, also tend to impact upon Ryanair's ability to raise fares to counteract increased fuel and other operating costs. A continued recessionary environment, combined with austerity measures by European governments [...] could restrict the Company's ability to grow passenger volumes, secure new airports, and launch new routes and bases, and could have a material adverse impact on its financial results.

"The Importance of the Economic Situation for Developments in Aviation".
Ryanair Annual Report (2015)

The economy proved to be a lot more positive in many countries than Ryanair expected in 2015, but the report shows the vulnerability of the industry to economic developments. And now, with the booming economy, Ryanair is confronted with a capacity issue: the company didn't have enough available pilots in autumn 2017, and for the first time in history had to cancel a large number of flights. This might damage the image of Ryanair as a cheap and maybe somewhat uncomfortable, but always reliable, carrier.

Finally, there is the threat of terrorism. This threat might make the consumer travel less. And if they are already travelling, they might be more likely to opt for the familiarity of their own car. Or, if they are environmentally aware, for a less polluting alternative. In short, there is a general uncertainty for aviation. The big question is: What will be the result of this uncertain situation?

Both Ryanair and the British low-cost carrier Easyjet saw the number of passengers grow by 6 to 11 per cent in 2015. As a result, the low-cost airlines perform considerably better than their established competitors. The 'traditional airlines' struggle with high personnel costs, and regularly collide with the pilots who want to defend their salary and other vested privileges. Strikes at Air France-KLM, for instance, have already cost that company a lot of money. And not only because flights fail; the market requires flexibility, while the necessary changes are stopped by the strikers.

In 2012, for the last time a larger European airline went bankrupt: the Hungarian Malev. Some experts expect the sector to be at the beginning of a major consolidation battle where only a few very large players will remain.

In a statement, Ryanair writes about the future with full confidence. For the time being, Ryanair also seems to be better able to handle the uncertainties in the market than the competition. The big question is obviously what the uncertain market will do with the market position of the price fighter in the longer term: Will Ryanair continue to grow in the future?

Questions

1. Treacy and Wiersema (1993) distinguish three value strategies. Which value strategy has been chosen by Ryanair? Explain your answer (see Chapter 7).
2. Which strategic groups can be distinguished in the European airline industry?
3. Make a macro-environmental analysis of the European aviation sector, based on the information in this case.
4. The case outlines major differences between traditional airlines such as Air France-KLM and low-cost carriers such as Ryanair.
   - In what phase of the product life cycle is the traditional airline company? Give reasons for your answer.
   - At what stage of the product life cycle is the low-cost carrier? Give brief reasons why.
   - What strategic consequences could you draw for a company such as Air France-KLM, based on the product life cycle concept? And do you think this is feasible in practice?
5. a) Do you feel that the aviation industry is sensitive to economic fluctuations? Why [not]?
   b) Do you consider the aviation industry sensitive to seasonal trends? Why [not]?

6. a) Determine the attractiveness of the aviation industry, from the point of view of Ryanair, by using Porter's five-forces model (1980).
    b) To what extent does this differ from the attractiveness from the viewpoint of Air France-KLM?
7. Give your own opinion: do you believe that the growth potential for Ryanair has reached its limits? Give reasons for your answer.

Chapter 7

Competitor analysis

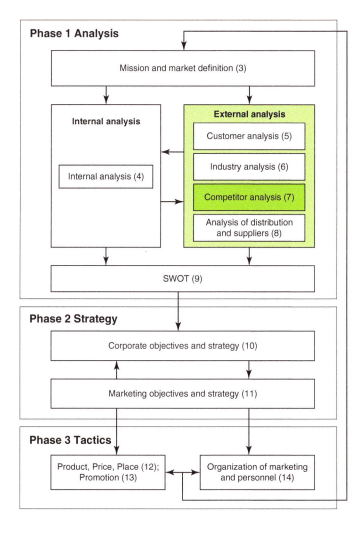

Phase 1 Analysis

Mission and market definition (3)

Internal analysis

Internal analysis (4)

External analysis

Customer analysis (5)

Industry analysis (6)

Competitor analysis (7)

Analysis of distribution and suppliers (8)

SWOT (9)

Phase 2 Strategy

Corporate objectives and strategy (10)

Marketing objectives and strategy (11)

Phase 3 Tactics

Product, Price, Place (12); Promotion (13)

Organization of marketing and personnel (14)

Key points in this chapter

- ■ Know the steps of a competitor analysis.
- ■ Be able to identify competitors by using the appropriate methods.
- ■ Assess competitors' strengths and weaknesses on the corporate and brand levels.
- ■ Know which qualitative and quantitative data sources may be used in a competitor analysis.
- ■ Put it all together in making a forecast of a competitor's strategy and reactions.

Introduction

A competitor analysis may be thought of as a competition analysis at the micro level: the behaviour of individual competitors is analysed with the ultimate goal of predicting the competitors' actions and reactions. It is important to maintain a clear structure in a competitor analysis. Without structuring, the problem may arise, as it often does in practice, that large amounts of data are collected about competitors without deducing the relevant *information* from the data.

Section 7.1 describes the goal and structure of a competitor analysis. The first phase in a competitor analysis is identification of the competitors. Section 7.2 discusses the methods that may be useful in that process. Sections 7.3 to 7.6 outline the other phases of the competitor analysis. Section 7.7 reviews a number of data sources that may be used.

7.1 Goal and structure of the competitor analysis

7.1.1 Goal

A competitor analysis examines individual competitors. Opportunities that may be expected from competitors are typically found in the weaknesses of those competitors. Those weaknesses provide starting points for the company's competitive advantages. The extent to which competitors are threatening the company depends on their objectives and strategies. If a competitor is satisfied with its position and has no new plans, there is relatively less danger to be expected. However, a competitor that wants to grow and starts an active competition battle for that purpose, with new products and intensive advertising efforts, presents an important threat to the company.

Therefore, the objectives of the competitor analysis are to obtain insight into:

- ■ The strengths and weaknesses of the competitors.
- ■ The future behaviour of the competitors.

The strengths and weaknesses of the competitors are compared with the company's own strengths and weaknesses to understand the extent to which the company is strong or weak in relation to the competitors. For example, a company's strength has little strategic value if the competitors have the same strength. However, a weakness is less serious if all the competitors have the same weakness. Therefore, the goal is to determine the company's relative strengths and weaknesses.

An understanding of the expected behaviour of competitors provides indications for opportunities and threats caused by competitors. In terms of the future behaviour of competitors, a distinction can be made between the 'autonomous' expected behaviour of the competitors – what they are planning to do on their own initiative – and possible reactions of competitors to the company's strategies.

7.1.2 Structure

In performing a competitor analysis, two approaches may be chosen: a rivalry approach and a partner approach.

1. A *rivalry approach* is to consider the competitor as a 'rival', another supplier that does battle for the favour of the customers and therefore should be 'fought'. Until the end of the 1980s this approach was the most common. The goal was to beat the competition, and the competitor analysis was therefore aimed at identifying the weaknesses of the opponent. By placing a company's strengths against those weaknesses, the company could achieve a competitive advantage.
2. In *a partner approach*, the company considers its competitors as future collaboration partners. Partly as a result of the trend towards internationalization mentioned earlier in this book, in many industries survival is possible only through collaboration with competitors, not through attempting to beat them. Examples of industries in which collaboration has taken on an increasingly important role are the airline industry, the banking and insurance industries, the printing and allied trades, and health care. In terms of the practice of performing a competitor analysis, a partner approach means that the analysis should be focused not only on searching for weaknesses of the opponent (to gain a competitive advantage for the company) but also on searching for starting points for collaboration. An opportunity presents itself when the competitor has an interesting strength in an area where the company has a weakness, and vice versa.

Five phases may be distinguished in a competitor analysis (Figure 7.1):

1. Identification and choice of competitors.
2. Objectives of competitors.
3. Current strategies of competitors.
4. Identification of factors that determine success and the strengths and weaknesses of competitors.
5. Expected strategies of competitors.

Phases 4 and 5 of this process provide the information mentioned in the description of the objectives of a competitor analysis (strengths and weaknesses, future behaviour). We will now discuss each of the five phases in turn.

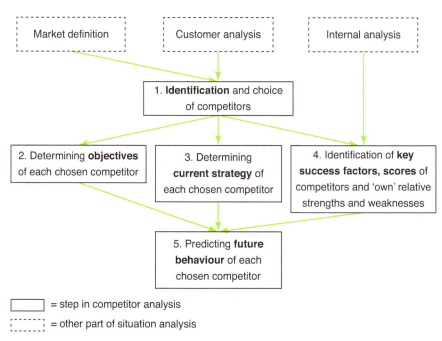

Figure 7.1 **Framework for a competitor analysis**

7.2 Identification and choice of competitors

In terms of a definition of what a competitor is, it may be another supplier that potentially fulfils the same need of the target audience. On the basis of this definition, the question of who the competitors are therefore depends on the definition of the need. That definition is connected to the market definition. Does Coca-Cola's top management consider that the company is active in the market for colas or the market for soft drinks, or in the market for luxury items?

7.2.1 Competition levels

With regard to competition, four levels may be distinguished (see also section 3.3.4):

1. *Product form competition.* This is competition among brands that are focused on the same market segment.
2. *Product category competition.* This is competition among products with comparable characteristics.
3. *Generic competition.* This is competition among products that respond to the same needs of consumers.
4. *Budget competition.* This is competition for the money of the consumer.

Figure 7.2 includes several examples of competition at these four levels.

Competition level	Low-alcohol beer	Low-priced TV	Chinese restaurant
1. Product form	Low-alcohol or alcohol-free beer	Low-price TV	Chinese restaurants
2. Product category	Beer	TV's	Restaurants
3. Generic	Drinks	Electronic devices	Eating at home
4. Budget	Drinks, food, entertainment	Durable goods, vacations	Food, drinks, entertainment

Figure 7.2 **Examples of competition levels**

In moving from product form competition towards budget competition, the market definition broadens and, consequently, the number of competitors increases. Therefore, a direct relationship exists between the definition of the market and the identification of the competitors. Because of this, there is also a relationship with the marketing decisions. *Different product characteristics* should be emphasized at the different competition levels. For example, if a manufacturer of low-priced televisions chooses the product form level of competition shown in Figure 7.2, the competitors are other low-priced TVs, and the manufacturer should emphasize why its TV is better than the other cheap TVs. However, if the manufacturer chooses the product category level, the manufacturer should position itself in relation to all TVs, for example, through price. At the generic level, the advantages of the TV over other devices such as PCs should be pointed out to the consumer. On the budget level, the company may communicate why using a television is more interesting than other leisure activities.

The choice of the competition level is therefore clearly connected to the market definition. The market definition in turn is determined, among other things, by two related factors:

1. The *planning level* in the company: company level, business unit level, or product level.
2. The *planning period*: Is it a matter of short-term plans (a year or less) or longer term plans?

Figure 7.3 shows the relationship between these two factors and the definition of competition and the market.

To the extent that a higher aggregation level in the company is involved, the planning period usually becomes longer, the market definition broader, and the level of competition higher. For example, at the company level, issues such as collaboration with potential partners play a role. This is a long-term issue that requires a broad market definition and therefore a high level of competition. After all, potential partners do not need to be active only in the direct market of the company but may also be active in adjacent markets. At the product level the annual short-term planning is relevant; this involves, for example, the daily threat of directly competing products and brands (product category competition and product form competition).

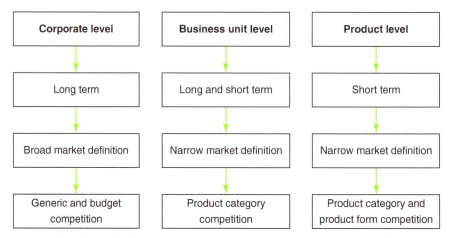

Figure 7.3 **Relationship between aggregation level, planning horizon, market definition, and competition level**

7.2.2 Methods for identifying competitors

The methods that may be used for identifying the competitors include competition-based methods and customer-based methods. In *customer-based methods*, data regarding the demand side of the market are used: the competition is analysed from the perspective of the customers. For example, customers may be asked which product or brand they would purchase if the preferred product or brand were not available. A *competition-based approach* means that the company identifies the competition on the basis of data about the competitors; for example, by examining which competitors follow a strategy similar to the one used by the company.

In general, competition-based methods are suitable for identifying the competition at the *company level*, whereas customer-based methods are appropriate for identifying competing *products*. We will review two competition-based methods and then three customer-based methods. We will conclude this part of the chapter with a brief discussion about the advantages and disadvantages of both categories of methods.

Competition-based methods

Two competition-based methods may be distinguished:

1. Management opinion.
2. Strategic groups.

Management opinion

By using his or her experience and knowledge of the market, a manager can often make a reasonable estimate of the identity of current and future competitors (management opinion). When necessary, the manager can also consult the company's representatives, distributors, and other internal experts. A tool that may be used for this purpose is the division of competitors into companies that:

- Bring the same *products* onto the market.
- Serve the same *customers* (markets and/or segments).

The most *direct competitors* are companies that supply the same products to the same markets. More *indirect competitors* are companies that supply the same products but focus on a different market. Companies that serve the same market but sell other products may be designated as *potential competitors.*

Strategic groups

A second competition-based way to identify competitors is to divide the suppliers in a market into *strategic groups*. A strategic group is a group of companies that employ similar strategies (see Case 7.1). A company can develop insight into how these groups are composed by determining which strategies the suppliers in a market have chosen; that is, by examining the choice of a target audience and the positioning, as well as the implementation of the elements of the marketing mix: product quality, assortment, price setting, distribution spread, use of representatives, and the communications mix. Furthermore, the strategies relating to other functional areas are important, such as the extent of research and development (R&D) efforts, production, purchasing, and finances.

The concept of strategic groups simplifies the identification and choice of competitors. After all, the competition will be strongest within strategic groups. If there are many competitors, a company may place the most emphasis on its own strategic group. The other strategic groups may then be analysed as a whole. In practice, sometimes all competitors or groups of 'small competitors' are defined as a strategic group; in this case the company makes the assumption that those small competitors all use strategies that are more or less comparable (this is often not the case).

Customer-based methods

We distinguish three customer-based methods:

1. Direct identification research with customers.
2. Brand switching.
3. Positioning research.

Direct identification research with customers

The most direct and simple method to identify the competition via customers is to ask directly who the competitors are; for example, by asking questions such as "Which other similar products do you know?" and "Which products did you also consider buying?" Insight into the most direct competitor may be obtained by asking, "If your preferred

Case 7.1 Strategic groups

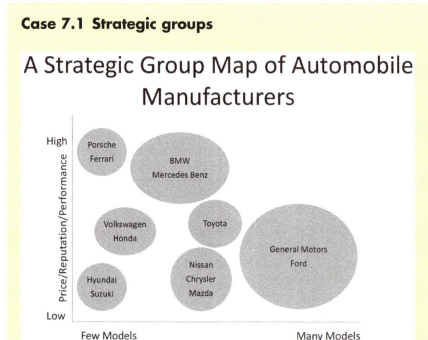

Figure 7.4 **An example of the automotive industry**

An example in the automotive industry

Based on the variables 'Number of models' and 'Quality/reputation', a distinction can be made in five strategic groups in the automotive industry. Figure 7.4 is an example, based on assumptions.

brand was no longer available, which brand would you buy?" A disadvantage of such questions is that the extent to which the opinion of the interviewee is actually a reflection of his or her behaviour is uncertain. The simplicity of this method is an important advantage.

A variation on asking a direct question is to make a connection with product usage. In approaches that entail *product usage associations*, users of the product are asked to name all usage situations or applications. They are then asked to name suitable products for each application. Other product users are then asked to indicate how suitable each product is for each usage situation. Finally, the products may be clustered on the basis of similarity of suitable applications. An advantage of this method is that it is possible to gain insight into less direct forms of competition, such as generic competition.

Brand switching

A more advanced customer-based identification method uses data about the extent to which customers switch between brands (brand-switching data). The advantage of this method is that it uses behavioural data. The data are usually collected through the use of panels of households. The assumption is that a high degree of brand switching indicates a strong similarity and therefore strong competition. For example, if it is observed that many households switch regularly between brands B, D, and E, it is concluded that those brands are competitors of one another. A disadvantage of these data is that they usually refer to households ('families'), leaving it unclear *who* actually buys the product. Because of this, there is the possibility that the switching behaviour is not caused by similarity but is done because different family members with different preferences make the purchases. A solution to this problem is to register the purchases made by individuals. This is being done increasingly often. For example, the increasing use of cash cards allows the retail industry to register who makes certain purchases. If these data can be combined with data on the purchases of articles that have been collected through scanning (reading bar codes), a detailed 'brand-switching' analysis is possible. In Chapter 4 we discussed developments in scanning. Brand-switching analysis is suitable only for fast-moving consumer goods, and as a result of the lack of data, it cannot be used for service and industrial markets.

Positioning research

It is also possible to obtain insight into the competitive situation in a market through a more indirect method of customer-based research: so-called *positioning research*. This method often uses multidimensional scaling (MDS) techniques. With research of this kind, customers are asked to compare the products or companies they know on the basis of similarity and/or preference. Using these data and software especially developed for the purpose, it then becomes possible to represent the different products in relation to each other graphically in a multidimensional space (a 'perceptual map; see Chapter 5). Products located close to each other are close competitors. In addition, positioning research produces other important strategic information, such as information about the image of the company's product and that of the competitors.

7.2.3 Choice of identification method

In practice, competition-based methods are used the most frequently. This is also the simplest technique: a company forms a judgement on the basis of its own market knowledge and is not required to perform additional fieldwork. However, competition-based methods have an important disadvantage: they are based on the assumption that what the company thinks about the competition actually corresponds to the perceptions of the customers. The danger is that a company may perceive certain businesses as being competitors, whereas in reality the customers do not consider those businesses in that light, and vice versa. This danger does not exist when a customer-based approach to identifying the competition is chosen. However, a customer-based approach has two limitations. First, it is difficult to gain insight into potential customers and indirect competitors. After all, customers know only the existing products and are not aware of competitors that have not yet entered the market. Second, customer-based methods typically have to be performed at the level of brands and products. That is, customers often do not know the suppliers of products.

Both limitations imply that customer-based methods are especially well suited to *short-term planning*. After all, in the short term it is unlikely that new competitors will enter the market, and the analyses may therefore be limited to the product or brand level. However, for longer term planning, both the company level and potential competitors also need to be considered. The competition-based methods are especially appropriate for this purpose.

Therefore, it is advisable to choose both a customer-based approach and a competition-based approach for the identification of competitors. In this way, the company will put into practice what Kotler articulated many years ago: "learn how your customers view your competitors rather than how you view your competitors" (Kotler, 1984).

7.2.4 Choosing the competitors

If, with the aid of the previously discussed methods, the competitors have been identified, the next issue is whether a detailed behavioural analysis must be performed for all possible competitors. In practice this is not necessary and is usually not feasible. It is also not possible to perform a separate behavioural analysis of all *potential competitors.* Therefore, the manager needs to choose the competitors that merit the most attention in the chosen market. But which one is the most important? The largest one or the one that is most similar to ourselves? And which one will be important in the future? Because these questions in principle will be answered in the subsequent analysis, it seems impossible to make a choice beforehand. A solution to this chicken-and-egg problem is to perform a global competitor analysis and then examine a number of competitors more closely.

For the first selection of competitors, two factors are important: market share and *similarity* with the company's product or the company. It is advisable to consider the competitors that are largest as well as those which have comparable products or focus on the same target audience.

7.3 Objectives of competitors

In the second phase of the competitor analysis, an attempt is made to deduce the objectives of the most important competitors. This involves two aspects:

1. What does the competitor want?
2. How much does the competitor want it?

The first aspect is related to the competitor's growth direction: Does the competitor want to maintain its market share or increase it? If it wants to increase its market share, does the competitor want to grow with the aid of existing or new products and with existing or new customers? The second aspect is determined by the 'commitment' of the competitor: the extent to which the competitor is involved with the product or market. Both aspects together determine the effort and aggression with which a competitor is active in the market. The largest threat may be expected from a competitor that is very involved with a market and wants to grow in that market. However, a competitor that 'only' wants to maintain its market share but strongly wants to maintain it also presents an important threat.

Indications of what the competitor wants may be obtained in the following ways:

1. *Comparison of the objectives of the competitor with the current results.* A difference between desired and achieved market share leads to an expected growth strategy.
2. *Application of a portfolio analysis to the competitor.* Assuming that the competitor also uses a portfolio analysis, a company can perform its own analysis of the position of the competitor's strategic business units (SBUs) and products in a portfolio model and use it to deduce the competitor's most logical portfolio decision (investments and growth direction).
3. *Determining how important a product is for the competitor.* This may be measured in terms of sales, profit, or number of employees.
4. *Studying the competitor's use of the marketing mix over time.* For example, a price reduction together with an increase in advertising expenses may indicate that the competitor is pursuing growth, and this may present a threat to the company's product. In contrast, a competitor's minimizing of marketing efforts may indicate a harvesting strategy, which means attempting to maximize profit. This type of competitor typically presents less of a threat in the long term.

7.4 Current strategies of competitors

In an attempt to discover the expected strategy of a competitor, the first step is to examine the competitor's current strategy (see Case 7.2). This involves, among other things:

- The marketing strategy: the choice of the target audience (segments) and the chosen positioning.
- The use of the marketing mix.

Insight into the marketing strategy is obtained by observing and analysing the elements of the marketing mix. Typically, a company will examine the competitor's use of the marketing mix and use that information to deduce its marketing strategy. An understanding of the segments targeted by the competitor may be obtained through market research (who are the customers of the competitor?) as well as through indirect methods such as the media choice and advertising expressions of competitors. The choice of distribution points also makes a statement about the choice of a target audience. Analysis of the target audiences defined by competitors is important to avoid segments with intense competition, whereas segments with little competition present an opportunity.

Insight into the competitive advantage pursued by the competitor can be provided by the competitor's advertising campaigns and all other offline and online communication.

Case 7.2 Strategy of competitors

Large brands increasingly compete with small brands

Large brands, such as brands of Unilever, Nestlé and Procter & Gamble, are confronted with increasing competition from successful small brands. There are three reasons for the growth of small brands. First, there is an increase in price competition, especially from distributor-owned brands (DOBs). But this is not the only reason. Well-known brands as Mars, Ariel, Magnum, and Andrelon not only compete with DOBs, but also with small brands such as Tony Chocolonely and ice cream brand Halo-Top. Consumers increasingly prefer authentic, local brands. Another important reason for the growth of small brands is that getting into the consumers' mind requires less investments using social media instead of developing expensive advertising campaigns. Halo-Top is an excellent example of this: with smart online campaigns they managed to get into the consumers' mind, and while not existing in 2012, they had a turnover of $100 million in 2017.

Source: *Financial Daily* (Financieel Dagblad), 16 May 2018

It is fair to assume that each company will communicate its supposed strength to the customers. Therefore, a detailed analysis of the contents of the competitor's communications is very important. In section 7.7 we review tangible data sources that may be used for the analysis of the competitor's strategy.

7.5 Factors that determine success and strengths and weaknesses of competitors

In this phase, three questions should be answered:

1. Which resources and skills are important in this market? In other words, what are the determinants of success (section 7.5.1)?

2.   What are the strengths and weaknesses of the competitors (section 7.5.2)?
3.   What summarizing conclusions may be drawn (section 7.5.3)?

7.5.1 Identification of key success factors

To avoid having to determine all possible strengths and weaknesses during a strengths–weaknesses analysis of the competitors, it is useful to determine which resources and skills are the most important in a particular market: the *key success factors*. For this purpose, the factors that determine success in a market should be identified; that is, the resources or skills that have a large influence on the results of a company. 'Result' in this context may refer to relative costs, customer loyalty, market share, profit, and so on (Day and Wensley, 1988). In other words, the focus here is on the strengths that lead to a better-than-average result. If a company possesses those strengths, it has an advantage relative to its competitors. Examples are: for a manufacturer of food items, efficient physical distribution; for a manufacturer of televisions, low labour costs; and for an insurance company, a good relationship with agents.

To be able to operate successfully, knowledge of the factors that determine success is very important for a company. As a starting point for the identification of these factors, a checklist similar to the one used for an internal analysis may be employed (Figure 4.7). Next, the question is which factors from that schedule are the most important. The following questions may be useful in this regard:

1.   Why are successful companies successful and unsuccessful companies unsuccessful?
2.   What are the most important motivations of customers? What do customers consider important?
3.   Which phase in the production process creates the highest added value, and which phase creates the highest costs?
4.   What are the entrance barriers in the industry and between segments in the market?

A method related to the first question involves doing a comparison of successful and less successful companies. By comparing the characteristics of successful and less successful companies in its own industry, a company can develop an understanding of the characteristics responsible for success. To arrive at reliable conclusions, sufficient data must be available. Because this is often not the case or only partly the case for a company's industry, such an analysis often has to be performed qualitatively and the conclusions are only indicative.

To answer the second question, a customer analysis should be performed. The goal is to discover what customers consider important. The simplest method is to ask directly how important customers consider certain product characteristics (attributes) to be. To prevent respondents from answering that they consider everything important, methods have been developed that take into account the 'trade-off' between characteristics. In this regard a suitable analysis method is *conjoint analysis* (see section 5.4.3).

A method related to the third question is an analysis of the *value chain* as it applies 'on average' in the industry. The activities that on average contribute the highest added value are factors that may determine success. In addition, the phases with the highest costs are the most likely candidates for pursuing cost advantages.

The fourth question implies that the *entrance barriers* should be analysed. The factors that make it difficult for a potential supplier to enter the market (e.g. obtaining the technology required for making the product, achieving a high degree of distribution, executing an intensive advertising campaign) are typically very important in the industry.

Based on the preceding analyses, for each factor a company can indicate its importance in the industry (see the first column in Figure 7.5).

7.5.2 Determining the strengths and weaknesses of competitors

The next step is to determine for each of the factors shown in Figure 7.5 the extent to which the chosen competitors are strong or weak in that factor. For this purpose a great deal of mostly qualitative data have to be collected, and in that process interviews with various 'experts' (representatives, customers, researchers, etc.) will be an important source. In Figure 7.5 a short description and designation may be added to each of the characteristics of competitors. Note that in this figure the strengths and weaknesses may apply to both the corporate level and the brand level of a competitor. Information regarding the brand level may be collected through marketing research.

7.5.3 Determining relative strengths and weaknesses

Chapter 4 reviews several methods for the internal analysis. If these methods are also used for the competitor analysis, a direct comparison can be made. For example, a manager may make an assessment of the performance of a competitor on the value strategies. A manageable method for comparing the company with its competitors is to summarize the essentials in a score chart: a *competitive grid* (Figure 7.6), which may be limited to the key success factors. Comparing competitors' strengths with the company's own strengths provides insights into *relative (unique) strengths*.

The following may be deduced from Figure 7.6:

- The own company is strong in quality and finance (last column).
- The relative strengths and weaknesses of the firm. Because competitor A also has a good financial position, this is not a relative strength for the focal company. The quality level, however, is a competitive advantage. The other factors show a not-so-innovative management and perhaps as a result of this an unclear image.

Figure 7.6 may also be used for selecting a partner. Innovation is weak in the focal company but is very strong for competitor B. For the financial position it is the other way around. Cooperation with B may be beneficial for both the own company and competitor B. See also Case 7.3.

Characteristics	Competitors			Other competitors*
	A	B	C	
Marketing and market position				
Customer orientation				
Product quality				
Market knowledge				
Relationship with distributors				
Sales promotion				
Service				
Market share				
Brand loyalty				
Brand awareness				
Customer satisfaction				
Innovation				
Technology				
R&D expenses				
Patents				
Production				
Resources				
Means of production				
Personnel				
Financing				
'Cash flow'				
Parent company				
Current position				
Management				
Flexibility				
Entrepreneurial quality				
Staff turnover				

*This might also be assessed for a strategic group.

Figure 7.5 Potential key success factors and strengths and weaknesses of a company or brand

Characteristics	Competitor A	Competitor B	Competitor C	Group of small competitors	'Own' company or brand
Ambition top management	2	2	5	4	1
Distinctive brand image	4	1	3	4	2
Innovation	1	5	2	3	2
Quality	4	4	1	2	5
Finance	5	2	4	2	5

Figure 7.6 Competitive grid: scores on key success factors of competitors and a company's own brand (1 = very weak; 5 = very strong)

Case 7.3 Partner analysis

Is the combination of Sainsbury's and Asda a logical fit?

The announced merger of Sainsbury's and Asda might have led to positive reactions of investors, but the question is whether it is a logical fit. Asda is a relatively cheap supermarket, with a strong position in the North of England. Sainsbury's has a somewhat higher image and is especially strong in the South of England. Their combination should lead to a new strong supermarket brand. Also, internally it is of vital importance that both cultures fit.

Source: *Financial Daily* (Financieel Dagblad), 1 May 2018

A more specific form of comparison of the organization with the competitors is called *benchmarking*. Benchmarking (sometimes called 'cheating') is best described as searching for best practices. By comparing operational processes in the company with those in other companies, one can gain insight into the company's performance and therefore also into starting points for improvement. These operational processes may range from administration and production to a comparison of commercial performance. This comparison may be made with competitors but also with non-direct competitors. Vorhies and Morgan (2005) show that benchmarking can be a fruitful tool for realizing a competitive advantage.

7.6 Expected strategies of competitors

In the previous phases, an answer was provided to the questions of who the most important competitors are and what the objectives, current strategies, and strengths and weaknesses of those competitors are. In the last phase of the competitor analysis, those elements should be used as a basis to answer the question of what the competitor is going to do in the future. In addition, this process should include an attempt to predict how the competitors may react to the strategies formulated by the company. In this phase, the assignment is therefore to draw a 'conclusion' about the expected behaviour of the competitors based on all previously collected information. It is therefore important to identify oneself with the competitor.

It is not easy to make tangible predictions during this phase. Among others, subjective forecasting methods will have to be used: methods through which, in one way or another, 'experts' generate prognoses based on the available information. Concrete methods that may be used for this purpose are Delphi research (attempting to arrive at a prognosis through several rounds with experts within the company) and *role-playing*. In a role-play, people are assigned the roles of market parties and everyone is required to create a plan based on his or her own objectives (which by definition are conflicting; not everyone's market share can grow). Armstrong (2001, 2002) has demonstrated that this forecasting method often creates accurate predictions of competitors' behaviour. As with the analysis of other environmental factors, it may be useful to define *scenarios* here; for example, the competitor does or does not react to our strategy.

Finally, it is important to take into account the importance of the customer. Some firms are so strongly directed towards their competitors that they seem to forget the customer. Academic research on price reactions of US retailers (Leeflang and Wittink, 1996; Steenkamp et al., 2005) shows that brands often overreact to competitors' actions. This may lead to a competitive battle that is bad for all brands. See also Case 7.4.

7.7 Data sources

Collecting data about competitors is sometimes called 'competitive intelligence' or 'business intelligence'. In effect, all this means is that a company tries to collect as much data about the competitors as it can in as inventive a way as possible. This may range from analysing all offline and online communication of a company to requesting university research reports or buying up an employee of the competitor. Obviously, companies can be very 'creative' in competitive intelligence. Taylor (1992) provides an overview, but in the current online world the possibilities of legal and illegal data collection have strongly increased.

In practice, several publicly accessible sources may be used. A distinction may be made between three types of sources:

1. What *other market parties* say about the competitor; for example, customers (for example, online), suppliers, its own representatives, and financial institutions.
2. What competitors say about *themselves*; for example, on their website, in annual reports, lectures, press releases, personnel advertisements, and advertising expressions or through 'bought-up' employees of competitors.
3. What *third parties* say about the competitors; for example, online, articles in newspapers and magazines, consumer organizations (product tests), industry studies, research reports, and universities.

It is important to collect all the data about the competitors that are being gathered in a company and to make the data accessible to others in the company. Only in that way

Case 7.4 Price reactions

Supermarkets' new price war risks damaging relations with food brands and consumers

The question over whether the supermarkets are embarking on a price war appears to be getting answered. This week, Tesco announced a further round of price cuts with the cost of items from baked beans to bacon to prepackaged cucumber falling. That is on top of the £200m it has already said it will invest. The Co-operative Food, meanwhile, has said it will invest £100m this year in cutting prices and is launching a 'Fair and Square' marketing campaign to get the message out. Morrisons and Asda have both announced £1bn investments. The investments are a reaction to a shift in consumer behaviour away from weekly shops in large out-of-town hypermarkets to a focus on value and convenience that has polarized the grocery industry. Aldi and Lidl are seeing double-digit growth while Waitrose and M&S's growth are outpacing the wider market. That has left all the big four experiencing falling market share. To defend their positions they are focused on price.

Source: *Marketing Week*, 24 April 2014

is it possible to arrive at a coherent picture of the current and expected behaviour of the competitors. To bring this about, two conditions must be met:

1. The *responsibility* for the competitor analysis is concentrated in one person. This person can ensure that the correct analyses are performed and that all data are gathered in one place.
2. There is a well-functioning *marketing information system*. Such an automated system should store not only the data about the company but also the data about its competitors. Everyone in the company should have the ability to request the most current data about the most important competitors and also to enter his or her own 'news items'.

In addition to qualitative data, there are several *quantitative* data sources. The most important data source is the internal marketing research of the firm. A company can and should investigate customers' perception of its competitors.

In some countries there may also be secondary quantitative data sources about the competitors. In section 4.6 we discussed the Nielsen, IRI, and GfK files that include data regarding sales, prices, and distribution of fast-moving consumer goods and some other product categories as well. Detailed data about *advertising* are collected in many countries by. Nielsen Media Research.

As was noted before, a limitation of the quantitative data sources mentioned here is that they relate primarily to markets for consumer goods. This implies that conducting a competitor analysis in the service or industrial markets requires a greater amount of ingenuity than is the case for consumer markets. Nonetheless, even for these markets an adequate competitor analysis is possible through the involvement of the appropriate people and the structured collection and processing of data.

Summary

The goal of a competitor analysis is to obtain insight into the strengths and weaknesses of the most important competitors and their expected strategies. The combination of those two issues, linked to the company's own strengths and weaknesses, determines whether a competitor should be considered a rival or a future partner. The answer to the question of how many competitors a company has depends on the level at which the competition occurs for the target audience: at the budget level, the generic level, the product category level, or the product form level. In the context of the annual marketing plan, the last two levels are usually considered. Next, the most important competitors at the chosen level should be identified. It is important to perform that identification process from the perspective of management but also to examine how the target audience perceives the competition (market research).

Subsequently, for the most important competitors the company will determine their current strategy and objectives and their strengths and weaknesses. Finally, all the information about a competitor becomes the input for a brainstorm session or role-playing setting in which a forecast is made of a competitor's strategy and possible reactions to the firm's strategies. Data regarding competitors are to a large extent qualitative in nature. Quantitative data regarding sales and advertising are sometimes collected by research agencies, and a firm's internal marketing research is also an important source of information on competitors.

Case *McDonald's versus Burger King: concept or taste*

You likely know more about the fast food industry than you realize. If you live in the United States – or pretty much anywhere else – it's everywhere. Off every exit on the highway, and at every rest stop. In the food court at the mall, and on the commercial strips on the outskirts of town. In cities and at airports.

What you may not have noticed, though, is the changing dynamics within the industry. The last several years have seen an absolute explosion of diversity in both restaurant concepts and menu choices. This evolution reflects an industry that has been responsive to changing consumer tastes as well as entrepreneurs finding niche opportunities to profit. An industry that needs to be responsive as consumers become more and more critical about what they eat.

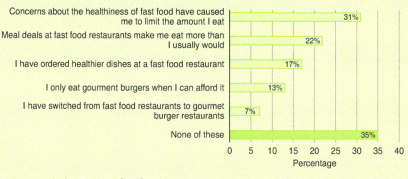

(a) Eating behaviours at fast food restaurants (Source: Lightspeed GMI/Mintel).

Figure 7.7 Eating behaviour

Thinking about the food you eat at fast food restaurants, how concerned, if at all are you about the following?

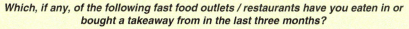

(b) Concerns about eating at fast food restaurants (Source: Lightspeed GMI/ Mintel).

Figure 7.7 **Eating behaviour (Continued)**

The fast food sector has been growing rapidly in the past decades due to the busy lifestyle of consumers. Hamburger giants, pizza chains, and sandwich restaurants all compete to favour the grazing consumer. But the growth has been slowing down over the past decade, partly due to the growing health consciousness of the consumer. The fast food market continues to be dominated by hamburger fast food restaurants in most countries. However that market share is sliding, and alternatives such as wok-to-go concepts have been gaining. A recent trend is the rise of 'premium' fast food: chains such as Five Guys, Byron, or Smashburger that claim to offer a better food or customer experience than the traditional chains.

Which, if any, of the following fast food outlets / restaurants have you eaten in or bought a takeaway from in the last three months?

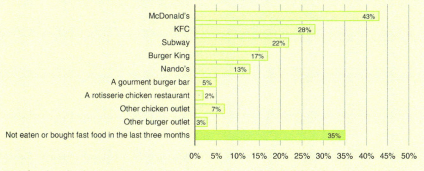

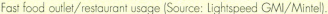

Fast food outlet/restaurant usage (Source: Lightspeed GMI/Mintel).

Figure 7.8 **Restaurant usage**

Especially in the US, this has led to price competition between McDonald's, BK, and other 'traditional' hamburger chains. But competition with 'dollar-menus' not only leads to financial consequences; the brand equity also suffers.

McDonald's still is the global market leader. The golden arches not only symbolize Big Mac and Happy Meal, but also a certain lifestyle. But there are negative associations as well. Especially in Europe, McDonald's is seen as an example of American imperialism, together with for instance Hollywood and Coca-Cola.

The brand is no longer the only kid on the block. One of the causes is the growing diversity in the fast food landscape. But there are also challenges in hamburger country itself. One of the competitors even claims to be king: the Burger King. Even though there are more McDonald's restaurants than Burger Kings worldwide (around 35,000 McDonald's restaurants against around 15,000 Burger King restaurants), both brands have established themselves firmly in the mindset of the customer.

The final word is up to the consumer: Does he love McDonald's or will he choose the BK-Way?

McDonald's

The good thing of being a market leader is that free publicity comes more or less automatically.

The campaign 'I'm lovin' it' is, according to McDonald's, more than just a slogan. "It's a way of thinking, with as [its] central theme how McDonald's can satisfy the needs of every individual customer," according to the global chief marketing of McDonald's Corporation. The intention of this approach is to check whether the product range still matches the diversity of desires of the client. Store design and service will be adapted to the taste of the customer as well.

The McDonald's strategy is visible in the worldwide campaigns. In the commercials a variety of people are enjoying the McDonald's products. At the start of the campaign reactions were mixed. Critics were surprised that McDonald's apparently had abandoned the 'think global-act local' approach. With this approach McDonald's had conquered the world, and a unique image in each country of the world.

"The campaign is loaded with people enjoying themselves, individually. A boy is playing the drums with McDonald's straws, a businessman is swinging in the streets. Sometimes the fun has a cynical touch, like when a kickboxing girl kicks a milkshake out of someone's hands. This type of fun is typical for individualistic cultures like in Europe or North America. In collectivistic cultures like in Southern Europe, Asia or Latin America people have fun with each other," according to the criticism.

Another critic: "This is a typical American feel-good campaign. This might not work with a European audience. I also wonder whether it is smart to target young people. Especially in a number of European countries the brand is doing very well with families with children. McDonald's has to be careful not to lose this audience."

Others, though, have more favourable opinions. A reaction is that the campaign fits a market leader. "The campaign is superficial, but demonstrates a vision. Apparently McDonald's has no identifiable competitive advantage. That's why – like with a fashion brand – McDonald's uses a non-tangible appeal to make the brand relevant and valuable. If there would have been a distinctive advantage it would be a lot easier to make a nice commercial, which gives the consumer a hint of what they can find at McDonald's. But fast food is not necessarily tasty or healthy. Whatever you say about it would not be believed by the consumer anyway. What remains is the ordinary, the day-to-day aspect of McDonald's. And because of this, McDonald's is part of our lives."

Even though the theme is global, execution of the campaign remains localized. The marketing director of McDonald's Netherlands, for instance, highlights that: "The specific contents will differ from country to country, especially because the strategy is focused at the individual consumer. The global strategy is localized in each country. In the Netherlands our main focus is on teenagers, young people, and families with children."

Burger King

The difference in positioning between Burger King and McDonald's was characterized once as 'concept versus taste', or 'brains versus belly'. The market leader, McDonald's, is communicating a lifestyle in its global campaign. Burger King, on the other hand, emphasizes its products. According to a marketing expert: "I think that in the fast food industry the best way is to communicate the product. Burger King has a distinctive way of making its products." The preparation (grilled, meaning less fat) has been a USP (unique selling position) for BK for years.

The Burger King campaigns have a local approach, although the supporting slogan is global. For a long time, this slogan was "Have It Your Way". This slogan was based on the idea that Burger King offers a specific snack for each moment of the day. "Nowadays, the consumer is changing its habits continuously," according to a marketing manager at Burger King. "Grazing patterns and tastes change continuously." Therefore, the slogan was changed in 2014 into "Be Your Way". In an interview, management of Burger King noted that "Have It Your Way" focuses on only the purchase – the ability to customize a burger. By contrast, "Be Your Way" is about making a connection with a person's greater lifestyle. "We want to evolve from just being the functional side of things to having a much stronger emotional appeal," according to BK's brand management.

Whether the new tag line can help Burger King's image over the long term remains to be seen. Real BK-lovers know the slogan. These people appreciate BK for its quality, the flame grilling as a way of preparing the food, and the Whopper. But the slogan is almost unknown for most people. A marketing specialist observed that "The problem is that people don't see themselves as living the Burger King lifestyle. You've got to be realistic with the place that your brand holds in real life. And it is not certain whether the consumer knows what the slogan 'Be Your Way' stands for." Brand management replies that "We will communicate this more in the future. The slogan puts the customer in the middle. The customer decides on the size of the menu, and whether he wants ingredients like cheese, ketchup, or bacon."

Next to a new slogan, part of BK's strategy is to directly challenge McDonald's products. In 2014, Burger King introduced the Big King sandwich, two patties, three buns and a 'special sauce', as a not-so-subtle replication of the successful Big Mac from McDonald's. When McDonald's brought back the McRib sandwich, Burger King responded by unveiling a $1 BK BBQ Rib as a cheaper alternative.

Next came a new fleet of coffee products from Burger King to challenge the McCafé menu. McDonald's made waves years ago by partnering with Starbucks to create a new morning coffee option, so Burger King targeted and acquired Tim Hortons, Inc., the leading Canadian coffee and donut outlet. Burger King management is clear about its value proposition. It is just as good as McDonald's, with the same products, just slightly more upscale and, possibly, cheaper. BK also subtly illuminates McDonald's oft-criticized nutritional value by offering the new 'Satisfries' or a healthier French fry option with "40 per cent less fat and 30 per cent fewer calories than the leading French fries." The leading French fries are, of course, McDonald's. At the same time, Burger King remains aware of the importance of its flagship: the Whopper.

Questions

1. Based on the case about the fast food market, explain what the difference is between the industry analysis and the competitor analysis.
2. Which strategic groups can be identified in the fast food industry?
3. Four levels of competition may be distinguished. Define for each of these levels competitors of McDonald's.
4. According to Treacy and Wiersema (1993), a company has to choose a specific value discipline in order to be successful. Do you think the McDonald's campaign matches the value strategy chosen by McDonald's? Explain.
5. The industry structure may be defined by using Porter's five-forces model. Execute this model for the fast food industry. Draw your conclusions about the attractiveness of this industry, from McDonald's point of view.
6. The case highlights the observation that "McDonald's has no identifiable competitive advantage". Do you agree with this observation? Explain your answer.
7. Suppose McDonald's would like to identify its most direct competitors by means of multidimensional scaling. Describe step by step what needs to be done to execute this analysis.
8. What would you favour in the fast food industry: A campaign focusing on the product (like the old "Have It Your Way" slogan of Burger King), or a campaign focusing on the lifestyle you want to create with your brand (like McDonald's)? Give reasons for your answer.
9. What do you consider to be the key success factors in the fast food industry?

10. a) What is the competitive advantage of McDonald's, as compared to Burger King?
    b) What is the competitive advantage of Burger King, as compared to McDonald's?
11. Imagine that McDonald's asked you to analyse and predict the strategy of Burger King by performing a competitor analysis. Start with the information in the case, but do additional desk research where necessary.
    a) Define the (marketing) objective of Burger King.
    b) Identify the current marketing strategy (target group selection and positioning) of Burger King.
    c) Determine the strengths and weaknesses of Burger King.
    d) Predict the future strategy of Burger King: How do you expect Burger King to proceed in the near future?
12. Imagine that Burger King asked you to analyse and predict the strategy of McDonald's by performing a competitor analysis. Start with the information in the case, but do additional desk research where necessary.
    a) Define the (marketing) objective of McDonald's.
    b) Identify the current marketing strategy (target group selection and positioning) of McDonald's.
    c) Determine the strengths and weaknesses of McDonald's.
    d) Predict the future strategy of McDonald's: How do you expect McDonald's to proceed in the near future?

Chapter 8

Analysis of distribution and suppliers

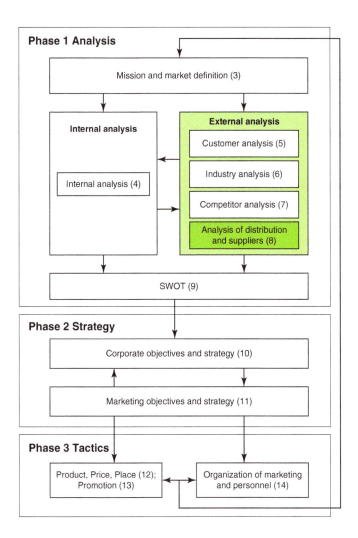

Phase 1 Analysis

Mission and market definition (3)

Internal analysis

Internal analysis (4)

External analysis

Customer analysis (5)

Industry analysis (6)

Competitor analysis (7)

Analysis of distribution and suppliers (8)

SWOT (9)

Phase 2 Strategy

Corporate objectives and strategy (10)

Marketing objectives and strategy (11)

Phase 3 Tactics

Product, Price, Place (12); Promotion (13)

Organization of marketing and personnel (14)

Key points in this chapter

- Know aggregation levels in the distribution analysis.
- Be able to analyse the distribution structure in an industry.
- Assess the role of disintermediation.
- Be able to analyse the distribution intensity by applying different criteria.
- Know the steps in an individual distributor and supplier analysis.

Introduction

With the increased focus on the strategic marketing concept described in Chapter 1, the purview of marketing has been broadened from customers to include other interest groups within and outside the company. Two interest groups play a central role: competitors and distributors. Chapter 7 discussed competitor analysis. This chapter focuses on the distributors. By 'distributors' we mean all stakeholders between the producer and the consumer. In addition, we pay attention to suppliers. We take the perspective of a producer.

The importance of a thorough distribution and delivery analysis lies in the opportunity to gain advantages from good relationships with those parties. Consumers seem to be becoming more critical, and availability is important for a brand. Of course many brands will nowadays follow a multi-channel strategy and be available all over the world when being offered online. But still, physical availability is important as well, and so a competitive edge may be gained through a good channel strategy. Section 8.1 focuses on the structure of the distribution analysis, after which sections 8.2 to 8.4 flesh out the distribution analysis on three levels: the macro, meso, and micro levels. Section 8.5 deals with the analysis of suppliers.

8.1 Goal and structure of a distribution analysis

In preparation for Chapter 11, we note that in the context of using the marketing mix element of distribution, three types of decisions have to be made:

1. Choice of the distribution intensity (objective).
2. Choice of the distribution channels.
3. Management of the distribution channels.

This chapter will not discuss these decisions; instead, it will focus on providing an analysis diagram with which the necessary information may be obtained to make those decisions in as well-founded a manner as possible. In the context of this book we will limit ourselves to several main points.

A distribution analysis occurs at three levels of aggregation:

1. *Macro level.* This involves mapping out the entire distribution column both vertically (possible levels, long or short channel) and horizontally (various types of

intermediate links within one level); therefore, this refers to a global distribution structure.

2. *Meso level.* This analysis is especially important in terms of the implementation of the desired distribution intensity, as was mentioned in decision type 1. It involves the following:
   - The more specific distribution structure within one type of intermediate link; for example, the distribution of the power of shop chains within supermarkets.
   - The position of brands within a single level, and especially within the group of retailers (analysis of the distribution intensity).

3. *Micro level.* The strategies and needs of individual distributors (e.g. retail brands such as Walmart) (distributor analysis). This information is required for the implementation of the daily marketing policy towards distributors (such as retailers).

These levels cannot be considered separately. For example, the distribution structure has a macro component as well as a meso component. Although this distinction is useful in an analytic sense, in reality both components belong to the distribution structure. In addition, an analysis of the distribution structure at the meso level (within a single group of intermediate links) requires information about the market shares of individual distributors. This information is obtained from the distribution analysis at the micro level.

Each of the three levels will be reviewed in the following sections.

8.2 Distribution analysis at the macro level

8.2.1 Dimensions of the analysis

The analysis of the distribution structure at the macro level involves two dimensions:

1. The number of levels in the distribution column (vertically: the length of the channel).
2. The type of intermediate links within a single level; for example, within the group of retailers the distinction between supermarkets, discounters, neighbourhood shops, and specialty stores or the 'grey circuit' of, for example, gas stations (horizontally: the width of the channel).

   Insight into this issue is important for the choice of the type of intermediate links.

In regard to the length of the channel there are two possibilities:

1. Direct delivery to customers without the use of 'intermediaries'; this includes all trade of producers who sell online.
2. Indirect delivery that does involve intermediaries.

Direct delivery to customers is increasing (online). Section 8.2.2 will discuss this further. With indirect delivery, potential intermediate links between producer and consumer include agents, importers, wholesale dealers (wholesale trade), and retailers. If a company chooses to deliver exclusively through retailers, this is called a short channel. In all other cases, it is called a long channel (Figure 8.1). Some of the criteria for choices

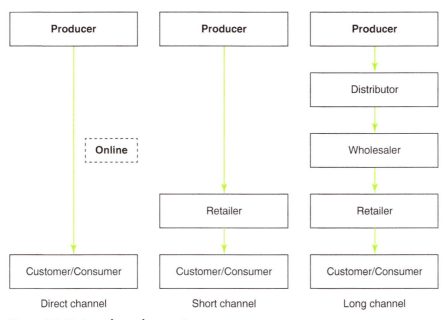

Figure 8.1 **Various channel strategies**

in this regard are the number of final customers the company wants to serve and the type of product (e.g. shelf life and complexity).

The choice does not have to be restricted to only one channel. Increasingly, companies choose a *multi-channel strategy*; for example, combining bricks (offline) and clicks (online).

In the analysis, the focus is not only on mapping out the various possibilities but also on the importance of each type of intermediate link. For this purpose, the company needs to figure out which share of the purchases in the product category occurs through which links. In other words, the sales (in terms of money and volume) of the various types of links should be estimated. Hard data are often not available in this area, and so estimates have to be made of the importance of various links.

8.2.2 Online channels

The internet makes it relatively easy to make direct contact with customers, and direct contact enables direct trade. Trade on the internet (e-commerce) has therefore expanded enormously and is an important component of what has been called the 'new economy' since the end of the 1990s. Direct delivery to customers by producers implies that intermediaries are 'cut out' (*disintermediation*). That strategy fits very well within but is not required for the value strategy of customer intimacy. For example, a producer of cat food may deliver cat food at a discount to a customer, as it is ordered online by that customer. If the producer has a sufficiently rich database of data on cat owners, it may deliver a certain amount of cat food every few weeks or months without the customer having to place a specific order. In doing so, the manufacturer could even take into account the age of the cat and, as the cat gets older, could recommend and deliver special food for older cats. Avoiding intermediaries means in principle that a manufacturer's power is increasing in relation to the retailer's.

However, e-commerce is challenging to implement for manufacturers. A manufacturer is responsible for delivery and therefore needs to set up its own logistic system for that purpose; the issue here is whether a sufficient volume can be attained to make it profitable. For example, it will not be profitable for the cat food manufacturer to use a car for each separate order. Another problem with disintermediation by manufacturers is the possible reaction of retailers. As a result of the large buying power of purchasing combinations, the threat of the elimination of these intermediary links may lead to undesired reactions, with the most extreme reaction being that the products of the manufacturer will no longer be placed on the shelf. For these reasons, online sales are mostly organized by 'lower levels' in the channel, especially retailers such as supermarkets or grocers. As shown in Figure 8.1, this means that in the final chain retailers use two channels: offline and online (bricks and clicks).

In the context of the distribution analysis, it is necessary to continue researching the possibilities and impossibilities of direct delivery to customers and to be neither too cautious nor too optimistic in the choice of strategy.

8.3 Distribution analysis at the meso level

8.3.1 Distribution structure at the meso level

In the previous section, an analysis was provided of the distribution structure at the macro level. However, more detailed information is required to determine the optimal choice of a channel. We briefly describe the role of the wholesale trade and then discuss the level of individual retailers in more detail.

The wholesale trade is positioned between the manufacturer and the retailer, and its core function is to tailor the demand and supply of goods in markets, both qualitatively and quantitatively. In light of developments in information and communications technology (ICT) that allow manufacturers and retailers to be attuned to each other's supply and demand more easily and more intensively (electronic data interchange (EDI)), there is evidence that the wholesale trade is being eliminated. For a supplier, this means that an analysis of the added value which the wholesale trade may offer is relevant.

Within a single level of intermediate links (e.g. retailers) or even within one type of intermediate links (e.g. supermarkets), it is important to understand the distribution of power (market shares) between individual companies and distributors. After all, this distribution also determines the importance of the individual retail brands (in addition to volume and margin), and therefore will determine the direction of marketing efforts in this regard. The analysis of the power distribution should obviously take into account the various forms of collaboration between retailers (purchasing combinations, franchising, etc.). In some countries a tendency towards concentration has occurred in the food retail industry. For example, in the USA Walmart is by far the largest food retailer, with a share of more than 30 per cent in some product categories (see the case on p. 92).

8.3.2 Analysis of the distribution intensity of a brand

The distribution intensity of a brand relates to the position of the brand within a single level in the distribution channel. For this reason, we consider the analysis of the distribution intensity to be an analysis at the meso level.

To determine the desired distribution intensity, the past and current distribution intensity should be analysed. We will now focus on the 'offline' distribution of a brand. As soon as a brand has a web shop (i.e. the brand may be bought online), the distribution intensity is by definition 100 per cent (assuming there are no regional constraints). So, for online distribution only two values exist: 0 per cent or 100 per cent. The review of distribution criteria that follows is therefore in some sense 'old-fashioned'. But it is still important to manage physical distribution as well, also in the light of the findings of Sharp (2010), who demonstrated that visibility strongly affects market share.

To measure the position within the distribution channel, two criteria are typically used:

1. *Non-weighted (numerical) distribution.* This is the percentage of shops in which the brand is available.
2. *Weighted distribution.* This is the market share in the product group of the shops in which the brand is available; in other words, the cover of the market.

The difference between the two criteria is that the weighted distribution takes into account the size (in sales) of the shops. Shops that sell a relatively large amount from the product group count more heavily. To calculate the size of the shops where the company is represented, the following measure is used. The *selection indicator* is the average sales in the product category at the shops where the company's brand is available, divided by the average sales in the product category in all shops where brands from the product category are offered. If the selection indicator is larger than 1, the company's brand is located in relatively large shops. The selection indicator may also be calculated by dividing the weighted distribution by the non-weighted distribution.

The criteria mentioned earlier make a statement about the distribution of a brand in the market as a whole. To measure the position of a brand in the shops where that brand is available, the following measure is used. The *sales share* is the market share of the brand within the shops where it is available (company's sales or sales divided by total sales, or sales in the product category in the shops where the brand is available).

It is easy to demonstrate that the following relationships exist:

Market share = weighted distribution ÷ sales share
Market share = non-weighted distribution ÷ selection indicator ÷ sales share

Another important indicator of the position of the brand in the shop is the *shelf position.* The shelf position has two important aspects: location and amount. Location (low, middle, high) cannot be quantified. Amount may be expressed in *facings*: the number of

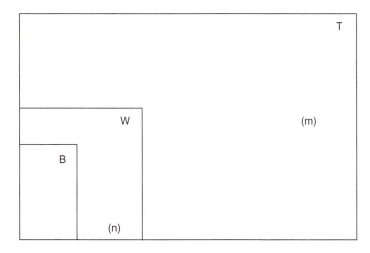

B = sales of brand   B/W = sales share
W = category sales of 'own' retailers   B/T = market share
T = sales total market   W/T = weighted distribution

(W/n)/(T/m) = selection indicator
n/m = numerical (unweighted) distribution
So: weighted distribution = numerical distribution x selection indicator

Figure 8.2 **Distribution criteria**

visible products. The number of facings is often related to the market share: the larger the brand, the more facings the retailer will allocate to it.

Figure 8.2 summarizes these issues schematically. We illustrate this figure and the preceding text with an example.

Suppose a brand achieves sales of €500.000 (B) in a market size of €5 million (T). The brand is located in 100 (n) among the 500 (m) shops where the product is being offered. Sales in the product category of these 100 shops are €2 million (W).

The non-weighted distribution is thus 100/500 (n/m) = 20 per cent. The weighted distribution is 2 million/5 million (W/T) = 40 per cent. The selection indicator is [2/100]/[5/500] ([W/n]/[T/m]) = 2. This could also be calculated by dividing 40 per cent by 20 per cent. The sales share is 500,000/2,000,000 (B/W) = 25 per cent. The market share of the brand is 500,000/5,000,000 (B/T) = 10 per cent. This is the same as 20 per cent × 2 × 25 per cent.

The conclusion is that the brand has a low degree of distribution and is located especially in large shops (measured in sales within the product category). The shops where brand A is located are dependent on that brand for 25 per cent of their sales in the product category.

The results of the distribution analysis are directly relevant for the use of the marketing mix. For example, if a company wants to increase the weighted distribution, it may choose to encourage retailers to include the brand in the assortment through a lot of advertising and visits by the sales staff. If the sales share is disappointing, this means that the position of the brand in the shops where it is located is weakening; for example, because of too little support in the shop. A strategy that provides more rewards to the retailer for support (push strategy) is an obvious choice.

Finally, we again mention the limitation of the previous analysis in that it pertains to the physical distribution.

8.4 Distribution analysis at the micro level: retail analysis

We now focus on the relation between a producer and retail brands. Retailers are in fact the customers of the producer; thus, for a producer, an important issue is to anticipate the retailers' needs. The final distribution goal is to obtain a good location on the shelf as well as a lot of positive attention from the sales staff of retailers in terms of personal sales to the final customers (consumers). Important tools in this context are the margins on products and promotional activities in collaboration with the retailer. The concept of *relationship management* has a central focus: the manufacturer attempts to realize its goals (and those of the retailer) through an optimal relationship with the retailer. Insight into the wishes and desires of retailers is the most important information source in this area. For that purpose, individual retail brands must be examined. Therefore, this involves a distribution analysis at the micro level (distributor analysis).

At the most disaggregated level (sales outlets), a manufacturer may be dealing with many hundreds of 'customers'. By far the largest proportion of these customers is in one way or another involved in joint collaboration. Thus, in reality, the 'salesperson' of a manufacturer (the sales manager) has to deal with a significantly lower number and often with only a few buyers.

For the purpose of organizing the analysis of a distributor it is important to determine which role the retailer actually plays for the producer. As already mentioned, the retailer is a *customer* that 'resells' the product to final users. Yet, in the food industry, retailers are increasingly also *competitors* of producers as a result of the *own brands* of those distributors (*distributor-owned brands*).

Therefore, a distributor analysis is positioned between a customer analysis and a competitor analysis (see Chapter 6). For each retailer, insight should be obtained into the following:

1. The importance and role of the retailer (section 8.4.1).
2. The position of the manufacturer's brand at the retailer (section 8.4.2).
3. The objectives, strategy, and wishes of the retailer (section 8.4.3).
4. The strengths and weaknesses and the expected strategy of the retailer (section 8.4.4).

8.4.1 The importance and the role of the retailer

The importance of a retailer may be measured by its sales in the product category. For the food products industry, relevant data may be obtained from Nielsen, IRI, or GfK. For markets for durable consumer goods, the position of retailers (e.g. the position of

Case 8.1 Building relationships with retailers

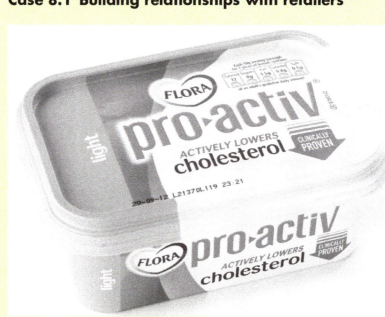

Butter brands seek greater collaboration with retailers to drive value

Butter and spread makers Arla and Dairy Crest are seeking greater collaboration from retailers to try to inject more creativity into their shopper marketing strategies after recent attempts to drive sales through deep discounting have failed to trigger growth. Unilever's Flora brand is using sampling and in-store promotions to help introduce a new creative platform that will see the return of its sunflower logo after 15 years. It is part of a £12m strategy for Flora, which will seek to remind consumers of the 'natural goodness' of the sunflowers used to make its products. The campaign will run until the end of November alongside TV, print, and digital activity.

Source: *Marketing Week*, 3 September 2013

Megapool in the market for white fabrics) should be estimated. In addition to sales, the margin is essential. For a manufacturer, the profitability of a 'relationship' is ultimately what matters.

With regard to the role of a retailer, the easily answered question is whether it is only a 'customer' or also a competitor. The retailer is a competitor if it carries its own brands (distributor brands, or D-brands), a situation that occurs in many markets for fast-moving consumer goods. In addition, it is important to determine the degree of freedom in brand supply for a retailer: Does the retailer have a 'preferred supplier' – a manufacturer within the product category that is preferred?

8.4.2 The position of the manufacturer's brand at the retailer

Measures of the position of the manufacturer's own brand at the retailer include the shelf position, the number of facings, and the sales of the manufacturer's brand at that retailer in relation to other sales outlets and/or in relation to other retailer brands. Shelf position and facings are tools of the retailer. Another tool is the personal sale, especially in lines of business that are not related to the food products industry. All these tools have an impact on brand sales. Relatively low brand sales may indicate insufficient attention to the brand on the part of the retailer; that may indicate an inadequate marketing policy of the producer towards that retailer.

The other way around it may be argued that for the retailer the producers' brand may also be important. This is especially true: if the producers' product contributes to the turnover of the retailer, if the margin is sufficient, if it meets the needs of consumers, and also if it helps the retailer to differentiate the product from competitive retailers.

So, there is a mutual dependency between producers and retailers. See also Case 8.1.

8.4.3 Goals, strategy, and wishes of the retailer

Objectives involve issues such as satisfaction of the retailer (and therefore the results up until the present time) and ambition (limited or fast growth, growth with existing or new activities, etc.). Strategy here involves the implementation of the marketing strategy (positioning and choice of the target audience): On which consumers does the retailer focus? For a manufacturer, it is important to choose a retailer with a marketing strategy comparable to its own. In addition, the use of the four Ps by the retailer should be examined. The 'P' of product in this regard is actually related to the wishes of the retailer: How wide is its assortment, which product categories are in the shop with how many varieties, and what proportions of those are A brands, B brands, and retailer brands? Other relevant questions include the following: To what extent and how does the retailer implement its own communication policy? How does the retailer handle promotional campaigns? In general, to what extent is the retailer willing to collaborate with the manufacturer?

The answers to all these questions will need to be provided, based mostly on observation and experiences with the relevant retailer. It may be expected that an account manager or another representative of the manufacturer will gain insight, through regular contacts with the buyers, into what the retailer does or does not want and how it behaves. All these issues are part of what is called *trade marketing*: the marketing of a producer to the retailer.

8.4.4 Strengths and weaknesses and the expected strategy of the retailer

Finally, an attempt is made, based in part on the foregoing steps, to deduce the strengths and weaknesses as well as the expected strategy of the retailer (see also Case 8.2).

In terms of the strengths (and weaknesses) of a retailer, two types may be distinguished: strengths that are interesting to any manufacturer (e.g. high sales per customer, friendly staff, and short waiting times at the cash register), and manufacturer-specific strengths. After all, for a manufacturer the issue is to choose a retailer that fits with the target audience and the positioning of the manufacturer's products. Characteristics of

Case 8.2 Strategies of a retailer

Co-op shifts strategy to become 'leading convenience food retailer'

The Co-operative Group is planning to double the size of its convenience store estate and invest in price, own-label food, and store refurbishment as it aims to shift perceptions of the brand from being the fifth largest supermarket chain to the 'leading convenience food retailer' in Britain.

The firm says it will open between 100 and 150 new convenience stores per year with the aim to double the number from the 2,000 it currently owns. Research firm IGD estimates that convenience is the fastest growing retail chain, with its worth set to increase to £46bn over the next five years, from £36bn last year.

Co-op will also roll out its new convenience store format, dubbed 'Generation Two' and currently on trial in 20 stores, to a third of its estate by the end of the year. The format includes a new in-store bakery and designated zones for grocery, chilled and on-the-go produce.

Source: *Marketing Week*, 5 March 2014

the retailer that are congruent present opportunities for the manufacturer (such as a good fresh produce department, high-quality positioning, and a large staff).

Weak points of an existing retailer (e.g. low sales per customer) may be an occasion for more intensive collaboration with the manufacturer (e.g. joint promotions).

The expected retailer strategy may also present opportunities (or threats) to the manufacturer. Expanded support and growth of the retailer's brands may have important implications for the manufacturer. Potential options vary, from strengthening the position and positioning of the producer's brands to starting to produce retailer brands.

Just as in section 8.4.3, statements can only be qualitative in nature and assumptions will probably have to be made if insufficient information is available.

8.5 Analysis of suppliers

This section provides a brief introduction to the analysis of suppliers. For more extensive descriptions, the reader should refer to the literature on *purchasing* and *business marketing* (marketing from one company to another company).

Purchasing occurs in many areas, such as the purchasing of the following:

- Supportive goods and services (office furniture, financial services, online support services, advertising agencies, etc.).
- Means of production (labour and capital goods).
- Semi-manufactured articles and raw materials.

Case 8.3 Analysis of suppliers

Many Chinese suppliers of clothing for retailer Zeeman not sustainable

Retail chain Zeeman found more than 50 failures in sustainable behaviour at Chinese suppliers. Many of them could not deliver reliable information about wages and workload of their employees, making it unsure whether employees are working under sustainable conditions. Checks like this are increasingly normal among companies since the 2013 disaster in a Bangladesh garment factory, leading to more than 1,000 casualties.

Source: *Financial Daily* (Financieel Dagblad), 6 June 2018

A good relationship with suppliers can be a source of a competitive advantage. This applies to all types of purchasing. For example, a good website which is easily found and has a strong 'call to action' may be very important for success. Good housing can have an impact on staff motivation. The usefulness of qualified personnel (labour market) is evident. Good and reliable machines determine the quality of production. Certainly in the case of semi-finished products and raw materials, savings in purchasing may be 'channelled' to the consumer. The requirements for purchased semi-finished products and raw materials depend on the chosen value strategy. A company that chooses customer leadership (*customer intimacy*) and direct delivery will require flexibility (many varieties) and reliability (timely delivery) in the deliveries. The strategy of *product leadership* requires a high and constant quality of the purchased products. A company that chooses a low price within operational excellence will have a strong need for inexpensive purchasing; for example, through agreements about quantity discounts.

Whichever demands are made for whichever type of purchasing, it will be easier to comply with those demands if good relationships are built with the supplying companies. Therefore, an analysis of current and potential suppliers is important. See also Case 8.3.

Purchasing by a company is in essence no different from purchasing by a consumer: there is a need that is satisfied through purchasing and/or acquisition. The most important differences are the following:

- In purchasing, the need is 'indirect'. It depends on the requirements that are made of the products, which in turn depend on the final needs of the final customer.
- The purchasing process is different and more complicated. Typically, a single person is not responsible for purchasing; instead, there are *decision-making units* (*DMUs*). In this situation, various people in a company are responsible for the final purchasing decisions.

In a supplier analysis, the following questions are answered:

1. Which needs within the company have to be met? The analysis of suppliers depends on the need that must be met. Therefore, an internal analysis to define that need is important. For example: Do we need a new website? Should we search for more sustainable suppliers?
2. Which supplier can best provide for that need? To arrive at a selection of potential suppliers, the company will have to examine the expected achievements of the suppliers in the following areas:
   - Quality: the concrete characteristics of the products.
   - Price (potential discounts, etc.).
   - Service.

The service component is very important in business markets, and includes both components such as warranty, repair service, and reliability, and additional service components such as training and information.

To be able to evaluate suppliers on these factors, information from the company's own purchasers is important: they know the market like no one else. In addition, suppliers may be asked to make 'bids'. This may occur through a call for tenders (e.g. construction combinations needed to create and present a building scheme), pitches (advertising agencies that need to write a campaign proposal), or normal quotes. Because trust plays an important role in purchasing markets, issues such as reputation, experience with suppliers, and personal contacts are often decisive in making a choice. This implies that branding and communication are also relevant in a business market. Therefore, in a supplier analysis, these qualitative elements play an important role.

Summary

An analysis of the distribution and suppliers is important, since building relations with retailers and suppliers may lead to competitive advantages. A distribution analysis is performed at the macro level, the meso level, and the micro level. At the macro level, the distribution structure is mapped out. Clearly, nowadays multi-channel strategies are often applied in the sense of offline as well as online. An analysis is made of which levels are used and to what extent and how many sales are made in the category through which channels. A specific point in that regard is what the potential development of online sales might be. The elimination of intermediary links is a way for manufacturers to avoid the increasing power of retailers. At the meso level the power of the retailers is analysed, along with the position of the brand at the various retailers. At the micro level, individual retailers (chains) are analysed; an important point is to discover how the best possible relationship with the retailer can be built. For that purpose, an understanding of the retailer's goals, strategy, and wishes is required. The company's account managers are an important data source for this largely qualitative analysis. For a supplier analysis, the goal is also to build relationships. An analysis will focus on the question of which purchasing needs the company has and which supplier can best meet those needs. The company's own purchasing needs will depend on the chosen value strategy.

Case challenges in food distribution: the Barika Story

An African perspective on distribution

Sub-Saharan Africa is often heralded as an important future growth area. In addition, with the rise of an African middle class spending power increases, creating the growth opportunities that are increasingly difficult to reach in the saturated European or American markets. But, in order to be successful, knowledge of distribution structure is of the highest importance: in order to sell, it is essential to reach the consumer!

The Western shopper is used to buying food in supermarkets, operating under familiar names like Walmart, Carrefour, or Tesco. This is where we spend the bulk of our money. But we easily forget that this pattern isn't the same everywhere. In sub-Saharan countries in Africa, big chains have a substantial lower relevance, often being virtually non-existent.

Nielsen retail sales data show that some 40 per cent of African consumers shop in small, local grocery stores, or 'dukas'. These dukas account for nearly 50 per cent of consumer goods spend. The average duka, often measuring only a few square metres, is loaded with a wide variety of goods and often forms the centre of a community. But this is not even the most relevant channel. The most common African shopping channel is the table top: a stall set up at the side of the road or in the local market to capture local and passing trade. In a recent Nielsen study of sub-Saharan countries it was found that 80 per cent of consumers shopped from table tops. For instance, in a country such as Nigeria there are no less than 200,000 table tops. At the duka, Africans tend to spend a lot more during each visit than at the table top. But this doesn't make the duka more relevant. An important factor is the frequency of visits: consumers tend to shop less frequently in dukas, since stores can be hard to get to without transport. In contrast, they often visit a table top or kiosk daily for smaller, top-up quantities. Shopping patterns also differ by country. In Madagascar, a Nielsen survey showed that consumers went shopping 70 times a month on average – more than twice a day! – while in Kenya the average was 38 times.

At the table top, consumers are familiar with both the vendor and the products, and the products are helpfully sold in decanted or single servings and in rounded denominations (e.g. 100 shillings in Kenya or 1,000 CFA francs in Burkina Faso). So, while the shop itself may be no more than a table or counter top, its products unbranded and the product range small – many might sell no more than four different items – these outlets perfectly meet consumers' needs. They offer familiar goods at the desired price and size, they offer convenience, and they are trusted.

Numbers give an average picture. Companies need to identify the best channels and retailers for their product category. In Lagos (Nigeria), for instance, Nielsen found laundry detergents in distribution in no less than 100,000 outlets, an impossibly large number to reach. But further analysis showed that 80 per cent of the sales value came from just 35,000 of those outlets, and a full 50 per cent from a more manageable 10,000. Similarly, in the same city, beverages are sold in 61,000 outlets, but only 24,000 of those outlets generate 80 per cent of sales.

But still, how to reach even the most effective dukas and table tops in an efficient manner? Getting close to the retailer in order to build distribution to support sales in such a fragmented retail market is a huge undertaking, particularly for international manufacturers lacking in local knowledge. Moreover, it is only the final stage of a meticulous process. First, manufacturers need to understand who shops where and for what; then they must identify the best retail outlets for a given product, and then they can turn to helping retailers build demand.

Companies also need to consider how to help build demand in an environment where consumers on limited budgets are ultra-cautious about trying new products. Consumers continue to show a powerful preference for products they know, have tried before, or that have been recommended to them – not surprising in an environment where budgets are tight and a disappointing purchase is an expensive loss.

But the creation of brand awareness and familiarity, a crucial step in introducing new products to the market, is a huge challenge. Small retailers have little or no display space, shopper loyalty is often to local manufacturers, and premium-priced branded packages are often split open and sold in unbranded singles or servings to meet consumers' needs. So, in a market where brand familiarity and recommendations from others are strong purchase drivers, how can you start with a new product that – by definition – does not have any familiarity or recommendations?

A close understanding of how smaller, traditional retailers operate is key for the right approach to building sales. For instance, a table-top vendor selling a small range of everyday basics will often stock only a very narrow range of products. With no transport and limited or no storage, the vendor will probably not visit even one distributor or wholesaler. Instead, everything is brought to the stall either on a bicycle, boda boda (cargo-carrying motorcycle), in a motor vehicle, or perhaps even on a pushcart or by foot. Sometimes it is a wholesaler who drops off supplies, sometimes another retailer; often, there is no record of what are all cash transactions. Cigarettes and sodas may be delivered as often as three to five times a day. Other goods, such as gum, sweets, biscuits, or analgesics, may be delivered every three days.

The vendors are masters at adapting their offerings to meet consumers' immediate needs, which change at various points during their day. In the morning, the commuting consumer may stop for breakfast – ready-made tea served from a flask, freshly squeezed juice, slices of bread, a cooked sausage, a single teabag and a serving of sugar; even super-glue for fixing a broken shoe. All of this must be understood by a manufacturer that wants to introduce its product to the table-top market and develop its success, particularly because it is the vendor and not a wholesaler intermediary that will make the ultimate decision. Meeting consumers' needs in this environment means not only being timely, but also thinking about the required pack size, format, affordability, and denomination. If a branded packet is too expensive, the retailer may open the pack, split it into smaller ones, and sell it unbranded, resulting in profit for the manufacturer, but weaker brand identity.

Sometimes it's the small things that have the potential to drive success. A number of these small suggestions to stimulate brand identity in the African market are:

- Repackaging and branding products into single servings or at least smaller sizes.
- Providing branded packaging such as wrappers or sachets that retailers can use if they spilt up larger portions.
- Branding the selling vessel; for example, the basin from which water sachets are sold.
- Providing branded cooler boxes for table-top vendors to sell products which require refrigeration.
- Providing small, portable display stands for kiosk vendors to stack products and add visibility.
- Branding reusable product packaging or containers for top-ups and repurchases.
- Providing free samples appropriate to the time of day and the way the outlet is used. Each table top may be seen as a location to trial new products with no risk to either the vendor or the consumer.

Barika

Barika is a medium-sized distributor in Burkina Faso, a francophone country in Western Africa. The company profiles with the following mission statement:

African urban societies are experiencing a social change that is reflected in a more individualized food experience. Styles and aspirations are diversifying while traditional community channels are showing more and more their limits. In order to overcome these changes, Barika proposes to facilitate access to quality essential products in partnership with local actors and committed suppliers.

According to its website, Barika offers an innovative distribution network based on:

- a triple principle of modernity, accessibility, quality;
- a wide range of products, emphasizing attractive products with social impact;
- a brand that caters to all, including the low-income segment;
- innovative products, previously unavailable on the market, to enrich the local offerings;
- collaboration with a wide variety of fully involved stakeholders.

The company promises a quality commitment:

- a guarantee of quality to give consumers the assurance of healthy products;
- a stable price guarantee;
- support to suppliers in improving their local distribution;
- quality of service: personalized support for customers in the choice and use of products.

The company proposes to work with a network of partners:

- committed suppliers;
- local stakeholders in the field of health, childhood, etc.;
- offers proposed in collaboration with partners.

Interview with the Strategic Manager of Barika

Question: Can you tell me something about Barika?
Barika is a brand specialized in distribution of innovative products. We aim at good products that are not too expensive with a focus on local quality products. We get our products directly from the producer, or through an intermediary. Barika has its own shops, two boutiques located in Ouagadougou (the capital of Burkina Faso). Besides, we distribute to a number of small shops and table tops.

Question: What is the role of the Barika store?
A strong local store is a proof of quality. We want to use the shop to increase the awareness of the Barika brand, so that the owners of the small shops will come to us.

Question: But why do you prefer the small shops to come to you? Wouldn't it be better if you go to the small shops?

A push strategy seems to make more sense than a pull strategy in our market. Going directly to the small shops and the table tops is very hard work as they are disseminated all over Ouagadougou with approximately 3,000 selling points. Currently we have only two sales people in our own service. That is why our primary focus is on making Barika a strong and trusted retail brand. Then the shop and top owners will come to us, instead of we to them.

Question: How important is relation management in the Burkina Faso market?

Very important. Work is not efficient without good relations. There is also a strong hierarchy issue – people are not really saying what they think: they will say yes in order to keep the relation, even if they mean no. The ideal sales person is someone that used to be a respected retailer with a well-established network. We are still looking for the ideal.

Question: I want to talk about one of the products you distribute: Grandibien. Can you say something about the product?

Grandibien is a product against chronic malnutrition. It targets pregnant women, as well as young children, in a couple of age categories. Awareness of the Grandibien brand is still limited. The target group doesn't know it too much. Currently it is available in 150 shops, mainly smaller ones. But there is a potential of 3,000 sales points for this type of product in Ouagadougou and way more in the whole country, so there is still a lot of work to do.

We found that kids like Grandibien. The sales price is relatively high due to the hiqh-quality ingredients. It pays off, as a healthy diet prevents medical costs due to malnutrition issues. But it's hard to convince our target of the importance of prevention of malnutrition. Prevention awareness is a global issue in the world anyway.

Question: African consumers are known to be ultra-cautious about trying new products. What is your experience with Grandibien?

Yes, consumers are very faithful and loyal. They trust big brands such as Nescafé, but above all they trust the person that sells them the product. But consumers here are also curious. We noticed that they try Grandibien, but we need to create more awareness around the brand and the benefits of prevention to create a rebuy.

Questions

1. Draft a global distribution structure for a consumer product in the sub-Saharan market, for instance, for a product such as laundry detergent in the Nigerian market.

2. A distribution analysis may be executed on three levels of aggregation. For which of these levels does the Barika interview provide useful information? Explain your answer.

3. Is Barika a wholesaler or a retailer? Explain your answer.

4. The manager states that *"A push strategy seems to make more sense than a pull strategy"*.

   a) Explain what the manager means by this statement. See also section 12.4.

   b) Do you agree that in the sub-Saharan market a push strategy makes – in general – more sense than a pull strategy? Give reasons for your answer.

   c) What is your opinion on the solution of the push/pull issue as proposed by Barika?

5. The choice for a focus on the Barika shop (a choice on the macro level) seems to be partly driven by issues in the sales force (micro level). Do you agree that micro-level issues should drive macro-level choices? Why (not)?

6. Describe the current distribution intensity of Grandibien.

7. Analyse the information about Grandibien: how would you advise Grandibien to increase its market position?

8. Which distribution intensity would you advise for Grandibien?

Chapter 9

SWOT analysis

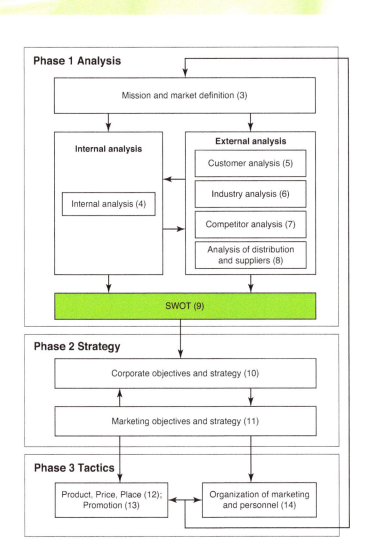

Phase 1 Analysis

Mission and market definition (3)

Internal analysis

Internal analysis (4)

External analysis

Customer analysis (5)

Industry analysis (6)

Competitor analysis (7)

Analysis of distribution and suppliers (8)

SWOT (9)

Phase 2 Strategy

Corporate objectives and strategy (10)

Marketing objectives and strategy (11)

Phase 3 Tactics

Product, Price, Place (12); Promotion (13)

Organization of marketing and personnel (14)

Introduction

In the earlier phases of the strategic marketing planning process, an internal analysis and an external analysis were completed. This is called a situation analysis. In this chapter, we describe how the insights from the situation analysis can be summarized, and what steps can be taken to come to strategic decisions. The tool reviewed is the SWOT analysis, where SWOT stands for strengths, weaknesses, opportunities, and threats. This chapter is structured as follows:

1. Definitions and forecasting.
2. Summarizing the situation analysis in a limited number of issues.
3. Choosing a vision about the environment.
4. Defining the main challenge.
5. The choice of the value discipline.
6. Formulating strategic options.
7. Selecting a marketing strategic option.

9.1 Definitions and forecasting

Before discussing the steps in the SWOT analysis we will look at two general guidelines in relation to the SWOT analysis: the need for clear definitions, and the need for a future perspective.

9.1.1 Definitions

First, we define what we mean by strengths, weaknesses, opportunities, and threats. There is a need for a good definition because we will otherwise encounter misunderstandings when we get into specifics. We have the following three characteristics:

1. *A distinction between strengths and weakness on the one hand and opportunities and threats on the other hand.* Strengths and weaknesses are internal: they are related to the brand for which the marketing plan is made. Opportunities and threats are external: They are related to the environment and would exist even *if the brand in question did not*. Therefore, a 'good image' (measured in terms of customers) is a strength and not an opportunity, despite the fact that it comes from the customer analysis.
2. *A distinction between opportunity and threat.* The distinction between an opportunity and a threat is that an opportunity is a positive development for an *unrevised*

policy and a threat is a negative one. We add the criterion of unrevised policy because, as is often said, "There is no such thing as a threat because a company can capitalize on anything." If that fundamentally correct assumption is made, there is no tenable distinction between opportunities and threats, and so it is better to use the term *issues* or *external points of attention*. Thus, we do in fact make a distinction. Therefore, an economic slump can be an opportunity for a quality product if the brand is in a position to lower the price. However, we still consider this a threat because there may be unfavourable influences in the case of an unrevised policy.

3. *A distinction between opportunities and strategies.* One difference between an opportunity and a strategy is that a strategy is something a brand *does* and an opportunity is not. Thus, "a peanut-flavoured beer developed for young people" is not an opportunity but a possible strategy. The underlying opportunity may be "expected increase in demand for specialty beers among young people". As another example, 'brand rejuvenation' is not an opportunity but a reaction to the 'corny image' weakness.

Finally, we sometimes use the terms *relative strength* and *relative weakness*, by which we mean that they are strong or weak not only in general but also *with respect to the competition*; that is, comparatively. Relative strengths can be determined by comparing the 'absolute' strengths and weaknesses (partly derived from the internal analysis) with those of the competition (derived from the analysis of the competition).

9.1.2 Forecasting methods

A marketing plan is by definition about the future, for example, for the next three years. This means that a manager should try to assess future opportunities and threats. Current opportunities and threats or even developments in the past are in fact irrelevant. The problem is that no one knows for sure what the future will bring. What a manager should do is to make his or her own forecasts, in the meantime making use of forecasts made by others as well as, for example, forecasts by research or governmental institutes.

A manager should not only predict environmental trends, but also the sales of the own brand. This is necessary for making financial projections in the marketing plan (see sections 9.7 and 14.3).

Since forecasting is important in a marketing plan, we now provide some guidelines for choosing the best forecasting method. We make extensive use of Armstrong (2001).

There are two kinds of forecasting methods:

■ *Objective methods* are methods where in one or another way a forecast is computed, so that if someone else applies the same method the same result will come out (replication possible). For these methods, quantitative data are used and mostly some statistical knowledge is needed. Examples are trend extrapolations and causal regression models.

■ *Subjective methods* are where a forecast is made 'in the head' of a researcher or expert, or customer. In this case quantitative data may also be used, as well as qualitative data, but the processing of these data is implicitly done. There are two kinds of subjective forecasting methods: expert opinions, and intention research (intentions are statements of customers about the likeliness of buying a product).

An important factor to consider in choosing objective or subjective methods is whether it is expected that 'the circumstances will strongly change'. Objective methods are based on patterns from the past and are thus less appropriate to predict changes in trends. But also subjective methods are not always suitable for predicting major changes. People have a natural tendency to be anchored to the past and thus underestimate likely changes. See also Case 9.1.

A general conclusion from research about the accurateness of forecasting methods is that *combining different forecasting methods* (called *eclectic research*) provides the best forecast. Armstrong (2001) therefore recommends not putting too much energy into one forecasting method but putting less energy into several methods. Preferably both an objective and subjective method should be chosen.

Finally, the question is how to come to one forecast if several methods are chosen and thus if several forecasts are available. This issue is also investigated and the surprising result is that simply computing the (unweighted) mean provides the best result.

Case 9.1 Forecasting is also difficult for experts

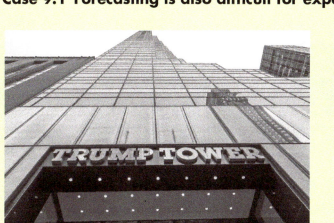

Three major forecasting errors leading to global changes

In the 2010s the world was confronted with three major unexpected events. First there was a major economic crisis after 2009, lasting for about six years. Then we had Brexit, chosen in a referendum by the British population. The most famous unexpected event was the election of Donald Trump as President of the USA: until the last moment none of the published forecasts predicted Trump to be elected. It seems that human behaviour can in the end be different from whatever research agencies predict.

We end with an example. Suppose an entrepreneur has an idea for a new product. For the bank, he has to make a projection of expected sales in the upcoming five years. He could then apply the following methods:

1. He performs an intention survey, asking a group of male and female potential customers how likely it is that they would buy his new product, given a specific price. Combining these two segments and taking, for example, only the 'sure buy' category provides an own forecast.
2. Benchmarking: have a look how comparable products have developed. The problem is whether other products are really comparable.
3. Expert forecasts (opinion research). The entrepreneur researches some objective experts and asks them to make a forecast.

This leads to three different forecasts of future sales of his new product. To get one forecast the entrepreneur computes the mean of the three.

It may be that certain environmental issues are very uncertain and at the same time potentially important. In the case of the entrepreneur, it may be that a competitor will come with the same product. In these cases, scenarios may be used. A scenario is a description of an environmental context; for example, two scenarios, "there will be no competitor in the upcoming five years" and "there will be a competitor right from the start". The most likely scenario will be chosen and a second scenario may be shown in the appendix of the plan. A scenario is not a real forecasting method; it is merely a way of dealing with uncertainty.

9.2 Summary of the situation analysis

The situation analysis potentially produces a long list of strengths, weaknesses, opportunities, and threats. Some of these are important; others are less important. In addition, some are related to each other. To keep the subsequent analysis well organized, the situation analysis should be *summarized* into a limited number of strengths, weaknesses, opportunities, and threats. The following tips may be useful (Dibb et al., 2003):

- Include only the most important factors ('issues'). Always limit the number to a maximum of five (a maximum of five strengths, five opportunities, etc.).
- Classify the points in order of importance.
- Ensure that sufficient supporting evidence is available at each point.
- Strengths and weaknesses should be relative to those of the competitors.
- Do not mix up strengths, weaknesses, opportunities, and threats (see the definitions in section 9.1).

Therefore, the most frequently stated 'issues' become the starting point for further SWOT analysis. The choice of what is relevant requires a high degree of caution and creativity. It requires caution because it may be assumed that the competition also indicates the most readily available opportunities, and the distinction may actually be in less noticeable 'brackets'. Creativity is also important: the ability to intuit what may be an opportunity. There should be a 'golden bracket' for the entire SWOT process. As it is fashionable to say, a 'big idea' is all it takes for a profitable strategy. That bracket

Definite strengths and weaknesses (SW)*	Core issues in the environment (future opportunities and threats) (OT)*
S1 Strong position with professionals	O1 Companies increasingly need quality photos
S2 Good in quality and innovation	O2 Economic growth
S3 Many features	O3 Growing importance for consumer of advice in the shop
S4 Good relationship with retailers	O4 Cameras pay little attention to style
S5 Specialist in photography	O5 Competitors are not focused
W1 High costs and price	T1 Improving photo quality mobile phones
W2 Low market share in consumer market	T2 Growing need for convenience
W3 Brand awareness relatively low	T3 Growth of Instagram
W4 Not very easy to handle	T4 Competitors strong in user-friendly cameras
W5 No brand extensions	T5 Competitors (e.g. Canon) have broader assortment (printers, personal computers, cameras, etc.)

*In total a maximum of 10 internal and 10 external items.

Figure 9.1 Selection of SWOTs for a manufacturer of digital cameras

or idea may often be found by listening carefully to buyers and not only paying attention to aspects that the customers like but also paying attention to what they don't like. Figure 9.1 summarizes the results of this sub-step.

As may be seen in Figure 9.1, all SWs are about the brand and OTs are about the market. In addition, some issues can be both positive and negative: not having brand extensions, so products other than photo cameras may be a limitation (W5) as well as a strength as being specialist (S5). And the 'growing need for convenience' (T2) may be a threat but also an opportunity but is placed in the threat part, since, if things are not changed (not easy to handle), it is a threat.

9.3 Vision on the environment

After and in addition to the summary of the situation analysis, it is desirable to carry out a further reduction of the situation analysis. This facilitates the choice of what is and what is not important at this point. This is actually about the development of a *vision on the environment*: a short and concise statement about what management thinks is important in the environment of the brand. We refer back to the categories in the situation analysis:

- Customer analysis.
- Industry analysis.
- Competition analysis.
- Distribution analysis.

Each of these components is accompanied by the question: What future development or trend does the manager think is the most important? If there is a lot of uncertainty with respect to one of these components involving a development that is also considered very important, we can describe *scenarios* and then select one as the most probable scenario. For instance, suppose there is a lot of competition. We can describe two scenarios here: The competition either does or does not introduce a hefty decrease in prices. We then use this as a basis for choosing one of the two options.

9.4 Problem conclusion and unrevised policy

In order to realize a focus, it is recommended to draw some kind of conclusion from the situation analysis in the sense of the core challenge. Also, a marketing goal may be chosen. If the goal deviates from the predicted results ('gap analysis'), something has to change in a company's strategy.

The *performance evaluation* (part of the internal analysis; see section 4.2) provides an initial impression of where potential problems are, based on an evaluation of the strategy being followed and its results. Some examples of possible results of this are as follows:

- The marketing target (such as a certain market share) of a new brand X is not achieved.
- This is due mainly to a disappointing percentage of repeat purchases.
- The cause should not be sought in the *implementation* of the planned strategy because there was an important difference between the planned implementation and the actual implementation.

This recognition of the problem is not sufficient, of course. The question remains: What are the specific causes of the disappointing results? More specifically formulated, what is the current 'core marketing problem' for which the market plan must provide a solution? The answer to this question may best be given as the conclusion of the summary of the SWOTs. After all, it is in this phase that all possible relevant internal and environmental factors are analysed, and problems are often a combination of internal and external factors. It has already been indicated that at this point the problem conclusion was reflected in the marketing plan and even in the first chapter of the plan (see section 2.4). A solid foundation is important for the core problem. A practical example of a core problem is that brand identity does not correspond to brand image. The brand wants to have certain associations, but the target group does not see them. This happens a lot, sometimes more than managers realize. It is often said that a brand "is very strong because it has a great deal of familiarity". However, an image is also important. If an image is moving towards 'trusted, familiar', there is the danger ('prognosis') of moving towards 'corny, old-fashioned'. Does the company want that? Therefore, a critical interpretation of the situation analysis is desirable.

During this phase we can also make a prediction of what is expected in the case of *unrevised policy*: a prognosis of sales and profits if nothing is changed in the strategy. Of course, subjectivity plays a major role here, and the marketing plan to be developed will have to lead to better results. An advantage of this kind of marketing plan is that it emphasizes the need for change. Incidentally, this is also frequently stated within the framework of *change management*: the first step in a change management plan is to

Vision of camera manufacturer

In the market of digital cameras in Argentina our market share decreased from 2.8% in 2017 to 2.3% in 2018. The main reason for this is the growing popularity of compact cameras, a submarket where we do not have a broad assortment. Our goal is to regain a market share of 3.0% in 2020.

We expect that the need for instant photos via social media will increase and that competition will respond to this trend. Our image is that we deliver top quality cameras but also that user friendliness can be improved. If we do not change our strategy, market share will likely decrease.

Figure 9.2 **Development of a vision on the environment and core challenge for a digital camera manufacturer**

become aware of the need for change. The best way to gain awareness is to have the conviction that if the company keeps going down the same path, this will lead to disastrous or at least not prosperous results.

Combining this with the issues from section 9.3 we provide an example for a producer of photo cameras (Figure 9.2).

9.5 Choice of a value strategy

The three value disciplines by Treacy and Wiersema (1993) were discussed in Chapter 3. Every company should choose to excel in one of the three value disciplines after ensuring that a sufficient level has been attained in all three aspects (innovation, smoothly running processes, and customer orientation). The value strategy should have been defined by the time of the drafting of the marketing plan for a brand. If this is the case, we can proceed to the next planning phase.

However, it is often unclear which value strategy has been chosen. In this case, an assumption must be made as to which value strategy has been chosen or a value strategy must still be chosen.

Figure 9.3 gives an example of a possible selection method. The following must be assessed for each of the value strategies:

- *The current level*. If one of the three is at a level that is too low, this will have to be dealt with before the company considers excelling. In practice, an insufficient level of operational excellence is often a problem: the internal processes simply do not run smoothly. There are innumerable possible causes for this. The company will have to improve in this area, but this does not mean that the company chooses the operational excellence value strategy. Solving a problem is not the same thing as excellence.
- *Feasibility of excellence.* Here we can estimate whether and to what extent excellence is feasible within the time constraints. What has to happen for the company to become the best?
- *Connecting to opportunities.* Which value discipline offers the best opportunities for the environment? More specifically, what are the future desires of the client and the weaknesses of the competition?

Value strategy	Current level	Possibility of excellence	Fit with environment
1. Operational excellence	Not yet at a sufficient level	High costs (W1) must be reduced (S2), but not to a great extent. Not in DNA.	Links up with T2 (convenience). Difficult to be better than competition (T5).
2. Product leadership	At a sufficient level	Fits well with S2 (innovation), S1 (professionals) and S5 (specialist).	Links up with O1 well and with T4 (competition is more focused on operational excellence). But it appears that other innovations can be chosen in the future (Canon).
3. Customer intimacy	Customer-oriented, but not strongly one-to-one	Already achieved in distribution channel (S4) but not yet with consumers. Fits in well with our image as a specialist (S5).	Links up with O1 and O3. Service and customer intimacy go well together.

Conclusion

- ■ Sufficient level?
  - ☐ Operational excellence is still insufficient, and costs must be further reduced; only then can we start thinking about excellence. Need for convenience and instant photos demands investments.
- ■ Excellence?
  - ☐ Product leadership suits us well, but quality and possibilities are found to be less important and position threatens to be difficult to defend in the future.
  - ☐ Customer intimacy would be feasible thanks to our good relationship with distributors. Demand for this unsure.

*Instead of using this approach, a manager can apply the SWOT matrix to the choice of value strategies.

Figure 9.3 Selection process for value strategy for a digital camera manufacturer*

9.6 Marketing strategic options

9.6.1 Relevance of brand identity

Once the situation analysis has been reduced to a few main points and the value strategy has been chosen, it is time to develop ideas for the marketing strategy. In the practice of marketing, often too little time is spent thinking about the brand image and the brand identity. It is precisely the *brand positioning* that must be the reason why people buy one brand and do not buy another. This part of the brainstorming process is therefore critical. See also Case 9.2.

9.6.2 Chosen SWOT process in this book

Weihrich (1982) developed a method where all strengths, weaknesses, opportunities, and threats are put in a 2 x 2 matrix and where each issue gets a number (e.g. S2, O3). For each quadrant (e.g. strengths/opportunities) ideas are formulated and for each idea it is indicated which SWOTs are used.

Case 9.2 Strategy development

How to develop a positioning for Lipton in Asia

Although quite a long time ago, this interview with Tex Gunning, in 2004 working for Unilever Foods Asia, sheds light on how to develop a brand positioning: "We are now conducting all of our large market studies in large collective processes. The figures come back, and then we lock ourselves inside for three or four days. Then we work through all the ups and downs in this kind of process, but after that, it is also a collectively supported positioning. It can result in a lot of frustration, but you end up with a conclusion that you could never have arrived at by yourself with two other smart people. Consumers and their relationship with a brand are so complicated that a marketer can't make a go of it alone. We always get 10, 20, or 30 people in on the rethinking and the work. And we do it all over again in four months until the brand positioning is crystal clear and relevant." He gives Lipton tea as an example. "It sounds simple, but everyone sells tea in China. I've been working on it for two and a half years, and it wasn't until two weeks ago that we thought we really hit on it. This is what we're going to do with Lipton: Young Asians know that the future belongs to them. Those economies are so large and the political influence of the Chinese is growing so fast that the collective self-awareness is becoming infinitely large. You get a whole group of young people who want to ride that wave. Considering this, we positioned Lipton as a *bright and vital outlook on life*. That means that you have to do more than just sell tea."

Source: Van Vugt (2004, pp. 13–16)

Some authors even structure the SWOT analysis more, for example, by first giving weights to the different SWOTs and then trying to 'compute' the best combinations.

A (too) structured way of coming to options has two disadvantages. First, it hinders creative thinking. Second, options may result which are not comparable; for example, "get more active on social media" (a tactical idea) and "reposition the brand" (a strategic idea).

So, a SWOT analysis should meet the following requirements:

1. *It is firmly in tune with practice and has sufficient space for creative reflection.* In practice, mechanical methods are never chosen for strategy development. A situation analysis is typically carried out, but after that there is never actually a consideration of opportunities to arrive at a choice of strategy. What is done is brainstorming, delving into and understanding the results of the situation analysis, discussion, brainstorming, rethinking, more brainstorming, and so on. This approach is considered productive and also has the advantage that it can be performed by a number of people at the same time. Case 9.2 gives an example of effective strategy development at Unilever; the approach outlined matches up well with the method we have proposed.

2. *It leads to strategic decisions with sufficient focus on levels within the company.* A SWOT analysis should be truly strategic and, in particular, should produce ideas for the value strategy (if it is not already defined) and the marketing strategy (brand positioning). This means that the SWOT analysis must involve rethinking geared towards these strategic decisions and that there should not be a free brainstorming process for all possible types of tactical ideas. For instance, there is no point in brainstorming ideas for communication until the brand positioning has been defined at the strategic level.

The SWOT matrix may be modified to satisfy the conditions set forth above. In this case, two modifications of the original methodology are necessary:

1. Two types of strategies are considered:
   a. *The value strategies by Treacy and Wiersema (1993).* This choice should have been made at the company level, but if this was not done, a brand can still make choices about the method of competition: product leader, a leader in low cost for the customer, or specialized in individual customer relationships. Alternatively, it can come up with an indication of what must be improved to attain a sufficient level.
   b. *The marketing strategy: target group (segment) and brand positioning.* The value strategy provides a further specification of the particular target group choice (existing and new customers, background features, and lifestyle of the target group) and the brand positioning (instrumental and emotional, brand varieties).
2. Coordinating alternatives are considered 'at the same time', and explicit indications are given for which strengths, weaknesses, opportunities, and threats link up with each alternative. In this context, 'at the same time' means that we do not deem it necessary to consider the alternatives on the basis of their quadrant in the

matrix; that is, separately for the strength-opportunity, strength-threat, weakness-opportunity, or weakness-threat quadrant. In our view, this limits creative thinking and makes it more difficult to see the mutual relationships between, for example, strengths and weakness or opportunities and threats. It also makes it difficult to narrow things down to a few alternatives, such as a maximum of three. A manager can try to amass various ideas under 'umbrella options', but this produces too few coherent options.

9.6.3 Stimulating innovation

When deciding on a marketing strategy, a manager should be innovative and also think from the core competencies of the company. The positioning will end up being an extension of the chosen value strategy. If, for instance, the value strategy 'product leadership' is chosen, there is not much point in considering low-price positioning. However, in this phase, the company should not let itself be guided by existing preconditions such as the vision of the environment or financial constraints. In principle, any strategy is possible, even outside the current activities. It is of the utmost importance to be creative.

Creativity can be stimulated in different ways. Aaker (2013) provides the following recommendations:

1. Do it in groups, since diversity increases the number of different ideas.
2. 'Get warm' before starting the creative session, for example, by letting everyone come up with some kind of story.
3. Be clear about the goals of the session, such as finding an extension.
4. Do not judge the ideas, only generate them.
5. Try to think 'laterally', for example, by posing the question "What should we do to realize …", instead of "Yes, but this is not feasible since …".
6. In later sessions do not judge the ideas only on hard facts, but also based on feelings.

The brainstorming phase of the SWOT analysis is crucial and requires a high level of *creativity and empathy*. The ideas the company comes up with should be as specific as possible. Thus, it does not make much sense to take on vague ideas such as "boost market share", "anticipate customer desires better", "diversify", and "reposition". At the very least, we must state exactly how the company will be able to do this. To get as many ideas as possible on potential strategies, it is advisable to hold *brainstorming sessions*. This should involve different representatives from the company, such as designers, production personnel, intermediaries, marketing, and top management. The brainstorming session can follow three steps:

1. Representatives could first be debriefed on the results of the SWOT analysis (the most important Ss, Ws, Os, and Ts).
2. Then they will brainstorm about possible strategies. From a marketing perspective, the positioning of the brand is an important point of discussion that must be brought to the fore. What is the level of brand familiarity, and what are the brand associations that the target group has now? To what extent is this in line with the brand identity?

In these phases we attempt to arrive at a few (e.g. three) alternatives. 'Alternatives' means that the options should really exclude each other. Otherwise, there is nothing to choose. For each alternative, we indicate in brackets the idea on which internal and external issues are based. It makes a difference whether this is based on a strength or a weakness. Strengths offer connecting points for a competitive edge, whereas weaknesses result in a defensive strategy. It does not necessarily have to be this way. A weakness can be worked out quickly by cooperating with a strong partner and thus forming the basis for an offensive strategy.

At every step you should always be creative and interpret each signal carefully and on the basis of your own possibilities.

Case 9.3 Innovation

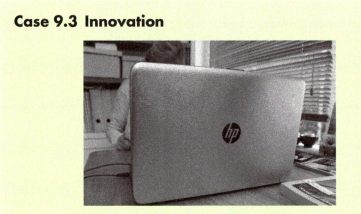

Product innovation or marketing strategy: What comes first?

'Innovate or die' is a phrase often used to describe the approach brands must take to stay ahead in an ultra-competitive market characterized by rapidly changing consumer demand. However, the way companies go about driving new product development depends very much on their structure, priorities, and where marketing sits within the innovation journey. Marketing's influence is key to ensuring new offerings fit with a strategy determined by customers' needs, so companies aren't stuck trying to sell something for which there is no demand. But brands have to balance being insight-driven with being able to launch products that no focus group would ever think to suggest. FMCG companies such as Unilever perform all kinds of qualitative and quantitative research and use these as input in product innovation.

Innovation is central to marketing's role within any organization, according to HP global chief marketing and communications director, Antonio Lucio. But he recognizes the approach differs depending on the category. So while in FMCG the fundamental premise is that the 'customer is king', in a technology business like HP the goal is to create products consumers have never even dreamed about. This means marketing is responsible for bringing invention to life from a consumer experience standpoint.

Source: Adapted from *Marketing Week*, 15 May 2018

Being innovative also means that *new activities* should explicitly be taken into account. In light of the fact that a situation analysis exclusively examines the existing market, this may appear strange. However, even a situation analysis may produce various signals that indicate opportunities outside of the existing, analysed market. Following the case of the manufacturer of digital cameras, examples of signals for new activities include the following (see also section 3.3.3):

- *Unmet needs*: Needs of existing consumers to which a company cannot respond with its existing products. An analysis of complaints and problems consumers have with products can be helpful; this is the most important source for new ideas, and so it is important to listen carefully to consumers. It must be noted, however, that consumers will not tell you what to do; you should listen carefully and translate the information into ideas. For example, you might develop a camera with a battery indicator that works properly.
- *New consumer segments* not served now, for example, cameras for children.
- Developments in the *macro environment* that may have a positive effect on other markets, for example, ageing, which stimulates the development of user-friendly cameras.
- The expected developments in *substitute products* within the industry factors, for example, the growth in mobile phones with a camera function, which could be a motive to become active in this market.
- What *competitors* do aside from their core activities, for example, selling copiers.

In order to enable a transparent choice process, it is recommended to not only come to one marketing strategic choice but to formulate three alternatives (options). Clearly, in the end, one has to be chosen. Defining three options has the advantage that:

- a manager is forced to think 'outside the box';
- it is easier to communicate internally why an option is chosen, leading to more support.

9.6.4 The SWOT matrix

To clearly show a link with the SWOT, for every option it is indicated on which SWOT issues it builds. Figure 9.4 provides an example with different positioning options. We have already mentioned the STP steps of marketing strategy: segmentation, targeting, positioning. Also, an application is possible about targeting. Suppose from segmentation research (Chapter 5) it appears that there are six segments with each having its own needs. Thus three alternative target groups may be mentioned: for example:

- segment professionals;
- segment children and youngsters below the age of 20;
- segment elderly above the age of 65.

If options have been formulated in this manner, in the last step a choice has to be made.

	O1 Companies increasingly need quality photos O2 Economic growth O3 Growing importance for consumer of advice in the shop O4 Cameras pay little attention to style O5 Competitors are not focused	T1 Improving photo quality mobile phones T2 Growing need for convenience T3 Growth of Instagram T4 Competitors strong in user-friendly cameras T5 Competitors (e.g. Canon) have broader assortment (printers, personal computers, cameras, etc.)
S1 Strong position with professionals S2 Good in quality and innovation S3 Many features S4 Good relationship with retailers S5 Specialist in photography	*Alternative marketing strategies for the next three years** Reposition on user-friendliness (T2, T4, W2, W5). Increase quality perception (S1, S2, S3, S5, W1, O1, O2, T1) Introduce a user-friendly and stylish sub-brand (S4, W4, W5, O4, T2, T4, T5)	
W1 High costs and price W2 Low market share in consumer market W3 Brand awareness relatively low W4 Not very easy to handle W5 No brand extensions		

*Two applications are possible: choosing a value strategy and choosing a more specific brand identity (as in this example).

Figure 9.4 SWOT matrix

9.7 Choosing a marketing strategic option

In this section, we deal with three steps. Section 9.7.1 reviews relevant criteria for making choices. Next we describe some considerations to be made during the choice process (section 9.7.2). Finally, we show how the net present value of a strategy can be estimated (section 9.7.3).

9.7.1 Criteria for judging options

In order to have a transparent choice process, ideally, every option should be judged along a fixed set of criteria. A company can choose their own criteria. In Figure 9.5 we present the steps and criteria we think are important during the strategy selection.

Criterion 1: *suitability* of the option to the vision:

does it fit with the value strategy, does it solve the core problem?

Criterion 2: *feasibility* of the option: is the option internally feasible? (preconditions FOETSLE):

· *Financial.* To what extent are sufficient financial resources available to implement the strategy?

· *Organizational.* Does the strategy fit within the organization? Is implementation organizationally possible?

· *Economic.* Is the strategy in line with the economic objectives of the company?

· *Technical.* Is implementation of the strategy technically possible?

· *Social.* Is the strategy socially acceptable?

· *Legal.* Are there no legal problems to be expected (e.g. in the context of trademark law)?

· *Ecological.* Is the strategy ecologically sensible (environment)?

Criterion 3: *results and risks*

expected realization of the objectives:

are the results acceptable to internal stakeholders

specifically: expected profitability, payback period and the accompanying risks?

Figure 9.5 **A selection process for strategies**

Suitability

A first evaluation of the strategic options concerns the extent to which an option:

■ Fits with higher strategic levels (vision, corporate strategy).
■ Resolves the core problem (if that has not happened already).
■ Fits with the most important *issues* in the external and internal environments.

For example, a company may have concluded on the basis of customer research that a market exists for significantly cheaper products. However, if the company has not chosen the value strategy of low price, offering cheaper products may not fit with the brand identity. In that case, the company, therefore, will not do what some customers would like it to do. This is in line with our opinion regarding the role of marketing as an intermediary between the customer and the brand.

The conclusion of the evaluation of the suitability of options may be that several are satisfactory (Figure 9.6).

Feasibility

Each of the potentially suitable options is then compared to a number of internal preconditions.

Evaluation based on the seven preconditions (financial, organizational, economic, technical, social, legal and ecological; designated with the acronym FOETSLE) provides insight into the feasibility: Is it possible to implement the specific option?

	Suitability	Feasible (FOETSLE)	Expected profit and risk
Option 1			
Option 2			
Option 3			
Choice			

Figure 9.6 Selection of a marketing strategy

Results and risks

A choice needs to be made from the options that remain after the process of elimination based on these preconditions. Selection occurs on the basis of *objectives*. These variables may be company objectives and/or marketing objectives. Company objectives are typically financial in nature (profit, cost recovery period, etc.; see section 10.1), whereas marketing objectives often relate to sales or market share (see section 11.1). Profit and market share are not always on the same line: with a high marketing budget, a high market share can be 'bought'. The issue of which type of objective is decisive depends on the internal and external situations in which the marketing plan is being written.

9.7.2 Forecasts and considerations in the selection process

When market share or sales is the selection criterion, a prognosis of sales to be expected should be made for each option. Although making these predictions is a perilous undertaking, the forecasting methods described in section 9.1 can be helpful in this area. The option with the highest expected market share will be chosen.

However, *financial considerations* are often decisive: the option that is expected to earn the most money is the preferred choice. A financial selection criterion implies that the profit figures for each option have to be predicted over a series of years. This means that the sales prognosis mentioned above has to be supplemented with assumptions about, for example, the required investments. In addition, the expected risk plays a major role.

Therefore, in the final option selection, an assessment has to be made involving expected revenues, risks, investments required immediately, and investments required over the long term. If financial goals are involved, the *payback period* is often used as a simple criterion: When will the immediately required investments be paid back? A manager can define a maximum for this; for example, four years.

A more advanced method for comparing alternative strategic options is *shareholder value analysis*, a method to determine the 'present value' (cash value) of a strategy. The concept behind the shareholder value analysis is that a strategy may be considered an investment that will produce a certain future cash flow. The 'expected shareholder value' can be determined by using discounting to calculate the expected cash flow back to the present time. The selection criterion is therefore entirely financial in this case and in effect is related to the value a strategy has for the shareholders. After all, shareholders can choose from various possibilities in investment capital, and in principle they will choose the option with the highest present value.

An important advantage of shareholder value analysis is that a link is made between the functional areas of marketing and financing: the strategies are evaluated on the basis of financial measures.

9.7.3 Estimating the net present value of options

To calculate the present value, the same formulas may be used that are employed in the investment realm. The present value of a strategy is the sum of the future cash flows converted back to the present (calculated back towards point 'zero' in time), plus the residual value at the end of the duration of the strategy, also converted back to the present. To calculate the *net* present value, the investment made at point zero in time should still be subtracted. The formula is as follows:

$$NCW = \sum_{t=1}^{n} \frac{CF_t}{(1+r)^t} - I$$

Figure 9.7 NCW formula

in which:

NCW = net cash (present) worth of a strategy
n = planning period (e.g. three or five years)
CF_t = predicted cash flow in period t (CF_n also contains the residual value of the strategy)
r = discount rate
$1/(1+r)^t$ = discount factor
I = investment amount

The variables mentioned here are calculated as follows:

- *Cash flow.* This is calculated in the usual manner: expected annual sales times gross profit margin minus taxes, increases in fixed costs (advertising, research, and development), and investments in working capital.
- *Discount rate.* The average capital cost rate for the company. If a certain strategy has a relatively high risk, the discount rate may be augmented with a risk surcharge.
- *Residual value.* The value after the completion of the planning horizon. This appears difficult to determine. A possible approach is to assume that the net receipts at the end of the planning period will continue forever or will change by a certain percentage.

In choosing a certain strategy, this procedure should be performed for a situation of 'unchanged policy' as well as for the options to be considered. The difference between the net present value of an option and the net present value of an unchanged policy is the value of the strategy. Figure 9.8 includes a calculation example. During the calculation, it is easiest to assume the expected *differences* between the strategy to be considered and the unchanged policy all at once. Figure 9.8 is based on the assumption (prognosis) that with the strategy to be chosen (investment 150), the cash flow will increase 10 per cent annually, whereas with the unchanged policy a stable cash flow (of 100) is expected. In this case, the strategy should be implemented.

	Current values	Forecast of differences between strategy and unchanged policy			Residual value
	2018 (t = 0)	2019	2020	2021	2022 and on
Cash flow* (annual growth 10%)	100	10	21	33	46
Discount factor (r = 15%)		0.87	0.76	0.66	3.81**
Present value of cash flow**		8.7	16.0	21.8	175.3*
Total present value	222				
Investment amount	150				
Net present value of strategy	72				

*For examples of how cash flow is calculated, refer to the literature.
**Eternity assumption: discount factor/discount rate = .57/.15

Figure 9.8 **Example of calculation of present value for a strategy**

An advantage of the shareholder value analysis is that the financial expectations of a strategy are summarized in one indicator. This simplifies the comparison of strategies. Another advantage is that it forces the planner to make all expected revenues from and costs of strategies explicit. Setting up financial indicators is always a necessity in a marketing plan. On the other hand, the shareholder value analysis depends on the reliability of the predicted results. So, it looks like an objective method, but it is based on a lot of subjective assumptions.

Summary

The SWOT analysis forms the link between the situation analysis (internal analysis and external analysis) and the strategy formation. From the results of the situation analysis (a listing of the most important strengths, weaknesses (both relative), opportunities, and threats), ideas for potential strategies are generated. It is important to do this systematically, be creative, be critical and customer-oriented, and make clear choices. Four steps are proposed:

1. The whole situation analysis is reduced to some core issues. A manager can do this by making a selection of at most ten relevant internal and external issues.
2. Coming to a conclusion. The company should explicitly formulate its vision on the environment: Which (customer) trends are considered most important in the future, and what is the core problem?
3. A thorough discussion is organized about the future positioning of the brand. Using the issues from the analysis as inspiration, alternative ideas are generated.
4. Selection is realized by applying three criteria: fit with the value strategy, suitability, and expected results and risks.

Although we propose concrete steps and criteria, it is an illusion to think that a strategy can be chosen in an objective way. For example, forecasting turnover for three years for an option and also for the situation of 'unrevised policy' is hardly possible. Since the best decisions in life are made based on gut feeling after doing homework, a SWOT analysis should be performed in a flexible way.

Case Pepsi Cola in the USA: strategic choices

The American market for (non-alcoholic) beverages is traditionally dominated by soft drinks, especially cola. However, the position of soft drinks has been under pressure for years as a result of, among other things, the pursuit of a healthier life-style, and continuous attention to the dangers of obesity. Other product categories, such as energy drinks and bottled water, are on the rise. The following segments can be distinguished in this market:

- (Carbonated) soft drink;
- Ready-to-Drink (RTD) tea (such as iced tea);
- Sports drink;
- Energy and health drink;
- Juices;
- Bottled water.

Carbonated soft drink

Sales of soft drinks have been showing a downward trend for years; sales have already dropped by 25 per cent in the past 20 years. And this trend continues: in 2015 there was a decrease of 1.2 per cent again. In money terms, there was a slight growth of 1.4 per cent in 2015 to a total of US$78 billion; this is about 166 billion litres. Consumers increasingly want 'non-cola' soft drinks. At the same time, people are increasingly buying drinks such as iced tea and mineral water instead of carbonated soft drinks.

Initially, companies such as Pepsi and Coca-Cola tried to counteract the down-turn by diet or zero sugar variants such as Pepsi Max or Coca-Cola Zero. But these drinks are also under pressure, partly because sweeteners such as aspartame are in the news since they are bad for health as well. In addition, producers are increasingly trying to turn the tide by innovating and putting soft drinks on the market with stronger flavours and/or other additions. Examples include Pepsi X Energy Cola and Dr Pepper Vanilla Float. Extra vitamins and minerals are also added to some soft drinks; a variant of Pepsi Max contains extra caffeine and ginseng, for example.

RTD tea and bottled water

Consumers in the USA are increasingly buying non-carbonated drinks. This is caused mainly by the increasing health consciousness and by product innovations in the non-carbonated segment.

Bottled water seems to benefit the most from this health trend. While soft drinks are increasingly seen as artificial in the eyes of the consumer and contain an excess of sugar, bottled water seems to benefit from its image of natural purity. In 2014, the sales of bottled water in the USA increased by 8 per cent to a total of more than 40 billion litres. The average American drinks more than 125 litres of bottled water per year.

Due to trends such as wellness, all kinds of product innovations arise with respect to bottled water with added vitamins and minerals, so that consumers can get their daily dose of vitamins by drinking bottled water. For the time being, product innovations will continue to generate growing consumption.

The producers of RTD tea have increasingly positioned their products as 'functional drinks', mainly due to the addition of useful anti-oxidants. Recent product introductions with additional extracts of green tea-leaves have benefited from the increasing interest in green tea. A number of scientific studies have shown that green tea contains many anti-oxidants. Functional drinks containing additives such as ginseng and ginkgo biloba are also becoming increasingly popular. Due to all these developments, RTD tea ('Ready-to-Drink tea') continues to attract attention, despite the fact that there is sugar in iced tea: in 2015 there was a growth of about 2.5 per cent.

Juice

Fruit juices are healthy, but they also contain sugar. Partly as a consequence of that, sales of fruit juice in the USA are under pressure: there was a 2 per cent decline in 2014. The high marketing activities in the other segments also have a negative effect on the sale of fruit juice, as well as the rising cost price of many fruits, and therefore of fruit juice.

Energy drinks on the rise

Energy drinks such as Red Bull contain – in contrast to functional drinks – no demonstrable health benefits. But they promote performance and concentration, or provide other physical or mental stimuli. Many consumers prefer energy drinks over soft drinks as 'energy boosters'.

A variety of viral marketing, especially for students and nightclub goers, in combination with 'traditional' campaigns via radio and TV, has stimulated the sales of these products. The market is growing fast. In 2011, around US$8 billion of energy drinks were sold; in 2015 this had risen to $13.5 billion. In 2014 there was a growth of no less than 6 per cent.

The sales of sports drinks have also risen sharply in recent years. This was mainly caused by product innovations and a repositioning whereby the link between sport and health has been strengthened. The growth in sports drinks in 2014 was approximately 3 per cent.

PepsiCo

PepsiCo is one of the leading food and beverage companies in the world. PepsiCo's product portfolio includes Frito-Lay (snacks such as Lay's chips, Doritos, Cheetos), Quaker Foods (Quaker Oatmeal and other nutritious (breakfast) products), and PepsiCo Beverages (brands like Pepsi Cola, Mountain Dew, Aquafina, Tropicana, Gatorade).

PepsiCo sees a number of important trends for its markets:

- The strength of the retail;
- The emergence of e-commerce as a new distribution channel for food and beverages;
- The consumer focuses increasingly on the values and ethics of a brand;
- Consistent consumer interest in health and wellness.

The company has split its portfolio to benefit from these trends:

- Good-for-you (Tropicana, Aquafina and Quaker Foods). The Quaker brand is one of the most important brands that Americans associate with healthy food.
- Better-for-you. Diet Pepsi can be considered 'better for you' than 'regular' Pepsi.
- Fun-for-you. Snacks and soft drinks.

PepsiCo is active in communicating the importance of fitness and a balanced diet to young people, for example, by sponsoring sports activities for children.

The mission statement of PepsiCo (source: www.PepsiCo.com, 19 September 2016) is:

[T]o provide consumers around the world with delicious, affordable, con-venient and complementary foods and beverages from wholesome breakfasts to healthy and fun daytime snacks and beverages to evening treats. We are committed to investing in our people, our company and the communities where we operate to help position the company for long-term, sustainable growth.

The main products in the PepsiCo beverage portfolio (figures for the USA, 2014) are set out in Table 9.1.

Table 9.1 **The main products in the PepsiCo beverage portfolio**

	PepsiCo's brands	Sales in billions of litres (1 litre is approx. 0.25 gallon)	Market share (%)	Competitors	Market share (%)
Soft drinks*	Pepsi Mountain Dew	28.2 19.9	17 12	Coca-Cola classic (Coca-Cola Company) Dr Pepper (Cadbury Schweppes) Sprite (Coca-Cola Company)	39 11 9
Sports drinks	Gatorade	4.2	77	Powerade (Coca-Cola Company)	20
Juices	Tropicana	3.0	30	Minute Maid (Coca-Cola Company) Private labels	29 25
Bottled water	Aquafina	4.5	11	Dasani (Coca-Cola Company) Private labels	10 13

Note: * Approximately one-third of soft drinks sales consist of light products. For Pepsi (Pepsi Max, Diet Pepsi) this percentage is slightly higher than for Coca-Cola (Diet Coke, Coke Zero).

Pepsi targets more than Coca-Cola at young people; not just the so-called 'Pepsi generation' of 20- to 35-year-olds but also at teenagers. Pepsi believes that if the company manages to persuade these young people to adapt to Pepsi, they will have a customer for life. Pepsi also profiles itself differently from Coca-Cola. Brad Jakeman (marketer at PepsiCo) has said:

> Coke represents happiness and moments of joy, while it preserves the culture and maintains the status quo. Pepsi, on the other hand, creates a culture and embraces individuality. For Pepsi loyalists, leading an exciting life is much more important than leading a happy one.

This insight led Pepsi to opt for a positioning in which the 'excitement' of the here and now is central. The brand thus seems to aim at a target group that has high expectations of life and is very mobile and active. In their lifestyle, they seize the day (*carpe diem*). With the slogan 'Live for Now' Pepsi tries to connect with this lifestyle. The Coca-Cola strategy is different. This is clear from the campaigns such as 'Always Coca-Cola'. The traditional values of the product are central here.

The new slogan 'Choose Happiness' allows the brand to join in an overall feeling of happiness, and focuses less on an 'experience' than Pepsi.

The position of private labels in the soft drinks market in the USA is getting stronger but is still a far cry from the position of private labels and cheaper brands in some European countries. In the USA, the choice of the consumer is determined more by image than by price. But a growing awareness of American consumers could make consumers more price-sensitive in the USA.

Pepsi has spent a lot of money on marketing and distribution and will continue to do so in the future. It has created a young and dynamic image, which has made product introductions like Pepsi Max possible. But continuous competitive pressure and the increasing importance of healthy consumption limits the growth perspective. Consumers seem to consume less and less cola. So ... What should PepsiCo do with the Pepsi brand?

Questions

1. Create a graphical representation of PepsiCo's business, using the method described in Chapter 3.
2. How is it possible that volume sales of soft drinks, expressed in litres, are falling, while sales in terms of dollars are increasing? Mention at least two reasons.
3. An industry can be described by using Porter's five-forces model. Execute this model for the soft drinks market in the USA, and then draw conclusions about the attractiveness of this market.
4. Apply the product life cycle concept to the soft drink market in the USA. Try to include the following product categories in your product life cycle:
   - Soft drinks
   - Ready-to-Drink (RTD) tea
   - Energy drinks
   - Bottled waters.
5. Create a portfolio analysis for PepsiCo Beverages USA, using the Boston Consulting Group approach. (The theory on portfolio analysis is covered in Chapter 10.)
6. Make a SWOT matrix for the Pepsi brand in the USA.
7. Analyse the strategic problem that PepsiCo has to deal with, with respect to the Pepsi brand.
8. What should PepsiCo do with the Pepsi brand?
   a) Define strategic options for the Pepsi brand by using the information in the case description and the SWOT matrix you created in question 6 above.
   b) Develop a strategy for the Pepsi brand, based on your strategic options. Use the strategy selection process to make your choice.

Part III

Corporate decisions and marketing decisions

10. Corporate objectives and corporate strategies
11. Marketing objectives and marketing strategies

In Part II the situation analysis was explained. These analyses form the basis for the decisions that are to be made (planning). Part III focuses on corporate objectives and corporate strategies (Chapter 10) as well as marketing objectives and marketing strategies (Chapter 11). Decisions at this level relate to the long term and are therefore strategic in nature.

Chapter 10

Corporate objectives and corporate strategies

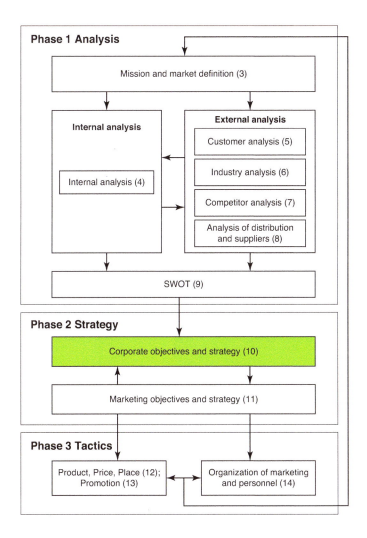

Phase 1 Analysis

Mission and market definition (3)

Internal analysis

Internal analysis (4)

External analysis

Customer analysis (5)

Industry analysis (6)

Competitor analysis (7)

Analysis of distribution and suppliers (8)

SWOT (9)

Phase 2 Strategy

Corporate objectives and strategy (10)

Marketing objectives and strategy (11)

Phase 3 Tactics

Product, Price, Place (12); Promotion (13)

Organization of marketing and personnel (14)

Key points in this chapter

- Know the difference between corporate strategy and marketing strategy.
- Apply a portfolio analysis.
- Know the different growth directions for companies.
- Know how to relate growth directions to development methods (partnering or not).

Introduction

As was discussed in Chapter 2, objectives and strategies exist at different levels within companies: the levels of the company, the strategic business unit (SBU), and the product. Brands play an important role at each of these levels. A central issue in this book is the development of a marketing plan for a brand. This can be a company, an SBU, or a product. In this chapter we assume that a company is active in different markets with different product brands. In that case there is a large difference between decisions made at the corporate level and those made at the lower brand levels. This chapter discusses the decisions made at the top level of the company: the corporate objective and the corporate strategy. In Chapter 11 the other types of decisions are reviewed: the marketing decisions and marketing instrument decisions. If there is no difference between the corporate level and the brand level (as with corporate brands or small companies), the decisions in this chapter and in Chapter 11 are made on one level.

There is a great lack of clarity, both in practice and in the literature, about the content of the concepts of corporate objective and corporate strategy. For example, one often encounters a 'mission' (*corporate mission*) instead of an objective at the point where one would expect to find the corporate objectives. In those cases, one does not encounter the designation of the corporate objective anywhere else. However, during later planning steps, corporate strategies may be encountered. In sections 10.1 to 10.4 the planning phases are reviewed. Section 10.1 reviews the corporate mission and corporate objectives. Section 10.2 deals with the portfolio analysis. We then discuss the two components of the corporate strategy: the issues of 'where to compete' (section 10.3) and 'with whom to compete (partnerships)' (section 10.4).

10.1 Corporate vision and corporate objectives

In Chapter 3 we reviewed the corporate vision and mission. At this stage of the marketing planning process (after the SWOT), it is time to evaluate the mission and vision and to check whether the SWOT provides arguments to update the mission or especially the vision. In section 10.1.1 we shortly review the vision. Then we go into corporate objectives.

10.1.1 Evaluation of the corporate mission and vision

Section 3.1 reviewed the mission and the vision. Here we summarize some main points. There are two important differences between a mission and a vision:

- A mission is merely a description of the current activities, such as the market in which the company operates. Also the values of the company may be mentioned in the mission, such as integrity, quality, and corporate social responsibility.
- A vision looks at the future. It reflects the 'dream' of the CEO.

This implies that a vision may contain 'the personal opinion' of top management. In Chapter 3 we explained that this 'opinion' can be about the environment and about the desired position of the company. Since a vision contains (or should contain) a 'dream', it can function as a way to motivate staff.

Often mission and vision statements are very generic. Then they will not function as a focal point for the staff.

10.1.2 Corporate objectives

In Chapter 4 we mentioned the demands for formulating objectives (SMART) and we argued that companies should not only choose financial goals but also objectives about innovation, customer satisfaction, and internal goals (balanced scorecard). Corporate objectives are mostly chosen for several years; for example, three years. In choosing corporate objectives, two decisions are made:

1. What are the most important variables for the objectives?
2. Which values of the objectives do we want to achieve at what point?

Prioritizing the variables used for the objectives is an issue for top management. This involves, for example, the question of whether the company wants to emphasize market share or profit. In developing the specific content of the chosen objectives, it is important that those objectives be supported in the organization by the people who will be responsible for achieving them. This means, among other things, that the various departments of the organization should be involved in the process of creating the objectives. In making both decisions (ranking and choosing objectives), the method of the balanced scorecard (reviewed in section 4.1.2) can be helpful.

10.2 Portfolio analysis

A portfolio analysis is a tool that can be helpful in making decisions about the allocation of the budget over products (or business units of brands). First we discuss the goal and content of portfolio methods (section 10.2.1). Then we review a 'classical' portfolio method (the BCG matrix; section 10.2.2), and a portfolio method that deals with 'more factors' (MABA analysis; section 10.2.3). Portfolio methods in fact deal only with existing products in existing markets. In section 10.2.4 we show how one can incorporate new markets into a portfolio analysis (trajectory analysis). Portfolio methods are useful mainly for companies that operate in different markets. However, companies often have several brands in one market. In section 10.2.5 we discuss a 'brand version' of the portfolio analysis. We conclude with several comments about the use of portfolio methods (section 10.2.6).

10.2.1 Goal and content

A company that is active in various markets with various products should strive for balance in its product–market combinations. In this context, *balanced* means that the total use of the financial resources is in balance with (and preferably is less than) the revenues of the various product–market combinations.

Although this may seem an obvious goal, its realization is not simple. Markets and market positions are continuously subject to changes, and that leads to the consequence that the appeal made by product–market combinations to the financial resources is always changing. After all, a product that is intended to grow costs a lot of money. If the company wants to maintain a constant market share in a growing market, that also requires investments. However, a product with a large market share typically makes a lot of profit, and products in stable markets require fewer investments. Having a balanced 'portfolio' of products may therefore mean that a company has products in various phases in the product life cycle; for example, a product in the introductory phase, several products in the growth phase, several in more mature markets, and several in a declining phase.

The method a company may use to achieve a balanced portfolio is to define goals for the market positions of the product–market combinations and subsequently attempt to achieve those goals by investing more or less in the various products. Portfolio methods are a tool for making a choice regarding the investments in various products. With portfolio methods, the positions of product–market combinations are represented visually in a figure or matrix in which the two axes represent approaches to the following factors:

1. *Attractiveness of the market.* The hypothesis in this case is that more should be invested in attractive (e.g. growing) markets than in unattractive markets. A reason for this is that without extra investments, the market share will decline in a growing market, partly due to the fact that the competition is typically stronger. The attractiveness of a market therefore indicates the extent to which cash is *required*.
2. *The market position of the products.* Products with a strong market position have a number of advantages in relation to smaller competitors. These advantages, such as economies of scale, cost advantages through experience effects (the so-called experience curve), better access to distribution channels, and higher awareness, lead to higher profitability. The market position therefore indicates the extent to which cash is made *available.*

Alternative investment strategies may be formulated on the basis of the visual overview of the positions of the various product–market combinations.

Portfolio methods can also be used to analyse the position of competitors and attempt to predict their future behaviour on the basis of that analysis. This is especially possible if the company knows that the competitors use portfolio methods. Portfolio methods are therefore also a tool for competitor analysis.

The *level within the company* at which a portfolio analysis is conducted involves two choices:

1. *Portfolio analysis at the company level.* This involves the assessment of the positions and the allocation of financial resources over strategic business units (SBUs): the choice of the company strategy (and SBU objectives). In the literature and in practice, the most attention is paid to this 'regular' application.
2. *Portfolio analysis at the SBU level.* This involves the assessment of the positions and the allocation of financial resources over brands and products: the choice of the SBU strategy (and marketing objectives). For this application, some adjustments to the tool are necessary.

First, we will review the regular portfolio methods. In section 10.2.5 we will pay attention to the latter category.

The two dimensions of 'market attractiveness' and 'market position of the products' demonstrate that in a portfolio analysis, results from the external analysis and the internal analysis are linked. For this reason, the portfolio analysis is a logical sequel to a SWOT analysis. However, the relationship between the portfolio analysis and the SWOT analysis differs with the level at which the portfolio analysis is performed. In Figure 10.1 the relationship between the SWOT analysis and the portfolio analysis is depicted at the *company level*.

Because a SWOT analysis is defined for a single market, a number of SWOT analyses for the same number of SBUs represent the input for the portfolio analysis. The attractiveness of the markets is the result of the industry analysis, whereas the market position of the SBUs (the collective position of the brands on a market) was examined in the internal analysis. *Countries* may be interpreted as segments or market segments. Thus, if a company is faced with an international investment problem within a market, a portfolio analysis may be very helpful.

Over time, various portfolio methods have been developed. We will review the following methods:

1. The portfolio matrix developed by the Boston Consulting Group (the BCG matrix; subsection 10.2.2). This is the first and most simple portfolio method, but because of its simplicity it has the most limitations.
2. The 'business screen' developed by General Electric (subsection 10.2.3).

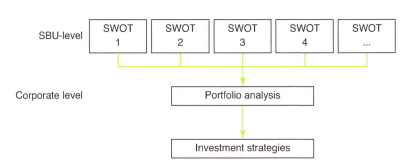

Figure 10.1 **Relationship between SWOT analysis and portfolio analysis**

Two other well-known portfolio methods are:

- The directional policy matrix developed by Shell. This method is no different in essential points from the portfolio model developed by General Electric and therefore will not be discussed here (see Kerin et al., 1990).
- The life cycle portfolio developed by Arthur D. Little. This matrix is based on the assumption that markets (like products) have a life cycle; the dimension of market attractiveness is treated as a phase in the life cycle: embryonic, growth, saturation, decline. The position of the competition is determined qualitatively as dominant, strong, positive, fair, or weak (see Patel and Younger, 1978).

10.2.2 The BCG matrix

This section reviews the portfolio matrix developed by the Boston Consulting Group. We will discuss the contents of the BCG matrix, the resulting recommendations, and some critics.

Content of the matrix

Figure 10.2 shows an example of a BCG 'growth share' matrix. The following two variables are placed along the axes:

1. Market growth.
2. Relative market share.

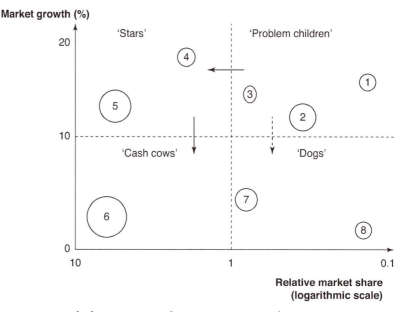

Figure 10.2 Growth share matrix and strategic recommendations

Market growth

The vertical axis represents *market growth.* This axis is divided into two sections: more and less than 10 per cent growth per year. The variable market growth therefore represents the attractiveness of the market. The choice of this variable derives, among other things, from the central role of market growth in the concept of the *product life cycle* (see section 6.4.2). Another advantage of using this variable is the fact that market growth is easy to measure.

Relative market share

The horizontal axis represents *relative market share:* the company's market share divided by the market share of its biggest competitor. The limiting value is at 1. A value greater than 1 implies that a company has the largest market share and therefore is the market leader. The highest value is typically defined on the left, and the lowest on the right. The fact that market share and profitability are positively linked is due partly to the existence in some industries of the so-called *experience curve* (learning curve). This concept states that the more a company has experience in producing a product, the more the costs per unit of that product will decrease over time as a result of various learning effects. The relationship between market share and profit may not only be argued 'theoretically' but has also been demonstrated through empirical research. The best-known studies in this area have been conducted with the Profit Impact of Market Strategy (PIMS) database, a file with financial data from a few thousand companies. One of the most remarkable results from the PIMS studies is the clear relationship between market share and return on investment (ROI).

In the BCG matrix, the SBUs are categorized by circles. It is customary to make the diameter of those circles proportional to the contribution of an SBU to the sales of the company.

Four types of products can be distinguished, depending on the placement of a product–market combination in one of the four quadrants:

1. *Stars.* These are products with a high market share in a strongly growing market. The cash resources used for and the cash resources required by these products are both high and therefore in principle in balance. If market growth decreases, the stars may turn into cash cows.
2. *Cash cows.* These are products with a high market share in a market that is not growing very much. As a result of the strong market position, they produce many cash resources, and they require few investments because of the limited market growth.
3. *Problem children.* These products (also called 'question marks' or 'wild cats') have a small market share in a rapidly growing market. As the name indicates, they can create problems: they produce little but require a lot of cash resources. If they are able to strengthen their position they can become stars, and, over time, when market growth decreases, cash cows.
4. *Dogs.* These are products with a low market share in a market that is growing very little. Therefore, they produce little but also require few investments. As with the

stars, for these products the financial balance is even. Because many markets are saturated and by definition only one brand can be the market leader, in practice most brands may be designated as dogs.

In Figure 10.2 the most important SBUs are numbers 5 (a star) and 6 (a cash cow). In addition, the company has a medium-sized star and several small problem children and dogs.

Strategic recommendations

Based on the previous material, several general investment strategies may be recommended. The following investment strategies are possible:

- Growth (build).
- Maintain position (hold).
- Harvest or milk (harvest).
- Liquidation (terminate).

The strong positions of the stars and the cash cows should be maintained. With the cash cows, part of the revenues may be used to strengthen the positions of problem children that have the potential to become stars. Therefore, for some problem children the company will use a growth strategy financed by cash cows. No investments are made for the other problem children, and so it is a case of harvesting or liquidation. Of course, a problem in this regard is selecting the problem children for which the company perceives growth possibilities. The choice depends in large part on which phase of the product life cycle a product inhabits: Is it in the introductory phase, the growth phase, or the maturity phase? A thorough industry analysis is important here.

In principle, the recommendation for the dogs is to milk them and remove them from the market. However, if dogs have a reasonable size, they may be an important part of a company's activities. In that case, a maintenance strategy appears to be possible.

In the example, the sizeable cash cow may be used to finance both stars and perhaps a problem child. The portfolio of this company appears to be relatively balanced.

Criticism

We will discuss the criticisms of portfolio methods in general in section 10.2.6. Here we consider several specific disadvantages of the BCG matrix. As was stated, an advantage of the BCG matrix is its great simplicity. However, that also causes disadvantages. The most important limitation that applies specifically to the BCG matrix is that for both dimensions only one variable is chosen: *relative market share* or *market growth.* Although these variables are very important for the determination of market position and market attractiveness, they form only a single underlying factor in this regard. Other underlying factors should also be considered.

To respond to this criticism, portfolio methods have been developed that take more factors into account (see the following section).

10.2.3 MABA analysis

An example of a *MABA analysis* (market attractiveness and business position assessment) is the 'business screen' developed by General Electric (Figure 10.3).

Instead of market growth, the vertical axis shows the *attractiveness of the market*. This variable is determined by a number of underlying industry factors, such as market size, market growth, profitability, the intensity of the competition, and the power of distributors. The attractiveness may be determined by assigning scores to each of the underlying industry factors, weighing each of those factors on the basis of the importance management attaches to it, and calculating a total score. We provided an illustration of the manner in which this may be accomplished in the discussion of the industry analysis in section 6.6. After all, the goal of the industry analysis is to determine the attractiveness of the market. The result of the industry analysis (an attractiveness score) may therefore be used directly as the 'input' for the 'business screen'. See also Case 10.1.

Instead of the relative market share, the horizontal axis shows the *competitive position/competitive power* of the product–market combination (relative strength). This variable is also determined from scores on a number of underlying factors. An example of such a calculation appears in Figure 10.4.

	Competitive position		
Market attractiveness	Strong (score > 3.33)	Average (1.67 < score < 3.33)	Weak (score < 1.67)
High (score > 3.33)	1 Invest/grow	1 Invest/grow	2 Selective investing
Average (1.67 < score < 3.33)	1 Invest/grow	2 Selective investing	3 Harvest/terminate
Low (score < 1.67)	2 Selective investing	3 Harvest/terminate	3 Harvest/terminate

Figure 10.3 **The 'business screen' used by General Electric**

Competitive position criteria	Weight	Value (1 = low; 5 = high)	Score
Market share	0.10	4	0.40
Price competition power	0.05	2	0.10
Growth rate of product–market combination	0.20	3	0.60
Experience curve effects	0.10	4	0.40
Added value	0.20	5	1.00
Production equipment	0.10	2	0.20
Quality of the product	0.10	1	0.10
Communication	0.05	4	0.20
Research and development	0.05	5	0.25
Labour productivity	0.05	4	0.20
Total	1.00		3.45

Figure 10.4 **Determination of the competitive power of a product–market combination**

Case 10.1 Market attractiveness

The most attractive markets: understanding China's market potential

With the ever-increasing complexity underlying trade openness, regulatory, and tax systems, among other factors globally, identifying the best target markets for a specific company remains part science, part art. Market attractiveness assessments cover demand, value chain, competition, innovation, regulatory environment, barriers to entry, risks, and security issues, among other critical measures. Companies also rely on composite metrics to compare markets across several dimensions simultaneously during the early stage of analysis preceding detailed analyses. One such metric is the Market Potential Index (MPI) published by Michigan State University.

- The MPI is a composite indicator assessing a country's market potential across eight dimensions: market size, intensity, growth rate, consumption capacity, receptivity, commercial infrastructure, economic freedom, and country risk. Each dimension is based on several indicators. For example, market size is based on the size of the urban population and the volume of electricity consumption whereas GNI per capita and private consumption serve as proxies for market intensity.
- According to the MPI, in 2017, China was the most attractive market in the world for the fourth consecutive year. Hong Kong, India, Canada, and Japan also made the top 5.
- Many countries in the top of the ranking are developed European countries. Brazil has steadily fallen in the ranking according to market attractiveness, dropping from 11th in 2010 to 35th in 2017.

Source: www.knoema.com, revealed 31 May 2018

Based on the scores for the factors market attractiveness and competitive power, the various product–market combinations are placed into the matrix. The axes are divided into three sections in this matrix. Therefore, there are nine possible cells (Figure 10.2). If we use the example of the market for candy bars from section 6.6 and declare the position determination from Figure 10.3 to be applicable to that market, the attractiveness score is 'average' (2.95; see Figure 6.6) and the position score is 'strong' (3.45; see Figure 10.3). This means that this SBU belongs in one of the cells labelled 'invest/grow' in the business screen. In depicting the SBUs in Figure 10.2, the sales of the SBU may be shown through the size of the circle that designates the SBU, as in the BCG matrix.

10.2.4 Trajectory analysis

Earlier in this chapter it was shown how the *current* set of SBUs (or products within an SBU) can be outlined with a portfolio analysis. A disadvantage of such an analysis is that it does not take into account any possible new activities. After all, for a new activity the market share is by definition zero at the starting point, and this means that it cannot be included in a portfolio analysis. To be able to consider potential new activities for a company (diversification) in a portfolio analysis, a *trajectory analysis* should be performed (Kerin et al., 1990, pp. 53ff.). This includes taking the following three steps:

1. First, the *current position of the SBUs* is analysed with a portfolio analysis. The most important question in this regard is whether the current portfolio of SBUs is balanced. In this context, questions such as the following should be answered: Are there not too many SBUs that require investments? Are there enough SBUs with positive growth perspectives?
2. Subsequently, a *prediction* should be made of the portfolio positions in the case of *unchanged policy.* This should take into account, for example, the expected growth of the various markets: even without taking action, the portfolio position of an SBU may change if the attractiveness of the market changes. Possible actions by competitors should also be considered because they may erode the market position of the SBU. In this regard 'success trajectories' and 'disaster trajectories' may be detected. In terms of the BCG matrix, a success trajectory means that a problem child turns into a star through market share growth, and if the market becomes saturated, it subsequently turns into a cash cow. A disaster trajectory is the reverse and occurs if a cash cow turns into a dog through a declining market share.

    Next, the results expected with unchanged policy are compared with the objectives (*divergence analysis* or gap analysis). If there is no difference, the current strategy does not require change, but if there is a difference, as is usually the case, the next planning step is taken.
3. The company determines the *desired portfolio.* For existing SBUs, the question is whether the expected positions are acceptable. For some SBUs (which top management considers promising), growth will be desired. For some SBUs in saturated markets with moderate market positions, disposal will be the best strategy. *New activities* may also be included in the desired portfolio. For example, if the expectation is that the existing markets will demonstrate little growth, perhaps new markets should be searched for to maintain a balanced portfolio.

The designation of the desired portfolio determines the development directions of the SBUs (or products), and in this process the corporate strategy is fleshed out.

10.2.5 Portfolio methods for brands

Portfolio methods seem to be useful only for companies that are active in *different markets and/or segments.* If a company is active only in a single market (segment), the same market growth/market attractiveness applies to every product. The positions of the products in that case are all on one line, and the market dimension is therefore no longer relevant. McDonald (1990) provides an adequate resolution for this problem. He recommends considering the various products as being markets and/or segments. The rationale behind this approach is that each brand and/or product has more or less its own target audience and therefore may be considered a separate 'market'. With this assumption (in the BCG application), the expected sales growth of the product may be placed on the first axis and the relative market share on the other axis. Figure 10.5 shows an example. In this figure, brand 2 is a small brand that has good possibilities to grow and become a star. Brand 4 appears to be an established brand with little chance to grow, and brand 1 appears to be in the final phase of the product life cycle.

Finally, we make another comment on the use of two dimensions. Both dimensions have to do with the attractiveness of a market for a brand. If there are possible new markets, then, as outlined above, a course analysis may be applied, but there is still the restriction that no focus be placed on *entry thresholds*: the thresholds for entry into a

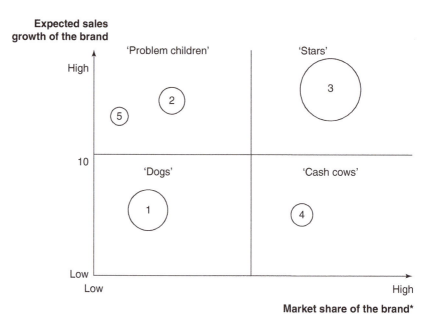

Figure 10.5 Portfolio method for brands with varying sales growth

*The scaling of the axes is in conformance with normal use: from low to high. Thus, it is different from the scaling shown in Figure 10.2.

market. In simple terms, there may be an extremely attractive market out there, but if there is a huge mountain in front of the market, it is still difficult to choose it. Entry thresholds include access to distribution channels, a minimum level of brand familiarity, and a physical location. In this case, a somewhat less attractive market with lower thresholds may be just as attractive.

There are three dimensions of importance in the choice of a development direction for a brand (see also Lehmann and Winer, 2008):

1. *Market attractiveness,* measured on the basis of features such as *expected growth of the market for the brand.* Information on this is gathered from the organizational analysis and the customer analysis.
2. *Position of the brand in the market*, measured as market share or competitiveness (in new markets, the possibilities for attaining and maintaining a defendable competitive edge). These possibilities are estimated on the basis of the competition analysis, the customer analysis, and the internal analysis. The interconnection is produced during the SWOT analysis. This criterion produces a reciprocal relationship with the choice of the marketing strategy.
3. *For new markets, the entry barriers: all means for penetration of the market or segment.* Insight into the entry barriers is gathered from the organizational analysis. Insight into possible means of penetration is obtained from the internal analysis.

The first two dimensions are part of a portfolio analysis. When new markets are being considered, the recommendations from a portfolio analysis must be offset against the resources needed to overcome the entry barriers (figure 10.6).

10.2.6 Pros and cons of portfolio methods

Applying portfolio methods presents some analytical and strategic problems but also offers advantages.

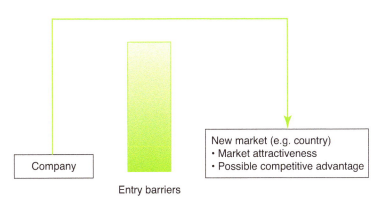

Figure 10.6 **Entry barriers and market attractiveness**

Analytic problems

Wind et al. (1983) have done empirical research on the extent to which different portfolio methods lead to different recommendations. They conclude that the classification of product–market combinations in portfolio positions as 'low share and low growth (dog)' or 'high share and high growth (star)' depends on four factors:

1. The definition of the dimensions.
2. The rule used to divide a dimension into high versus low.
3. The weight of the underlying factors if a multiple-factor method is used.
4. The specific portfolio model.

This means, among other things, that if the chosen limit values of a dimension are changed or if different weights are chosen for the underlying factors, another classification of product–market combinations is obtained and, with it, different recommended strategies. Based on this, Wind et al. recommend:

- Using several portfolio methods rather than just one.
- Examining how sensitive the classifications of the product–market combinations are for the choice of the definitions, the limit values, the weights, and the portfolio model to be able to judge the reliability of the recommendations. Subsequently, the company should make the choices that are the most appropriate for its own situation.

Aside from these factors, the results of portfolio methods depend strongly on the *market definition.* If the market definition is changed, the positions of the product–market combinations are altered. Suppose, for example, the market for toys is growing 5 per cent each year and a certain brand of computer games has a share of 7 per cent in this market. This brand may be classified as a dog. However, if the relevant manufacturer redefined the market as the market for computer games, the situation might turn out to include market growth of 15 per cent and a share of 30 per cent. In that case, the brand would be a star. Because of the direct relationship with the market definition, the results of a portfolio analysis are quite arbitrary in nature.

Strategic problems

Schnaars (1997) has articulated fundamental criticisms of the strategic implications of portfolio methods and especially of the BCG matrix. His criticisms come down to the fact that the recommended strategies are not always truly desirable. For example, a low market share does not by definition have to lead to low profitability, particularly for companies that focus on a segment in the market (focus strategy). Markets with low growth may be interesting. In that case, companies do not milk their products or battle for market share but focus all their attention on improving quality and lowering costs.

Advantages and applications in practice

In terms of the *way in which* portfolio methods are used, the benefit of the models is not limited to decisions about investment strategies. In fact, in light of the analytic and strategic problems of portfolio methods outlined above, it appears undesirable to base investment decisions only on a portfolio analysis. However, portfolio methods have two additional important advantages:

1. Portfolio analyses improve the quality of strategic thinking at the SBU level.
2. At the 'corporate level', portfolio analyses lead to a better understanding of the various SBUs and the product–market combinations (Hamermesh, 1986).

Therefore, portfolio methods are suitable for use as one of the diagnostic tools employed by a company and are also a very effective tool for internal *communication* within a company.

10.3 Corporate strategy: where to compete

10.3.1 Components of the corporate strategy

Chapter 1 indicated that at every level two decisions have to be made: where to compete (markets) and how to compete (competitive advantage). At the corporate level we add a third item: with whom to compete. Thus, at the corporate level the following choices are made:

1. *Where to compete.* Choice of scope of activities: SBUs and investments per SBU.
2. *How to compete.* Choice of value strategy.
3. *With whom to compete.* Alone or in collaboration.

In this section we discuss the first component. Value strategies were discussed in Chapter 2. In section 10.4 the third component will be reviewed.

10.3.2 Portfolio of SBUs

The core of the corporate strategy is the question of where and to what extent the company wants to compete. In other words, in which markets does the company want to be active and to what extent? In effect, the issue here is the composition of the portfolio of SBUs ('markets') of the company and the importance of each of the SBUs. The method that may be useful in this task is the portfolio analysis (discussed in section 10.2). The advice given there is to use a portfolio analysis in combination with a path analysis in three steps:

1. Determination of the current portfolio.
2. Forecasting and evaluation of the portfolio if policy remains unchanged.
3. Determination of the desired portfolio.

In the last step, ideas about new activities should be considered explicitly. This cannot occur without creativity, brainstorming, and deliberations with lower management. Ideas

Case 10.2 Corporate strategy: acquisitions

Unilever extends its skincare brands with Dermalogica acquisition

Described as a "superior skin health brand" by Unilever's CEO Paul Polman, the acquisition follows the FMCG giant's move to acquire British skincare brand Ren Skincare back in March.

Dermalogica – which generated total sales of $240m in 2014 and is currently sold in over 80 markets – will be incorporated within Unilever's prestige brand division. Designed to address skin problems such as acne and sensitive skin, the brand's products are a mix of professional and in-home. However its focus is more on skin health than beauty and pampering. "Dermalogica enjoys an outstanding reputation and incredible awareness among skin care professionals and consumers alike that complements our Prestige offering," said Polman. "It is a company with great distribution and presence globally and shares our belief in the role of business as a force for good in society."

Source: *Marketing Week*, 25 June 2015

about new activities in practice often originate from within the SBUs. In the discussion regarding the SWOT analysis (Chapter 9), we discussed the analysis of new activities at the SBU level.

The process of generating ideas for new activities in effect corresponds to the first phases of what is often referred to in the literature as the process of new product development. Empirical research on the success of new products has shown that often many dozens of ideas are required for just one of them to succeed. The chance of success of a new activity is larger if the new activity is attracted from the outside (for example, through acquisition; see also section 10.4 and Case 10.2) than it is if the company decides to develop it from within.

Finally, if a company is considering entering new markets, it is probably necessary to perform a situation analysis for those markets. Thus, there is a feedback loop to the situation analysis. Only if the attractiveness of the relevant market outweighs the investments required to enter that market does a decision to enter the market make sense.

With the definition of the desired portfolio of SBUs, the *development directions* are determined. The following development directions are possible:

1. Dismantling.
2. Harvesting.
3. Maintaining position.
4. Growth in existing activities.
5. Growth in (setting up) new activities.

The first four directions apply to existing SBUs, and the last one to new activities.

Among the five growth directions mentioned, the most attention in the literature is paid to growth with existing SBUs (*expansion*) and growth with new activities (*diversification*). Within both development directions, a total of eight specific growth directions may be chosen (Figure 10.7). These growth directions are based on the well-known matrix by Ansoff (1957) (Figure 10.8).

Growth direction	Customer groups	Product*	Example of rusk manufacturer**
Growth with existing SBUs: expansion			
1. Market penetration	Same	Same	■ Increase brand loyalty at expense of competitor (quality improvement, promotional action) ■ Stimulate usage by current users (e.g. increase communication) ■ Other segments (youth)
2. Market development	New	Same	■ Other markets (business: cafeterias) ■ Geographic (exporting)
3. Product development	Same	Modification	■ Modification: wholemeal rusks
4. Horizontal diversification	Same	New related or unrelated	■ Related (expansion): rice waffles, knäckebröd (Swedish crackers) ■ Unrelated: rusk tins
Growth with new activities: diversification			
5. Market widening	New	Modification	■ Small rusks as 'toast'
6. Vertical diversification	Company becomes customer or supplier	New	■ Backward: take over supplier ■ Forward: take over store chain
7. Concentric diversification	New	New related	■ Production of cookies
8. Conglomerate diversification	New	New unrelated	■ Production of candy, laundry detergent

*Relatedness may be in marketing and/or technology.

**Starting point: market definition is rusk manufacturer (product) for final customers and especially women (customers) for use at home (function).

Figure 10.7 Growth opportunities for a company

	Current products	New products
Current customer groups	Market penetration (1)	Product development (3–4)
New customer groups	Market development (2)	Diversification (5–8)

Figure 10.8 **Growth directions in the matrix by Ansoff (1957)**

Source: Ansoff (1957).

Expansion

There are four types of growth direction by which a company can grow with its existing SBUs:

1. The first and most obvious way to grow is *market penetration*: increasing sales with the current products in the current markets. In a growing market, a sales increase may be obtained by maintaining market share. In stable markets, a sales increase can be achieved only if market share grows. Market penetration is usually achieved through the use of the marketing mix.
2. If market saturation occurs, management will research other growth opportunities, such as *market development*: growth by finding new customers for the current products. A well-known form of market development is geographic expansion of the market; for example, through exportation. See also Case 10.3.
3. *Product development* may also be considered: new modified products in addition to or instead of the current products for the current customers.
4. A more extreme form of product development is *horizontal diversification*: new products for the existing customers (e.g. a tea manufacturer who starts producing coffee). In this case there is some synergy (both in technology and in marketing), but there is a limited spreading of risk. Another example of this form of product development is a food retailer that is also going to sell computers or mobile phones.

Diversification

When a company expects that it will not be able to achieve its objectives through expansion, it may consider diversification: an exploration of new roads and areas. Four forms may be distinguished. The choice of one of these forms is determined mostly by the degree of synergy and the extent to which a company remains dependent on a limited number of activities (risk). The four forms of diversification are as follows:

1. The least extreme form of diversification is *market widening*: reaching new customer groups with modified products. This growth direction is the opposite of horizontal diversification: The 'newness' is limited to such an extent that in practice this direction is often not described as diversification but as a type of expansion.
2. *Vertical diversification* (or vertical integration) means that a company takes over links that are higher (backward) or lower (forward) in the supply chain. The biggest advantage is an increase in market power: a company is less dependent on suppliers and/or customers.

Case 10.3 Market development

Buoyant Ikea gears up for more store expansion in China

Ikea Group plans to open three new stores in China in its new financial year, which has just started, the head of the Swedish furniture and home accessories group in China said on Thursday. Angela Zhu, country retail manager of Ikea Retail China, told China Daily in an interview in Shanghai, that the group would also enhance its distribution networks and e-commerce presence in the mainland.

Ikea's store expansion plans come in the wake of strong results that saw revenue in China, in its full 2017 financial year to August 10, surge 14 per cent to more than 13.2 billion yuan ($1.98 billion). Zhu said the new stores would be located in Guangzhou in Guangdong province, Tianjin municipality and Xuzhou in Jiangsu province. Next year marks the 20th year for the Swedish company in China, where it already operates 24 stores.

Source: *China Daily*, 8 August 2017

3. The last two growth directions have the least synergy but the largest opportunity to spread risk. In *concentric diversification,* the company starts to bring new, related products (related in terms of technology or marketing) into the market for new customers.

4. In *conglomerate diversification* there is no synergy at all: the company brings new products into the market for new customers.

We note the following regarding the choices of growth direction in practice.

1. *Be careful with unrelated activities.* Several empirical studies have been conducted to examine the success of related versus unrelated diversification. For example, Porter (1987) analysed 2,021 acquisitions of 33 strongly diversified companies in

the period 1950 to 1980. More than half the acquisitions had ended by 1986, whereas in fact 74 per cent of the 931 unrelated acquisitions had been ended. These studies indicate that the more foreign the activities are, the smaller the success usually is. The conclusion is therefore that companies should be very careful in starting up entirely new activities and that if diversification is chosen, the presence of synergy in, for example, technology or marketing is definitely preferred.

2. *Perform additional SWOT analyses if diversification is considered.* If a company considers expanding its activities, this may involve another defined field of strategic activities with other market characteristics, other competitors, other customer wishes, and so on. To be active in such a different market and to find a sustainable competitive advantage, the new market should be analysed in detail. This means in effect that an external analysis should be completed for a second time. Only after that can the actual growth direction be chosen and the next steps in the planning process be completed.

3. *The stranger the activities, the higher the decision level in the company.* If we compare the two growth directions – expansion and diversification – it may be argued that the implementation of the direction of *expansion* will take place more on the *SBU level*, whereas in the case of *diversification* the involvement of management at the *corporate level* will typically be larger. For example, top management will not concern itself with the question of whether growth of an existing SBU is achieved through more intensive advertising efforts (market penetration) or by bringing improved products into the market (product development). The elaboration of the direction of expansion will therefore be determined to a great extent by the choice of the marketing strategy. However, setting up completely new activities will require so important a commitment that the decision-making process should involve high levels of the organization. This is also due to the fact that in diversification, collaboration strategies will be more likely to be considered than is the case in expansion (see section 10.4). An exception to this is *export.* Decisions about this geographic form of market development are always made at the corporate level.

The difference in decision levels does not mean that *ideas* for new activities will come primarily from top management. In practice, these ideas come both from within the SBUs and from the top of the company. Still, the innovative power of a company is determined in large part by the extent to which *top management* is open to new ideas. There are companies in which managers from an SBU left the company because of insufficient support for their new ideas and started successfully in business on their own.

10.4 Corporate strategy: with whom to compete

'With whom to compete' refers to the choice of partners. The following subjects are dealt with in this section:

- Internal or external growth (section 10.4.1).
- External development: competition-decreasing strategies (section 10.4.2).
- SWOT analysis and collaboration (section 10.4.3).
- Collaboration in practice (section 10.4.4).

10.4.1 Internal or external growth

If the choice of a growth direction has been made, the next question is whether the company wants to achieve growth through its own development (internal) or through 'others' (external). This decision must be made for both expansion and diversification. In both cases, the choice could be to 'do it ourselves' or to 'do it together with others'. There are three possible *development methods*:

1. Internal development.
2. External development through collaboration. This involves various possibilities, such as joint ventures (joint interest in another company), strategic alliances (long-term collaboration agreement), and licences (approval for others to sell a company's success formula or product).
3. External development through takeovers (acquisitions): the 'purchasing' of new activities.

Internal development is the most risky: There is no certainty about the results. In addition, it takes a long time. However, there is more flexibility: everything is kept under the company's control. With acquisitions, the reverse is true: it can be achieved quickly, it offers a fair degree of certainty regarding the result, but it leads to a decrease in flexibility. In addition, acquisitions usually require a lot of financial resources. With external development through collaboration, the advantages and disadvantages lie between these two extremes.

In choosing the manner in which growth is to be achieved, a company should weigh the advantages and disadvantages. In general, the less a company is familiar with the market and technologies of the new product, the less it should do on its own (Roberts and Berry, 1985). When we translate this into the growth directions shown in Figure 10.6, it may be concluded that the more a company approaches the direction of 'strange' activities in terms of the choice of growth direction (i.e. towards the direction of conglomerate diversification), the more the choice of a development method should lean towards external growth. Except for explicitly named exceptional situations, such as the time factor and the availability of financial resources, expansion should in principle be based on internal growth, whereas concentric and conglomerate diversification should be based on acquisitions. For horizontal and vertical diversification, internal development or external development through collaboration is recommended. Export is also the exception in this regard: this type of expansion can occur quickly and effectively through mergers and acquisitions of companies that are already active on site.

Because of the great importance of competition-decreasing strategies such as collaboration and acquisition, we devote attention to those issues in the following section.

10.4.2 External development: competition-decreasing strategies

In the literature about corporate strategies and marketing strategies, typically most of the attention is paid to strategies to improve the company's position at the expense of the competitors: *position-strengthening strategies* (internal development). The issue here is to claim a position in the market that is stronger than the competitor's position; that is, to 'beat' the competition.

In addition to a position-strengthening strategy, a company may choose a *competition-decreasing* strategy (external development: all forms of collaboration). Examples of such strategies include the following:

- Strategies in which the concentration in markets is increased through mergers, acquisitions, and other forms of collaboration, such as purchasing combinations, franchising, and strategic alliances.
- Market agreements; for example, price agreements, agreements regarding the division of the market, and cartels.

A competition-decreasing strategy may also be a possibility if a position-strengthening strategy is not feasible: "If you can't beat them, join them." It can also be a tool to achieve a desired competitive advantage; for example, a price reduction resulting from important synergistic advantages. The choice of a competition-decreasing strategy typically has far-reaching consequences for the entire company. Therefore, decisions in this area are made at the corporate level.

A company's attention to position-strengthening strategies is also discussed in this book. A central concept in the analyses and analysis methods described in the previous chapters is the attempt to find and maintain a sustainable competitive advantage. This attempt is based on the finding that only companies with such an advantage are able to withstand the competitive forces in the industry in the long term. Without a competitive advantage, a company will achieve relatively low profitability over time. The implicit assumption here is that a company should strengthen its own position at the expense of its competitors: The goal is to be 'better' than the competitors on an ongoing basis. However, there may be circumstances in which it is better to choose some type of collaboration with a competitor. These circumstances may be deduced from the situation analysis described in this book. The results of the analysis should simply be interpreted from a different perspective. Especially in the SWOT analysis, another viewpoint needs to be chosen. We now discuss this issue further.

10.4.3 SWOT analysis and the competition-decreasing strategy

In Chapter 1 and in the material on SWOT analysis in Chapter 9, we indicated that a company should search for a combination of the following:

1. A strength of its own that
2. Is a weakness for the most important competitors and that
3. Is difficult to obtain for the competitors and that
4. Is important to the customers.

This combination implies a sustainable competitive advantage.

A competition-decreasing strategy is appropriate when the first two requirements are reversed (Figure 10.9; cf. Figure 2.3):

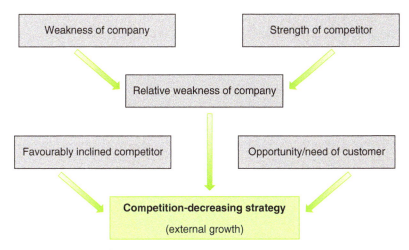

Figure 10.9 **SWOT analysis and competition-decreasing strategy**

1. The company has a weakness that is
2. A strength of one of the competitors and
3. That competitor is favourably inclined and
4. It is a response to an opportunity in the external environment and/or the issue is important to the customer.

In terms of the 'favourable inclination' of the competitor, the same thing applies to the competitor that applies to the company seeking the initiative for collaboration: it is especially interesting if the other party has a strength in an area that is a weakness for the company. This means that a relative weakness of the initiating company should preferably be counterbalanced by another relative strength in relation to the competition. This means that there should be a 'win-win' situation.

This mutual dependency is especially important if there is an equal collaboration (e.g. a merger). If there is an unequal collaboration (e.g. a company that 'adds' another, smaller company to its divisions through an acquisition), the requirement of a mutual advantage is less important.

An example will clarify Figure 10.9 and the relationship of the growth options described therein. Suppose bank institution A has a strong position in the consumer market but a weak position in the industrial market (e.g. granting credit to companies). The company is looking for growth options and chooses market development: development of the industrial market. In principle, there are now two possibilities:

1. Internal growth: attempting to strengthen its position with companies through sales promotion; however, because of the strong position of a number of competitors in the industrial market, this appears to be a risky route that will also take a lot of time.
2. External growth.

The second option can provide bank A with a strong position immediately. To find a merger candidate, the bank analyses the competing banks. This analysis indicates that for bank B, the reverse of the situation of bank A is true: B is strong in the industrial market but relatively weak in the consumer market. Bank B is approached and appears willing to consider merger talks. After some time, a merger is completed and bank BA is created.

10.4.4 Competition-decreasing strategies in practice

In various industries (such as the printing and graphics trade, the banking and insurance industries, the aviation industry and health care), there have been 'merger waves'.

Case 10.4 Mergers and acquisitions

So many M&A deals fail because companies overlook this simple strategy

An analysis of 2,500 such deals shows that more than 60 per cent of them destroy shareholder value. Perhaps such deals should come with an official warning: "Acquisitions can result in serious damage to your corporate health, up to and including death."

As our research has shown us, the core of the problem is not the high number of M&A deals in itself, but rather that too many executives bring insufficient discipline to the evaluation process that fuels these deals – as a result, they often get deals wrong. For instance, despite the importance of accurately identifying and calculating company synergies, diligence work frequently results in an overly optimistic view of the revenue synergy opportunity. Often the weakest assumptions involve estimates of how much additional revenue the companies can generate when combined. This, in turn, leads bidders to overpay.

Ultimately, the key is discipline. By rigorously and relentlessly asking two questions – "How will the deal help our customers to complete their journey?" and "How is the deal using our foundational assets to create value in a different context?" – an edge strategy approach to M&A can mitigate the risks of an inherently risky business.

Source: *Harvard Business Review*, 10 May 2016

An important reason for the expanded use of competition-decreasing strategies is the expected increase in competition resulting from the fact that international markets are becoming increasingly open. Especially if the collaborating companies complement each other's strengths and weaknesses, the collaboration may be a better match for the competition than is either of the companies on its own.

However, there are three dangers of a merger: (see also Case 10.4)

■ First, a merged company is larger and therefore less flexible than a small company; this may make it more difficult to react to actual developments in the environment (e.g. an action by a competitor).
■ Second, if the corporate cultures do not fit together well, there is no balanced fusion. In that case, the merger can lead to large internal problems.
■ Third, collaboration may make it more difficult to brand the new company. In the case of mergers, an important question is which brand name to use. Often a new brand architecture is needed (see Chapter 11).

Summary

When working on a marketing plan, corporate decisions are largely given: others in the company set the corporate boundaries for marketing. In this chapter, after the situation analysis and the SWOT, we want to show what subjects corporate decisions are about.

At the corporate level, the mission and vision are determined first. The main components of these decisions are determining the core business and choosing the value strategy. Based on the vision, the corporate objectives are chosen. This involves setting not only financial goals but also customer-oriented goals, internal goals, and innovation goals (the balanced scorecard discussed in Chapter 3).

Subsequently, it should be determined where (in which markets) the company wants to compete: the portfolio of SBUs and the desired development for each SBU. A portfolio analysis is a tool for decisions about investments in SBUs or product–market combinations. In a portfolio analysis, the various SBUs or product–market combinations are depicted in a two-dimensional space in which one axis represents the expected cash flow (through a representation of the market position) and the other axis represents the extent to which cash flow is required (through a representation of the expected market growth). Various portfolio models exist, of which two were reviewed: the Boston Consulting Group matrix and the business screen. Both methods require quite a few arbitrary assumptions; this means that the investment recommendations are not always as desired. The entry barriers must also be considered for new markets.

A company may grow with its existing SBUs (expansion); the possibilities then are market penetration, market development, product development, and diversification. Growth can also be achieved with new products and services (diversification); this may occur through market widening via vertical diversification, concentric diversification, or conglomerate diversification. The managers of a brand can influence corporate decisions through the internal marketing of a plan (see Chapter 14).

At the corporate level, a decision needs to be made about with whom the competition will occur: alone or in collaboration with others.

Case chocolate of Barry Callebaut

Two-thirds of the world's cocoa is produced in West Africa. Côte d'Ivoire has the biggest share. The market price for cocoa, like other raw materials for the food industry, is subject to strong fluctuations. The price was under $1,000 per tonne in 2000, rose to over $3,000 per tonne at the start of the credit crisis in 2008, and stands about $2,800 at the end of 2016. When the price of cocoa falls, a number of farmers in West Africa may turn to lowering production costs by using child labour or even slave labour. The importance of sustainable, 'fair' cocoa may be clear, but an increasing demand for sustainably sourced and 'fair' products does mean that production prices will rise. The unstable political situation in many countries in West Africa also includes a risk for price developments.

In chocolate, two important types of companies may be distinguished: the chocolate maker and the chocolatier. The chocolate maker processes cacao beans into basic chocolate. The production of basic chocolate is dominated by two chocolate makers: Barry Callebaut and Cargill. A large part of the chocolate in our world is supplied by one of these two chocolate makers.

Chocolatiers use this basic chocolate to make products (in the form of bars, bonbons, etc.). These are partly large companies, such as Cadbury or Nestlé, and partly small specialized businesses such as certain bonbon makers.

The supply chain is shown in Figure 10.10.

The total chocolate confection market (the sales of all chocolatiers together) is estimated at about $100 billion. The market growth per year is approximately 3 per cent. On the one hand, there are large chocolatiers in this market, with their global brands. Well-known brands are, for example:

- Kraft – Milka
- Nestlé – Nestlé, Kitkat
- Cadbury – Cadbury

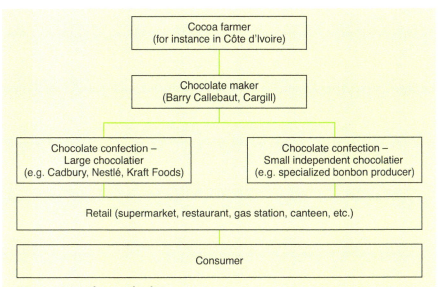

Figure 10.10 **The supply chain**

Competition among these companies is intense. Due to the high marketing costs, new brands are rarely introduced. But the importance of private labels of the most important supermarket chains is growing. In addition to these large companies, however, there are also many small, specialized producers, particularly in the luxury segment: production of chocolates and the like.

Many chocolate products are seasonal products. This is mainly due to holidays such as Easter and Christmas. Hot summers have a slightly negative effect on the sales of chocolate.

Chocolate is partly an impulse product. It is sold through various channels, such as supermarkets, gas stations, canteens, etc. In many markets, large retailers account for less than 50 per cent of sales. There is a tendency towards concentration in the retail, but the large variety of channels makes the pressure of the retail sector less strong than in many other markets.

Nowadays the choice for consumers 'on the go' is enormous. This also applies to 'premium indulgence': we can choose from a large amount of luxury snacks.

Market developments and trends

The chocolate market in Western Europe is mature. However, an important growth segment within the market is formed by the premium products. Consumers are also becoming increasingly aware of the effects that chocolate can have on health. This has led to an increase in the sales of organic and dark chocolate with a high content of cocoa. Preferences have shifted to dark, high-quality chocolate: people are looking for a more intense taste experience, and at the same time people are becoming increasingly aware of the positive influence of the cacao bean on health. In addition, the value-for-money segment is also growing. Increasing lack of time leads to more consumption 'on the go'. Chocolate has become a popular snack.

A large growth in chocolate sales may be found in the so-called 'emerging markets'. The increasing relevance of the middle class in Eastern Europe and Russia, but also, for example in China, is responsible for the increasing sales.

The chocolate sector is sensitive to price increases in the raw materials market, in particular of course the price development of cocoa. In addition, the following trends may be distinguished:

- increasing price awareness of the consumer;
- growing pressure on margins due to concentration in retail;
- increasing importance of discount retailers in Europe;
- increasing importance of private labels, and the resulting pressure on the margins;
- changing consumer preferences: 'diet and health' trend, wellness;
- increased government legislation: food safety, regulations concerning genetically modified products, etc. This could lead to increasing costs.

In the premium segment, the following trends can also be mentioned:

- *Health: the growing need for healthy chocolate*
  Dark chocolate contains more cocoa, and therefore more anti-oxidants. But producers do not rely on only cocoa for the health effects, so healthy ingredients such as acai or pomegranate were added to chocolate.
- *Premium chocolate ('gourmet trend')*
  In recent years, the market has been flooded with innovations in the luxury segment. A popular gourmet trend is 'single-origin chocolate': premium brand chocolate that comes from just one source, such as Venezuela, Ecuador, or Vietnam.
  Many large producers have called in the help of expert truffle makers. For example, Nestlé has partnered with the Belgian specialist Pierre Marcolini. Nestlé also invests in its Black Magic products: a luxury indulgence.
- *Ethical chocolate*
  Sustainability is also an important trend. Most chocolate makers have promised to buy only 'honestly produced' cocoa.

Chocolate in Asia

Markets such as China and India, where the economy has grown considerably in recent years, have a rapidly growing middle class. This has led to a significant increase in the total consumption of chocolate. In these markets the middle class increasingly discovers the Western lifestyle and associated eating patterns. Other markets, such as Japan, are more mature, but show a clear trend towards premium chocolate. The consumption of chocolate in Asia varies greatly, depending on prosperity, climate, and culture. But even in Singapore and Malaysia, where the bitter-sweet product is well established, per capita sales are far below the European level. Chocolate consumption in China and India is still low.

Sweet snacks such as chocolate are traditionally unknown in China. But consumption is increasing. *"You used to see people in a Chinese office eat dried fruit, dried fish or dried meat,"* says the Asia director for Barry Callebaut. *"Now you see more and more yoghurt, cookies, and chocolate."* The Chinese chocolate market is therefore growing fast: a growth of more than 60 per cent is expected from 2015 to 2020. The market is dominated by Western multinationals (Mars, Nestlé, Ferrero): Chinese people have much more confidence in Western producers than in Chinese chocolate suppliers.

In India the market is growing very fast: in the year 2014, for example, the market grew by around 25 per cent. With these growth figures, however, we must not forget that chocolate consumption per head of the population in these countries is only a few 100 grams, compared with 8 to 10 kilos per person in countries such as Switzerland and Germany. So there is still a great potential. The consumption of chocolate is lower in India than in China: The Chinese market is almost three times as large as the Indian market. In India, however, people are more used to a sweet taste. The market is growing mainly in the big cities; however, there is also great potential in rural areas. After all, people are used to a sweet taste. As in China, Western companies are also dominant in India; the market leader in India is the British Cadbury. However, local brands are gaining popularity in India. Important for Barry Callebaut is that the tendency towards higher quality (dark) chocolate is already visible in China and India.

And what do people in India say about dark chocolate? Malini Suryananayan, a Bangalore-based baker, says:

> I prefer dark chocolate over mithai [traditional Indian sweets]. People here are still worried that chocolate contains eggs or other forms of animal fat. Indeed cheaper chocolate varieties use animal products as emulsifiers. It has been proven that eating dark chocolate releases endorphins into the human brain, and that puts people in a good mood. But dark chocolate works poorly in India simply because we do not accept bitterness as taste experience.

Other observations in the Asian market:

- Chocolate is primarily seen as a Western taste.
- India is a country where the mentality and preferences are as diverse as the country itself; China mainly has a big difference between city and countryside.
- Especially in the higher middle class in China, chocolate is seen as a gift item.

- Chocolate is considered a surrogate of parental love for their children: "The perfect expression of parental love." Chocolate is mainly regarded as a surprise for the kids.
- Chocolate is seen as a luxury indulgence, and not good for health.
- The Cadbury and Nestlé brands are well-established brands among Indian middle-class consumers.

Barry Callebaut

The almost 200-year-old French-Belgian-Swiss company Barry Callebaut AG is the largest chocolate maker in the world. One in four chocolates eaten in this world was produced by Barry Callebaut. The company has more than 50 production facilities. Some 9,000 people are employed; half of them work in the so-called 'emerging markets'. Annual sales in 2016 amounted to some 6 billion Swiss francs, an increase of 5 per cent compared to the previous year.

The vision of Barry Callebaut: "*Heart and engine of the chocolate and cocoa industry.*" The company is the only fully integrated chocolate producer in the world, with a product range varying from 'raw' cocoa to high-quality chocolate bonbons. Barry Callebaut focuses on two market segments:

- Multinationals and other major chocolate brands that use semi-finished and 'raw' chocolate as ingredients for their consumer brands.
- Artisanal and professional users of chocolate, including chocolatiers, bakers, as well as restaurants, hotels, and caterers.

The business model of the company is ambitious, according to the 2015 annual report:

> We are the world's leading manufacturer of chocolate and cocoa products, by mastering every step in the value chain from the sourcing of raw materials to the production of the finest chocolates. We are able to provide our customers with added value products and services adapted to specific market needs, ahead of trends and at a competitive price. We serve the entire food industry – from global and local food manufacturers to artisanal and professional users of chocolate, such as chocolatiers, pastry chefs, bakers, hotels, restaurants or caterers. We are committed to a growth significantly outperforming the global chocolate market.

The strategic ambition of the company is described in the annual report of 2015 as: "*Our continued above-market growth is the result of the consistent implementation of our long-term strategy based on four pillars:*

- *Expansion,*
- *Innovation,*

- *Cost Leadership,*
- *Sustainable cocoa."*

Under the header *expansion*, the company mentions three major growth directions:

- Emerging markets. In addition to the saturated markets in Europe and North America, the company wants to take advantage of the growth opportunities in countries such as China and India.
- Outsourcing and partnerships. The possibilities of outsourcing are described in Barry Callebaut's annual report as: "*Increasing competitive pressure in confectionery opens up interesting doors for our brands, which are now offering ready-to-use concepts and solutions in addition to the chocolate ingredient itself.*" In other words, Callebaut not only supplies the basic chocolate, but partly takes over the work of the chocolatier by making chocolate products. Shifting part of the chocolatier's work to the chocolate maker is of course in favour of Barry Callebaut. Barry Callebaut itself has a cost advantage by being able to realize economies of scale.
- Gourmet and specialties. With this, the company tries to respond to the aforementioned gourmet trend.

Innovation. Barry Callebaut has played a pioneering role in the trends in the chocolate industry. The company has successfully launched an impressive range of innovative products that meet the demand for better and healthier taste experiences. The company works closely with customers to develop tailor-made products that meet specific customer needs. This takes place in, among other things, so-called chocolate academies, innovation centres where, together with clients, they try to translate Barry Callebaut's expertise into new chocolate products.

Cost leadership is especially important when it comes to outsourcing. By optimizing production flows, economies of scale, and tight cost management, Barry Callebaut tries to become the favourite choice of its customers with respect to outsourcing the processing of basic chocolate to end product.

Sustainability is an important issue in the industry. Barry Callebaut believes that it is crucial to pay the cocoa farmer a fair price and encourage the cocoa to be harvested in a responsible manner, with attention for the environment and for the welfare of the workers. To achieve this, the company takes part in all kinds of programmes in this area, and Barry Callebaut tries to maintain direct contact with the cocoa farmer himself.

The former CEO, Patrick de Maeseneire, summarizes the strategy of Barry Callebaut in the following way:

> The successful interplay of these strategic focal points has convinced multinational confectionery makers to choose Barry Callebaut as their preferred partner. Our wide product range and strong innovation platform are among

our greatest competitive advantages. In addition, our global geographic reach allows us to better serve our customers. However, innovation and geographic expansion are only possible if we succeed in maintaining cost leadership in the long term. To achieve this, we are constantly optimizing our cost structure at every step of the value chain, while refining our production processes and technologies and improving our use of energy. This strategy has served us well so far, and we expect to continue to reap the fruits of our investments.

Interview with Andreas Jakobs, Chairman of the Board of Barry Callebaut, and Mr Jürgen Steinemann, CEO of Barry Callebaut, 2011.

How did Barry Callebaut perform in fiscal year 2010/2011?
Andreas Jacobs, Chairman (AJ) We saw another year where we delivered on our targets. With our top-line volume increase in all regions and with all our product groups, we grew more than twice as fast as the global chocolate market. Thanks to the higher operating result in combination with lower income taxes, also our net profit shows a result we can be proud of.

Juergen Steinemann, CEO (JBS) The positive result is all the more impressive given the recent crisis situation in Côte d'Ivoire when, due to political conflicts following the presidential elections, cocoa and semi-finished products couldn't leave the country for four months. We are extremely proud of how our local colleagues handled the crisis. With the tireless efforts of our Global Sourcing and Cocoa team and thanks to our worldwide network, we were able to honour all customer contracts.

How did your product groups develop?
JBS Our Food Manufacturers Products business showed good growth, including specifically good results in specialty products and fillings. Some of our emerging markets in various regions performed at double-digit growth rates. The gourmet and specialties products business achieved strong growth in all segments throughout the year, especially in Asia-Pacific and Europe. Our global gourmet brands Cacao Barry and Callebaut as well as the various local brands contributed to the overall volume growth. The global sourcing and cocoa products business reported double-digit growth driven by the strong demand for cocoa powder and the sales of cocoa products to strategic customers.

While the demand for high-quality, responsibly grown cocoa seems to increase steadily, the supply side appears to become insufficient mid-term – how do you react to that?
AJ Our answer to this dilemma is our new, fourth strategic pillar Sustainable Cocoa, which stands for more volumes and better quality, aiming to secure our future growth ambitions. With this, we will also scale up our certified volumes.

JBS In order to get this done, we have launched a dedicated initiative that mainly consists of three action areas: improving farmer practices with so-called yield enhancement services, farmer education through the setup and implementation of an education curriculum for secondary schools and farmer health. All this is aiming to improve the livelihood of farmer communities with which we work directly. We will establish several farmer academies and implement a series of showcase farms.

Besides expansion, cost leadership and the new strategic pillar Sustainable Cocoa, you also have a strategic focus on innovation. How did your Research & Development (R&D) department contribute to the group's growth?
JBS I am very satisfied with the contribution of our global R&D teams. The R&D project success rate reached 50 per cent. Over 70 per cent of all products sold last fiscal year were innovations or optimizations for recipes developed in the past five years!

How do you take care of people development in your high-performance environment?
JBS In order to shape future growth, we have to have the best people and we have to continuously develop our people. Today, we are thinking in a kind of life cycle that starts at employer branding, comprises a recruitment and trainee programme, and includes performance management and engagement as well as various development measures. Another important element is succession planning. The ultimate driver of our growth and the basis of our success are our employees. I am very proud to lead such an enthusiastic, innovative, intense, and eager group of people who are dedicated to go the extra mile.

What are the main challenges for the future?
AJ Our main focus is on the successful implementation of the recently gained outsourcing and long-term partnership agreements as well as on the completion of the measures to support the acceleration of the growth of our Gourmet & Specialties Products business. Additionally, we will emphasize on people and systems while maintaining our efforts on continuous improvement and cost leadership. As mentioned before, we will also have an increasing focus on the mid-term and long-term sustainability of the cocoa supply chain.

Questions

1. Treacy and Wiersema (1993) distinguish three value strategies. At Barry Callebaut, elements of each of these three strategies are visible.
   a) With the information in the case, show for each value strategy how it has been integrated into Barry Callebaut's activities.

b) According to Treacy and Wiersema, every value strategy must be performed to a certain minimum level, but the company should excel in one of the three value strategies. Explain which value strategy for Barry Callebaut is the 'key value strategy'.

2. Describe the market definition for Barry Callebaut. Make a three-dimensional drawing, and add a brief explanation.

3. Analyse the attractiveness of the chocolate confection market for a large chocolate confectioner (such as Cadbury). Use Porter's five-forces model.

4. a) What is the core competence of Barry Callebaut? Briefly explain your answer.

   b) Show the connection between the core competence of Barry Callebaut and the competitive strategy (value strategy) used by the company.

5. Make a SWOT analysis for Barry Callebaut.

6. Indicate how Barry Callebaut could use a portfolio analysis when making strategic decisions.

7. Develop objectives for Barry Callebaut by using the balanced scorecard. Use information from the case, but make your own assumptions where necessary.

8. According to the book, different growth directions are possible for an organization. Which growth directions do you consider central to Barry Callebaut's expansion strategy? Please explain your answer.

9. To expand its market, Barry Callebaut considers strengthening its activities in the Chinese and/or the Indian market. Advise Barry Callebaut about this. How should this market development be carried out? Please include in your answer:
   - Internal and/or external growth
   - Target group selection
   - Positioning.

Chapter 11

Marketing objectives and marketing strategies

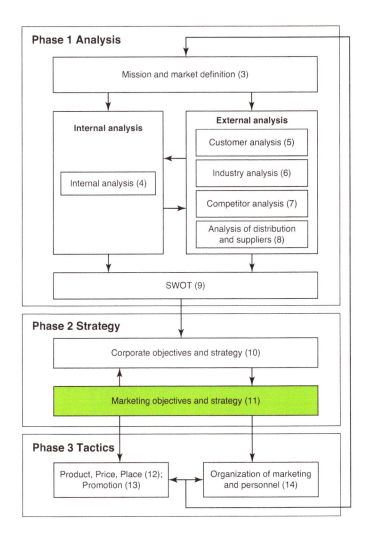

Phase 1 Analysis

Mission and market definition (3)

Internal analysis

Internal analysis (4)

External analysis

Customer analysis (5)

Industry analysis (6)

Competitor analysis (7)

Analysis of distribution and suppliers (8)

SWOT (9)

Phase 2 Strategy

Corporate objectives and strategy (10)

Marketing objectives and strategy (11)

Phase 3 Tactics

Product, Price, Place (12); Promotion (13)

Organization of marketing and personnel (14)

Key points in this chapter

- Know how to formulate marketing objectives.
- Apply methods for targeting customers.
- Know the principles of and methods for positioning.
- Know the role of the brand.
- Know how to choose a brand name and brand design.
- Apply guidelines for managing brands over products (extensions), internationally, and over time (crisis management).

Introduction

In Chapter 2, the hierarchy of objectives and strategies in a company was illustrated. In Chapter 10, the first two phases in that hierarchy were reviewed more closely:

1. Corporate objectives.
2. Corporate strategies.

The results of these steps include the choice of markets in which the company wants to be active; that is, the answer to the question of *where to compete.* This chapter reviews the two subsequent phases:

3. Marketing objectives.
4. Marketing strategies.

These phases specifically provide an answer to the question of *how to compete.*
Chapters 12 and 13 are devoted to the following phases:

5. Marketing mix objectives.
6. Marketing mix strategies.

These phases represent the elaboration of the issue of how to compete. In the context of the marketing strategies, a central concept is that positioning should be based on a sustainable competitive advantage. Marketing plays a central role in finding and achieving such an advantage: searching for a sustainable competitive advantage requires a careful analysis of the market and the competitors (market research), whereas its achievement depends to an important degree on the use of the marketing mix, such as communication. To achieve marketing strategies, strategies for other functional areas in a company should be formulated, such as strategies for purchasing, human resource management, and ICT. After all, the choice of a sustainable competitive advantage is so important that there may be consequences for the entire company or strategic business unit (SBU).

Section 11.1 reviews the marketing objectives. Section 11.2 is devoted to targeting, the first dimension of the marketing strategy. Section 11.3 reviews brand positioning.

Section 11.4 is about brand architecture. Section 11.5 deals with brand naming. Section 11.6 is devoted to house style. Section 11.7 is about managing brands in time (such as in rebranding), over products (extensions), and internationally.

Figure 11.1 shows the relationship between some of these subjects.

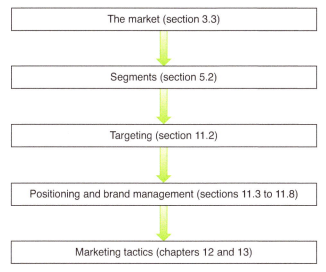

Figure 11.1 **Segmentation, targeting, and positioning (STP)**

11.1 Marketing objectives

Marketing objectives are objectives for which the functional area of marketing may be held primarily responsible. These objectives may be formulated on different levels: at the company, business unit, or product level. In practice, marketing objectives occur most frequently at the product level. Marketing objectives are expressed in measures that relate to the following

1. Customer-oriented variables, such as market share, sales, customer loyalty.
2. Brand-oriented variables, such as brand awareness, or brand associations.

Although profit is not a marketing objective but a corporate objective, profit objectives may also be incorporated into a marketing plan. Examples include the following:

- Sales of brand X should increase 10 per cent next year.
- After the introduction of brand Y, in three years a market share of 10 per cent and a profit of 1 million euros should be achieved. The loss in year 1 may not exceed 0.5 million euros, and in the second year a profit of 0.5 million euros should be achieved.

As mentioned in section 4.1.1, objectives should be SMART: specific, measurable, ambitious, realistic, and time related. Three of these are related to the form of the objective, and two of them (acceptable and realistic) are related to the contents of the objective. Regarding the contents, a manager should take into account:

- *The available budget*: an ambitious goal demands more money.
- *The corporate objectives*: the marketing objectives should fit into a timeline that leads towards a long-term objective.

11.2 Segmentation and choice of a target group

This section deals with the following topics:

- The importance of segmentation (section 11.2.1).
- The steps to be taken in segmenting and targeting (section 11.2.2).
- The evaluation of market segments (section 11.2.3).
- The selection of market segments (section 11.2.4).
- Customer intimacy and loyalty programmes (a segmentation strategy) (section 11.2.5).

11.2.1 Importance of segmentation

The definition of the market, followed by the choice of the company strategy, has determined items such as which products the company wants to make for which customers (markets); for example, clothing for women. Although this means that the target group has already been determined to an important extent in the choice of the company strategy, several more specific choices about the target group should be made during the formulation of the *marketing strategy*, such as the following:

- Does the company want to approach the entire market with a single product or with different products and varieties?
- Does the company want to attempt to reach the entire market or emphasize several segments, or even only a single segment?
- Can the chosen segments be categorized by general characteristics (age, income, etc.) and by situation-specific characteristics (product usage)?

These questions are all related to *segmentation:* Should the customers be split into groups? If they should, which positioning should be chosen for each segment? The segmentation decision is therefore a closer, more specific interpretation of the choice of a target group: in the company strategy this choice is made on a global level; in the marketing strategy on a specific level. The most important reason for splitting the market into groups is that different people may have different preferences, and this may lead to higher profitability than would be the case if different groups were approached with the same strategy. Whether segmentation is useful depends on the size of the segments and the higher costs associated with the use of different strategies.

A 'different strategy' in theory means a difference in one or more of the four Ps: product, price, promotion, and place. In practice, segmentation almost always involves differences in the 'supply' (product). After all, product changes allow a company to respond to specific needs. For example, a manufacturer can bring several different brands of laundry detergent onto the market with several varieties within each brand.

It is not inconceivable to approach different segments with a single product, but this should be done, for example, with different advertising campaigns. For example, a newspaper could recommend its fashion columns in women's magazines while promoting its sport attachments in men's magazines. However, a disadvantage of attempting to present different characteristics of a single product to different segments is that the product will have an unclear image in the market; in other words, no clear positioning. Without clear positioning, the company will not have a clear competitive advantage. Thus, if a company discovers segments with different needs in a market, in practice segmentation will mean a different product (or product variety), perhaps supplemented with the use of another price and/or promotion and/or distribution. In other words, segmentation has direct consequences for product decisions and *assortment decisions*: Does the company offer the market a single product or a line of different products?

Aside from assortment decisions, segmentation may have consequences for the rest of the marketing mix. Examples include the following:

- *Variety only in product.* Many laundry detergent manufacturers bring different varieties into the market (with or without colourfastness, liquid or solid, etc.) that do not differ or hardly differ in price and are not always subject to different advertising.
- *Variety in product and price.* A car manufacturer may bring various types into the market without doing separate advertising for the different varieties.
- *Variety in product, price, and promotion.* The car manufacturer may use different advertising campaigns, such as advertising on a specific television station for the cheaper models and in a glossy magazine for the more expensive ones.
- *Variation in all four elements of the marketing mix.* A manufacturer of baby clothing produces more expensive and cheaper clothing, advertises separately for those varieties, and distributes the expensive clothing through baby specialty stores, and the cheaper clothing through warehouses and lower price textile stores.

11.2.2 Steps to be taken

Several steps need to be taken in choosing target groups on the basis of segments. Figure 11.2 shows the steps (refer back to Figure 11.1).

Market segmentation involves dividing the market into buyers' groups that may require different products and different marketing mix strategies. For this purpose, the company first identifies ways to divide the market into segments and then creates a 'profile' for each segment: a description based on general and situation-specific characteristics. The second step is choosing *market target groups:* defining the characteristics to be used as a basis for determining the attractiveness of each segment and choosing which segments the company wants to enter. The third step is *product positioning:* finding a clear 'place' for the product in the minds of the customers and in relation to the competitors.

The steps in market segmentation were discussed in Chapter 5. This section reviews the choice of target groups, and sections 11.3 to 11.7 discuss brand positioning and brand management.

Market segmentation (section 5.2: Segmentation research)

1. Identifying segmentation variables and segmenting the market
2. Developing profiles per segment

Market target groups (section 11.2: Segmentation and targeting)

3. Evaluating the attractiveness per segment
4. Selecting the segments

Brand positioning (sections 11.3 to 11.8: Positioning: managing a brand identity)

5. Identifying potential positioning concepts for each chosen segment
6. Choosing, developing, and communicating the chosen positioning concept

Figure 11.2 **Steps for market segmentation, determination of target groups, and positioning ('STP')**

11.2.3 Evaluation of the market segments

The result of the segmentation analysis as reviewed in section 5.2 is that a manager divided the potential group of customers into subgroups (segments). Let us take as an example that the manufacturer of photo cameras used two segmentation variables: age and price sensitivity (a benefit). Age is classified into three groups: 0–25, 26–49, 50+. And price sensitivity is assumed to be low or high. Combining these levels there are six segments (Figure 11.3).

The next step is to judge whether this segmentation is useful. To this end, we use the segmentation criteria from section 5.2:

1. *Homogeneity/heterogeneity*: Are the preferences of customers within the segments more or less the same and between the segments different? In this case partly, since a benefit is used to split the group. One could wonder whether the age classification is the most appropriate. Perhaps using 65+ is better to make a more accurate distinction between age groups
2. *Size*: Are the segments large enough to be profitable? Some segments may be quite small, for example, the whole group 0–20, since they perhaps hardly ever buy an expensive camera.

	0–20 years	21–49 years	50+
Low price sensitivity	Segment 1	Segment 2	Segment 3
High price sensitivity	Segment 4	Segment 5	Segment 6

Figure 11.3 **Example of result of segmentation**

3. *Measurable/identifiable*: Is it possible to describe the segments? Using additional research it may be possible to identify which customers in these groups buy our cameras.
4. *Reachable*: Are the segments reachable, for example, with specific media? This may be the case with specific magazines or online using search behaviour data.

After different potential segments have been identified and described, a choice has to be made: Which segments will the company focus on? In other words, what are the target groups in the market? See Case 11.1.

11.2.4 Selection of the market segments: targeting

For selecting segments three *segmentation strategies* may be used:

1. *Concentrated marketing (focus/niche strategy)*. This entails choosing a single segment in the market. The advantage of this strategy may be that there is little competition in that segment. The disadvantage is the high risk: the company is dependent on only a single group of buyers.
2. *Selective marketing.* This entails selecting several segments. The advantage of this strategy in comparison with concentrated targeting is lower risk through spreading activities. An example would be car manufacturers with types that differ in price.
3. *Complete market coverage.* This means that a company attempts to serve all customer groups. This may be achieved by bringing a large number of different brands and/or products into the market. An example is Procter & Gamble in different product groups such as hair care and laundry detergents. This strategy is possible only for large companies. Another possibility is to bring one or several products onto the market aimed at a broad target group, such as Coca-Cola.

The naming of the segmentation strategy depends on the market definition (see Chapter 3). For example, if a car manufacturer like Mercedes-Benz uses a broad market definition (e.g. the car market) and chooses a single segment in that market, it might be called a niche strategy. If that manufacturer chooses a narrow market definition (e.g. top-quality cars) and explicitly maintains that definition in its situation analysis, it would count as complete market coverage. So, the classification of segmentation strategies is actually quite subjective.

The ultimate choice of target groups also depends on the branding strategy (section 11.4), since it may be easier to serve different segments by using sub-brands. In addition, it should be mentioned that the choice of the target group is strongly related to the brand positioning. A brand positioning describes the relevant attributes of a brand and the brand's personality, and these should fit with the personality and values of the target group.

11.2.5 Loyalty programmes

After target groups have been chosen, the next issue is whether the target group should be approached as a whole or one on one. In section 5.6 we paid attention to obtaining data

Case 11.1 Targeting

Targeting Asian-American consumers

Asian-American consumers are on the cutting edge of everything digital. Their preferences, habits, and adoption of devices are indicative of a larger US trend that is seeing consumers turn to their devices for their favourite content. By studying the unique consumer preferences of Asian-American consumers, marketers and advertisers can gain insight into reaching other consumers, while also continuing to make progress with one of the most powerful consumer groups in the USA.

Source: www.nielsen.com, 30 May 2018

from individual customers (after approval: *permission marketing*) and to the selection of the most profitable customers. To strengthen the bond with the most important customers, a choice can be made to use loyalty programmes (Dowling and Uncles, 1997). These are programmes in which the marketing mix is used in such a way that customers are directly rewarded for loyalty to the brand. This is a tool for the seller to increase the *bond* between the customer and the brand and reduce the chance that the customer will switch to a competitor. For this purpose, the organization requires a database with individual customer data (*a CRM system: customer relation management*). The next step may be that the seller actually starts rewarding loyalty: gives a reward for brand loyalty. See for an example Case 11.2.

Before a loyalty programme can be started, individual customer data are required. With online shopping this is easy to organize. Simply register who buys online and what they buy. In retail *customer cards* are also a widely used tool for this purpose. A customer card may be provided for free or for a fee. Free cards have the advantage

Case 11.2 Loyalty programme

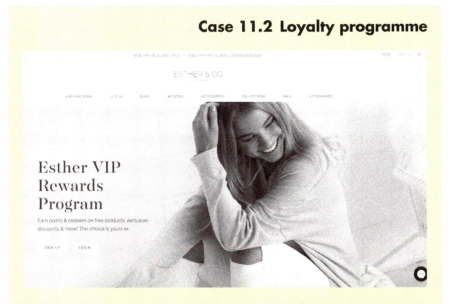

Esther & Co. stimulates ambassadorship

Esther & Co. VIP Rewards members earn points in a variety of ways, including purchases, referrals, and when they sign up. The best part? They reward generously! At a glance reaching the highest tier in Esther's programme might appear to be difficult, but once you see how much they reward for social sharing you quickly realize that's not the case!

Of all the sharing options offered, Esther is particularly focused on Instagram. Brands around the world are using Instagram to build brand awareness and loyalty because users are eager to share their latest purchases with their followers. Instagram is an especially effective platform for clothing retailers, whose customers look forward to posting about their outfit of the day.

Source: blog.smile.io, Top ten customer
loyalty programs of 2017,
2 January 2018

of high participation but have low involvement. For a paid customer card (becoming a 'member'), the reverse is true. In both cases, customers should be rewarded with, for example, discounts, early notice of special actions, and/or a magazine or journal.

It should be noted that a CRM system in itself is not a loyalty system, although it is often described as such. A CRM system is merely a tool that the seller may rely on in attempting to *build* customer loyalty. A real loyalty programme exists only when loyalty is truly rewarded; on the basis of demonstrable brand loyalty (determined with a specific measure), a customer is offered a reward of some kind (in the form of a specific interpretation of the marketing mix).

In practice, the following measures are used for customer loyalty:

■ How long someone is a paying customer: the length of the brand 'membership'. This measure is often used for magazines: the longer someone has a subscription, the more attractive discounts can be used. This is also used frequently with 'clubs' (whether or not in the non-profit area); the longer the membership, the lower the price.
■ The cumulative purchasing amount, such as the *frequent flyer* programme of KLM with which points are collected. Online registration is easy, the old way of registering purchases are 'stamp cards' of retailers. If the data are used subsequently to provide rewards to loyal customers, it is indeed a loyalty programme.

The rewards may relate to each of the four elements of the marketing mix:

1. *Product*: free premiums (extras), service in the form of advice, maintenance, and so on.
2. *Price*: discount on new purchases, accessories, and so on. This is the form of reward used most frequently in loyalty programmes.
3. *Place*: home delivery for loyal customers.
4. *Communication*: A magazine can be a reward for brand loyalty if non-loyal customers have to pay for it and loyal customers do not have to pay or can pay less. Specific information based on the purchasing behaviour of customers may also be a reward for loyalty.

Figure 11.4 summarizes the essence of a loyalty programme. In practice, loyalty programmes for individual brands increasingly occur due to online shopping.

Based on academic research (Dorotic et al., 2012) about the effects of loyalty programmes, it appears that:

■ Loyalty programmes often have a positive effect on both attitudinal loyalty and behavioural loyalty.
■ Members of a loyalty programme are less sensitive to the actions of competitors.
■ A loyalty programme is especially effective for 'low users' and less effective for 'heavy users'.
■ Ending a loyalty programme gives customers a negative feeling.

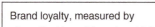

Figure 11.4 **Characteristics of a real loyalty programme**

11.2.6 Behavioural targeting

Online behaviour enables a new form of targeting, the so-called behavioural targeting. This entails that data about the online behaviour of people is used to target them with specific communication messages tailored to their online behaviour. When you Google to search for information about a new shaver, and when you click on a certain brand, the following day you will probably receive tailored ads about shaving. In fact this type of targeting is the main business model for online platforms like Google, Facebook, and Instagram. Of course, privacy is an important concern and customers should be explicitly asked permission for doing so. In 2018 Facebook challenged a big issue when it became clear that an organization used personal Facebook data from 50 million people to influence them in the presidential elections in 2017 as well as in the voting for Brexit. The fact that they did this is in itself a common marketing targeting strategy, but of course this cannot be done without permission. Section 13.9 will go deeper into online media.

11.3 Brand positioning

First, we outline the definition and goal of positioning (section 11.3.1). Since positioning is strongly related to 'values', in section 11.3.2 we review needs and values. Section 11.3.3 provides some models that may be used for choosing brand values. Finally, we show in section 11.3.4 how a positioning statement can be made.

11.3.1 Definition and goal of positioning

The word *positioning* that has been used several times in this book was emphasized by Ries and Trout (1981) in their classic book *Positioning: The Battle for Your Mind.* The title indicates the message of the book: the goal of positioning is to capture a place for the brand in the mind of the target group. Positioning is striving to create a perception in the mind of the target group. The final result is the brand image (associations). An image may be both functional and psychosocial. The desired image is the positioning (also designated as the brand identity, the proposition, or even the 'strategy'). Obviously, the goal is for image and positioning to correspond; for example, the safety image of Volvo is also the core of Volvo's identity rather than sportivity.

Positioning is directly related to brands. A brand (name) can have no more than one identity and vice versa: an identity should always be related to one brand (name). Just as in human life, brands cannot have two personalities.

What is a brand? A brand may be defined from the supply-side perspective (the company) and from the demand-side perspective (the customer). The supply-oriented definition of a brand is "a name, designation, sign, symbol, design, or combination thereof intended to identify the products and services of a supplier and distinguish them from competing products and services" (Keller, 2013). So, in fact, anything with a name is a brand. A brand may also be defined from the perspective of a customer: A brand is a set of associations linked to a name, mark, or symbol. This definition stresses the consequence of the use of a brand and is applied in this book. A brand is much like a reputation. Not only are products and services brands but also shops, shop formulas, people, places, organizations, ideas, and events.

Brands fulfil different functions for customers:

1. *Identification.* Brands make products and services recognizable.
2. *Trust and quality.* The customer knows what to expect and where it comes from, and there are no risks.
3. *Symbolic function.* By purchasing brands, people show who they are or what they want.

Although consumers will not easily admit to researchers that they are strongly influenced by brands during purchasing decisions, research shows that this is in fact the case. The most striking forms of evidence in this regard are blind taste tests. For example, in research by de Chernatony and Knox (1990), 51 per cent preferred Pepsi and 44 per cent preferred Coca-Cola. When the tasters were told what they had been drinking, only 23 per cent preferred Pepsi and 65 per cent preferred Coca-Cola.

But what is 'stronger'? To define this we use the Keller model, already depicted in Chapter 2. The basic assumption in the Keller model is that a brand derives its power from the knowledge about the brand that resides in the minds of groups of customers. The more knowledge (awareness), the more brand equity. Next to awareness, people should have strong, relevant, and unique associations with the brand (Figure 11.5).

It may be concluded from Figure 11.5 that a company should try to realize:

1. High awareness among the target group: a strong 'mind share'. Mind share is the level of being 'top of mind' among customers. So, how strong will a customer think of a brand (for example, Heineken) when a certain category need (I want a beer) pops up?
2. A distinctive image (by positioning). This is related to 'heart share': the degree to which the associations fit with the needs of the customer. Does the brand feel good for the customer? For example, what are the unique associations Heineken has for a customer? Or is Heineken just one brand of beer, comparable with other brands?

The need for high awareness is in line with the findings of Sharp (2010), already reviewed in section 1.2.4. Keller, as have many authors, explicitly mentions the need for also a clear and unique brand image. In Keller's model these two dimensions are in his view the sources of brand equity: the knowledge effects.

The tools to achieve this knowledge in the target group (Figure 11.6) are the fixed brand elements such as brand name and logo, the four elements of the marketing mix

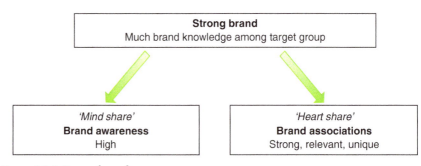

Figure 11.5 **Strong brand**

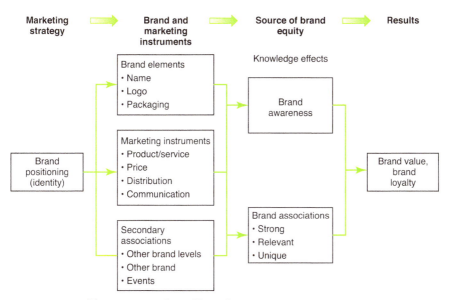

***Figure 11.6* Building customer-based brand equity**

Source: Keller (2013).

(product, price, place, and communication), and so-called secondary associations such as linking the company name to the brand (*endorsing*), linking with a completely different brand (*co-branding*), and linking to events. The *result* of strong sources of brand equity includes brand loyalty. Aaker (1991, 1995) also developed a brand equity model that is often used and that contains components similar to those in Keller's model: brand awareness, brand associations, perceived quality (a specific association), brand loyalty, and other elements, such as patents.

11.3.2 Needs and values

There are two meanings of the phrase *brand value*:

1. Brand values are the intended brand characteristics, such as cheap, friendly, feminine, or honest.
2. The brand value (without an s) means the financial value of the brand. Measuring the financial value of a brand is important in, for example, acquisitions of brands.

We will now discuss brand values (attributes). Positioning requires choosing a specific brand value (attribute). The chosen brand value should fit with what customers consider important: customer values and brand values should correspond. It is important to note that 'values' exist on several levels. In Chapter 5 we briefly reviewed the means–end chain. Figure 11.7 shows a summary of that model.

The essence is that attributes of the product or service will lead to benefits for the customer, and that these benefits will be perceived as more beneficial if they fit with the values of a customer. There are several enumerations of values in the literature. A

Figure 11.7 **Means–end chain**

well-known list of values is that by Rokeach (1973), who makes a distinction between terminal ('end') values (what someone considers important 'in life', such as an exciting life, happiness, friendship) and 'instrumental' values (personality characteristics such as ambition, clean, honest, responsible) (Figure 11.8). The distinction between those two categories is sometimes difficult to make. The list by Rokeach is very old and should not

End values	Personality characteristics*
A comfortable life	Ambitious
An exciting life	Broad-minded
A sense of accomplishment	Capable
A world at peace	Cheerful
A world of beauty	Clean
Equality	Courageous
Family security	Forgiving
Freedom	Helpful
Happiness	Honest
Inner harmony	Imaginative
Mature love	Independent
National security	Intelligent
Pleasure	Logical
Salvation	Loving
Self-respect	Obedient
Social recognition	Polite
True friendship	Responsible
Wisdom	Self-controlled

* Called instrumental values by Rokeach.

Figure 11.8 **Values according to Rokeach (1973)**

Source: Rokeach (1973).

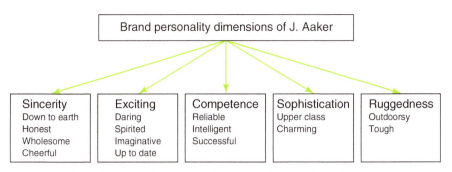

Figure 11.9 **Brand personality characteristics according to Aaker (1997)**

be used exhaustively. For example, the value 'a sustainable world' is not included, which nowadays is almost a generic value.

Where Rokeach developed a model for consumer values, other authors focused on values of brands. We discuss two of these other models. Aaker (1997) did research into the personalities of brands. Using extensive empirical research, she found that the brand personality characteristics may be organized into the five factors mentioned in Figure 11.9. Although Aaker's model has been criticized (Austin et al., 2003; Azoulay and Kapferer, 2003), it is still helpful for positioning.

Recently, Kostelijk (2017) argued that for positioning decisions brands better focus on values rather than on personality, since values better determine the needs of customers. Kostelijk empirically investigated a number of countries where values consumers relate to brands and he empirically reduced the set of values to 11 dimensions, which are summarized in the so-called Value Compass (Figure 11.10).

In the Value Compass the values that are near to each other are more or less related (for example, 'care and affection' and 'intimacy'), whereas values that lie opposite each other (such as 'functionality' and 'joy') are in fact opposite values that are hard to combine.

Consumers will not always be consciously aware of their values. But values do affect behaviour. For example, when visiting Disneyland, a consumer with a value 'safety' will have different needs from a consumer with the main value 'stimulation'.

11.3.3 Tools for choosing a positioning

Positioning is striving to create a perception in the mind of the target group. Figure 11.11 illustrates what positioning is by depicting the *positioning triangle*: A central concept in positioning is the selection of those 'values' for which:

- The *target group* considers them important.
- The *organization* or brand is strong in that area.
- The *competitors* are less strong in that area.

In the choice of positioning, four strategies may be followed in theory. These strategies are based on the *means–end chain* of meanings. Figure 11.12 shows this chain as well as the potential positioning strategies.

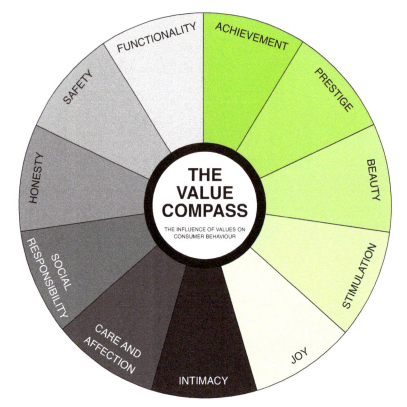

Figure 11.10 **Value Compass**

Source: Kostelijk (2017).

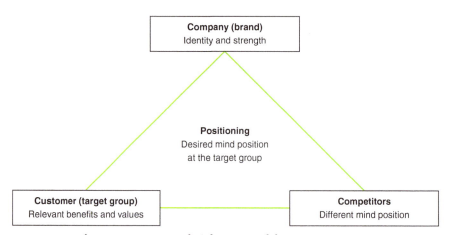

Figure 11.11 **The positioning triangle ('three-C model')**

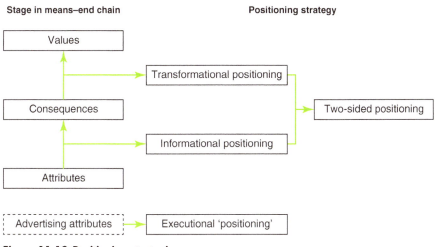

Stage in means–end chain   Positioning strategy

Figure 11.12 **Positioning strategies**

Informational positioning

Informational positioning involves an emphasis on communicating a tangible advantage of using a brand, perhaps connected to a physical characteristic of the product ('reason why'). For example, Freedent sugar-free chewing gum prevents stomach acid and damage to the teeth (benefit) because it has a pH-reducing effect (functional characteristic). This positioning strategy is often used for new products (e.g. Philips wide-screen television) and products with a problem-solving character (e.g. laundry detergents, dishwashing detergents, lime deposit cleaners). Informational positioning is particularly effective when there are clear differences between brands; in short, when brands have or are able to claim a USP (unique selling position). In light of the fact that brands increasingly look like one another, the effective application of informational positioning is becoming more difficult (Carpenter et al., 1994).

Transformational positioning

In this strategy (also called lifestyle or image positioning), the emphasis is on communicating values, perhaps linked to product advantages. Values are issues which the consumer considers important in life, a type of ideal. Examples are being healthy, caring for children, living responsibly, enjoying oneself, convenience, being good to others, and making a career for oneself. An example is Starbucks coffee. In this kind of positioning, often it is not the values that are shown but various possessions and forms of behaviour of the consumer. The values are the binding element in this regard. The choice alternative (brand) is placed in an environment that is clearly dominated by certain values. The consumer asks him- or herself: Am I such a person or do I want to be such a person? If the answer is yes, the brand may be considered for purchase.

In this type of positioning, psychosocial aspects play a large role. This strategy is often used for products that are purchased for pleasure (such as soft drinks and beer), products that hardly differ from each other (such as cigarettes), and products in which characteristics do not play a role (such as perfume). In general, transformational positioning is difficult to achieve for new products: it takes a lot of time and money to build up a psychosocial image. Maintaining this type of positioning also requires persistence.

Case 11.3 Transformational positioning

Durex launches new positioning

Durex is to reposition to build a stronger emotional connection with consumers, following the recent acquisition of the brand by Reckitt Benckiser. It is introducing a new brand strapline to mark a shift in strategy from a safe sex brand to an emotional brand. Durex hopes that the new 'Love Sex. Durex' brand signature will help shift perceptions of the brand and drive associations with 'sexual connection'. It will be introduced for the first time in a global campaign for Durex's premium 'Feeling' condom range.

Source: *Marketing Week*, 4 November 2010

Two-sided positioning

This type of positioning relies on the entire means–end chain: The product advantages are linked both to the functional product characteristics and to the values of the consumer. An example is Apple, which distinguishes itself through user-friendliness but also through an impertinent personality. Many other lines of business also try to combine 'reason' and 'feeling'. Think of brands such as McDonald's and KLM. Also, in the fast-moving consumer goods branch it may be noticed that brands that for many years strongly relied on functional positioning (laundry detergents, diapers, feminine hygiene products, etc.) are increasingly working on building a brand personality. Those 'characteristics' definitely do not have to relate only to the physical product but also may be found in added characteristics such as service, advice, customer friendliness, and knowing the customer. Since two-sided positioning entails the whole means–end chain, it is preferable to try to apply this positioning strategy.

Execution positioning

Execution positioning means that a brand is being positioned on the basis of the execution of the campaign. The distinction from the competition is sought mostly or partly from an advertising characteristic. In effect this is not truly a case of positioning, since advertising associations rather than brand associations are created. The brand or product is linked to a unique element or symbol in the communication.

According to Rossiter and colleagues (1991), the choice of informational versus transformational positioning depends on the product category (problem solving or value adding) and from customer involvement (low or high). Their recommendations are summarized in Figure 11.13.

Category	Low involvement	High involvement
Problem-solving category	Informational	Informational
	Example: laundry detergents, insurance	Example: health care, mortgage
Adding value category	Informational and transformational	Informational and transformational
	Example: beer	Example: cars

Figure 11.13 **The Rossiter–Percy matrix**
Source: Rossiter, Percy and Donovan (1991).

Positioning statement

If a brand positioning has been chosen, the entire package may be summarized in a positioning statement: within the category _____ brand A will be better for target group _____ than competitor B for goal _____ (usage goal) because it _____ (advantage, benefit). This is demonstrated through _____ (characteristic) and leads to the brand personality _____ (core value).

In this positioning statement we end up with 'the core value'. Core value simply means the most important value. In their book Ries and Trout (1981) pose that the most ideal situation is that a brand claims 'one word'. Of course, this word of value should be unique and relevant.

11.3.4 Guidelines for positioning: the brand laws

In Chapter 4 we laid the base for positioning: searching for the identity of the brand. A positioning should always fit with the current culture of the company. This does not mean

Figure 11.14 **The four brand laws**

that ambition cannot play a role: striving for an improvement may be motivating for the staff. So, a positioning should logically fit with the brand.

In practice, companies have considerable difficulty in coming to a proper positioning. One of the problems is that positioning demands 'making a choice', and that also means 'making a choice of what not to communicate'. We think that there are four main recommendations for positioning (and communication), which we call the four brand laws (Figure 11.14).

1. Focus

Many companies want to talk about all the things they are good at. However, there are two reasons why focusing is important. The first is that a message to a target group can only be clear if it is indeed a clear message. And when a company is talking about several unique things, people will not remember the main promise. In communication, a basic principle is: KISS, Keep it Simple, Stupid (and repeat). The second reason is that also for the company itself, trying to be the best in many different areas is not possible and may even be frustrating for the staff. This is what Porter (1980) mentions: 'stuck in the middle'. As already mentioned, choosing also implies 'choosing what not', and that demands guts.

2. Be different

Daring to choose is difficult. In addition to revealing too much, many companies also make promises that are made by many others. 'We offer top quality products', 'we offer the best service', 'we listen to you', etc. Great, but nobody will get enthusiastic about this. Everyone claims to be the best. What is really different? The difference can be sought in what you do (products), but it is probably easier to seek how you do it or even 'why'. This is the main insight of the simple and well-known 'Golden circle' by Simon Sinek (2009) from his book *Start with Why?* (Figure 11.15). The recommendation of Sinek is in line with the previous section where we recommend using 'values' in positioning, which is strongly related to 'motivation'.

Being different also means staying different. This can be done by innovation: doing something new. Talking about popular books, we would also like to mention the

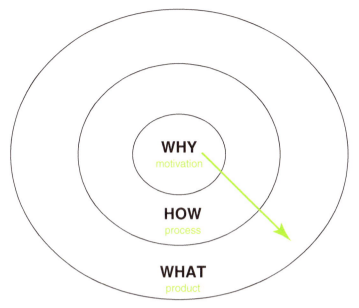

Figure 11.15 **Golden circle of Sinek**

Source: Sinek (2009).

well-known publication by Kim and Mauborgne (2005), *Blue Ocean Strategy*. Their main message is: 'create a new market space', which is the same as 'innovate'. Their best-selling book actually is not telling a new message but also shows that claiming and promoting a new message can lead to success.

3. Relevance

Relevance is relevant at the level of the marketing strategy and of marketing tactics. At the strategy level it is important to choose a positioning that meets customers' needs. If needs change, the positioning may also need to change. On the level of communication, it is important that there is some logical relation between the way of communicating and the brand. What sometimes goes wrong is that creativity is leading in communication without a logical link with the brand; for example, a great joke, but no relation with the brand. People will perhaps remember the joke but not the brand. A pretest of an ad can help in preventing this problem.

4. Consistency

Building a strong brand costs time. So, be patient, and be consistent over time. Brands that try to 'change their personality' from one day to another should wonder how credible this is for consumers. Not being consistent is also confusing. This has also to do with the portfolio of products. How many different products can be promoted using one brand name? Consistency is also important across communication channels, for example, online/social and print.

11.4 Brand architecture

Many companies have more than one product or service: a portfolio. New products may be the result of own development but may also be the result of a merger or acquisition. In all of these cases, a company should decide how to name the new products and especially whether to use the existing brands and whether and how to use brand levels. We first discuss brand levels and then we review the choice of the brand architecture.

11.4.1 Brand levels

Brands and brand names exist at different levels. Figure 11.16 gives an overview with examples.

The company level refers to the supplier of the brand. A supplier is sometimes part of a larger group. A company may choose to use or not use the group name in terms of positioning. In the insurance industry these days, it is clear that group names are increasingly being used as a source of trust. This is related to the idea that consumers increasingly consider it important to know who is behind the brand and how that entity behaves (in social terms). A good reputation and a good corporate image are therefore very important.

A family brand is a brand that is used for various product categories. A family brand may be different from the corporate brand.

Level	Fast-moving consumer goods	Durable consumer goods	Services
Company brand (corporate brand)	Procter & Gamble	Volkswagen	ING Group
Family brand (umbrella brand)	Crest	Volkswagen	ING Financial services
Individual brand	Crest toothpaste	Volkswagen Passat	ING Direct
Type of variety	Crest Sesame Street Kids' Cavity Protection	Passat 2.0T Value Edition	Orange Home Loans

Figure 11.16 Brand levels

An individual brand is limited to a product category. The emphasis in this book is on the individual brand. An individual brand has its own image and its own target group.

The lowest brand level indicates the type of product (item or variety).

This classification into levels is arbitrary. For example, the distinction between type and individual brand is often difficult to make. In the car industry some brands work with type numbers (Peugeot 501, Mercedes A), but these numbers may also be considered individual brands. For example, there is a great difference between a Mercedes A (small) and a Mercedes D (large). In the same industry 'real' individual brand names are increasingly being used (Toyota Corolla, Toyota Yaris).

Often there is a relation between the brand level and the way in which the brand is positioned. At the higher levels positioning is often done on emotional values. On lower levels functional benefits are (also) important.

11.4.2 Choosing a brand structure

Companies may decide to use several brand levels at a time; for example, by using a corporate brand as support for an individual brand, or the other way around: an individual brand with a variety. When a company uses two brand levels, the main brand is the *primary brand* and the 'lower' brand is the *sub-brand.* Designing the combination of brands and brand levels is called the *brand architecture.* The chosen combination of brand levels is called the *brand structure* (see Case 11.4 for an example). The brand portfolio is the combination of brands and brand levels in a company. There are four possible brand structures:

1. *Mono-branding*: there is one (corporate) brand used for all products, for example, Philips.
2. *Branded house*: the 'mother brand' is the main brand name for all products, but the separate products also have their own sub-name (e.g. Siemens Health Care, Ford F150).
3. *Endorsed brand structure*: two brand levels are used, where the individual brand name is the main brand, followed by the corporate brand who is the owner. The difference with branded house is that the two brand names are used in the opposite way: first the individual brand than the corporate brand. Unilever, for example, started with this way of branding a few years ago: they show the logo of Unilever in ads of their many brands, such as Bertolli.
4. *House of brands*: a brand structure with only individual brands. This is how Procter & Gamble is working: all its brands, such as Pampers, Tide, Bounty, Always, are communicated without any reference to the mother brand.

In choosing a brand structure several factors should be taken into account. First, keep it simple. The more names a consumer should remember, the more difficult it is for that consumer. On the other hand, an advantage of using a corporate brand and an individual brand as 'owner' (dual branding) is that it makes brands more reliable: a product is coming from a reliable manufacturer. Another advantage of dual branding is 'cross-selling': the possibility of communicating from a manufacturer to customers about several brands.

A brand structure is combining brands owned by a company. Brands can also decide to cooperate with brands of other companies. If both brands continue to exist in this form of cooperation, it is called *co-branding*: two 'independent' brands are put on one product. See Case 11.5. The advantage of co-branding is that brands can make use of each other's strengths. Empirical research shows that in co-branding situations the weaker brand gains more of an advantage from co-branding than does the stronger brand (Simonin and Ruth, 1998). A specific form of co-branding is *ingredient branding.* This occurs when a brand communicates as part of another brand, for example, 'Intel inside'.

11.5 Brand names

11.5.1 Developing a brand name

According to Trout and Rivkin (1996), "The most important marketing decision you can make is what name you give to your product". "The most important"

Case 11.4 Brand architecture

Is Facebook building a P&G-style house of brands?

With the acquisition of WhatsApp and Instagram, Facebook appears to be using the Procter & Gamble playbook for building a 'house of brands'. P&G says its purpose is to "provide branded products and services of superior quality and value that improve the lives of the world's consumers, now and for generations to come." Facebook on the other hand says it wants "to give people the power to share and make the world more open and connected." With the addition of WhatsApp and Instagram, you could argue that these purposes are becoming more and more similar. Facebook now has three superior branded products to improve consumers' lives and connect the world better.

Source: *Advertising Age*, 20 February 2014

might be an overstatement, but it is definitely important and underappreciated. In many situations, the brand name is already determined. But sometimes, as in the case of introductions, a new brand name needs to be chosen. Mergers and take-overs entail name changes (rebranding), and so the question of what name or names should be used arises here. Despite its vast importance, the choice of a name is often poorly thought out in practice. Two dangers in choosing the 'wrong' name are as follows:

1. It is difficult to link the desired associations with the name.
2. The name turns out to be legally invalid.

The brand name is the main bearer of identity. In fact, the same thing applies to people: a person's name gives one a good idea of his or her character. This character (brand personality) is typically learned along with the name over the course of time. Similarly, it is true for people that a name such as Carol, for instance, has different associations than does a name such as Elizabeth. One could say that a name does not have a 'charge' at

Case 11.5 Co-branding

Starbucks and Nestlé come to a licence agreement

Nestlé will pay Starbucks just over £5bn to enable it to exclusively sell the Starbucks brand of coffee beans, capsules, and ground coffee products around the world. That money is, without question, the greatest benefit of brand equity. It's 100 per cent marginal income and comes without any expectation that Starbucks will provide any form of product to aid Nestlé in its business.

Let's hope it is a long-term agreement. When the licensee starts to take liberties with a licensed brand, things can turn litigious very quickly. Indeed, Starbucks knows all about this. It was forced to pay $2.8bn to Kraft when it decided to end an earlier licensing arrangement in 2011 after a 12-year partnership. Starbucks argued that despite increasing sales of its beans and packaged coffee more than tenfold, Kraft embarked upon inconsistent marketing efforts that led to an "erosion of brand equity". Despite the enormous fine, Starbucks' then CEO Howard Schultz described the resolution as "the right strategic decision for Starbucks, our brand and our shareholders".

Source: *Marketing Week*, 8 May 2018

birth; the charge develops over time. One could also say that each association must be learned for each name; this is partly true. Names may also have meaning built into them. This is true for two reasons:

1. The phonetic characteristics (sound, length, letters) may in itself lead to associations with a name or word, for example, a word sounding 'Italian'.
2. A name can provide some information about a product; for example, a Duracell battery will probably last for a long time.

11.5.2 Types of brand names

One can distinguish between the following types of brand names:

1. Functional names.
2. Associative names.
3. Abstract names.
4. Abbreviations or numbers.

1. Functional names

A functional name is a name that almost literally describes what the brand is about. Examples of functional names are the University of Groningen, the *Journal of Marketing*, and the *Northern Gazette*. A special category of functional names includes questions, sentences, and specific promotions, such as www.iwantacheaperloan.us. Clearly, an advantage of a functional name is that it is easy to learn what it is about. A disadvantage is that it is rather more difficult to link emotional values to a functional name.

2. Associative names

Associative names are names that provide some information about the brand, without literally saying what it is; for example, by providing information about the category or brand, such as Transavia, Facebook, and Microsoft.

3. Abstract names

Abstract names are names that do not provide any clue about the brand. These names may be existing words (word names) or new words. Perhaps the most famous example is Apple. Apple has shown that using a 'random' word can be very successful: no one thinks about an apple when he or she thinks about the brand, even though the name and the logo are still literally an apple. An abstract name can also be the name of a person, for example, Heineken. Abstract names can also be new words, without any information about the brand, such as Sony. Many brands have abstract names. Initially, the names do not have any link with a brand (they are existing or new words, not linked to a brand), but after a while the target group begins to associate the name with something.

4. Abbreviations or numbers

Examples are KLM, HP, TNT, and 501. These names work similarly to the way functional names work: it is difficult to create emotional distinctiveness. Another disadvantage is confusion: abbreviations are easily confused with each other, for example, KPN (telecom) and the paper manufacturer KNP. Companies considering a name that is longer than two words must take into account the fact that people will abbreviate it, even if the company does not. This may be a reason to keep the name short.

Brand	Name	Brand	Name
1. Apple	Abstract	11. General Electric	Functional
2. Google	Abstract	12. McDonald's	Abstract
3. Microsoft	Associative	13. BMW	Abbreviation
4. Coca-Cola	Abstract	14. Disney	Abstract
5. Amazon	Abstract	15. Intel	Abstract
6. Samsung	Abstract	16. Cisco	Abstract
7. Toyota	Abstract	17. Oracle	Abstract
8. Facebook	Associative	18. Nike	Abstract
9. Mercedes	Abstract	19. Louis Vuitton	Abstract (person)
10. IBM	Abbreviation	20. Honda	Abstract

Figure 11.17 **Top brands, 2017, and name category**

Which names are the most common in practice? Probably abstract names. Figure 11.17 lists the 20 most valuable brands in 2017, and with an indication of the name itself.

11.5.3 Criteria for choosing a name

There are four criteria that should be taken into account in choosing a brand name:

1. Fit with marketing strategy.
2. Meaningfulness.
3. Distinctiveness.
4. Protectability.

1. Fit with marketing strategy

The name should fit, or at least not be in conflict with the marketing strategy of the brand: targeting and positioning. This means, for example, that for a typical local product, an international (sounding) name will not be logical. Or that for a health care provider a very fancy name will be chosen.

2. Meaningfulness

Research shows that the meaningfulness of a brand name is affecting the speed of acceptance (Kohli et al., 2005). This is quite logical: if a name has some meaning, people can easily recognize what it is and thus easily adapt the brand. See Case 11.6 for an example.

3. Distinctiveness

A brand should be different from its competitors. This is perhaps the essence of branding in general. So, preferably, the name should also be really different from its competitors. A related issue here is that the url (including the countries' extension) should preferably

Case 11.6 Meaningful brand name

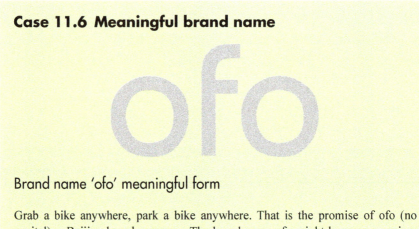

Brand name 'ofo' meaningful form

Grab a bike anywhere, park a bike anywhere. That is the promise of ofo (no capital), a Beijing-based company. The brand name ofo might have no meaning, but the form of the word 'ofo' looks like a bike.

be available. If the countries' extension is not available, name.com can also be chosen depending on how international the brand is.

4. Protectability

From a legal perspective, virtually all visible distinguishing characteristics of brands (names, logos, symbols, colours, and packaging forms) are considered 'brands' on their own and may be registered as such within the framework of trademark law. Because of the strong associative role of brand names and signs, it is indeed important for companies to register them. Without registration a competitor can easily misuse the brand signs of another company. For registration, the registration office (in Europe, the Office of Harmonization for the Internal Market (OHIM)) looks closely at the distinctive power of a brand sign. For example, the colour combination yellow-blue of the Swedish Ikea was judged to have too little distinctive power to be registered as a 'brand'. The same holds for the names 'Super Champion' for computer games and 'Fitline' for clothes. Philips successfully registered the form and varieties of this form of its coffee machine Senseo. See also Case 11.7.

Some long-existing brand names are so successful that people start to use them as category names (for example, Luxaflex, aspirin, spa). A risk of using a brand name as a *category name* is that it loses its distinctive power and cannot be legally protected.

A related issue is whether the url is available (see also the previous criterion). This is easy to check using specific apps.

When we have a look at the four criteria, it may be seen that they are not independent from each other. There is a trade-off between meaningfulness and distinctiveness/protectability: the more meaningful and thus descriptive a name is, the less it will be distinctive and the less easy it may be to find a free url. Another disadvantage of a

Case 11.7 Protectability of brand elements

Dutch retailer Hema condemned for copying Levis logo

The Dutch department store Hema has to pay 4.3m euros to Levis for illegally copying a Levis design element in their jeans. It is about a V-form on the back pockets of the jeans. The Brussels court judged the Hema design looked too much like the Levis jeans. Hema has to pay €20 for each pair of jeans sold.

Source: *Financial Daily* (Financieel Dagblad), 16 May 2018

meaningful name is that it may make it more difficult to do other things than the name suggests. Since it is possible to link every association to almost every name, the recommendation could be to use own, new words. On the other hand, for finding a website it is easy to have a simple, logical name. In current practice, it is quite common to choose an associative name, for example, CompliMints. Another solution is to choose a name that is in some sense associative but is 'misspelled'; for example, Greetz for a website to send cards.

11.5.4 Brand name process

The same thing applies to coming up with a brand name for developing an advertising campaign: First, a briefing must be drafted with the following major points: the vision on the environment, the product, the target group, and the brand positioning. If these points need clarification, it is not yet time to consider a name. The reason for this is that the name should fit with the marketing strategy. See Case 11.8 for an example.

There are three ways to come up with a new name:

- *Invent it yourself.* This is the quickest and least expensive method but typically produces the worst names. The problem is that managers often cannot step outside themselves and may have trouble imagining how the name will go down with the customer.

■ *Hold a competition among personnel and/or customers*. The biggest advantage here is that a foundation is created for the name or name change. Personnel and customers must learn to accept and spread the name, and so it is wise not to surprise them with it. The disadvantage is that only obvious, bad names come out of the box. You can hold a contest, but it should be explicitly stated that it is not guaranteed that one of those names will be used; they will be submitted to a professional agency for assessment, for instance.

■ *Use a brand name agency*. There are a few agencies that specialize in this service. Enlisting the services of an agency is typically the preferable course of action, possibly in combination with a contest.

A brand name agency usually takes the following steps:

1. Request a briefing from the client. There must be complete clarity with respect to various strategic decisions in addition to brand levels and use in other countries.
2. Come up with a large number (approximately 50) of names. These names are submitted to the client. The agency learns from the feedback what appeals to the client and what does not. This may also include names from a contest.
3. Submission of a smaller quantity, including old and new names. Using the same process, an attempt is made to narrow the list to three names.
4. Test the three names with the target group. This is not necessary, but it is recommended if quick acceptance is important to the manager.
5. Conduct a connotation and legal study of the three names. A connotation study attempts to determine whether a name creates undesired associations in another country. For instance, a detergent was introduced to the market in Spain that denoted the Spanish word for a whore. A legal study attempts to determine whether the names are already in use elsewhere (and are registered) and, for instance, whether the corresponding website is still available. For domain names, registration is a common problem. Sometimes large companies have to fight in court for their domain names.
6. Selection of the name by the client.

11.6 Design and logo

Because the design and logo are strongly related to brand positioning, we discuss these elements not under the marketing instrument product in Chapter 12 but in this chapter on marketing strategy. Design relates to the design of all external appearance forms of the brand: the logo (form, colour, etc.), brand signs, and packaging. Since these product elements are directly linked to the brand, they are important carriers of the brand personality. A logo should be an extension of the brand personality. A good example is the logo of the Rabobank: a person in the middle of a circle who portrays the positioning of the Rabobank: "you as customer have a central place and we as bank are located in the middle of society." However, in the case of more abstract logos a manager should be aware of the spontaneous associations a logo has. In practice, logos are often dealt with too lightly. Often it is said that a certain logo 'is outdated' or 'not

Case 11.8 Changing the name

How one software company rebranded to break down silos

When Braze rebranded from Appboy last year, it wasn't just trying to broaden perceptions of its expertise to more than apps, it wanted to improve collaboration, explains its senior vice-president of marketing Marissa Aydlett. "Appboy is a fine name for a new company – fun, light, a little cheeky. But not necessarily built for the long haul. As we became the dominant startup in our space and started to challenge marketing cloud incumbents, our name led some brands to sell us short. Having 'app' in the name meant that people often missed that we were capable of working our magic in email and on the web, too. We needed a change, a new name and new branding that spoke better to the company we'd become."

Source: *Marketing Week*, 14 June 2018

appealing enough', and that the 'house style' should therefore be modified. Then a new logo is designed, and if the management likes the new logo, a new house style is born. However, this approach ignores the function of the logo as the carrier of the brand personality. A new logo can be designed only after a discussion has taken place about the brand personality: What does the brand or company want to represent? A similar issue applies to brand signs.

Brand signs are symbols, colours, spelling, and the like that are 'own' to the brand; for example, the special way in which the name Coca-Cola is written or the colour 'canary yellow' associated with Post-It from 3M. Brand signs, just like logos, are strongly connected to the brand personality. For example, colours have their own radiation: blue

Case 11.9 Meaning of a logo

New Reebok logo indicates shift from pros to cross fit

The new logo coincides with the brand's 'singular' focus on fitness. "Through the millennia the delta has been a symbol of change and transformation," the company explained in a press release. "The Reebok Delta has three distinct parts each representing the changes – physical, mental, and social – that occur when people push themselves beyond their perceived limits and embrace an active and challenging life."

Source: *Adage*, 28 February 2014

is perceived as mild, red as lively and fierce. Colours are important for the brand and for varieties. For example, colours play an important role in the recognition of coffee varieties (red brand, gold brand, silver brand, etc.).

Packaging obviously plays not only a functional role but also a strongly communicative one. The packaging design therefore has a relationship with the brand and sub-brands.

Not only for products but also for retailers, design is important, perhaps even more important. The house style of a retailer is literally the style of his house/the shop, which is determining a large part of the shopping experience of customers. And with the growing competition of online shopping versus offline shopping (clicks and bricks), realizing a good shopping experience is increasingly important. Not only does the design of a shop affect the experience but also the scents and the sounds; and, of course, the products and the service.

11.7 Managing brands

Brand values have to be managed over time, over products (extensions), and over countries. Specific issues related to this include:

- repositioning (section 11.7.1);
- rebranding (section 11.7.2);
- crisis management (section 11.7.3);

- extensions (section 11.7.4);
- internationalization (section 11.7.5).

11.7.1 Repositioning

At a certain moment a company may want to change the main communication message of a brand. Changing a communication message can pertain to:

1. The level of positioning, so a new positioning (*repositioning*);
2. Another communication aspect, for example, a promotional campaign;
3. The execution of the communication, for example, the creative concept.

One of the brand laws is about consistency. A repositioning looks dangerous because the brand is claiming to change its core message. This may not be credible for customers. In practice, there are examples of beer brands (that are strongly dependent on building image) that change their brand personality from one day to another. Clearly, such an action lacks credibility.

On the level of specific messages, changes are not necessarily a problem. This also pertains to changing execution, although a consistent execution leads to easier recognition of the brand. For example, a simple piece of music consistently linked to a brand may lead to spontaneous associations for customers who just hear the music. Execution can thus be a kind of fixed part of a brand. However, a disadvantage of consistency in execution is that attention will decrease. Research into the effects of TV advertising shows that regular changes in execution lead to an increase in market share (Lodish et al., 1995a). Probably this is caused by higher attention to new advertising. A risk of new, attention-attracting executions is the lack of a logical link with the brand. In that case, no or a wrong brand name will be remembered. The conclusion is that changes in execution may be good for the brand as long as there is a link with the brand.

11.7.2 Rebranding

Rebranding means changing the brand name. This is a more narrow interpretation than is sometimes used, since repositioning is sometimes called rebranding (see Case 11.10).

Changing a brand name is a rare occasion. This is logical, since the name is the most important carrier of the brand knowledge people have. This brand knowledge is, according to Keller, the essence of 'brand equity'. Changing a brand name does not imply that the brand knowledge with customers is lost. Only the link changes. This is still a big step.

Reasons for rebranding include:

1. *Mergers and acquisitions*: in these situations brands sometimes disappear and become part of another brand.
2. *Legal problems*: a new name already used by another may lead to a new rebranding.
3. *Crisis*: a brand can have a severe image problem and for that reason decide to rebrand.
4. *Efficiency*: international companies may rebrand products to have the same name in different countries.

5. *Marketing strategic motives*: a company may want to reposition the brand and also change the name.

What is the best way to organize rebranding? First, it is important to be clear in communication about the motives of rebranding. Information facilitates acceptance. This is investigated for non-fitting extensions, and is probably also true for rebranding. Then still, there are two possibilities:

Case 11.10 Repositioning

Kipling rebrands as it looks to do 'fewer things, but bigger'

Belgian bag brand Kipling is hoping to ramp up its appeal among millennials by ditching the pink and tapping into an 'on-the-go' lifestyle, 30 years since its products first hit the shelves. Known for its lightweight fabric bags in a variety of sizes, shapes, and colours, Kipling is hoping to give its customer base a boost by targeting the millennial market, developing its relationship with existing consumers and investing in key categories like back to school. The new brand vision will roll out in July across 3,000 points of sale worldwide, with the launch of the autumn/winter 2018 collection and will continue into spring/summer 2019. Global president Vera Breuer, who joined fashion conglomerate VF Corporation in January to head up Kipling, describes the rebrand as an evolution rather than a revolution. This evolution will involve stripping back the colour palette, revamping the monkey keychain on some styles, and focusing on pieces that fit an 'on-the-go' mentality.

"I think we've been a bit pink in the past and this is not what the heritage of the brand is, so we'll go from a pink brand to a much more inclusive brand," Breuer explains.

Source: *Marketing Week*, 4 June 2018

■ Slow change. In this case first a new name will be put on the product next to the old name or the new name is announced on the old product. After a while the old name disappears. The advantage is that the target group can get used to the new name. The disadvantage is higher marketing costs and perhaps some confusion with two names.

■ Change at once. With a 'big bang' the company is clear: the name is changed due to some specific reasons.

11.7.3 Crisis management

Another aspect of managing brands over time is dealing with a crisis. True stories include beer bottles that were discovered to contain pieces of glass, cat food that killed cats, poisoned spinach, and an insurance company that distributed sex films instead of informational films. Failing to respond adequately to such a crisis is very damaging to trust in a brand and in a company, and is therefore damaging to brand equity (and brand value).

The characteristics of successful crisis management are *speed, openness, and responsibility*. The longer a company waits with communication, the more speculation occurs, and the more vague a company is and/or the more it places the blame on others, the more suspect it becomes. Figure 11.18 offers several tangible guidelines for good crisis management (see e.g. Seymour and Moore, 1999). The goal of crisis management is to use open communication to build a foundation for restoration of trust in the brand and the company following the crisis. A threat such as a crisis, if adequately handled, may even strengthen the brand (see Case 11.11).

11.7.4 Managing brands over products: extensions

Many companies have a tendency to 'hang' new products under existing brands (extensions). In doing this, they hope to address other customer needs and to have the success of the brand rub off on the new product. There are two types of extensions:

1. *Category extensions*. Under an existing brand name ('parent brand'), a company brings new products onto the market outside the category of the parent brand; for example, a manufacturer of watches brings cars onto the market.
2. *Line extensions*. These are assortment expansions under an existing brand within the same category as the parent or flagship brand; this involves the introduction of varieties (flavours, forms, package sizes, etc.).

The major type of new product introduction is extensions, of which line extensions constitute the majority. The difference between a category and line extensions is arbitrary: it depends on the definition of the product category. If Coca-Cola is defined as a soft drink, a new variety containing alcohol is a brand extension. If Coca-Cola is defined as a drink, it would be a line extension.

Ries and Trout argue that extensions are fundamentally objectionable, since broadening a brand may confuse consumers and weaken a brand's image (Ries and Trout, 1981). This is indeed a serious risk of extensions, but we do not want to take the argument that

Case 11.11 Crisis management

Crisis handling by Tylenol

Although a very long time ago, the next story is illustrative for how to handle a crisis situation.

It was a crime that forever changed the way we buy over-the-counter medications. In 1982 seven people in the Chicago area died after taking Tylenol capsules that had been randomly laced with cyanide. No one was ever charged with the murders. However, James Lewis was released from prison in 1995 after serving 13 years of a 20-year sentence for trying to extort $1 million from Johnson & Johnson, Tylenol's parent company. About a month after the deaths, Lewis wrote to Johnson & Johnson demanding money or he'd strike again. As a result of the case, regulations were adopted that require tamper-resistant packaging. The crime cost Tylenol's makers $100 million for the recall of 31 million capsules. Johnson & Johnson decided to stop all Tylenol advertising until several weeks after the seven deaths. In December 1982 the company aired 'You can trust us' commercials that received high visibility. Tylenol finished third in top-of-mind awareness of all advertising behind Coca-Cola and Burger King that month.

Source: Lucy Howard and Carla Koehl, "Release in the Tylenol Case,"
Newsweek, 23 October 1995, p.8; "'Trust Us' Tylenol Ads Working,"
Advertising Age, 6 December 1999, p. 77

far. Much research has been performed on the success of extensions which has shown that under certain conditions, extensions can indeed be successful. An important finding is that in the eyes of the target group, the extension should fit with the parent brand: There should be a logical fit between the extension and the brand (Aaker and Keller, 1990; Reddy et al., 1994; Kirmani et al., 1999). For example, the extension BIC perfume in addition to BIC pens turned out not to be a success; the extension 7-Up Ice Cola (a clear

Crisis preparation

- Have a team of experts (lawyers, doctors, etc.) available.
- Prepare a crisis plan (including making a single person responsible for contact with the media).

Crisis management

- As fast as possible (after the first relevant information has arrived) present a statement externally (press, retail, competitors, etc.) but also internally (staff). The information supply should be under the company's control as much as possible.
- Open communication and no shifting the blame to someone else.
- If the crisis is serious, enact a 'recall' (calling back products).
- Stop all current marketing communications of the brand.
- Be accessible for complaints with, for example, a free 800 number and via email and the internet.
- If applicable, pay compensation to victims.
- Have a 'renewed' product available as soon as possible.

Figure 11.18 **Example of crisis management by a manufacturer of consumer goods**

cola from 7-Up) was not successful for the same reason. Research, however, shows that the perceived fit between a parent brand and an extension can be improved by communication (Lane, 2000).

There is a relationship between the positioning strategy and the possibility for extensions. Brands with informational positioning are more strongly linked to the product than are brands with transformational positioning and have less room for extensions. In practice there is the temptation to bring many extensions onto the market, yet from the perspective of maintaining the brand image (and also for the 'parent brand'), this is often not wise.

Managers considering brand extensions should thus ask the right questions (partly based on Braig and Tybout, 2005):

1. How is the parent brand currently positioned?
2. Will consumers understand the logic for the extension? Which elements of the positioning are extended?
3. Is the positioning element that is extended relevant in the new extension category?
4. If there is no logical fit, can communication help lead consumers to such an understanding?
5. What is the impact of the extension on the parent and other existing extensions?

To answer these questions, appropriate market research and continuous monitoring of effects (tracking) are necessary (see Chapter 4). If this is done and if companies introduce extensions step by step and facilitate perceptions of fit, extension strategies can be very profitable (Figure 11.19).

If research indicates that an extension is too risky, a manager may consider choosing another brand portfolio strategy: introducing the new product by using a new brand name or applying sub-branding.

Case 11.12 Brand extensions

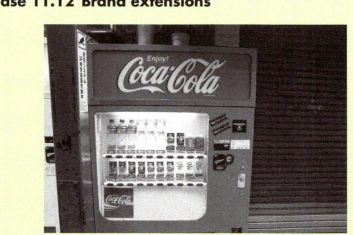

Coca-Cola introduce their first alcohol drink ever

It is far away from their homeland, but it is a structural break with 130 years of history. Coca-Cola is working in Japan on a soft drink containing alcohol. With this novelty, the company becomes active in the popular market of mixed drinks in Japan, locally known as Chu-Hi, most popular among women. In Japan, there are many varieties of all kinds of mineral drinks with some kind of taste and alcohol.

Jorge Garduno, CEO of Coca-Cola in Japan: "Until now, we did not do any experiments with low alcohol drinks. This is a small experiment, only here. I do not think the product will be available outside Japan."

Coca-Cola is faced with lower demand for its sweet soft drinks, and is thus experimenting in new markets, such as low sugar drinks, sport drinks, and water.

Source: *Financial Daily* (Financieel Dagblad), 2 June 2018

11.7.5 Managing brands over countries

The internationalization of business is occurring very quickly. Retail businesses, producers, and service providers are developing into multinationals. Through mergers and acquisitions, companies seek reinforcement from each other, and local brands (brands limited to a single country) are increasingly becoming part of international groups that subsequently use those brands for a global brand strategy. Consumers are also becoming increasingly international, both physically (travelling) and from the home base (television, internet).

In light of these developments, the question is how far an international brand should go in the standardization of marketing communication. An advantage of having the same communication in all countries is efficiency and consistency. A disadvantage is that differences among countries are not taken into account. Four international advertising strategies may be distinguished (Floor and Van Raaij, 2011):

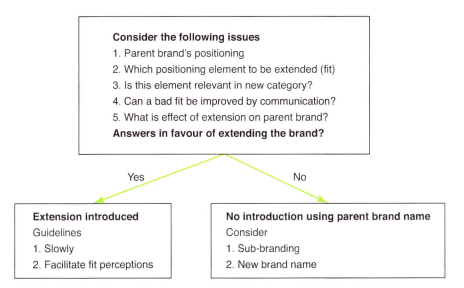

Figure 11.19 **Guidelines for brand extensions**

1. *Global strategy.* This strategy uses the same positioning, the same creative concept ('campaign idea'), and the same execution in each country. This strategy is used by, for example, Coca-Cola, Marlboro, Levi's, and Carlsberg beer ('probably the best beer in the world').

2. *Adaptation strategy.* This involves adapting only the execution, usually in the form of a translation (dubbed or produced again). This strategy is used by, for example, Philips and KLM. This strategy requires a high degree of coordination between company divisions and communication consulting firms in the various countries. This may be difficult because the local companies and agencies usually prefer more autonomy, since they know the local market better.

3. *Differentiation strategy.* With this strategy, the central message of the campaign (the proposition) has already been determined but the implementation of the communication is delegated to the countries. The advantage of locally imagined creative concepts is that they take into account the cultural differences between countries. McDonald's, Pepsi Cola, and all brands of Procter & Gamble use this strategy.

4. *Local strategy.* In this strategy, nothing is standardized, but a positioning, a concept, and execution are chosen for each country: "Think globally, act locally." Many Japanese brands use this strategy. Also, brands such as Heineken appear to have chosen this strategy: in the USA this brand has a very different positioning (top-quality import beer) than it does in The Netherlands (beer for everyone).

The choice about the degree of standardization depends on issues that include the nature of the products and the differences in preferences, purchasing behaviour, and values among countries. A balance must be found between the necessity of a consistent international brand policy and the differences in customer values among countries. A well-known model for characterizing the culture of countries is that by Hofstede (2011). Hofstede distinguishes six dimensions of culture:

1. *Power distance*: the extent to which the less powerful members of institutions and organizations within a country expect and accept that power is distributed unequally.
2. *Individualism vs. collectivism*: the degree of interdependence a society maintains among its members. In individualist societies people are supposed to look after themselves and their direct family only. In collectivist societies people belong to 'in-groups' that take care of them in exchange for loyalty.
3. *Masculinity vs. femininity*: a high score (masculine) on this dimension indicates that the society will be driven by competition, achievement, and success, with success being defined by the winner/best in field – a value system that starts in school and continues throughout organizational behaviour. A low score (feminine) on the dimension means that the dominant values in society are caring for others and quality of life.
4. *Uncertainty avoidance*: this has to do with the way a society deals with the fact that the future can never be known: Should we try to control the future or just let it happen?
5. *Pragmatism vs. long-term orientation*: this dimension describes how people in the past as well as today relate to the fact that so much that happens around us cannot be explained. In societies with a normative orientation, most people have a strong desire to explain as much as possible. In societies with a pragmatic orientation, most people don't have a need to explain everything, as they believe that it is impossible to understand fully the complexity of life.
6. *Indulgence*: this dimension is defined as the extent to which people try to control their desires and impulses, based on the way they were raised. Relatively weak control is called 'indulgence' and relatively strong control is called 'restraint'.

Figure 11.20 shows the scores for China and The Netherlands.

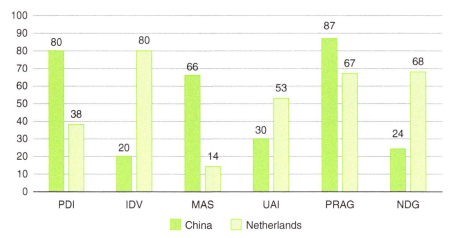

Figure 11.20 **A comparison of China with The Netherlands according to Hofstede's cultural dimensions**

Source: https://www.hofstede-insights.com/country-comparison/china,the-netherlands.
Note: PDI = *power distance*, IDV = *individualism*, MAS = *masculinity*, UAI = *uncertainty avoidance*, PRAG = *pragmatism*, NDG = *indulgence*.

It may be seen that the largest difference is in the level of individualism (high in The Netherlands) vs. collectivism (high in China). Also power distance and masculinity score quite high in China, while the indulgence dimension shows that in The Netherlands people prefer to follow their desires, while Chinese culture is restraint. Clearly, cultural dimensions play an important role in marketing, communication, and sales in and with China and in general in and among countries. See also Case 11.13.

Case 11.13 Cultural values

China's low individualism increases implementation power

China's culture is strongly based on Confucianism. This means that the role of the group is much more important than the role of the individual and also that power distance is large. The strong hierarchical system increases the implementation power of China. An example is that to lower smog all scooters in China had to be made electric. Which happened. So, all the millions of scooters are electric nowadays, which would be impossible in Western countries where individuals have much more power. For marketing purposes it is important to make friends in China. Take time and build relations: it is all about 'Guanxi' (networks).

Summary

Marketing objectives are usually expressed in terms of sales or market share. The choice of a target group and brand positioning forms the core of the marketing strategy. Target groups may be chosen after research has been performed into which target group is the most attractive, based on the segmentation research described in Chapter 5. It should also be determined whether the target group will be approached as a single entity or one on one. In the latter case, loyalty programmes may be used to strengthen the bond. A brand positioning must be chosen for the identified target group. Values have to be identified as well as a focused, distinctive and relevant message. Consistency is also important. A combination of a functional and emotional promise is preferable. The positioning is the starting point for all decisions about brand elements: the name and logo, the product/ service itself, and the other marketing instruments as well as the brand structure and secondary associations. Brand values should be managed over time (with issues such as repositioning, rebranding, and crisis communication), over products (extensions should fit with the parent brand), and over countries (think globally, act locally).

Case Audi: Vorsprung durch Technik

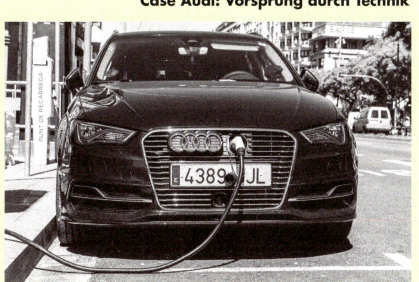

The German car brand Audi is part of the Volkswagen Group, just like the brands Volkswagen, Skoda, and Seat. The Audi brand is looking to the future with confidence. On its corporate website, Audi defined its strategy for 2020.

Strategy 2020: The vision of Audi

Audi has a simple but at the same time clear mission: "We delight customers worldwide." The company desires to be the largest premium car brand in the world.

In its Strategy 2020, the Audi Group emphasizes that it is ready for the challenges of the future. Audi represents values such as sportsmanship, progress, and 'style'. Audi makes technologically advanced cars, but the brand also strives for customer delight in other ways. The brand's success recipe consists of four key components:

– Focus on Research & Development. Audi's ambition to deliver high-quality innovative cars is expressed in its slogan Vorsprung durch Technik. The brand continues to pioneer through, for example, the use of intelligent combinations of materials, such as aluminium or carbon-fibre reinforced polymers.
– "We create experience." To continuously please its customers, the brand aims to create positive experiences that consumers associate with the Audi brand. One example is the Audi Innovation Award, an annual contest in Dubai where young designers are challenged to develop innovative car design solutions for the future. The challenge in 2017 was 'autonomy': to develop mobility solutions that can autonomously improve everyday life with minimal human intervention.

- "We live responsibility." Corporate social responsibility is central to Audi. For example, Audi has already combined its activities in electric mobility in the Audi e-tron brand.
- "We are Audi." The Audi brand continues to pay a lot of attention to product development. Growth is achieved through continuous attention to flexible, efficient production processes, combined with a strengthening of expertise and global presence.

Audi aims for global image leadership. A strong brand is the basis for sustainable success. The Audi Group wants to strengthen the emotional bond with its customers. The image position is constantly being strengthened with a wide and continuously growing model range.

Audi in Europe

The Netherlands is a relatively small car market in Europe, but an interesting one, as the country does not have any 'native' car brands. Consequently, there is fierce competition among all big international car brands to favour the Dutch consumer. And in creating a strong image position, Audi seems to be in the lead in The Netherlands.

A real ambassador for the Audi brand in this market is Henk de Hooge. He is a man with wide interests. He is an online publisher in a number of trendy Dutch blogs such as DutchCowboys and the Blog Idea Factory, he is a marketing strategist, storyteller, and internet evangelist (a top-five 'Blogger of the decade', with 6,125 Twitter followers). But Henk de Hooge is also a convinced Audi lover. And that's what this is about here. He owns an Audi A4 six-cylinder with seven gears ('fast as lightning and super safe'), but when you put Henk de Hooge in an Audi showroom he has his story for every model. *"I have already had a lot of Audis. The Audi Quattro, for example, is more than a car, it is an experience. Audi supports the driver with specific training days all over Europe; the car has a low gas mileage. And then that red-lit dashboard, that is so beautiful that it makes really the maximum out of a car experience."*

Audi's are modern cars, according to De Hooge. *"Many people in the Dutch internet and startups community have an Audi. Audis are also so much more popular than ten years ago. It is that design that they do well. All those models have a completely individual identity. Man, I am in love with Audi."*

Audi is the most popular car brand among business people in The Netherlands. But Audi is not only popular with business people. In the annual Dutch election of cool brands, Audi is the only car brand in the top ten, besides brands such as Apple, Google, and Heineken. In a survey among 4,000 Dutch people the question was asked which car brand they would like to own. Nine per cent answered an Audi. None of the other high-end brands, not Porsche, neither BMW, nor Jaguar, nor Aston Martin, nor Volvo could match that. In a brand image survey, Audi stands out as reliable and solid with class, as 'pre-eminently business' (no other brand comes into the neighbourhood), as self-assured, and as 'someone who has everything under control'.

An Audi is cool, a dream car. Literally. Because despite all the positive associations, the Dutch roads show a completely different picture. Only 3 per cent of Dutch car owners actually have an Audi. The Dutch mainly drive mid-sized family cars such as Volkswagen or Ford, or French brands such as Peugeot or Citroën. But the high desire factor does impact on the sales success of Audi in The Netherlands. While the car market was dropping in the past years, the German car with the four Olympic rings looks as recession-proof as the iPad.

Audi cool? Some people still have to get used to this idea. Not long ago, Audi was a fairly insignificant part of the big Volkswagen group. A brand that was always ranked after luxury Germans such as BMW and Mercedes. But those times have changed. "*Audi is a sympathetic brand. Everything is right. Product quality, design, image – they have filled it very well*," according to a brand expert. This is even emphasized in the German home market: "*German prime minister Angela Merkel does not drive a Mercedes or BMW, she consciously chose an Audi. That is a significant signal and has certainly helped the brand.*"

The management of Audi is doing more well, according to another marketing expert. "*They have the willingness to cannibalize. Many companies do not dare, for fear that their new product will be at the expense of the old. But if you dare to market models that partially cannibalize your own offer, it will only make you stronger. Another plus is the recognizable design. Every model is unmistakably an Audi, but with its own touch. Unity in diversity. That's really important. It gives consumers guidance in creating a homogeneous brand image. A few years ago the design of Audi was still a bit middle-of-the-road. But now they have a line that people find really cool, with which people like to be associated.*"

Audi in the rest of the world

The year 2015 was a record year for Audi globally, with 1.8 million cars delivered, an increase of 3.6 per cent compared to 2014. This growth is mainly due to the increasing sales in Europe, where more than 750,000 Audi cars were sold, 4.8 per cent more than in 2014.

But the Asian market is also of great importance for Audi. In China, German cars represent quality and luxury. In the case of Audi, there is still a distinct kind of prestige: the Audi has been the favourite car of the Chinese party elite for years. A black Audi in Beijing stands for power and prestige. Who drives a black car, of course with tinted glass, gives the signal that he is top of the bill in China. Audi's Chinese sales figures reflect that the Chinese economy is growing less rapidly than before: the sales stabilized at some 570,000 Audis. Despite the stabilization, China remains a much larger market for Audi than the USA: 'only' around 200,000 cars are sold in the USA.

Source: Corporate website Audi (www.audi.com) in combination
with a number of newspaper articles

Questions

1. Which value strategy (Treacy and Wiersema, 1993) is applied by Audi? Explain your answer briefly.
2. Which segmentation variable(s) would you use if you were to segment the market for Audi? Explain briefly.
3. Which segmentation strategy is used by Audi? Explain briefly.
4. The book distinguishes four brand levels. Use Audi as an example to illustrate each of these levels.
5. a) Which brand values of Audi are discussed in the case?
   b) Use the Value Compass to show whether Audi has positioned its brand consistently.
6. Which brand personality dimensions of Aaker are used by Audi to profile itself? Explain briefly.
7. a) Give an example of what a commercial for Audi would look like if informational positioning were used.
   b) Give an example of what a commercial for Audi would look like if transformational positioning were used
   c) What would be your preference for the Audi brand: informational positioning or transformational positioning? Give reasons for your answer.
8. Use the information in the case to describe the positioning of Audi. Keep in mind the choice you made in the previous question.
9. The book distinguishes four types of brand names. What kind of brand name is Audi? Explain your answer
10. a) Provide an example of a category extension for Audi.
    b) Give an example of a line extension for Audi.
11. The book distinguishes four international advertising strategies. Which international advertising strategy would you advise for Audi, given the image of the brand in The Netherlands and in China? Explain briefly.

PART IV

Implementation

Following the discussion of the situation analysis in Part II, corporate and marketing objectives and strategies were reviewed in Part III. These decisions are strategic in nature and in principle are related to a time frame longer than a single year. Chapter 11 stated explicitly that brand decisions require a long-term vision. Part IV will focus on the implementation of strategic decisions. We distinguish two phases in the implementation: the elaboration of strategies into tactical marketing decisions and then their execution. The elaboration of strategies in marketing tactics is related to the use of the four Ps: product, price, place, and promotion. This is the subject of Chapters 12 (first three Ps) and 13 (communication). Chapter 14 discusses guidelines for the organization and implementation of marketing.

Chapter 12

Product, price, place

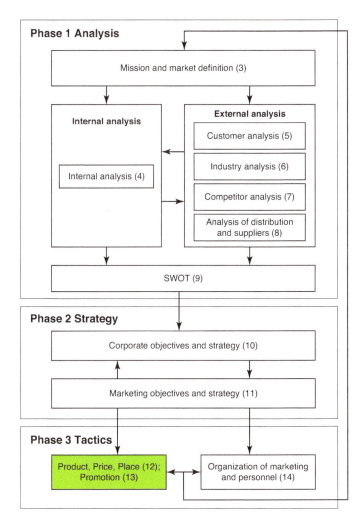

Phase 1 Analysis

Mission and market definition (3)

Internal analysis

Internal analysis (4)

External analysis

Customer analysis (5)

Industry analysis (6)

Competitor analysis (7)

Analysis of distribution and suppliers (8)

SWOT (9)

Phase 2 Strategy

Corporate objectives and strategy (10)

Marketing objectives and strategy (11)

Phase 3 Tactics

Product, Price, Place (12); Promotion (13)

Organization of marketing and personnel (14)

Introduction

Chapter 11 provided an answer to the question: How are we going to compete with the brand? We paid attention to choosing the target audience and the brand positioning on the basis of the value strategy and the competitive advantage the company pursues. The brand elements (name and logo) were also dealt with. The marketing strategy provides the direction for the four marketing instruments (the marketing mix). Figure 12.1 shows the hierarchy of decisions within a company.

Within the framework of this book, the review of the four Ps has been limited to a brief overview. For a more extensive description, see e.g. Kotler and Keller (2016). First, we discuss some general guidelines for the choice of the marketing mix (section 12.1). Next, in sections 12.2 to 12.4, we discuss all possible decisions that need to be made for three of the four elements of the marketing mix. In light of the important role of

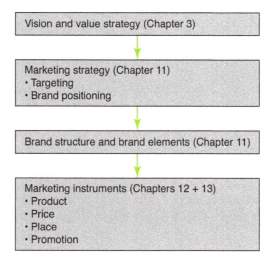

Figure 12.1 **From vision to the four Ps**

communication in building brand and customer loyalty, a separate chapter (Chapter 13) is devoted to marketing communication.

12.1 Guidelines for the marketing mix

We propose that companies use three guidelines for choosing the marketing mix (Figure 12.3):

1. Strategic: think from the DNA and positioning of the brand (section 12.1.1).
2. Innovative: stay ahead of competition (section 12.1.2).
3. Positive: think in possibilities, not in limitations (section 12.1.3).

12.1.1 Strategic thinking

In the previous chapter the marketing strategy is formulated. All tactical decisions should be in line with the chosen target group and the brand's positioning (Figure 12.1). This is the only way to create a coherent brand image.

If, for example, a manufacturer of dog food has decided to focus on high-quality food (*product leadership*), the four elements of the marketing mix could be used as follows:

1. *Product.* Goal: quality product. Strategy: quality food in an exclusive and smaller package with a classy name.
2. *Price.* Goal: price perception: high price in relation to regular dog food. Strategy: price setting based on the market: higher price than regular dog food.
3. *Channels.* Goal: within half a year a non-weighted distribution spread of 95 per cent in pet specialty stores and 70 per cent in other retail businesses, and also available online. Strategy: high margin for retailers.
4. *Communication.* Advertising goal: within one year an assisted name awareness of 90 per cent among people with a dog. Strategy: television advertising with the message "If you truly love your dog, you give it ____." In addition, hire three influential vloggers to spread the message online. And advertising in women's magazines. Action goal: generate 40 per cent 'trial' within half a year. Strategy: an introductory discount of €1.

Thus thinking from the DNA of the brand and consistency is important. However, this does not mean that things never have to be changed: on the contrary.

12.1.2 Innovation

To stay ahead of the competition and to meet changing demands of customers, it is inevitable to innovate. So, innovation, creativity, thinking 'out of the box', it is all part of entrepeneurship. Also it appears from research that innovation is important. Barczak et al. (2009) show that successful companies achieve about twice as much profit from innovations than do less successful companies. O'Cass and Ngo (2007) show that an innovative culture has an even stronger relation with performance than market orientation. These

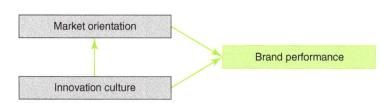

Figure 12.2 **Relation between innovation culture and brand performance**
Source: O'Cass and Ngo (2007)

authors also show that an innovative culture stimulates market orientation (Figure 12.2), so innovation has both a direct and an indirect effect on performance.

Talking about innovation, one should be clear about what innovation means. The most logical meaning of innovation is 'product innovation'. But there are other forms of innovation. In Chapter 3 we presented the Brand Benefiting Model. Linking the five possible benefits from this model to innovation, the following forms of innovation may be distinguished:

1. *Product innovation*: the 'classical' meaning of innovation, developing, for example, technological innovations to make better products (e.g. Apple), but also new food products are examples.
2. *Services innovation*: trying to improve the experience of customers, by taking more time, being more customer friendly, providing better guarantees, etc.
3. *Cost innovation*: every company wants to have low costs, so striving to optimize the production process to minimize costs is always important. Technological innovations may help, but also trying to buy at lower costs.
4. *Convenience innovation*: lowering other 'costs' of customers may also be a source of innovation; for example, lowering waiting times, facilitating availability (online), easier packaging, etc.
5. *Emotion innovation*: improving 'emotion' is mostly a task of communication, for example, by focusing on other values, and by adjusting advertising. Innovation in communication is by definition 'creativity' which we will review in Chapter 13.

In literature a distinction is often made between product innovation and process innovation. The innovation forms 2 to 5 may all be seen as process innovations.

Companies can also choose combinations of these forms. The urgency for innovation and the choice of forms of innovation depends on the value strategy of a company. Not every company has to excel in product innovation: especially companies following product leadership will be continuously dealing with product innovation. Companies focusing on operational excellence will focus on costs and/or convenience innovation. Companies focusing on customer intimacy will focus on service and/or emotion innovation.

12.1.3 Positive approach

Marketing is about finding and creating opportunities, and about making customers happy. This means that marketers should have a kind of positive mindset. What great things is this company about and how can we involve customers in the nice things that we do? Of course, being realistic is also important, but primarily an optimistic marketer will see threats as opportunities.

A positive approach can be implemented in at least two ways: focusing on the 'pearls' of the company and creating so called 9+ experiences.

The *pearl principle* means that a company should stress the pearls from the portfolio of products and services. These pearls may be successful products, but they can also be small successes such as a testimonial of a happy customer. Focusing on these things is not only important towards customers, but also towards the staff. Good news stimulates being proud of the company where you work. The pearl principle has consequences for at least two marketing instruments:

- product/service: products/services should be developed to provide customers with the best ('9+') experience;
- communication: the best products should receive most attention in communication.

The principle of a '9+' experience is related to the Net Promoter Score (NPS) introduced in Chapter 5. On the NPS scale of 'ambassadorship' it was noted that according to the theory only scores of 9 and 10 would lead to 'Promoters'. So, companies should do their best to offer customers the best experiences. This can be realized with unexpected service, for example, a free gift.

Figure 12.3 summarizes this section with guidelines for marketing tactics. We will now go into the four marketing instruments: three in this chapter and the fourth, communication, in Chapter 13.

Figure 12.3 **Guidelines for marketing instruments**

12.2 Product

12.2.1 Overview of product decisions

A product is an item offered in a market to satisfy a specific need. A product may be physical (a good such as a car) but also a service (a hairdresser), people (politics), places (vacation country), organizations (an employment agency), or an idea ("a good environment starts with you").

1.   Product mix decisions: choice of product groups (corporate strategy)
2.   Product group decisions: brand portfolio (marketing strategy)
3.   Product element decisions:
     ▪   brand elements: name, logo and design (marketing strategy)
     ▪   product development and product improvement
     ▪   packaging
     ▪   services

Figure 12.4 **Product decisions**

Decisions for the marketing instrument product are made at various levels in the company (Figure 12.4). This is different from the other three marketing instruments which are all real tactical decisions.

We now elaborate on the types of decisions mentioned in Figure 12.4.

Product mix decisions

Decisions at this level relate to the composition of the product mix (or the assortment) and therefore to the investments in strategic business units (SBUs) and product lines (introduction, growth, maintenance, harvest, elimination). Such decisions are made at the company level and are included in the formulation of the *corporate strategy* (see Chapter 10); for example, the decision by Unilever to stop producing margarines, thus changing their product mix.

Product group decisions

Decisions at this level are related to the composition of the product group; that is, to the introduction, growth, and elimination of brands and/or products. The choice of the number of brands or products within a product group is determined to a large extent by the marketing strategy: the choice of the target audience and the desired positioning. After all, if the company wants to serve several segments, each with its own positioning, it may do this with different brands or products.

Connected to this issue is brand management: the choice of potential line extensions, and so on. Decisions about the composition of a product line and brand policy therefore correspond to a large degree to the *marketing strategy* and are made at a minimum at the SBU level; for example, the decision by Unilever to introduce a new brand in the soup category.

Product element decisions

This relates to decisions about *individual* brands or products. Only these decisions may be considered *element decisions* with regard to the product, and they are typically the responsibility of a 'product or brand manager'. These decisions include the following:

1.   The brand elements: name, logo, and design.
2.   Product development and product improvements.
3.   Packaging.
4.   Service level.

Brand elements: name, logo, and design

These decisions are strongly related to the brand and are described in Chapter 11 (marketing strategy).

Composition of the product and product improvements

This involves questions such as the following: What characteristics should make up the product (functional and symbolic)? To what extent should each characteristic be present? Which varieties should be chosen? This decision therefore involves 'technical' product development: the transformation of the product idea into a concrete product. Small product changes (product modifications such as taste alterations) are also included with composition decisions. In addition to decisions about the physical characteristics of a product, decisions about the 'added' characteristics are important, including the symbolic characteristics. All these decisions are closely related to the chosen brand positioning and in principle were determined at that stage. Because new product development is a very important part of product decisions, we deal with this separately in section 12.2.2.

Packaging

Packaging has typically been mostly 'technical /functional' in nature: Packaging serves as protection for the product and as such is of essential importance in the logistical trajectory (transport, storage, etc.). However, the increasing importance of positioning and brand policy has led to the process by which a second function of packaging is becoming increasingly important: the *communicative* function. Especially because of the increase in impulse shopping behaviour, the external appearance of a product is playing an even larger role. This applies not only to fast-moving consumer goods such as chips and shampoo but also to the packaging of durable consumer goods such as household appliances. As a result of the communicative role, packaging design has a relationship with the brand and sub-brands.

Service provision

Each product may be perceived as a service. In the context of building customer loyalty, it is desirable to bring about higher customer satisfaction through forms of service provision. This involves not just requested service provision such as giving warranties and processing complaints; it also involves unsolicited service provision with the eventual goal of exceeding the expectations of the customer (9+ experiences). For example, a detergent brand can provide online advice about cleaning. Providing service is strongly related to the personnel of a company: Is the staff really customer friendly?

12.2.2 New product development

New product development is part of product innovation. We have already argued that an innovative culture is positively related to performance. But how should a company organize this? Cooper (2008) argues that new product development should be an organized process:

1. The proces starts with generating ideas. At this stage as many ideas as possible should be generated. Every idea is welcome and should not be criticized. However, there should be goals for the brainstorming, not creativity in general, but in the line of the strategy of the brand.
2. The ideas are then screened.
3. At the next stage business plans are made for the remaining ideas. Some ideas will be deleted.
4. Then, the ideas are really transformed into products. Also at this stage ideas can be deleted.
5. Then, some products will be tested; this can be a technical test and a market test.
6. Finally, the remaining products are launched.

With respect to the Cooper model, some notes can be made about how to discover new ideas: the role of the customer and the role of 'coincidence'. In practice, the development of new products is often initiated from a technological perspective. Creative entrepeneurs try to figure out which new products can be made. The first thing we want to stress is that customer orientation, although being an important perspective in marketing, cannot always be taken as the starting point of innovation. For customers, it is difficult to imagine things that do not yet exist. Market research many years ago showed that hardly anyone would want to be reachable always and everywhere. So, companies should be *inspired* by customers, rather than being driven by their needs.

The second note we want to make is that new products can also pop up 'by coincidence'. This is what is called '*serendipity*': the fact that researchers are looking for new products but that they find other new products than they were looking for. A well-known example is Louis Pasteur, who coincidently found a vaccine against cholera. Serendipity does not mean that innovation should not be organized: knowledge (such as about customers) and experience is needed to transform ideas and products into successful innovations.

Finally, we make a note about the testing stage in product innovation. Testing implies making a 'prototype' and finding out whether the prototype works and/or is meeting customers' needs. At this testing stage design science can be applied. *Design science* (or design thinking) entails that testing is done in a number of rounds: first a basic version or even a draft of the new product is made and tested, then an improved version is made and tested (Figure 12.5), and so on, until a product is developed that is convincing enough to launch (see also Case 12.1).

12.3 Pricing

12.3.1 Pricing decisions

The price is a characteristic of a product. Therefore, the marketing mix element of price cannot be considered separately from the element of a product. If the company alters the physical characteristics of the product, this will almost automatically have consequences for the price. There is also a direct relationship with positioning: a quality image is often

Case 12.1 Process of new product development

Drinkfinity not the result of systematic new product development

PepsiCo's Drinkfinity is an idea of Hernan Marina, of PepsiCo Latin America. The brand, which describes itself as a 'movement', is designed to mirror how a startup operates, from innovation all the way through to execution. Marina and his team were entirely independent from the rest of PepsiCo, working in an office separate and using different manufacturers. That is reflected in the brand and its communication – PepsiCo is barely mentioned on Drinkfinity's website and there is little to link the brand with its parent on its packaging or marketing activity. Marina explains how this startup culture influenced the product. He feels Drinkfinity was "truly co-created with consumers" as his team set up focus groups of 50 people who stayed in rented homes while feeding back about the product. He explains: "We called them alpha users. We started in Sao Paulo. We rented a house called the Drinkfinity Lab and we got people that were really passionate about the idea. We ran all the ideas through them, we changed the vessel, flavor, everything because of them."

Source: *Marketing Week*, 12 March 2018

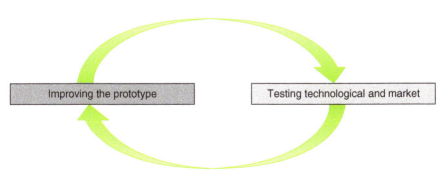

Figure 12.5 The principle of design science

1. Price policy
2. Price strategies
3. Determination of the price

Figure 12.6 **Price decisions**

related to a high price. Conversely, many consumers use price as an indicator of quality: a high price indicates high quality.

Figure 12.6 shows three pricing decisions that have to be made.

Price policy

Price policy involves the description of policy rules in relation to price. The goal is to create a framework of parameters that the various decision makers in a company can use to make price decisions. In the price policy, items such as the following are determined:

- The relation of the price to that of *competitors.*
- Rules about any *reactions* to price changes by competitors.
- The extent to which price promotions are used.

In section 7.6 we argued that companies sometimes react too much to each other, leading to too many promotions. We also argued that price promotions might dilute the brand. So, price policies could be stricter on these issues.

Price strategies

Price strategies involve long-term decisions about the price. These strategies concretely involve decisions regarding the following:

- The pricing of products in a *product line* (e.g. the choice of the price difference between types of video cameras of a single brand or between different types of packaging of one laundry detergent).
- Price agreements with *retailers*: recommended retail price, minimum price, and so on.
- *New products:* using a *skimming strategy* or a *penetration strategy.* In skimming, the company begins with a high price and then gradually drops that price over time. This strategy serves to recover the development costs quickly and is often used for durable consumer goods such as mobile phones. With a penetration strategy, the company starts with a low price that is increased over time. This strategy has the goal of quickly achieving a high market share by simulating trial purchases and is often used for non-durable consumer goods, for example, the introduction of a new snack.
- *Existing products:* price increase, price decrease, maintaining the price: decisions about these issues depend on, among other things, the phase of the product life cycle the product is in.

Case 12.2 Price strategies

The truth about discounting

According to market research specialists IRI, more than 50 per cent of food and non-food products are sold at a discount, meaning it is more common to buy a product in the UK on a sales promotion than on non-sales promotion. This is in spite of the fact that discounts decimate profits, even if they improve sales and market share – as Samsung can testify.

"I believe that too often price is left to the sales team, who are chasing volume rather than value," says Ozimek. "It shows once again that marketing really needs to be a consideration at every point of a product life cycle."

It comes back to the importance of value in marketing, and how ill-considered pricing can negate an otherwise brilliant marketing strategy, and waste a lot of hard work.

But doing your research and finding the pricing sweet spot is one thing – sticking to your guns is another: "I have one single piece of advice when it comes to discounting – don't," concludes Ritson. "Hold the line."

Source: *Marketing Week*, September 2017

Determination of the price

After the price policy and the price strategy have been formulated, the highness of the price should be determined. The definitive price determination is decided by the following elements:

- The costs (source: internal analysis).
- The market: What is the status of the price knowledge, price perception, and price sensitivity of the final customers?
- The prices of the competitors.
- The price policy and the price strategies.
- Other factors, such as psychological price borders ($199 instead of $200).

12.3.2 Investigating price sensitivity

Since consumer needs are the core of marketing, knowing how customers perceive your pricing is essential. There are various methods for researching the price sensitivity of products, including the following five:

1. *Causal models.* This involves analysing time series of sales and price (and other elements of the marketing mix) with the aid of *regression analysis*: a researcher tries to find relationships between variables by applying statistical methods. This is the only method that uses actual behaviour. All the other forms may be seen as types of experimental research.
2. *Conjoint measurement (see also section 5.4.3).* Respondents are asked to arrange a number of 'products' (combinations of characteristics, including e.g. the price) in order of preference; this is followed by a subsequent calculation of which characteristics are the most important. This can also indicate the influence of price changes on the preference.
3. *The Gabor-Granger method.* This method uses a number of direct questions about purchasing decisions and prices to determine the price sensitivity curve of a product.
4. *The brand–price trade-off (BPTO) method.* In this method, respondents have to choose from several brands at certain prices, after which the price of the chosen brand is increased and the respondent has to make a new choice, after which the price of that brand is increased, and so on. Based on the various choices the respondents make, it is possible to calculate preference shares (a type of market share) of the brands at various prices, which in turn measures price sensitivity.
5. *Price acceptance research.* This involves asking people which prices they consider cheap, expensive, too cheap, or too expensive, after which an acceptable price range can be determined.

Among these methods, the last one is the most simple. A disadvantage of this method, as with the Gabor-Granger method and the BPTO method, is that respondents are asked more or less directly to indicate the price sensitivity. Such a strong focus on the price apart from other product characteristics may have an impact on the reliability of the results. Conjoint measurement does not have that disadvantage, since it approaches the choice method of consumers closely without placing the emphasis on a single characteristic such as the price. Causal models have the advantage of measuring real behaviour but can be used only for markets with sufficient data (especially food products). Conjoint measurements may be used for all product categories.

12.4 Distribution

12.4.1 Overview of decisions

Channels ('place' or distribution) form the connection between the company and the final users of the product. Until some years ago this was about physical distribution via intermediate stakeholders. The possibility of online shopping changed the world. As we have already argued in Chapter 8: make your own web shop (including logistics) and you have a distribution ('reach') of 100 per cent. Having good distribution is very important and may even produce a sustainable competitive advantage. For example, the global and very intensive distribution of Coca-Cola is a clear competitive advantage for this product. Even in remote locations in the Himalayas, Coca-Cola is for sale. From academic research it appears that the distribution elasticity is large (Hanssens, 2015). This means that sales are strongly affected by the level of (physical) distribution. Figure 12.7 gives an overview of distribution decisions. These decisions will for a large part be based on the distribution analysis, reviewed in Chapter 8.

1. Level of availability (objective)
2. Determining preference for distribution channels
   - Number and type of channels (e.g. online or not)
   - Length of channel
   - Type of intermediate link
   - Shelf position
3. Management of the distribution channels
   - Push and/or pull strategy
   - Collaboration

Figure 12.7 **Distribution decisions***

Note: * We do not include logistic decisions with marketing mix decisions.

12.4.2 Level of availability

An important strategic decision for the marketing instrument distribution is stated in terms of *availability*: "To what extent and where should the product be available so that those in the target audience are able to obtain it?" So, availability consists of two elements: quantitative (the extent to which: this section) and qualitative (where: section 12.4.3). The quantitative element may be measured on the basis of the *non-weighted or weighted distribution* (see section 8.3.2); also, visibility on the shelf is measurable. An example of a distribution objective is: "With our brand B, we want to increase the weighted distribution from 80 per cent to 90 per cent within one year."

With respect to the intended level of physical distribution, a distinction is made between three possibilities:

1. *intensive distribution* (as large a number of distribution points as possible);
2. *selective distribution* (a limited number of distribution points);
3. *exclusive distribution* (in a certain region only a single distributor).

Case 12.3 Importance of distribution

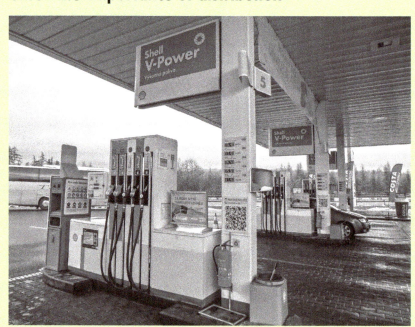

Shell will strongly increase distribution

Shell announced it will open 11,000 new gas stations and 5,000 new shops in the upcoming seven years. This should increase the profit of the 'downstream' activities (such as marketing and sales) from 4 to 6.5 billion dollars. About half of the growth of the number of stations will be realized in emerging countries such as India, China, Mexico, and Russia. According to Shell, there will be a strong growth in the need for transportation in these countries. But also in other countries Shell wants to increase distribution and thus the availability of their products.

Source: *Financial Daily* (Financieel Dagblad), 21 March 2018

A 'good' distribution does not have to be an intensive one. The intensity decision depends particularly on the type of product being offered. In this context, a distinction is made between three types of products:

1. *Convenience goods.* These are products which consumers will take little trouble to purchase. Examples are almost all food products. These products should in principle be distributed intensively. See Case 12.3.
2. *Shopping goods.* The consumer is prepared to make an effort (travel time, collection of information) to purchase this kind of product. This mostly involves higher priced products such as furniture and clothing. Such products require selective distribution.

3. *Specialty goods.* These are products with a very high attractive value to the customer. The customer is therefore prepared to make great efforts to purchase them. Examples are exclusive cars and warehouses with a strong attraction. These 'products' can succeed with exclusive distribution.

For realizing a certain level of (physical) distribution, a company is dependent on other stakeholders. The choice of intended availability may thus be seen as an 'objective', and together with the other decisions (management of the channels: section 12.4.4) this has to be realized. But first we pay attention to "Where do we want to be available?"

12.4.3 Where to be available

A company should first determine what the 'ideal' distribution picture looks like. Whether this is possible depends partly on the management strategies that will be used in the third step with regard to distribution channels. In designing the optimal distribution structure, four elements are relevant.

1. The number of channels

Especially if a company serves different markets, a choice of several channels is possible. For example, a drinks manufacturer may supply the hospitality industry via the wholesale liquor trade, whereas a food products retailer is supplied with its products via the food products wholesale business. An insurance company may choose more than one channel: direct delivery to customers, via insurance brokers, via banks, and via employers. Clearly, online channels are increasingly used. Every company will have to decide on the importance of offline and online channels. Many companies nowadays use both and are thus applying *multi-channel distribution* (Case 12.4 shows a remarkable exception).

2 The number of levels, or the length of the channel

Several intermediate links are possible between the company and the final customers: representatives, agents, importers, wholesalers, and retailers.

3 The types of intermediate links

A food products manufacturer should choose from within the group of retailers; for example, supermarkets, discounters, neighbourhood shops, and specialty stores. A company should make choices from within these types about specific retailers. These decisions may be seen as targeting distributors. An example is Unilever who decided in 2016 to also be available at European discounters such as Lidl.

4 The shelf position

The position of a brand on the shelf and the number of *facings* (visible units of the product) may have an important impact on the purchasing opportunity. The optimal place

Case 12.4 Channel decision

Picnic: an online-only Dutch supermarket

Picnic was started in 2015 by some young entrepreneurs. In 2018 Dutch consumers are queuing to be a customer of Picnic, since their success is enormous. The concept is clear: Picnic delivers your daily supermarket products at home at a lower price then all other (offline and online) supermarkets, including market leaders such as Albert Heijn and Jumbo. Picnic is able to do this, since its DNA is among others in big data analytics. Picnic is continuously seeking the optimal model for ordering and delivering, and is, for example, not delivering 24/7. Also they strongly innovate in their apps to enable simple and personalized shopping for their customers. Finally they have a less broad assortment than competitors but broad enough to fulfil consumers' needs.

on the shelf depends on issues such as the positioning in relation to competitors that was determined in the marketing strategy.

12.4.4 Management of the distribution channels

If an 'ideal' channel has been designed, the next step is an attempt to achieve the established objectives. Since distribution channels consist of companies and people that are typically not under the company's control, strategies need to be chosen for that purpose. This also applies if the company wants to make changes in the existing distribution channel. As a result of the strong concentration in the food retail business in some countries, manufacturers of food products have two target audiences: the distributors and the final customers. In principle, two distribution strategies may be used:

1. *A push strategy.* With this strategy, the company tries to 'push' the product through the channel. Tools that may be used for this include trade margins and trade discounts and the efforts of the sales staff.
2. *A pull strategy.* With this strategy, the company tries to 'pull' the product through the channel because an important demand for the product is created at the consumer level. The most important tools here are advertising and promotional actions.

In current practice, push and pull strategies are used in combination: it is important to establish a strategy towards the distributors and also to strengthen and maintain a consumer need. In this area, there is an increasing amount of *collaboration* between manufacturers and distributors. The interests of distributors and manufacturers are also parallel to a large extent: obtaining the highest sales (and profit) possible from the final customers. These objectives can be achieved better through a collective and therefore synchronized effort rather than without consultation. If a retailer is not sufficiently involved in the planning of, for example, a promotional action of the manufacturer, there is a chance that the retailer will run out of stock.

A manufacturer should therefore see the intermediate links as collaboration partners; this leads to a collective effort, and the distribution structure becomes an effective competition tool. In lines of business where the power of distributors is concentrated (such as the food industry), *account management* is often chosen: an organizational structure that holds individual people at the manufacturer responsible for the relationship with and sales to a single customer (an 'account', mostly a retailer such as Walmart). The relevant account managers then take over some responsibilities from the 'classic' sales managers (sales staff, representatives). In the food industry, collaboration with retailers is so advanced that some manufacturers attune their decisions about the breadth of a product group (such as new product introductions and their timing) to the wishes of the retailer. This is called *category management.*

The essence of category management is that both the manufacturer and the retailer no longer think in terms of brand and products but instead consider the interest and profit of product groups as a whole. In addition, they need to consider each other's interests. Category management implies that the manufacturer and the retailer jointly determine and manage the assortment within a product category. The planning of promotional actions is also increasingly attuned to the wishes of retailers. In general, promotions (if paid for by the manufacturer) are an important tool for retailers, especially if the promotions are made exclusively with the retailer.

The most far-reaching collaboration between a manufacturer and a retailer is that the one company can 'see' how many products are in stock at the other company. So they share their data (Electronic Data Interchange (EDI)). If both category management and EDI play a role, this is called *efficient consumer response (ECR).* In this strategy, the wishes of the final customers are responded to as efficiently as possible through collaboration between the manufacturer and the retailer. Typically, the following decisions are synchronized:

- Breadth of the assortment (e.g. number of varieties) of the manufacturer and the retailer (category management).

■ Production and distribution of the manufacturer, and the inventories and orders at the retailer (synchronization of production and logistics: *product replenishment*).

■ Promotional actions.

This section was about the management of, among others, retailers from the perspective of the manufacturer. A manufacturer has to develop marketing activities towards consumers and retailers. Retailers also have their own marketing to get consumers into their shops and to optimize the shopping experience of consumers. Sometimes the word '*shopper marketing*' is used to indicate the combination of both forms of marketing towards shoppers, which in our view is a little confusing, since every consumer is a 'shopper' when he or she buys something (online or offline).

Summary

In deciding on the elements of the marketing mix three principles are important: strategic thinking (on the basis of the chosen target audience and positioning), be innovative, and be positive (among others focusing on pearls). Product decisions relate to decisions about the choice of varieties, the design, and the service. As a result of the necessity to pursue customer satisfaction, competitive advantages based on products and services are very important. In addition, the development of improved and new products and thus innovation contributes to better performance. Price decisions relate to the interpretation of the price policy, price strategies (such as skimming and penetration), and price determination. Because price is often seen as an indicator of quality and therefore is directly related to brand positioning, it is often said that these days too much attention is paid to price actions. Distribution decisions relate to the required availability, the choice of channels, and the management of channels. Online channels are increasingly important in reaching the shopping consumer. Since in many countries retailers are powerful, a good relationship between manufacturers and retailers is important.

Case Nespresso: exclusive coffee

Nespresso – 'exclusive coffee' for a mass market - is the first coffee to be presented as a fashion brand: with its own shops and George Clooney as 'Mr. Nespresso'.

No, it was not easy to make a nice cup of Nespresso at home, according to an older lady who tastes a 'new taste' at the bar of a downtown Nespresso boutique. "Not *new taste* but *variety*," emphasizes the girl behind the bar. "It is not coffee with a taste, it is a bean from the Kivu lake in Rwanda with a subtle refreshing taste and delicate aftertaste."

"Variety," repeats the 60-year-old lady submissively. Anyway, at first she was struggling with her Nespresso machine at home; she kept pressing the button and there was only such a small stream of water. "The Umutima is a limited edition," explains the barmaid imperturbably about the new coffee variety, "with a fruity initial taste and a full body afterwards."

The Goroka is not just coffee, it is a grand cru. A whole wall of the Nespresso shop is designed for the lilac cups of the new kind and it has its own website, where the terms 'unique', 'sophisticated', and 'precious' dance on the screen. In the slick atmosphere of the Nespresso coffee shops ('Boutiques'), the spicy early taste can be judged free of charge. On a regular Monday afternoon, there are already dozens of customers trying the new variety.

Nespresso is for everyone, and yet there is an aura of exclusivity around the brand. What do you want, with a stylish and politically correct superstar like George Clooney as the face of the advertising campaign, own stores in the world's most expensive shopping streets and prices that are both towering and accessible; 30 euro cents can be extremely expensive for a cup of home coffee – a basic coffee prepared at home will cost you 2 cents per cup – but still 30 cents sounds to most people like close to nothing, and certainly much cheaper than a double latte macchiato in a trendy coffee shop. Democratized luxury, marketing experts call it: pricey, but feasible, just like the Chanel lipstick and the Prada sunglasses for the consumer who dresses himself at H&M. Additional information about the Nespresso introduction campaign may be found in the text box below.

The introduction campaign of Nespresso in 2006

Nespresso was launched in 2006. Back then, George Clooney was already the central figure of the brand.

Nespresso hired actor George Clooney for the introduction campaign for a role in the film *The Boutique*. The film lasted 50 seconds and was directed by Michel Gondry (*Eternal Sunshine of the Spotless Mind*).

The film marks the kick-off of Nespresso's first-ever Celebrity Campaign. In the film Clooney (himself drinking Nespresso, of course) is involved in a comical misunderstanding with two nice ladies in a Nespresso boutique.

The film was shot in Los Angeles but the production company had the Paris Nespresso flagship boutique on the Avenue Victor Hugo rebuilt on the film set specifically for this purpose. For the realization of the film, a large quantity of coffee, machines, and accessories was shipped, with which 38,500 cups of coffee could be prepared.

Olivier Quillet, International Marketing Director of Nespresso, explains: "The Nespresso brand represents a number of values, such as style, refinement, and charm. George Clooney also embodies these qualities, making him a perfect ambassador for our brand."

From May 2006, the film was shown in cinemas and on television through-out Europe. George Clooney could also be seen in the Nespresso print cam-paign. The photography for the print campaign was in the hands of celebrity photographer Michel Comte.

It is therefore no coincidence that Nespresso coffee and appliances are marketed as a fashion brand. For example, there is an own glossy magazine, complete with a Vogue-like appearance in which the 'legendary star photographer' Michel Comte is presented, fashionably posing with his chin in his hands. He prefers to capture 'humanitarian images' in war-torn countries like Afghanistan, but he also signed for Nespresso's most recent advertising campaign.

Then there are the Nespresso flagship stores. For example, there is a large flagship store of the brand on the Paris Champs-Élysées, right next to prestigious neighbours such as Louis Vuitton and Hugo Boss. More than 1,500 square metres of coffee in shiny aluminum cups, espresso machines – only suitable for Nespresso of course – and mocha-scented candles at €35, in a decor of gold leaf, mirror walls, and chandeliers. The festive opening a few years ago, in the absence of George Clooney, was cheered up by movie star Sharon Stone and went according to the best traditions of the Paris fashion world: flashy cameras, long lines, and cham-pagne. 'Brilliant' and 'superslick', applauds a branding expert about the Nespresso marketing strategy. He talks about 'emotion' and about customers who want an 'experience' instead of an old-fashioned cup of coffee. "Nespresso radiates: we are unique. Look at the fancy design of the Nespresso boutiques, the colours of the rows of cups. Who wouldn't like to spoil himself with that?"

Nespresso – part of the Swiss company Nestlé, with brands such as Nescafé, Maggi, Buitoni, and Perrier, the largest food group in the world – has been a growing brand for more than ten years. Nespresso is the European market leader in packaged coffee. In 2016, sales of an estimated 4.6 billion Swiss francs were achieved (around 4.2 billion euros), a growth of around 6 per cent compared to the previous year. For 2017, a turnover target of 5 billion francs is set.

The Nespresso club counts more than five million members worldwide. Customers order their coffee via the internet or by telephone. Because that's how it works: the coffee – per serving packaged in an aluminum cap and only suitable for Nespresso machines produced by a limited number of manufacturers including Krups, Siemens, and DeLonghi – is not for sale in the supermarket, but is delivered at home. Or you buy it in the Nespresso stores. With this distribution system, Nespresso keeps the price at a certain level, because supermarkets cannot offer the product at a discount. He compares it with the chocolates brand Australian, which until recently were only sold in their own shop: not only do people pay 28 euros for 24 chocolates, they pay the price because they feel that they are buying something special. The price level of the corresponding coffee machines, however, varies as much as the profile of the target audience. Prices vary from the Essenza of less than 150 euros to Porsche designs of almost 1,000 euros. But you can also get them for free: in many subscription plans of glossy magazines the coffee machines are given away for free. But Nespresso is more than just marketing. Friend and foe agree that you make an excellent espresso, macchiato, or cappuccino with it. Otherwise Michelin-starred restaurants like the world-famous The Fat Duck in London would not offer Nespresso.

The secret is the aluminium portion packaging, which ensures that the coffee does not lose taste. Coffee that is exposed to the air loses most of the aromas within 72 hours. The disadvantage of all that aluminium is that it is not good for the environment. But there are recycling systems for that, according to Nespresso. In Switzerland, next to practically every glass container, there is a container for the cups. The company also strives for corporate social responsibility in the field of coffee production. Thirty-five per cent of the beans come from the AAA programme, which guarantees sustainable cultivation and a good price for coffee farmers. Once upon a time in the 1970s, Nestlé struggled with an image problem, after the group had put milk powder for baby food on the market in developing countries. Because of the contaminated water on the spot – water was needed to make milk out of the milk powder – breastfeeding was a safer choice. A call for an international boycott was the result. Nestlé wanted that type of publicity never again.

But George Clooney also received some critical questions from the press. How he thought he could justify advertising for a multinational, a journalist once asked. Clooney replied that he works for Nespresso, not for Nestlé. When that turned out not to be enough, he replied annoyed: "*I am not going to apologize to you for trying to make a living once in a while. I find that an irritating question.*"

Questions

1. The case specifies a target for 2017. Is this a corporate, a marketing, or a marketing mix objective? Please explain your answer.
2. The book distinguishes five forms of innovation. Under which form(s) of innovation would you label the introduction of Nespresso in 2006?
3. Nespresso does not sell through the supermarket. As a result, supermarkets cannot offer the product at a discount, and the 'sophisticated' image is not affected. Why does Nespresso then allow that glossy magazines offer the coffee machines for free to attract subscribers?
4. Define a price objective for Nespresso.
5. Would you recommend a penetration strategy for the coffee cups when introducing a new taste variety for Nespresso? Why (not)?
6. Which functions does the packaging of the Nespresso cups fulfil?
7. a)   Does it make sense to define the distribution objective for Nespresso in terms of non-weighted or in terms of weighted distribution? Explain your answer.
   b)   Define an appropriate distribution objective for Nespresso.
8. Describe the distribution structure (channel selection) of Nespresso.
9. Describe the distribution intensity of Nespresso. How does this relate to the type of product (convenience, shopping, or specialty good) that Nespresso wants to be?

Chapter 13

Marketing communication

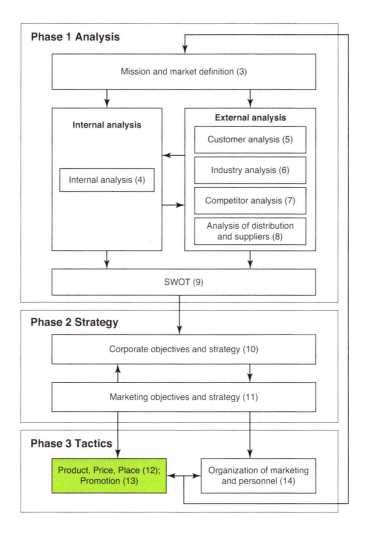

Phase 1 Analysis

Mission and market definition (3)

Internal analysis

Internal analysis (4)

External analysis

Customer analysis (5)

Industry analysis (6)

Competitor analysis (7)

Analysis of distribution and suppliers (8)

SWOT (9)

Phase 2 Strategy

Corporate objectives and strategy (10)

Marketing objectives and strategy (11)

Phase 3 Tactics

Product, Price, Place (12); Promotion (13)

Organization of marketing and personnel (14)

Key points in this chapter

- ■ See the relationships between the marketing strategy and communication.
- ■ Know how to formulate objectives for communication.
- ■ Know the steps in the communication planning process.
- ■ Understand the role of companies and advertising agencies.
- ■ Be able to make a communication plan, including online communication.
- ■ Know how to measure communication effects.

Introduction

The 'P' of promotion consists of communication and 'actions' (promotions). Communication then involves informing and convincing the target audience of certain characteristics of the brand; thus, it has not only short-term goals but also long-term goals. 'Actions' (*sales promotion*) refer to all short-term efforts to achieve more sales by making temporary changes in the four Ps. To connect with daily usage, we use marketing communication as an umbrella concept that includes all sale promotion tools. We call the steps that have to be taken to arrive at the execution of the marketing communication the communication planning process.

Clearly, the way in which companies and people communicate has drastically changed since the invention of the internet. So, online communication, including social media, became an important part of marketing communication and will be treated in this chapter as such. In the first section we provide an overview of the steps in communication planning. Then in sections 13.2 to 13.10 all steps are reviewed, where a separate section (13.9) is devoted to online communication.

13.1 Steps in communication planning

In the planning of communication, the concept of integrated communication plays a central role. This concept means that a company should synchronize their communication instruments (such as social media and TV advertising) in such a way that a consistent and clear message is given to the target groups. Clearly the positioning of the brand should be the starting point for integrated communication. This sounds quite logical, but companies have relatively limited experience with online communication including social media, and still have to learn how to logically incorporate these media into their communication mix. At the same time, integration with, for example, personal selling is sometimes a challenge: if in external communication a certain brand personality may be 'portrayed' (e.g. "You are the central focus for us"), but if that promise is not fulfilled at the first telephone contact because of long waiting times and less than friendly telephone operators, the company loses credibility. Oddly, especially with many service providers, the harmonization of external and internal communication leaves a lot to be desired.

A company itself can organize communication, but in practice this is mostly not effective. The reason is that companies often lack the necessary effective communication skills:

1. Developing a so-called 'creative concept'.
2. Planning the communication instruments (for example, deciding on the media schedule and the media formats).
3. Buying media space (for example, in print and on TV).
4. Developing 'own' communication instruments such as a website.

In practice, companies can hire agencies to help them with these specific skills. In this chapter we assume that a company will do that. This means that some steps in the communication planning process will be taken by the company and some by external agencies. Of course, there are circumstances where a company will do everything, for example, in the case of small or medium-sized enterprises (SMEs). Figure 13.1 gives an overview of the steps taken in the communication planning process.

The company (or 'advertiser') has the primary task of choosing a communication target audience and proposition (message), and determining the communication goals and a corresponding budget. In practice, the actual 'imagining' and elaboration of the communication expressions and the selection of the media are delegated to a communications consulting agency (also called an advertising agency). Ideally, the advertiser will subsequently perform the measurement of results.

Tasks of the company
1. Determination of the target audience (section 13.2)
2. Selection of a proposition (section 13.3)
3. Communication objectives and communication budget (section 13.4)
4. Briefing for the communication consulting agency (section 13.5)

Tasks for the communication consulting agency
5. Creation and execution (section 13.6)
6. Pretesting (section 13.7)
7. Communication instruments (section 13.8 and 13.9 (online))

Task of the company
8. Brand tracking and advertising tracking and effect research (section 13.10)

Figure 13.1 Steps taken in the communication planning process

13.2 Determination of the target audience

The first step to be taken by the company is to define the communication target audience: To whom do we want to tell something? The communication target audience does not have to correspond to the marketing target audience (see section 11.2). Often the communication target audience is broader: not only should the potential buyers be reached but also the most important influencing groups. In this context, it is relevant to know who plays which role within a household in the purchasing process of a product category (initiator, decision maker, etc.). For example, in toys the mother or father is the final decision maker, and women have a large input into the brand choice for cars. Older people often let themselves be guided by the opinions of their children and grandchildren for certain purchases. Another item that plays a role is whether the goal is to hold onto existing users or to attract new buyers.

The communication target audience should be described in as much detail as possible so that the advertising agency has as much information as possible for the development of the campaign. The best results are obtained by describing the target audience as an individual based on the dimensions reviewed in Chapter 5:

- general background variables;
- product category-related variables;
- brand-related variables.

A different categorization is more related to communication decisions (Figure 13.2):

1. Strategic dimensions.
2. Creative dimensions.
3. Media dimensions.

Strategic dimensions are related to the actual use of the brand or product. For example, an important choice is whether the manager wants to communicate mostly with users or with non-users. Creative dimensions are those that in effect relate to customer values: the 'reasons' for brand use. These dimensions give the creative types at the advertising agency an impression of the relationship between the target audience and the brand. The so-called media dimensions refer to the general characteristics of the target audience (independent of the brand): 'hard' background variables such as age and income class as well as qualitative variables such as habits, hobbies, and interests ('lifestyle'). These dimensions are important in the creative process: What kind of person is the average user? This is closely related to the brand personality: an average user may also be portrayed by describing the brand as a person. The second use for media dimensions is related to the formulation of communication objectives and the execution of media planning. For both steps it is desirable to describe the target audience in measurable terms.

1. **Strategic dimensions: brand use**
   - Users or non-users
   - Trial purchases, habit purchases, brand loyalty
   - Preference for our brand or for that of the competitor

2. **Creative dimensions: relationship between brand and user**
   - How, when, and where does the target audience use the product?
   - What does the brand mean to the target audience?
   - What is important to the target audience?
   - What are the current brand associations?

3. **Media dimensions: users' profile or 'brand personality'**
   - What is the demographic and socioeconomic profile?
   - What is the 'lifestyle' (including media consumption)?

Figure 13.2 Dimensions for formulating the communication target audience

Comparing Figure 13.2 with the three categories from section 5.2.2, it may be seen that in the end the same variables are used.

13.3 Selecting a proposition

The proposition is the message of the communication: What does the brand or product provide to the consumer to make his or her life a little easier or richer or to solve a problem? The proposition proceeds from the positioning that has been chosen for the brand and is in effect the simplified-language version of the promise that is being made. In section 11.3 we formulated a positioning statement: *Within the category _____ brand A will be better for target audience _____ than competitor B for goal _____ (usage goal) because it _____ (advantage, benefit). This is demonstrated through _____ (characteristic) and leads to the brand personality _____ (final value).* The proposition may be deduced from this type of positioning. Many designations for the choice of the proposition are used in practice, such as 'advertising strategy', 'copy strategy', and 'creative strategy'. The last designation incorrectly creates the assumption that the proposition has to be created by the advertising agency.

In practice, choosing a proposition is a challenging process. A positioning or proposition is often too broad. A brand wants to excel in too many elements, and the relevant managers want to say as much as possible in the communication. However, in communication, it is essential to be clear and therefore to focus on a single message. In selecting the core message, it is important to reason strongly from the perspective of the target audience. In effect, only two questions need to be asked:

1. How does the target audience perceive our brand now (*image*)?
2. How do we want them to perceive our brand (*identity*)?

When image and identity correspond, there is no communication problem. However, if there are differences, it is the role of communication to adjust the image. The way in which both questions are elaborated depends on the level of customer values that is important in the product category: Is the main focus on instrumental values (physical product characteristics) or on final values (abstract product characteristics)?

Instrumental values are very important in 'problem-solving' product categories such as laundry detergents and feminine hygiene products. Procter & Gamble is very active in these markets. In choosing a communication message Procter uses the so-called Admap (Figure 13.3).

The Admap entails that four simple questions have to be answered:

1. What is the target group currently doing? For example, using competitive brand G.
2. What is the target group currently thinking? For example, competitive brand G removes potato peel better.
3. What should the target group think? For example, our brand X removes potato peel better.
4. What should the target group do? For example, buy our brand X.

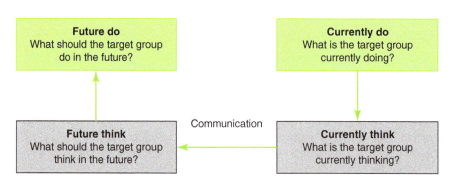

Figure 13.3 **Admap: a method for choosing a functional communication message**

The gap between questions 2 and 3 can be resolved through communication (a campaign which shows that potato peel is removed).

This method is suitable for adjusting instrumental values but less suitable for adjusting abstract values. The reason for this is that an abstract image cannot be easily adjusted with communication, since a brand cannot suddenly start portraying a different personality (consistency; see section 11.3.4).

To develop a proposition in which *abstract values* play an important role, the technique of *perceptual mapping* is often used (see section 5.4.4). In such depictions it is easy to represent a 'desired position' (identity) and therefore include the way the company wants to adjust the image. The fact that this is possible only on a limited scale implies that only limited movements are feasible in such image pictures. The *semantic differential* (section 5.4.4) is also a useful tool in this regard.

13.4 Communication objectives and communication budget

13.4.1 Measuring results and effects

A *communication objective* is a desired communication effect. Communication objectives are a tool for the communication planning process. If the requirements for useful objectives are met (Specific, Measurable, Ambitious, Realistic, Timed: SMART), communication objectives are the standards that can be used to evaluate whether a campaign has been successful. Communication objectives are therefore very closely related to the *measurement of results*. Conversely, measuring results has little value if no objectives have been formulated. Thus, the measurement of results means that a measurement is taken of the extent to which the objectives have been achieved. To make it plausible that the measured results have actually been 'caused' by the communication, *effect research* should be performed in addition to the measurement of results. Effect research generally involves a search for a causal relationship between an 'input variable' (in this case communication) and an output variable (communication goal). Figure 13.4 summarizes these issues.

Although formulating goals and measuring results are necessary from a planning perspective, in practice this is done infrequently. Usually objectives are mentioned, but they are often not quantitative. Sometimes quantitative 'advertising goals' are formulated, but

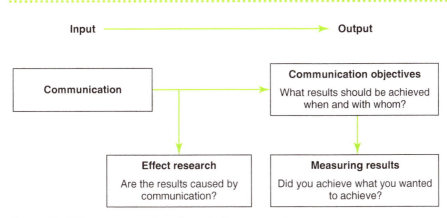

Figure 13.4 **Measurement of results and effect research**

they often appear to be related to coverage. Although coverage is a required condition to achieve real effects, coverage goals in themselves cannot be interpreted as effect objectives. Examples of true communication (effect) objectives include advertising awareness, brand awareness, and brand associations.

13.4.2 Choice of communication objectives

In choosing communication objectives, the question is "What do we want to achieve for whom and when?" We have already discussed the 'for whom' question. We now discuss the question "What do we want to achieve?"

A goal of communication will always be to achieve more sales, make more profit, attract more visitors, and so forth. Yet goals such as market share are not suitable as a communication objective, since those types of items are determined by many factors besides communication. Sales variables may be mentioned as objectives in communication, but then they should be marketing objectives. 'True' communication objectives are deduced from the marketing goals.

Various diagrams are presented in the literature for the purpose of selecting variables that may be used as communication goals. Most are based on the classic hierarchy of communication effects: knowledge (cognition), feeling (affection), and behaviour (conation). Quantifying these knowledge, feeling, and behaviour effects is very useful, but research shows that a hierarchy of effects cannot be demonstrated (Vakratsas and Ambler, 1999). Another disadvantage of classifications that are based on hierarchical models is that no explicit relationship is established with the input: the communication itself. A diagram that actually does this is the so-called 'Advertising Response Matrix' by Franzen (1998), which is shown (in a revised form) in Figure 13.5.

The Advertising Response Matrix indicates that in effectiveness research (and therefore also in the formulation of objectives) three levels should be distinguished:

1. Communication input.
2. Output at the individual level.
3. Effects at the market level.

Communication input

A.	Characteristics of the advertisement (campaign) Choice of media	▪ Rough drafts, creative execution variables ▪ Physical variables (length of advertising spot, format, colour, etc.)
B.	Communication expenditures	▪ Volume: millimetres, seconds ▪ Expenditures: money (share of voice: spending share)
	Confrontation (exposure) and reach	▪ Reach: absolute or relative [e.g. gross rating points (GRPs): per cent viewing figures; unique visitors (online)] ▪ Contact frequency

Output on the individual level

C.	Communication responses	▪ Communication awareness ▪ Communication attitude (likeability)
D.	Brand responses	▪ Brand awareness [top-of-mind awareness (TOMA), spontaneous, aided] ▪ Brand associations (strength, relevance/ importance, distinctiveness)
E.	Brand behaviour responses	▪ Purchasing intention ▪ Trial purchases ▪ Brand loyalty and repeat purchases

Output at market level

F.	Market responses*	▪ Sales ▪ Market share

Figure 13.5 **Communication objectives and measurable variables**

* Not communication objectives but marketing objectives.
Source: Adapted from Franzen (1998).

1. Communication input

The communication input level represents the communication effort. It consists of a qualitative component (category A: the characteristics of the campaign) and a quantitative component (category B: the weight of the campaign). Qualitative aspects are the substantive characteristics of the campaign (e.g. in advertising at McDonald's a menu or a Big Mac in the picture or not, using humour or not) and the physical variables (the length of the advertising spot, using outdoor advertising or not, etc.). Quantitative aspects are the efforts expressed in terms of volume (number of seconds) or money (e.g. the advertising budget portion *share of voice;* McDonald's share in total fast food advertising expenditures is 50 per cent) or the achieved coverage (e.g. gross rating points (GRPs): percentage of viewing figures; a campaign by McDonald's has been shown, for example, 20 times in one month with an average viewing figure of 10 per cent and produced 200 GRPs; if the average number of times people have seen the spot was, for example, four (average contact frequency of four), the net coverage is 200/4 = 50 per cent). With online communication, coverage is the number of unique visitors.

2. Output at individual level

The second level is a representation of individual responses; that is, the responses of people from the target audience that the company has to measure itself through market research. These responses consist of three main groups:

1. *Communication respon*ses. These are reactions to a single expression, such as the appreciation (*likeability;* the percentage that enjoyed a particular commercial by McDonald's, or the number of likes of a Facebook message) and reactions to a series of expressions such as advertising awareness (e.g. the percentage of people from the target audience who know that McDonald's is running a campaign with soccer teams that are visiting McDonald's).
2. *Brand responses*. This is brand awareness (already very high for McDonald's) and brand associations (percentage of people from the target audience who know that McDonald's offers a soccer menu, percentage of people who consider McDonald's to be child friendly, etc.).
3. *Brand behaviour responses*. These are behavioural intentions with regard to the brand (percentage that expects to be visiting McDonald's within one week), trial purchases, and information behaviour, purchasing behaviour, usage behaviour, and brand loyalty (e.g. percentage that indicates recommending McDonald's to friends). Online behaviour is, for example, clicking behaviour: clicking and ordering. This is called *conversion*: the percentage of viewers taking the intended action. Reactions to online messages are also brand responses. The interesting issue of online media is that reach and responses are easy to collect. In effect, it may be interpreted as *single source data*: a number of data from the same source for each individual site visitor.

3. Market responses

The third level consists of the aggregated effects at the *market level*. This refers to the size and strength of the brand preference in the market, the sales, the market share, the price elasticity, the profit margin, and the cash flow. Both at this level and at the second level the issue is the effects over time: direct effects (after a single expression), short-term effects (within one year), and long-term effects (after one year).

In terms of the Advertising Response Matrix, market response (sales, category F) is the most important goal that needs to be achieved. However, this is a marketing objective. Individual purchasing behaviour (category E) is also a marketing objective. An exception to this is *trial*. Trial purchases are influenced mostly by communication and may thus be considered communication goals. The clearest communication objectives are represented under category D: brand awareness and brand associations. The reason for this is that these objectives are influenced primarily by communication. A second reason is that these are also the sources of *brand equity* according to Keller (2013). In addition, the communication responses may be presented as communication objectives

	Total		Target audience A		Target audience B	
	1/1/19 (current)	1/1/20 (plan)	1/1/19 (current)	1/1/20 (plan)	1/1/19 (current)	1/1/20 (plan)
Aided advertising recall	__%	__%	__%	__%	__%	__%
Top-of-mind brand awareness (TOMA)	__%	__%	__%	__%	__%	__%
Percentage of people who associate (aided) brand with "adventurous"	__%	__%	__%	__%	__%	__%
Percentage of people who consider brand at purchase	__%	__%	__%	__%	__%	__%
Percentage of people who purchase brand for the first time (trial)	__%	__%	__%	__%	__%	__%

Figure 13.6 **Communication objectives for a brand**

except for the fact that this is never sufficient: communication is a tool used to achieve something with the brand. However, communication responses are very important in pre-testing: testing beforehand how an advertisement or commercial comes across to people in the target audience.

In summary, the middle part of the Advertising Response Matrix (categories C, D, and E, with the exception of brand loyalty and repeat purchases) contains all possible communications objectives. Which variables are chosen from this range depends on where the largest bottlenecks are. At this point the 'classic advertising models' are useful. These models assume that consumers progress through three phases: cognitive (knowledge), affective (attitude), and conative (behaviour). The oldest model is the *AIDA model*: attention, interest, desire, action. If spontaneous brand awareness is low, there may have to be a campaign to increase it. If the price image is unfavourable, improvement in this regard may be necessary. If the desire is doing well but the trial purchases are not, planning an action is conceivable. Research in combination with the desired proposition will therefore be the basis for the choice of the specific communication objectives. Each campaign will also have a marketing objective, and it is therefore conceivable to incorporate the marketing objective into a communication plan.

To meet the requirements for objectives, the objective should be quantified and should contain a time designation. Examples are as follows:

- Within half a year, 80 per cent of our target audience (women over the age of 30) should have heard of our brand at some time (*aided brand recall*).
- Within one year, the percentage of the 4 million households with a washing machine that identifies brand X as a low-foaming detergent that is effective in cleaning laundry should increase from 10 per cent to 40 per cent.
- By 1 October of the following year, 70 per cent of our target audience should have purchased the product at least once, and the average report mark that the 'trial purchasers' give our product at a minimum should be equal to that of our competitor Q (combined objective).

If a company has different target audiences, the objectives may be summarized (see Figure 13.6). This figure also shows that to measure the progress and success of a campaign, a measurement of the variables for the objectives should be taken both before (zero measure) and after.

13.4.3 Budget determination

Once the communication objectives have been determined, the available budget is also determined. These steps are closely linked: ambitious objectives cost a lot of money. In practice, various methods are used to determine the communication budget. The most common methods are the following:

1. A percentage of turnover (last year's sales or expected sales).
2. Closing entry: what the company can afford.
3. Comparable share to that of a competitor.
4. Based on objectives and tasks.

The disadvantages of the first two methods are that reverse reasoning is applied: the turnover determines the sales promotion instead of the opposite. This leads to *cyclical budgeting*. Moreover, the budget then is not based on opportunities in the market and the specific required promotion of products. A disadvantage of the third method is that it is uncertain whether the competition is doing well. A company is better off looking at its own resources, opportunities, and objectives. Budgeting based on *objectives and tasks* is therefore the best method: What do we want to achieve, and how much does it cost? For that purpose, items such as desired coverage should be determined and the number of required contacts per consumer reached. Since the link between objectives other than coverage and budget is not always easy to indicate, this will require making assumptions about effectiveness on the basis of past experience. See Case 13.1 for an example.

In this phase the budget is usually tentative. Depending on the concrete plans that are developed in later phases (e.g. by the advertising agency), the budget will often be modified. In addition, sometimes the company has already made a global allocation for resources; for example, for advertising, consumer promotions, and trade promotions.

13.5 Briefing and requirements for communication

Earlier in this chapter we indicated that an advertising agency is almost always engaged in elaborating campaign development and media choice (see also Case 13.2). In presenting the assignment, a briefing is used: a description of what is expected of the communication consulting agency. The marketing or brand manager is primarily responsible for this process. After consultation and deliberation with the advertising agency, the agency should declare its agreement with the briefing. The components of a briefing are briefly listed in Figure 13.7. A lot of information for the briefing may be obtained from the marketing plan.

In an introductory section, a description is provided of the company, the brand or product, the characteristics, technical data, and so forth. There follows a reproduction of the objectives and an elaboration of the other Ps: product, price, place, and promotion/communication (to the extent that they have been determined already). A description

Case 13.1 Budget determination based on objectives

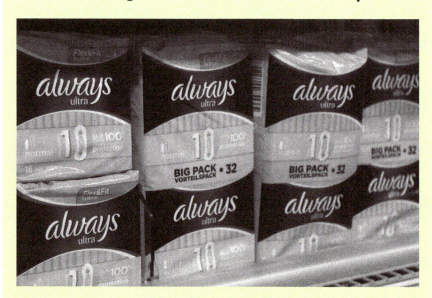

Procter & Gamble and Unilever cut in digital ad spend

As part of P&G's recent work to re-evaluate its marketing spend and weed out spend that is ineffective, the CPG giant said it cut $200 million in online spend in 2017. Last year, P&G revealed during an earnings call that it cut between $100 million to $140 million between April and July due to bots and brand safety concerns. The measures then continued for the rest of 2017, with the brand cutting roughly another $100 million between July and December. P&G's $200 million digital cut was re-invested into areas with 'media reach' including television, audio, and ecommerce.

Source: *Adweek*, 1 March 2018

Marketing background
1. What it is about: company and brand or product
2. Environment: summary of SWOT analysis and key problem

Campaign goal
3. Communication target audience
4. Promise and proof
5. Brand personality
6. Measurable communication goal and budget

Preconditions
7. Media and resources
8. Other preconditions (e.g. style and time planning)

Figure 13.7 **Components of an advertising briefing**

of the strengths, weaknesses, opportunities, and threats (SWOT) analysis provides the framework within which the campaign is developed. The perceptions of the target group are very important. The core problem often has to do with the difference between image and identity. For the competition, the central focus is the content of their communication, the media allocation, and the budget. The media behaviour of the competitors may sometimes be analysed by the agency on the basis of advertising expenditure figures by Nielsen (see section 7.7). Components 1 and 2 form the marketing background of the campaign. Components 3 to 6 are the core of the briefing. First, the communication target audience is described, for example, based on the dimensions mentioned in section 11.2. Component 4 is the focused proposition (with any evidence), and component 5 contains the brand personality.

Then there is the communication goal: What does the manager want to achieve with that target audience, and how much money is available (draft budget)? The budget mentioned in the briefing may sometimes be modified on the basis of the creative ideas of the agency.

In component 7 (media and resources), the wishes of the company are indicated in relation to any other sales promotion tools (e.g. online) and the media choice. Some companies determine a budget allocation for this (e.g. division of print/television); others do it qualitatively or delegate it entirely to the agency.

The final component contains the other preconditions within which the campaign has to be developed, such as necessary elements in advertising expressions (house style and layout), whether or not to use humour, and legal regulations. In this component time planning is also described.

A clear and well-defined briefing is very important for the advertising agency. Advertising agencies often complain that companies do not know how to write good briefings. The biggest problem is that companies cannot or do not make a choice. They want too much. This leads to briefings that are broad and therefore vague. A vague briefing means insufficient direction, which means the advertising agency can go in any direction with the campaign and brand consistency is no longer feasible. The disadvantage of this is that the campaign may go in a different direction from what was planned originally, and there is also a risk that subsequently a lot more work may need to be done if certain designs are rejected by the advertiser. A good advertising agency will therefore refuse to approve a briefing that has not been completed. At this point, the task of the client is finished and the baton is passed to the advertising firm.

13.6 Creation and execution

The simplest way to transmit a message is to just tell the message. However, in advertising this mostly does not work, since simply telling the message does not create enough attention. Therefore, creativity is needed. *Creation* involves inventing a 'fun' way to sell the message to the target audience. The goal of creativity (in this context) is to come up with a so-called *concept*: an idea to tell the message See for example Case 13.3. The concept is the link between the message and the media (Figure 13.8). *Execution* is the elaboration of that method and the development of the campaign.

We will now discuss the creative process. In advertising agencies, two people are usually involved in the creative process: a *copywriter* (text writer) and an *art director*

Case 13.2 The role of advertising agencies

Companies increasingly do their own advertising

Some companies choose to organize their communication themselves, without the use of an external advertising agency. The reason may be that online communication is becoming extremely important and that this part of the communication is more difficult to outsource: it has to do with direct customer contact, including using social media. Hiring an advertising agency may then make it more difficult to coordinate all forms of communication. And integrated marketing communication is still the key to effective branding.

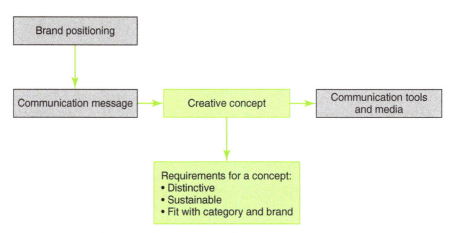

Figure 13.8 **Development of a concept in advertising**

(designer). Sometimes one of them thinks of the idea, and sometimes it is a joint effort. The goal is to find a 'hook' on which to hang the campaign. Few tools are available for the invention of a creative idea. Creation has been called a 'handicraft'. A creative type needs to have a 'feel' for it. One creative type is also different from another. Some advertising agencies are well known for their surprising, innovative campaigns, yet that is not appropriate for every brand. A copywriter will mostly come up with a slogan (if needed). Many brands do not use a slogan, although it is an effective way of summarizing the core value of the brand. Geursen (1990) has developed a 'model' that may be used in the process of creation (Figure 13.9).

Creation starts with considering 'something about the brand' ("Nike shoes are fast"). This 'something' should ideally be invented by the company (proposition), and if it is not, the agency will think of something about the brand. Most often, an advertiser comes up with many 'unique selling points' of the brand and the agency then has to choose one on which to focus. Agencies have commented that this is simplest when the brand actually has something to say, for example, something new. Research on television advertising (Lodish et al., 1995a) has shown that the effect is the strongest when a brand has something new to announce. If there is no instrumental message, a search can be made for something more abstract (transformational positioning): an element of the brand personality. The creative type subsequently ponders the way in which that can be communicated. The creative idea may be an illustration, a piece of text, a parallel ("a greyhound is fast"), an incident, and so on, that can logically be linked to the message and the brand. From this central idea (concept) the campaign is developed (such as a picture of a greyhound with sneakers) and the 'something' of the brand is communicated in an enlarged fashion (hence the triangle).

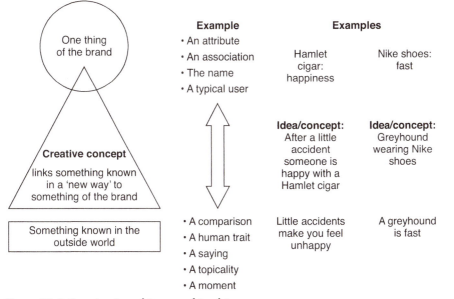

Figure 13.9 **Creation is making one thing big**

Source: based on Geursen (1990).

Case 13.3 Creative concept

Budweiser unveils its biggest ever global campaign ahead of the FIFA World Cup

Budweiser is launching its biggest ever global campaign ahead of the FIFA World Cup, which kicks off in Russia next month. Speaking on a conference call today (8 May) Miguel Patricio, the global CMO of Budweiser's parent company Anheuser-Busch InBev, says its new campaign will champion Budweiser's dream of bringing people together while energizing and inspiring the 3.2 billion football fans watching the World Cup.

The campaign, titled 'Light up the FIFA World Cup' and produced by the company's lead agency Anomaly, aims to "encapsulate the unparalleled euphoric energy of the world's biggest sporting event". It features the largest beer delivery to date, plus the deployment of noise-activated red light cups. Budweiser, the official beer sponsor of the World Cup for 32 years, will launch its new campaign in more than 50 countries, marking its biggest ever global activation. The campaign features a video of an ambitious beer delivery which shows drones carrying Budweiser from its Brewery in St Louis, Missouri (USA) to World Cup watching parties, from Shanghai to Rio de Janeiro, and to Luzhniki Stadium in Moscow.

Source: *Marketing Week*, 8 May 2018

Figure 13.9 listed the requirements for creative ideas:

■ *Distinctive*. Many ads for cars show beautiful landscapes with a car. This is not distinctive and can hardly be called a 'concept'.
■ *Sustainable*. This means that ideally the concept may be used in different ways, with different examples, and also stay interesting in the long run. Ideas that can be developed to go beyond a single campaign into a campaign that will run for years are very valuable. Case 13.4 gives an example of such an enduring concept. Sometimes good creative ideas are thrown out because of imagined 'wear-out'. The true cause of this

problem is often a change in managers or advertising agencies. Continuing for a long time with a creative idea requires a long-term vision.

- *Fit with the category and the brand.* There should be a kind of logical relation between the creative concept and the message. This is one of the biggest shortcomings of creative ideas. To be noticed among the enormous amount of communication expressions, agencies continually come up with 'creative' approaches. This makes advertising entertaining, and commercials may hold people's attention. However, the lack of a logical link with the brand leads to a situation in which the advertising is remembered but not the brand. In that case, advertising is by definition not effective. For example, a viewer who watches a television commercial in which a dog with dirty paws walks into the kitchen and a child dries the dog with a towel would not automatically think of candy bars.

Case 13.4 Consistent advertising

Sustaining an advertising concept for a long time: Hamlet cigars

An example of a brand that elaborated on the same creative idea for more than 30 years is British Hamlet cigars. The concept (advertising idea) was the accident around the corner. Something went wrong for someone, but by lighting a Hamlet cigar after the incident, the person still developed a satisfied feeling. With the supportive slogan "Happiness is a cigar called Hamlet, the mild cigar" and always with the same music, both an instrumental value (light) and especially a final value (happiness) were communicated; therefore, this was a two-sided positioning. In the years 1961 to 1994 the company made endless variations on this theme (after that time, television advertising for tobacco products was outlawed), and the Hamlet campaign won many prizes with famous commercials such as "Man in photo booth" and "Free kick in soccer", and was a successful cigar brand for many years.

13.7 Pretesting

There are three forms of pretesting:

1.   Qualitative testing of a design for an advertising expression: *concept test*.
2.   Qualitative testing of a fully developed advertising expression: *qualitative pretest*.
3.   Quantitative testing of a fully developed advertising expression: *quantitative pretest*.

13.7.1 Concept test

In the consultation between the advertising agency and the company there is usually a moment at which a design for an advertising expression (based on the 'creative idea') is submitted for approval to the advertiser. In print advertising the concept is then an advertising sketch, and for television advertising a *storyboard* is made: drawings of all the scenes with corresponding indications of the audio support (music and text) that is planned. In this phase it may be desirable to ask several consumers for feedback on the design. This could involve questions regarding intelligibility and attractiveness. An advantage of concept testing is that after this stage it is still relatively easy and cheap to make changes. A disadvantage is that the final expression is different from the concept. Especially in television advertising this is a problem: a commercial including music, editing, and so on may produce completely different feelings than does a storyboard.

13.7.2 Qualitative pretest

A test similar to a concept test may be performed with a ready-made expression. An advantage is that the actual expression is being tested and the respondents therefore receive a faithful image of the advertising. A disadvantage is the high cost of modifications.

13.7.3 Quantitative pretest and A/B testing

Quantitative pretests have the following goals:

- ■   To obtain insight into the expected effects of one or more advertising expressions.
- ■   To obtain insight into which components of an expression receive the most attention.

Online quantitative pretesting is popular and easy. Simply make, for example, two different websites, banners, vlogs, etc. and track the number of page views and clicks. This is called *A/B testing*: testing two online communication vehicles. For offline communication quantitative pretesting demands more effort. The most direct way to do quantitative pretesting is to ask a group of respondents to give their opinion about an expression with the aid of closed questions (e.g. with so-called *Likert scales*: scales with opposite values at either end, for example, very unclear … very clear or completely disagree … completely agree). This way of pretesting is used by Procter & Gamble (see Case 13.5).

Aside from questions about the expression to be tested, questions may be posed about the brand, for example, the brand personality. In this way a quantitative pretest can easily be used to perform a 'zero measurement' of the variables included in the objectives.

Case 13.5 Pretesting

Quantitative pretesting at Procter & Gamble

Procter & Gamble is one of the largest advertisers. Procter is strong in television advertising. Given the enormous investments, it is no wonder that P&G makes sure to pretest the majority of its commercials. The pretesting focuses on three factors: persuasiveness/credibility, uniqueness/distinctiveness, and trial intention. Through doing this pretesting for many brands for many years, P&G has compiled a large data file with pretest results. This database also contains the results following the closure of a campaign. By comparing the pretest and the actual results of brands within product categories, P&G gains a detailed insight into the predictive power of pretests. Based on these experiences, standards have been developed that a commercial must meet in a pretest in order to be approved.

Some research agencies offer quantitative pretesting tools using eye movement analysis. In 'laboratory circumstances', the eye movements of respondents who watch websites, advertisements in magazines, on television, and so forth, are documented. With these data it may be detected which components of the expression are watched the most, how long the expression as a whole is watched, and what influence of the 'environment' of the expression (the context, such as editorial pages in a magazine). The scores are compared with those of competitors and with the medium as a whole. In all of these cases attention is measured, which is not a communication-effect objective, though it is a condition for achieving communication effects.

13.7.4 Limitations and use of pretesting

Pretests have two important limitations:

1. *Often no actual circumstances.* With the exception of online A/B testing, pretests are conducted only in research circumstances. The issue here is whether respondents in 'laboratory conditions' will behave in the same manner at home. A danger is that if respondents know why they are included, advertising expressions will receive too much attention.
2. *Bad predictive value.* Research by Lodish et al. (1995a) demonstrated that the results of quantitative pretests are poor predictors of achieved brand equity and market shares. The results of pretests should therefore not be used in absolute terms, especially not in comparative terms.

In light of these limitations, the question may be raised whether pretesting has any value. The simple answer is that it does. Research by Lodish et al. (1995b) into the long-term effects of television commercials shows that if commercials do not have an effect in the short term, they will also not have an effect in the long term. This implies that it is important from the very beginning to measure the results of a campaign and compare them with the starting situation. If no short-term effects can be detected, action should be taken.

13.8 Communication tools and media

A company has a multitude of communication instruments at its disposal to stimulate customers to purchase its products. Figure 13.10 gives an overview. We make a

Brand elements
1. Brand name and name url
2. Design and logo
3. Packaging and location communication

Communication in service
4. Face-to-face communication of the staff

Promotional communication
5. Advertising
    - Print
    - TV, radio, cinema
    - Outdoor
6. Online communication
7. Promotions
8. Sales and personal selling
9. Direct marketing communication
10. Public relations
11. Sponsoring and events

Figure 13.10 **Marketing communication instruments**

distinction between 'fixed' brand elements, communication in service, and promotional communication.

Since online communication is relatively new and growing, much attention is given to online communication. But this does not mean that other ('offline') communication such as advertising on TV is no longer important. The studies by Sharp, reviewed in Chapter 1, show that dominance in visibility is strongly affecting sales. So, online and 'normal' marketing have to be integrated. Case 13.1 showed that companies as Procter & Gamble and Unilever cut their online spending in 2017.

We now analyse the communication instruments listed in Figure 13.10 and pay special attention to online communication (section 13.9).

Brand name, design, and packaging

The brand elements brand name, logo, and design are part of marketing strategy and are discussed in Chapter 11. They are the more or less 'fixed' communication tools that will not change yearly. Another characteristic of brand elements is that some of them can be legally protected, since they are legally defined as a 'brand' (such as the name or a logo). We also mentioned that design in the context of a shop is part of retail marketing, and strongly affects the shopping experience of consumers.

Packaging is part of the marketing instrument 'product' and is reviewed in section 12.2.

Communication in service

Communication in service is the personal contact between an employee and a customer. It can be related to providing information through the telephone, but it can also be the core of the product such as in education, consultancy, health care, retail, etc. If communication is an important part of the 'product' the quality of the 'product' will be strongly related to how the communication is experienced by customers. For example, the perceived quality which health care provides is sometimes strongly affected by how the doctors and other staff members communicate, rather than by the real outcomes of the health care process.

All other communication tools are part of promotional communication.

Advertising

Advertising includes every paid form of non-personal presentation and promotion of ideas, goods, or services by an identified sponsor. Advertising messages are communicated through media: public communication channels. Examples are magazine and television advertising, cinema commercials, outdoor advertising (billboards, bus shelters, etc.), and online advertising. Media themselves are also brands, and can also have 'sub-brands' such as TV programmes, specific magazines (titles), websites/platforms (Facebook, Google). Every medium has advertising income. Some media also have income from consumers, such as paid newspapers, magazines, and paid TV channels.

If a company or an advertising agency has developed some kind of communication message and concept, media have to be chosen. The choice of the media strategy is closely linked to the development of the campaign. Some concepts are appropriate exclusively for television, and others primarily for print. In practice, a combination of media is usually chosen. Factors that determine the media choice include the following:

- *Coverage.* Which medium can we use to reach the target audience as efficiently as possible?
- *Communication ability.* Suitability of the medium to the message: Is an explanation required? Does an 'atmosphere' need to be created? Is the message mostly *thematic* (informative) or action-oriented?
- *Contact frequency.* How often can we reach the target audience through the medium?
- *Costs.* What are the costs per 1,000 readers reached (print) or percentage viewing figures (gross rating points (GRPs): television and radio), and what are the total costs?

In choosing a combination of media (media 'schedule'), software may be used to 'compute' how many people will be reached and how often, with different combinations of media. These data are available, since in many countries, the coverage of media is measured through panel research: research with a fixed group of consumers who are willing to regularly provide information about what they read or watch (measured online).

Online communication

Section 13.9 is devoted to online communication.

Sales promotion

This includes all short-term actions directly targeted towards stimulating sales. There are three types of promotions (Blattberg and Neslin, 1990):

- *Consumer promotions.* These are promotions by manufacturers aimed at final customers, such as discount actions, money-back actions, and 'premium' actions (a temporary free gift with purchase); these actions are sometimes supported by in-store communications paid for by the manufacturer, such as special article presentations (*displays*).
- *Retailer promotions.* These are promotions of the retail trade targeted at the consumer, such as discount actions (paid for by the retailer).
- *Trade promotions.* These are actions of the manufacturer aimed at the retail trade, such as competitions for the highest sales or temporarily providing bonuses.

In the past few years, there has been a shift in consumer markets from advertising to promotions; increasingly, companies are choosing to stimulate sales in the short term. The causes of this include a greater acceptance by companies of the instrument of promotions, more pressure on product managers to achieve higher sales, and increased competition: more brands that are starting to resemble each other. Another factor may be that the availability of more data and more detailed data (scanning) makes it easier to measure the effects of promotions.

Three comments about the use of promotions follow:

1. Frequent use of promotions may have negative consequences for brand equity in the long run. Consumers start to doubt the quality and get used to *brand switching*. Therefore, it is recommended to use mostly value-adding promotions and fewer price discounts. Another recommendation is to make a promotion fit as much as possible with the brand; for example, by offering extras that fit logically with the brand.
2. Effect research into promotions shows that promotions are often not profitable for manufacturers (Van Heerde et al., 2003). Often there is a sales peak during the promotion, but afterwards the sales are typically lower (hoarding by consumers), and promotions do not always lead to effects that are favourable for the manufacturer, such as increased sales in relation to the competition and extra consumption. Another market effect is that competitors often react to each other's price promotions, thus decreasing the mutual market share effects.
3. Retailers are often not happy with actions because they lead to irregularities in demand and therefore make extra demands on logistics, inventory, and administration.

Some of these effects are summarized in Figure 13.11, which depicts the price promotion doom loop. Generally speaking, this circle shows the risk of a short-term (cash) orientation of companies instead of a long-term brand and customer orientation.

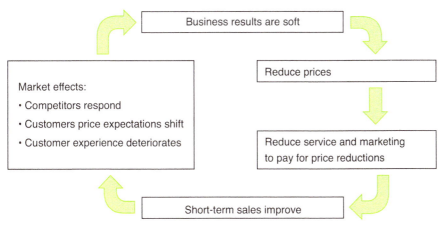

Figure 13.11 **Price promotion doom loop**

Source: Calkins (2005).

Sales and personal selling

Sales is aimed at realizing a transaction. It may be seen as the final step in getting the customer to buy your product, for example, a car. Personal selling is an oral presentation in a discussion with one or more potential customers to generate sales. Examples are representatives, product presentations, company days, exhibitions, and shows. Sales is related to account management. An account is a (large) customer of a company. An account manager is responsible for specific customers and has to take care of good relations with that customer. Account management is used by manufacturers, where the accounts are retailers, such as Walmart. Clearly, in order to be a good sales manager, personal communication skills are important.

Direct marketing communication

Direct marketing is a form of marketing aimed at obtaining and maintaining a structural, direct relationship between the supplier and the customer. Direct marketing communication is one-to-one communication used for this purpose. The forms most frequently applied are online communication, promotional messages sent directly to people (direct mail), and telephone sales.

Public relations (PR)

PR refers to the systematic promotion of mutual understanding between a company and its public groups. The goal is the creation and maintenance of a positive image in the public groups (customers, employees, suppliers, capital suppliers, shareholders, the government, and the general public). The tools of public relations include press releases, publicity, annual reports, sponsoring, and sponsored media (e.g. magazines of retailers).

PR is aimed at target audiences both outside and within the company. Although it is difficult to include internal PR with marketing, let alone with sales promotion, there is an overlap in activities. Marketing PR entails informing the company about its brands and products, and is applied on occasions such as the introduction of new products. In the case of 'calamities' PR is important (see the material on crisis communication in section 11.7.3).

Sponsoring and events

In sponsoring, the sponsor provides money, goods, services, or know-how to the party that is being sponsored, which in turn contributes to the achievement of the communication objectives of the sponsor. Sponsoring is a thematic communication instrument that may be used both for marketing communication and for corporate communication. Among all sponsoring revenues, the majority (70 per cent) goes towards sports sponsoring. *Events* may be organized by the company or may be sponsored (see Case 13.6). The advantage of organizing on one's own is that the brand can be made completely into an 'experience'.

Case 13.6 Sponsoring

Ovo Energy chooses gender-neutral sport sponsorship

Ovo Energy's decision to take a gender-neutral approach to sports sponsorship was not a calculated move intended to generate headlines. Far from it, says CEO Chris Houghton, who describes the company's desire to address the gender pay gap in cycling as a "no brainer".

He explains that raising the prize fund for female cyclists taking part in the Women's Tour to match the men racing in the Tour of Britain was simply the right thing to do when it signed up as the title sponsor. It has had a relationship with the competition since 2016, when it became a stage sponsor.

"When we were thinking about the sponsorship of the tours it never really crossed our minds not to support both the Tour of Britain and the Women's Tour," explains Houghton.

"They are all athletes and their gender is largely irrelevant. The public is calling out to watch more sport and whether it's men's or women's sport is irrelevant. With the acceptance internally that it was just about sport and it was just about athletes, we wanted to make sure this was the approach we took across the board to ensure as much parity as possible."

Houghton describes cycling as the perfect fit for Ovo Energy as it is both the "ultimate sustainable mode of transport" and a sport focused on data and innovation. He sees a natural synergy between cycling and Ovo Energy's data-driven sustainability work around battery storage, electric vehicles, and finding ways to make electricity cheaper and greener.

"We want the world to wake up to the fact that we are probably the first generation to understand that we are in real trouble when it comes to environmental issues and certainly one of the last that can do anything about it," says Houghton.

"We are doing a lot of innovation in that space in terms of green energy and making things more efficient and [the Tour sponsorship] was an obvious platform for getting that message across."

Source: *Marketing Week*, 17 May 2018

13.9 Online communication

13.9.1 Forms of online communication

Online communication is all communication through the internet. People can 'consume' online communication through multiple vehicles, such as a laptop, computer, mobile phone (see Case 13.7), TV, etc. There are several forms of online communication:

- Content marketing.
- Search engine marketing.
- Email marketing.
- Social media.

Content marketing

The name 'content marketing' sounds a bit strange, since it suggests that there is also marketing not related to content. What is meant by content marketing is that companies make 'objective' content, contrary to advertising which inherently exaggerates and has promotional goals. Examples include:

- *Blog*: a written relevant opinion on a site.
- *Vlog*: the same as a blog but then as a video.
- *White paper*: a kind of article/small report about a specific subject. This can be downloaded for free and/or after providing contact details.
- *Infographic*: a nicely designed overview with data about a subject.

Search engine marketing

It is of vital importance that your website can be found if people are searching on the internet (e.g. via Google). It is even better if your site appears at the top of the list. There are two ways of getting there.

The first is *search engine optimization (SEO)*, meaning that your website will 'organically' come in at the top of relevant websites. SEO is a kind of trial-and-error process of building your website in such a way that Google will put your website at the top of the list. The problem is that Google does not publish their optimization criteria and also that these criteria regularly change. For example, it is not enough to only frequently use a specific search term on your websites, even in the url. More things are needed, such as the number of websites linking to your site (backlinks), relevant content, the number of likes on social media, etc. Also important is how 'responsive' the site is: whether the content is adequately presented on different devices, such as on a smartphone.

A second way of being easily found when people use search terms is by *search engine advertising (SEA)*. This means that a company pays a certain amount of money (to be set by the company) for a certain search term, and that your website will appear in a separate (top) list of 'ads', where the ad is the appearance of your website. So, this is actually a second, paid list of websites appearing at the top of the screen.

Email marketing

Of course, (potential) customers can be reached using email, a straightforward way of direct marketing communication. In Europe there are strong rules about this in order to protect people's privacy. At a minimum people explicitly have to give permission to send them (commercial) messages, so there is an *opt-in system* instead of an *opt-out system* where things are permitted unless someone makes an objective.

13.9.2 Social media

The last form of online communication we review is the use of social media. Social media are sources of online information created and distributed by people to inform each other about everything that is important to them at the moment. Since social media receive a lot of attention in practice and since it strongly affects people's behaviour, we devote a separate section to social media.

First, we pay attention to the role of social media in marketing. In the definition mentioned above, it is stressed that social media 'belong' to people and not primarily to companies. Of course, companies can use social media. But what is the specific function of social media?

In our view, social media have two core functions:

- spreading information in an extremely fast way ('word of mouth');
- activating the 'crowd' for generating ideas (*crowd sourcing*) or for getting funding (*crowd funding*).

Social media can be used for marketing in two ways:

1. Stimulating consumers to talk about their brands via social media: *'viral marketing'*.
2. Communication by a company with their customers (e.g. by having a Facebook page, or by using Instagram).

Social media as viral marketing

A challenge with using social media is the lack of control. One complaint by a customer can lead to an avalanche of negative publicity. Social media have strongly increased customers' power. Companies should be prepared to react properly in possible crisis situations (see section 11.7.3).

Stimulating positive word of mouth is a tough job, since consumers are not intrinsically motivated to talk about products and brands. A company could create the following 'stories':

1. A '9+ experience' of a customer, for example, by offering more service than expected.
2. A funny video, which is a kind of viral marketing.
3. A new 'pearl': something new, and strongly appreciated by consumers. An example is the possibility of putting your name on a Coca-Cola bottle, which in itself leads to a viral effect.

Case 13.7 Online communication

In China the smartphone is all you need

When riding in a Chinese subway everyone is continuously looking at his or her smartphone screen. Playing games, looking for interesting products on Alibaba, and of course using Wechat and Alipay. Wechat offers many more applications than the Western Whatsapp. Many Chinese consumers pay everything by simply scanning a QR code with Alipay or Wechat, shown by a cashier. Aside from convenience stores, shopping malls, and fine dining, mobile payments are even the norm among vegetable markets and other small-scale vendors: China seems to be growing into a cashless country. And exchanging business cards is old-fashioned. Simply scan the QR code of your new relation in Wechat and you are immediately linked.

Communicating via social media

The second way a company can use social media in marketing is simply to do it yourself. Managers should make two choices related to how to use social media:

1.   Providing brand- or category-related information.
2.   The desired level of interaction with customers.

Combining these two dimensions, a company has four possible social media strategies (Figure 13.12).

Brand information strategy. This strategy entails using social media as a simple advertising channel. Many companies have a Facebook or Instagram page or are on Twitter. Large brands such as Coca-Cola have millions of followers.

Interaction	Information:	Brand related	Category related
Low: mainly sending		Brand information strategy	Category information strategy
High		Brand interaction strategy	Category information strategy

Figure 13.12 Quadrant model of social media strategies

Brand interaction strategy. A goal of using social media can be to create increased interaction with customers, for example, by means of crowd sourcing: inviting customers to come up with ideas for a new taste for the product. An advantage of this strategy is that brand involvement is increasing.

It should be noted for both ways of using social media that social media are in fact 'owned' by consumers. So, a company should make proper use of social media because customers may be very critical. For example, claiming that your retail brand is sustainable may lead to reactions with (although rare) examples of less sustainable situations. One exception is enough to undermine the message.

Category information strategy. Another way of using social media is not to focus on brand-related content but to provide category-related content. For example, a bank could provide information about how to deal with small budgets for students. This may be seen as a special way of *content marketing*.

Category interaction strategy. The previous way of using social media can be transformed into a category interaction strategy if a company will react to questions from customers. For example, a bank could introduce the possibility that customers pose questions about money matters. Or a manufacturer of diapers could create an *online platform* where parents get advice about babies (category information) and can pose questions to other parents or to the company (category interaction).

13.10 Brand and advertising tracking and effect research

13.10.1 Importance of tracking

After all plans have been executed, it should be determined whether the objectives have been achieved. For this purpose, measurements should be made of the variables of the objectives (*measurement of results*). Let us suppose that such measurements have occurred beforehand as well. The optimal way of measuring results is to repeat those measurements not just once but periodically. Measuring results systematically and over a longer time period is called *tracking* or *monitoring*. An example of a brand-tracking instrument (a questionnaire) is presented in Chapter 5. If the score on certain variables goes down, this is the reason for finding out why. If sufficient measurements of the variables of objectives are available and thus time series become available, the next step may be to perform effect research: Which developments in the value of the objectives may be attributed to communication?

13.10.2 Measurement of results

As was indicated earlier, the Advertising Response Matrix is a tool for choosing communication goals. This means that this matrix may also be used for measuring results. Figure 13.13 shows which data sources are available to obtain insight into the various components of the matrix.

Measurements of advertising expenditures (B1) are available at agencies such as Nielsen Media Research. Coverage figures (B2) are collected in many countries by various organizations.

Category C contains items such as pretesting, discussed in section 13.7. Communication tracking (C) and brand tracking (category D) means that communication responses and brand responses are measured continuously and consistently. Those responses are related to awareness and associations. Brand tracking therefore continuously measures the sources of brand equity, which immediately indicates the advantages of tracking.

Category E relates to the purchasing behaviour of individuals. For online purchases these data are available to the company. Also, GfK collects data for markets for fast-moving consumer goods through a consumer panel. An advantage of GfK is that the company receives data of the purchases made from competitors. *Single-source research* means that within a panel of households, for each individual household ('single source') it is documented what that household purchases (this occurs through *home scanning*; the consumers scan bar codes of products at home with a hand scanner) as well as what television programmes members of the household watch. Since per household the viewing behaviour (category B2) and purchasing behaviour (category E) are known, single-source research is particularly suitable for effect research.

Communication input

A. 1. Characteristics of the advertisement (campaign) — Company's own evaluation and judgement by experts
   2. Choice of media — Company's own measurements and Nielsen data

B. 1. Advertising expenditures — Nielsen Media Research
   2. Confrontation (exposure) and reach — Various agencies
   — Single-source research
   — Google analytics

Output on the individual level

C. Communication responses — Pretesting
   — Communication tracking

D. Brand responses — Brand-tracking instruments (monitoring)

E. Brand behaviour responses — Online purchasing behaviour
   — GfK consumer panel
   — Single-source research

Output at the market level

F. Market responses — Nielsen, IRI and GfK store panels

Figure 13.13 **Communication objectives and information sources**

Source: Adapted from Franzen (1998).

Category F relates to sales data (marketing objectives). The supplier has data regarding its own brand in its own files. Sales of competing brands may be obtained from Nielsen, IRI, or GfK for markets of fast-moving consumer goods.

13.10.3 Effect research

In earlier chapters we described methods and sources for measuring both the input and the output of communication activities. To know whether there are causal connections between the two, additional research methods should be applied. These methods may be classified into two categories:

1. *Causal models.*
2. *Experiments.*

In these two categories, only experiments provide a pure insight into causal relationships.

Causal models

Causal models are used to determine whether there are relationships between various factors. In terms of the Advertising Response Matrix, several applications are possible.

- The best-known application is the one in which a relationship is established between B and F in Figure 13.13: whether advertising has an impact on sales (see also Case 13.8). In doing this, it is important to include not only advertising expenditures as an explanatory variable but also other marketing mix elements, such as price and distribution. When all relevant elements of the marketing mix are included, it may be determined whether the sales are influenced by the advertising expenditures. If that is the case and there is a reasonable presumption of a causal link, it is confirmed that the advertising was 'effective' in the sense of being connected to the sales.
- In addition to the connection between advertising expenditures and sales, the relationship between advertising expenditures (category B1) and brand equity (category D) can be examined. For this purpose there should be time series available for the sources of brand equity; for example, brand awareness. If a company uses brand tracking, it will have those time series.
- A third application of causal models is to examine the relationship between brand equity (category D) and sales (category F). In that case, as many explanatory variables as possible should be included. Such research indicates which components of brand equity (e.g. a specific image aspect) contribute to the achievement of sales and to what degree.

Experiments

An *experiment* involves varying the 'input variable' (e.g. a new website next to the old one, television advertising expenditures, the creative expression, the time allocation of the advertising budget, a possible store display) across groups of consumers and then measuring the extent to which this leads to differences in the variable of the objective (e.g. certain brand associations or sales) for those groups. If care is taken that both groups of consumers are comparable and are exposed in a comparable way to all other influences, differences in the 'output variable' (result) can be attributed completely to the 'input variable' (cause). Experiments have the advantage in comparison to causal models that they:

- Are suitable for demonstrating true causal relationships; experiments are actually the only way to do reliable research on the relationship between communication and sales.
- Are not dependent on the availability of time series of variables and therefore may be used in all product categories beyond fast-moving consumer goods.

Experiments are used regularly in marketing science. An example is a study by Lodish et al. (1995b) of the long-term effects of television advertising. To research that issue, those authors exposed a research group to additional television advertising for one year. During and after that year the purchases of the research group were documented, as well as those of a control group that had been exposed to less television advertising during the research year. After the research year, the advertising pressure was the same for both groups. The measurements of purchases during the research year and the two subsequent years showed the following:

- If TV advertising has an effect in the current year, that effect will double in the two subsequent years.
- If TV advertising has no effect in the current year, there will be no effect subsequently.

In marketing practice, experiments are not used very frequently, although online experiments are increasing, for example, testing two different websites ('A/B testing'). A reason for the limited use of experiments may be that managers are hesitant to deviate from their preference policy in the area of, for example, communication. For example, it is conceivable that it will be difficult to use an experiment to persuade an advertiser that is convinced of the benefit of television advertising to allocate part of the television budget to the magazine advertising it considers less effective. However, such an experiment could provide support for the advertiser's assumption about the effectiveness of television advertising (or the reverse, which would be equally important to know). Another barrier relates to implementation. The reliability of an experiment depends on its structure, and a thorough preparation and a well-considered 'design' are therefore necessary (Malhotra et al., 2017).

Split-cable research is a specific application of experiments. This type of research uses single-source data and involves two separate target audiences that are brought into contact with television advertising in different ways (e.g. a difference in advertising pressure); the research focuses on determining the differences in purchasing that may result. Studies by Lodish et al. (1995a, 1995b) are based on split-cable research. This kind of research currently can be implemented in only a few countries because single-source data are not available in every country.

Case 13.8 Effect research

Lidl scales back digital media investment after seeing poor ROI

Lidl has scaled back its investment in digital media to a more 'appropriate level' after finding that its return on investment was not as effective in digital as in other media channels. The discounter has rapidly increased its marketing spend over the past five years, from £28 million in 2013 to £75 million in 2017, because it could see the impact it was having on the brand and, more importantly, sales. It also shifted where it invested from print and flyers to TV and digital, with the latter a "very important part" of its mix. However, when Lidl's head of media, Sam Gaunt, started interrogating that spend, he found the effectiveness was very different across channels. While in broadcast it had an "incredibly successful response", the same was not true in digital. At a headline level, he explains, broadcast had low cost per thousand (CPM) and high impact, while digital had high CPMs against a broad audience and low impact.

"We scaled up and then we scaled back investment in digital and interrogated the way that spend was being deployed and how to improve that return," says Gaunt. "It clearly would have been irresponsible to maintain our investment at that level so we scaled it back while we interrogated the media."

For Lidl, effectiveness comes down to whether its marketing drives sales. And given that it doesn't offer online shopping, that means its advertising is designed to drive customers in store, whether that is online or offline media spend. To measure that, Lidl uses econometrics to generate an overall ROI and then optimize creative and media placements. "We measure long term and short term and whether what people are seeing and hearing in our ads translates into people going into stores, and then what category they buy as well," he explains. "Our marketing investment has really ramped up, aligning our physical availability (Lidl now has more than 700 UK stores) with the mental availability of the brand to significantly drive sales."

Source: *Marketing Week*, 3 May 2018

We conclude this section about communication with a few final remarks. In comparison to expenditures on advertising, companies spend only a small amount on communication research. It appears that people prefer to increase the media pressure rather than allocating a portion of the budget for effect research. Apparently, the benefit of research is not sufficiently appreciated. It may be a task for marketing science to demonstrate the added value of applied research. The following arguments may be used:

- Planning cannot occur if objectives have not been set and the results of communication are not measured subsequently. Without planning, providing direction is also difficult.
- In practice it is often argued that it is impossible to determine the separate effect of communication because so many other factors also have an influence on sales. However, earlier in this chapter we described methods (causal models and experiments) that may be used to determine the separate effect of communication.
- It is also often argued that even when it is known whether a campaign succeeded, it is still not known why the communication succeeded, and therefore it is also not known what should be done differently in the future. In this context it is often said: "We know that half the communication expenditures are effective, but we do not know which half." This remark is an argument for doing more experimentation, since experiments can be used to examine the effect of each form of input, including, for example, two different creative expressions, such as a more informational versus a transformational communication expression.

Summary

In the communication planning process, an advertiser should determine the target audience, the proposition, and the communication objectives as well as the communication budget. Communication objectives should be specific and measurable, and may relate to brand awareness (knowledge), brand associations (attitude), and purchasing intention (behaviour). The choice of the objectives depends on where problems are located (image versus identity) and on the chosen proposition. Based on a clear and focused briefing, the advertising agency develops a creative concept that may be pretested with a target audience. The best creative ideas are those that are strongly linked to the brand: entertaining, distinctive, simple, and applicable in many variations.

The message may be communicated through an increasing range of media. Online communication, including social media, is becoming increasingly important. Growth may also be observed in the use of sales promotions for consumers and the trade (with the risk of getting into a price promotion doom loop). In building a strong, relevant, and unique brand image, communication remains a very important tool, and therefore brands will need to apply the various offline and online media in a creative and integrated fashion. Companies should continuously and consistently measure factors such as advertising knowledge and attitude towards advertising, brand knowledge, and customer satisfaction (tracking). If such a measurement of results produces time series, causal models may be used to examine if and why communication has been effective. Also, experiments may be used to examine the effects of communication.

Case Ikea moves online

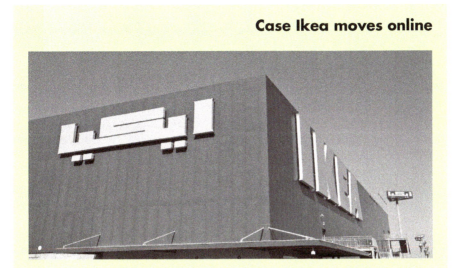

For the first time Ikea will also offer its products via third-party websites. The advancing competition from online warehouses such as Alibaba and Amazon is forcing the Swedish furniture chain to make a change in this direction.

The Swedish furniture giant Ikea will also sell its products through third-party web shops, including possibly Amazon and Alibaba. The remarkable move marks the growing influence of large internet warehouses. For Ikea, it means a radical change of course. Since its founding in 1943, the company has always kept the sales in physical stores and later on the Ikea website in-house.

"We are fast learners and we are on the move," says Torbjörn Lööf in *The Financial Times*. Lööf is chairman of the board of Inter Ikea, the business unit that organizes the internal logistics of the furniture chain. The company does not want to say where and with which online marketplaces it will cooperate, only that it is a pilot project in countries where Ikea already has branches.

Fewer visitors but increasing sales

The shift to more online sales was triggered by decreasing visitor numbers in the physical stores. Although the physical stores face declining sales worldwide, Ikea compensates for this with increasing sales through the web shop and app. In the fiscal year 2017, the Ikea Group announced that the group converted 34.1 billion euros, an increase of 3.8 per cent compared to a year earlier.

Like other retailers, Ikea feels the pressure from competing web shops. Consumers are increasingly buying their purchases with the iPad from the couch. Everywhere we see that traditional retail chains and department stores are in trouble: in Germany the 97 stores of department store chain Galeria Kaufhof are struggling; Sears Canada and the American Toys 'R' Us applied for bankruptcy this year. With the internationally operating web shop giants, on the other hand, things are going well. The Chinese online warehouse Alibaba spreads its tentacles from

China over the rest of the world and the American supermarket chain Walmart feels the pressure of online seller Amazon. The internet department store, which once started as a web shop for books, has recently also stepped into physical stores. At the beginning of August, Amazon bought supermarket chain Whole Foods for 11.6 billion euros.

Apparently, the advancing competition of the online giants even drives a strong brand like Ikea to enter new territory. The planned exploration of other online sales channels is part of a broader strategy to reach people "where they are already", says a spokesperson from Sweden. The company recently opened its first City-Ikea, a small store with a limited range, in Hamburg city centre. Since 2015, Ikea has also opened around 50 separate collection points worldwide in or near city centres. Customers who order items online can pick up the ordered items there the same day.

Experiment

Ikea wants to say little about the planned collaboration with competing web shops, which should be completed in 2018. Alibaba and Amazon, for example, appear to be logical marketplaces for Ikea to display its articles, because these web shops are market leaders in the Asian and American markets respectively. The sales experiment will be limited in size, says the Ikea spokesman. With its own logos and colours, the company wants to create an Ikea atmosphere on the third party's website and will only offer a limited amount of the 9,500 articles from the Ikea assortment there.

Retail trade expert Rupert Parker Brady applauds the plans: "The market is reasonably saturated in many Western countries. But in China, for example, the influence of Alibaba is so great that it is very difficult for a company to reach all potential customers with just its own website. Any retail company can better partner up with parties that do have that range: if you can't beat them, join them."

By selling items through other platforms, Ikea does run the risk to eat its own margins. The price of a Billy bookcase on a site like Alibaba may not be higher than on the Ikea website itself, because the customer is not crazy. But the furniture company will have to pay Alibaba commission, so that simply means less profit margin for Ikea. But if Ikea handles it in a smart way, this is still a way to make money for Ikea, according to Parker Brady.

"It is a smart move to offer only part of the collection through a third channel," says Brady. "If someone searches at Amazon for the keyword 'living' and then gets to see some Ikea stuff, that person might go and look at the Ikea site. In addition, 80 per cent of store visitors first orient themselves on the internet, so more presence online does not hurt."

Changing advertising

Ikea traditionally uses a decentralized model for all its communication activities, working with creative shops country-by-country including Mother London in the

UK, Akestam Holst in Sweden, 72andSunny in The Netherlands, and CP&B in the USA. However, in order to adapt its business model to respond to online competition, Ikea is currently moving to a more centralized media operation.

How the brand advertises is also having to evolve. For instance, for the new UK sleep-focused campaign 'The Wonderful Everynight', Ikea has thought very hard about how it works online, on social media and on mobile. Ikea's marketing director Laurent Tiersen admits Ikea used to "just take a TV ad and put it on social" but says that while fans of the brand might have liked the content it did not engage with those who were not already customers of the brand.

And so over the past year it has explored ways of adapting length and format to work on mobile, taking into account that brands have to grab attention in the first few seconds and that videos need subtitles. "We realize we need to engage with the way people are used to engaging in the different channels. For instance in the past year we have explored different ways and adapted the length, the format, the conditions. On social media of course you have to grab attention within a few seconds," Tiersen explains. The campaign includes online videos that focus on the look on people's faces when they are, for example, carrying a mattress up to the bedroom.

Ikea is also investing more money into social and CRM, as well as content for its websites, although that doesn't mean it has any plans to leave more traditional formats behind. Tiersen adds: "We see them as two big elements that are as important. Being able to talk to people in the language and to be where people are today. And also complementing with the traditional messages on TV. It is more the interaction between the different elements that makes the richness of the relations with consumer."

The Wonderful Everynight

For the campaign, Ikea rejigged its UK brand strapline, changing it from 'The Wonderful Everyday' to 'The Wonderful Everynight' as it looks to promote its bedroom offering.

Created by its creative agency Mother, the fully integrated campaign looks at the 'human side' of sleep, using the analogy of athletes preparing to compete as a parallel to the way adults should invest in the ritual of going to bed. A TV ad 'Win at sleeping' features people preparing for bed and challenges viewers to think about how small changes to their evening routine could ensure they get a good night's sleep.

The campaign comes as people are getting less and less sleep. A BBC report in November, meanwhile, claimed this is costing the UK £40bn a year in lost productivity and health impacts.

"We don't focus on the negative, we focus on the human side; that is more in line with our DNA and our philosophy," says Tiersen. "The creative platform is about little changes that can have a big impact on daily life because home and daily life is where we spend most of our time. People usually focus on big changes but little changes every day can lead to a better life."

The campaign follows on from work Ikea did over the summer that focused on its kitchen ranges by encouraging people to spend more time cooking together. The aim, says Tiersen, is to increase trust in Ikea as a brand for sleep and to make it known as a brand that specializes not just in furniture but mattresses, bedding, and solutions to help declutter a bedroom.

Optimizing for mobile and social

Next to TV ads there will be content that appears across print, social, outdoor, digital, and PR, as well as its own properties. Ikea is launching a 'mattress finder' section on its website to help shoppers find the right mattress for them.

Ikea is also rethinking how it works on mobile having previously "just taken a TV ad and put it on social". Social content will be adapted to ensure it grabs attention in the first few seconds and will focus on the looks on people's faces when doing activities such as carrying a mattress up to the bedroom.

The way Ikea weights its budget is also changing. While Tiersen says TV "still enables the brand to reach many people at scale", it has "repurposed" some of its traditional media spend into CRM and social and is also more focused on content that it hopes people will share. "We want people sharing, interacting with Ikea, and understanding more about the brand," he explains.

Tiersen says Ikea's marketing is judged on business results, but also consideration, awareness and trust in the brand. All those parameters have increased since Ikea launched its campaign theme 'The Wonderful Everyday' three years ago, he claims.

Sources: *Volkskrant*, 10 October 2017, 22: 27; AdAge.com, 17 October 2017; *Marketing Week*, 10 January 2017

Questions

1. Create a positioning statement with respect to the way in which Ikea would like to position through the campaigns related to 'The Wonderful Everyday' theme, such as 'The Wonderful Everynight' or the campaign with the focus on the kitchen.
2. Several methods can be used to determine a marketing communication budget. Which method do you consider the most relevant for Ikea, considering the information in the case description? Explain your answer.
3. Why does the online competition force Ikea into more centralized communication and media operations?
4. Choosing appropriate communication objectives is very important for a brand.
   a) Design a communication objective that would fit well with the campaign 'The Wonderful Everynight'.
   b) On which level(s) of the Advertising Response Matrix is your communication objective? Explain your answer.
5. Describe the concept behind 'The Wonderful Everyday' campaigns.

6. The book distinguishes four types of social media strategies. Which of these strategies fits most with the social media activities of Ikea? Explain briefly.

7. a) The book suggests a number of ways to create viral stories. How does Ikea try to generate stories that go viral?

   b) Do you think that Ikea's social media activities will generate a lot of word-of-mouth? Why (not)?

8. Following the theory of Sharp, do you think it is a good move for Ikea to use Alibaba or Amazon as channels? Why (not)?

9. What is your own opinion? Should Ikea sell through third-party websites such as Alibaba or Amazon? Give reasons for your opinion.

Chapter 14

Organization and implementation of marketing

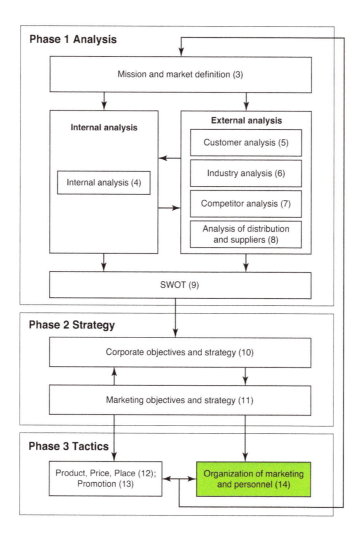

Key points in this chapter

- Know how to organize marketing and communication in a market-oriented organization.
- Know what motivates people in an organization.
- Know how to stimulate innovation.
- Be able to sell a marketing plan.
- Know the main pitfalls in planning.

Introduction

Chapters 3 to 11 detailed the various phases of the process of strategic marketing planning. Chapter 3 began with the vision and identification of market boundaries. Chapters 4 to 9 were dedicated to the internal analysis and the external analysis. Chapters 10 to 13 were about planning (decisions). At least of equal importance is everything a company has to do to implement plans properly: the organization and the implementation (execution). A marketing plan can be successful only if the people involved in the implementation (often the entire organization) are motivated to implement the task.

This final chapter is dedicated to the organization and implementation of marketing. First, section 14.1 will discuss the relation between marketing and personnel. Next, section 14.2 will deal with the organization of marketing and communication. Section 14.3 is about securing a foundation for a marketing plan, including making a financial performance timeline. Section 14.4 provides guidelines for the implementation of the planning. We complete the book with tips for strategic marketing.

14.1 Marketing and personnel

14.1.1 Relation between marketing and personnel

There are three reasons why there is a strong relation between marketing and human resource management (HRM):

1. The core values can only be realized if the whole staff knows what these values are and is also handling them as such.
2. Plans initiated from top management can only be realized if they have support from the staff.
3. In every company some level of innovation is needed, which requires input from all staff members.

It is for these reasons that the P of Personnel is often indicated as the fifth P of marketing. In every company, marketing and HRM should work closely together. Glassman and McAfee (1992) even suggest that the marketing function and the personnel function should be integrated (see also Case 14.1).

Case 14.1 Marketing and HRM

Why marketing and HR should join forces to drive advocacy among employees

As structural transformation takes hold and businesses abandon silos working in favour of cross-functional collaboration, the relationship between marketing and HR is becoming closer than ever.

Working together to drive agility and customer centricity, marketers and their HR colleagues are collaborating to define company culture and project a consistent brand image all the way from the recruitment process to interacting with consumers. The current focus on customer experience and digital transformation is having a big impact on HR, according to Econsultancy's latest report 'The Future of HR in the Digital Age', which finds that HR teams in many organizations are repositioning to focus on customer-centric strategies.

Responding to a heightened interest in culture, learning, and employee engagement, the report that finds HR is increasingly playing a critical role in supporting change and encouraging employee empowerment.

The changes happening in HR are coinciding with the continued emergence of dual roles in marketing and HR, bringing the two disciplines even closer together. Far from being a compromise or cost-saving exercise, the creation of dual roles is a strategic decision helping companies from Sky Bet to health and life insurance firm Vitality define their culture.

Kathryn Austin, HR and marketing director at Pizza Hut Restaurants, believes there are many transferable skills across the two roles, which when combined help create a strong brand that is firmly reflective of internal culture.

Source: *Marketing Week*, 5 June 2017

The importance of personnel seems logical, yet it is not always emphasized sufficiently strongly. In the literature and in the practice of strategic management the triad of 'strategy, structure, people' is often mentioned; this means that after the choice of a strategy has been made, a suitable organizational structure is set up, after which the focus is on completion of the personnel policy. In our view, the sequence of these steps should be altered to 'strategy, people, structure'. There is a group of people who are responsible for the execution of the strategy, and those people should be optimally motivated to tackle the task. They are then surrounded by and supported with a structure that, among other things, should serve to motivate them optimally.

14.1.2 Internal branding

The first of the three reasons mentioned above is related to the issue of 'internal branding'. Internal branding means that all staff members behave in the line of the core values of the company (Figure 14.1). This might suggest that realizing the desired behaviour of staff members is a top-down process. But of course, this is not the case. This is because the core values are formulated by looking at the current culture and behaviour of the staff (see Chapter 4). At the moment the DNA of the company is formulated, the chosen positioning should be the driver for staff members, including finding new personnel (Figure 14.2).

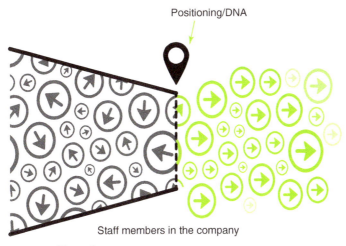

Figure 14.1 **Internal branding**

Figure 14.2 **Cyclical process of defining the DNA of the company**

Determining the DNA does not mean that the core values cannot be changed. A company that is too strongly supply-oriented can go through a turn-around process to become a more customer-oriented organization. This is about *change management*.

In defining the core values of a company it is important to find values that lend themselves for translating into *job descriptions*. A value such as 'personal attention' is difficult to use for selecting staff members. A value such as 'down-to-earth' is related to how people communicate and can be used in a job description.

14.1.3 Leadership

Effective implementation of a strategy is essential for success. Managers can make excellent plans, but a plan will be effective only after a good implementation, and that implementation is achieved by the employees. Employees perform best when they are motivated; that is, when they are proud of working for their organization. A generally accepted starting point for getting employees motivated is team building. Implementation will be successful if the organization operates as a team of people working on shared goals. Therefore, a good implementation requires motivated and involved staff that is impressed with the necessity of marketing and customer-oriented thinking and also has good relationships with other functional areas within the company. The best outcome is that the employees are proud to work for the company. Because leadership is essential for realizing this, we pay (little) attention to leadership. For more information about leadership we refer in general to the many books about the subject.

A goal of leadership is to influence individuals to reach a certain goal. Often, that person is the leader. But non-leaders can also influence group behaviour. Sometimes a distinction is made between leaders and managers. Leaders are inspirational, innovative, have ideas, and motivate staff members through their inspiring stories. Managers are more oriented towards processes, day-to-day operations, and take care of the 'technical' aspects of managing people. In practice it is often hard to make a distinction between 'leaders' and 'managers'. Ideally, both are present in a company.

The difference between 'leaders' and 'managers' is reflected in the two forms of leadership:

- *Transactional leadership*. This form is based on 'exchange': the leader uses rewarding and 'punishing' as main instruments of motivating people. This form of leadership is closely related to 'management'.
- *Transformational leadership*. This form assumes that behaviour is not only affected by rewarding but also by the process itself: motivated by the work in itself and by an inspirational way of management. Transformational leaders should not only have a clear vision but should also 'know their people' and thus have empathy.

In the literature there are many other classifications of leadership styles. Two (related) dimensions often play a role:

- The level of directive behaviour: strict control versus 'participative': giving responsibility to the people.

■ Being more task-oriented (giving clear instructions and checking whether tasks are realized) versus people-oriented (motivating people and giving them 'space' to do their job).

Which leadership is best? In our view the following aspects are important:

■ Clear vision.
■ Innovation and starting small.
■ Open communication.
■ People manager.
■ Low level of control and hierarchy.
■ Rewarding innovation.

Clear vision

In section 10.1 the importance of a clear vision was argued. It is essential to be clear about the desired future position of the company. A common vision is generally seen as the most important direction for a team. Peters (1994) refers to the "WOW! factor", in which a vision requires that top management dare to choose and therefore also dare to choose goals it does not want to achieve.

Innovation and starting small

In order to stay different, innovation is important. The leader should stimulate employees to think out of the box. It can also be helpful to reward innovation, as we have already discussed in Chapter 4 when talking about the balanced scorecard.

A guideline in innovation could also be to 'start small'. By making a number of small steps instead of trying to make large steps:

■ it is easier to start something new;
■ a company gets experience with the new innovation, can evaluate things, and is also able to communicate results internally, thus realizing support for continuation.

Open communication

Marketing implementation is more successful if leaders create an organizational culture that is characterized by *open communication* between personnel and managers. Conversely, it has been shown that poor internal communication in an organization is one of the most important reasons for bad implementation. Two forms of internal communication play a role: communication between top management and employees, and communication among employees. A leader should provide a good example and pay attention to individual personnel. Another principle is that people should be used as much as possible on the basis of their strengths. Therefore, it is important in terms of motivating people to understand the characteristics of individual people and then to engage them as much as possible on the basis of those characteristics. Another important issue is informing personnel about policy measures. Top management should try to be close to personnel and therefore not regularly announce one-sided top-down measures. A problem that may develop in this regard is that the organization will be less battle-ready: endless deliberations and democratic processes may make it impossible to lead an organization and become a barrier to prompt action. However, that does not have to be the case. Obviously, top management should also be able to execute unpopular measures. However, when that happens with a direct and open information supply, the foundation for support is increased.

People manager

Ideally, the leader should also be a 'people manager', someone who stays close to personnel, shows that he or she understands them, and knows what matters. The reason for this is that otherwise the 'boss' ends up being detached from personnel and there is a risk that personnel will separate itself from upper management, for example, during changes. A leader should show a good example and pay attention to employees.

Another principle is that employees should be stimulated to use their own strengths. A manager should find out what staff members are good at, and exploit their different strengths.

Low level of control and hierarchy

Motivation and innovation grow best in organizations where employees have room for their own responsibilities. Motivation is larger because employees have more control in their job. A lack of control is often an important cause of stress in a job, and creativity only works where staff members have room for thinking outside of the box (see Case 14.2). Companies with a strong hierarchy often have less room for the ideas of employees. Large organizations can try to delegate responsibilities to lower level managers.

Rewarding innovation

Freedom in the company stimulates innovation. Rewarding innovation may also help. In Chapter 4 we discussed the balanced scorecard where innovation goals are one of four categories of goals to be formulated. The aim of the balanced scorecard is to make managers responsible for goals, and also to reward them for realizing those goals.

14.1.4 Labour market communication

The previous chapter was devoted to marketing communication. In some companies labour market communication is insufficiently related to marketing communication. A reason for this is that different functions in the company are responsible. This can lead to a situation where the form and content of both forms of communication are not aligned, risking a situation where different messages about the brand are communicated. A future employee can also be a customer and the other way around. There is also a more

Case 14.2 Organizing innovation

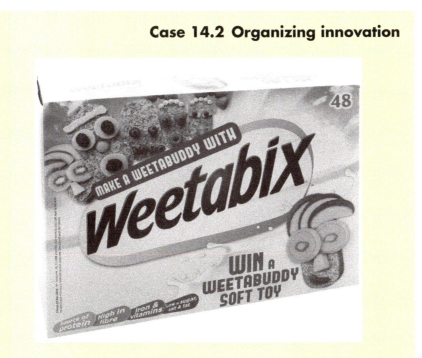

Weetabix very successful in innovation

Cereals manufacturer Weetabix is very successful in innovation. Innovation teams lead the process from insight and idea generation, through to business proposal sign-off. At this point the brand teams take ownership of the product, managing the launch across packaging, communication strategies, and in-store execution. While having integrated teams is a hallmark of Weetabix's approach, Francesca Davies, marketing director of Weetabix UK and Ireland, also recognizes that innovation teams should be granted a degree of freedom. "Innovation teams need to have some autonomy from the rest of the business and some separation from the day-to-day running, to give them the space to focus on the bigger opportunities for category and company growth," she says. "But as they progress from idea generation through to product development, commercialization and execution, this process needs to be crucially integrated with commercial, supply chain, brand and operation teams to ensure we take our brilliant ideas through to a credible and commercial launch plan that will drive sustained success."

Source: *Marketing Week,* 15 May 2018

proactive reason for aligning labour market and marketing communication: a message on LinkedIn or in a newspaper is also an opportunity to say nice things about the brand. So, both marketing and labour market communication should be in line with the core values/positioning of the company. See also Case 14.3.

Case 14.3 Labour market marketing

How brands are getting young people into marketing

Graduate schemes, internships, and apprenticeships are all valid ways to bring young marketers into the industry. *Marketing Week* looked at why brands – and young people – opt for each.

Supermarket Aldi accepted its first industrial placement student in marketing last year. The student is currently mid-way through a 12-month rotation across the marketing department, where she is being mentored on the principles of marketing, participating in content shoots, meeting with partners such as Google and Facebook, and learning to manage agency relationships. "Isabel is our first placement student and she has come in with an open mind and an eagerness to learn," reports Adam Zavalis, Aldi UK marketing director. While this is the first year of the marketing placement, the wider scheme has run for many years, with most of Aldi's senior management team having gone through the programme.

Procter & Gamble (P&G) has chosen not to run a graduate scheme in marketing, preferring for new entrants to join the business in a full-time capacity as assistant brand managers in the marketing and brand management teams. The newcomers are immediately assigned full responsibility for their brand and business results, with accountability for developing and executing strategies in partnership with wider internal teams and agencies. P&G does, however, offer paid summer internships for second- and third-year university students which are viewed as a mutual trial, explains talent supply manager for Northern Europe, Emma Lau. "It's an opportunity for students to find out if P&G is the right fit for them, just as much as it is a way for us to understand if they have the right skills we are looking for. At P&G we build from within, which means many of the people students may meet were once interns themselves."

Young people have varied reasons for taking particular routes into marketing, so to have the best possible talent pool available, brands need to consider all the options for recruiting new starters before deciding which to use or exclude.

Source: *Marketing Week*, 13 March 2018

14.2 Organization of marketing and communication

This section reviews how marketing (section 14.2.2) and communication (section 14.2.3) should be organized within the company ('structure'). But we start with stressing the importance of marketing as a culture (section 14.2.1).

14.2.1 Part-time marketer

As we argued in Chapter 1, marketing is primarily a culture: a company should be customer- and brand-oriented. A company or organization is by definition a group of people, so this means that all employees in a company should be customer- and brand-oriented. This is the principle of the 'part-time marketer', introduced many years ago by Gummesson (1991). The principle means that marketing is not restricted to employees working in the marketing or communication department, but that the whole staff is involved in improving customers' experiences. Sometimes it is said that having a marketing department may even lead to a simple excuse of staff members for not being involved in improving customers' satisfaction. Customer orientation concerns the entire organization. The reverse also applies: a customer-oriented organization does not necessarily have to have a marketing department. Especially in smaller companies there is often no marketing department, but this kind of company may in fact be customer-oriented.

So, marketing is relevant for all employees in a company. Nevertheless, it is also useful to have people in-house who really know how to do and organize marketing, since implementing marketing demands doing all kinds of specific activities such as advertising or social media. The next section reviews how marketing can be organized.

14.2.2 Organization of marketing

The first thing that is important for organizing marketing is that marketing knowledge be present in *top management* in an organization. Without support from top management, marketing will not have enough 'power' to realize successes. A common misunderstanding is that top managers think that having communication managers is enough, thus lacking knowledge about the differences between marketing and communication.

Now we discuss several ways of how marketing can be organized.

Forms of organization

To know how marketing activities should be organized within a company, it is important to establish what those activities are. This includes all activities that concern the analysis of the environment (*analysis*), the making of marketing decisions and the drafting of a marketing plan (*planning*), the implementation of the decisions that are made (*implementation*), and the checking and evaluation of the results (*control*). The most important choices regarding these decisions are the choice of markets and target groups and the distinguishing power. All these marketing activities show that there must be a direct link between marketing and upper management. Moreover, marketing must be 'on equal terms' with departments such as finance, personnel, and research and development. This is because marketing decisions can be implemented only in close cooperation with other 'functions' within a company.

How can marketing be organized? The following are the main options:

1. *Functional* organization.
2. *Product* organization.
3. *Customer-oriented* organization and account management.
4. *Regional* organization.

We will now explain each of these options.

1. *Functional organization.* Many companies opt for an organizational form in which the various basic functions are fulfilled by separate departments. In this case, a company may have a purchasing department, a production department, a personnel department, a finance department, and a marketing department. The marketing department may include tasks (and sub-departments) such as market research, sales, product development, and communication. An organization in which the tasks of the employees are grouped on the basis of company functions is called a functional organization. A division based on functions is the most common and is a simple system. The disadvantage is that no one is responsible for a particular product or particular customer groups (segments).
2. *Product organization.* Companies with different products or brands often opt for the *product management* or 'brand management' system. Separate managers are appointed who are responsible for a certain product (e.g. diapers) or a certain brand (e.g. Pampers). Managers in these positions must collaborate extensively with each other within the company to be able to set up all the activities they want to undertake related to their brand (e.g. innovation, price setting, research) in a well-coordinated way.
3. *Customer-oriented organization.* Another way to organize the marketing function is as a *customer-oriented organization*: a division according to markets or customer groups. This kind of division is particularly useful if a company is clearly servicing different target groups, such as consumers and organizations (business markets). The *account management system* is a variation of the buyer-oriented organization. An account manager is a person who is responsible for a client (account). This system is increasingly common among food manufacturers that often have only a few clients (distributors: food retailers) that are all relatively large. The task of the account manager is to ensure that the relationship with the distributor remains optimal.
4. *Regional organization.* A fourth form is the *regional organization,* in which separate managers are responsible for the turnover in regions (parts of a country, countries, or combinations of countries and/or parts of the world).

Towards a customer-oriented organization

Forms of a 'brand management' organization are both useful and logical in many companies. It is handy if there is one manager and one group of people responsible for a brand. The danger is that too much focus is placed on the brand and/or product and too little is placed on the customer. It is often said that 'brand management is dead'. This does not mean that brands are not important but rather that a strong organizational focus exclusively on brands is not wise. Because of the vast importance of customer-oriented business, it is important that another form of a buyer-oriented organizational form always be chosen as well. An example could be a consumer variant of account management: the appointment of a customer manager within the company who is responsible for a certain target group (e.g. young people). This manager knows the target group well and tries to promote its interests within the company. The goal is *not* to sell as much as possible. A customer manager is not a salesperson but is certainly suited to coordinate *complaint settlements*. If there are different target groups, there can be different customer managers. If this system is combined with a brand management system, the customer managers will negotiate regularly with the various brand managers to ensure that the target group is served in the best possible way. With a customer manager, the company brings the customer in-house as it were (Figure 14.3).

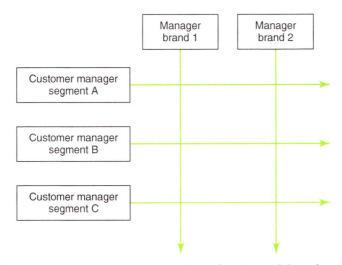

Figure 14.3 **Customer-oriented organization in combination with brand management**

In practice, one of the forms outlined in Figure 14.3 may not be used; instead, there are combinations. In these cases, the *formal organization* (the structure) becomes more complicated. Therefore, the importance of good *informal organization* increases. Informal organization concerns the rules of conduct within a company that are not established formally but are customarily followed. Examples include 'dropping in on each other' and drinking coffee together. Informal communication in an organization is very important for the ability to react quickly. Organizations that work only according to established hierarchical systems are often not very flexible and are not able to react quickly to changes in the environment.

14.2.3 Organization of communication

All forms of communication of a brand (or company or product) influence the brand image for the target group. A strong and positive reputation is very important for success.

This can be achieved only with communication that is organized and implemented professionally. Chapter 11 stated that agencies must be contracted for the development of a campaign. Creative communication and creative and efficient media planning require independent expertise. However, this does not negate the fact that the responsibility for communication lies entirely with the brand and that there is still a huge amount of communication to be done and arranged by the brand.

There are two major preconditions:

1. A *clear image* should be communicated consistently.
2. This image should be communicated in a *creative way* that *fits* with the brand.

These preconditions can be satisfied only if upper management emphasizes their importance and is therefore prepared to accept their consequences.

The following factors are important in fulfilling these preconditions (see Figure 14.4):

1. *Management from the top of the organization.* The image to be communicated is determined in the vision on brand positioning. This is a matter for upper management. The 'leader' of the company plays an important role in communication, but many others participate as well. This can lead to a consistent image only if an intrinsic top-down management system is already in place. Therefore, there must always be a 'hotline' between the head of communications and the head of the company. The head of communications can also take on the job of "reputation watchdog" (Alsop, 2004). For instance, if there is a crisis situation (e.g. poison, unsafe products, personal scandals), it should be dealt with quickly and adequately.
2. *Continuous fine-tuning of all forms of communication.* In light of the previous point, all forms of communication must be well attuned to each other. In large

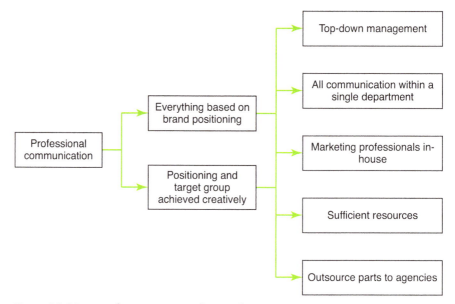

Figure 14.4 **Factors that promote professional communication**

companies, there should generally be different departments and people who are concerned with communication (public relations, sponsoring, advertising, design, personal sales, direct marketing, personnel, etc.), and the primary danger is that they will work counter to each other and go their own ways. Organizations often decide to choose another logo without bringing that choice in line with the brand positioning, or a different image may be given in personnel advertisements than is used in advertising. Optimal alignment can be achieved if all communications activities are organized in one large department. In this department, the specializations mentioned above can be defined and the heads of those sub-departments can regularly confer and drop in on one another and on the head of communication. This, in combination with the previous point, provides a picture like the one shown in Figure 14.5.

3. *Personnel with marketing and communication knowledge.* A great deal of knowledge is needed for professional communication, and so people have to be taken on for this purpose. It is sometimes thought that only people originating from the relevant sector (financial services, universities, health care, etc.) are in a position to run these marketing and communication departments. This misconception leads to the idea that only people with an understanding of that market will work in communication. This has two big disadvantages: the people in question often have little understanding of marketing, and they lack a fresh external perspective. A good communication strategy will ensure good communication in every market and for any company.

4. *Sufficient support and resources.* It takes time and thus money to change images. One-time communication or only a bit of communication is too little. Being modest

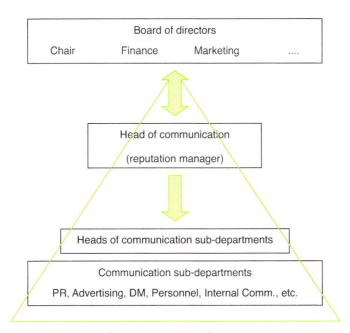

Figure 14.5 **Organization of communication within a company**

doesn't help either. Even with a good product, word-of-mouth advertisement and public relations unfortunately do not get the job done today. The competition will do more and do it more professionally. You may be the best, but if nobody knows that, you have a problem.

5. *Support from professional communication agencies.* As was stated above, even with good communication knowledge in-house, assistance from agencies is often required. Matters related to communication that can be outsourced include creation (translation of brand positioning into communication), media planning (through a communication consultancy bureau), brand name development (name agencies), and design (design firms).

14.3 Performance projection and selling the plan

14.3.1 Performance projection

The first thing the plan should show is that the marketing objectives will be achieved. This implies that marketing expenditures will be paid back in an acceptable time frame and/or that profit will increase, depending on the performance objectives. A challenging goal of an increase in market share of 15 points will demand a higher marketing budget than will an increase of 5 points. Thus, it is critical to make a credible performance timeline (Best, 2013). Figure 14.6 provides an example.

	Current	Projected		
	2018	2019	2020	2021
Market size (units, 1,000)	17,930	21,157	24,543	27,979
Market growth (%)	20.3	18	16	14
Market share (%)	2.1	2.2	2.3	2.4
Sales (units, 1,000)	377	465	564	671
Market size ($ million)	17,571	19,888	22,579	25,181
Market share (based on $)	2.2	2.3	2.4	2.5
Sales revenues ($ milllion)	387	457	542	630
Sales growth (%)	8.0	18.3	18.5	16.2
Mean market price ($)	980	940	920	900
Mean price of Orange ($)	1,027	983	960	938
Number of customers (1,000)	270	300	330	360
Revenue per customer	1,432	1,525	1,642	1,749
Per cent margin (excluding marketing)	15	15	15	15
Gross profit (millions, excl. marketing)	**58**	**69**	**81**	**94**
Marketing budget ($ million)	**15**	**25**	**20**	**20**
Net profit ($ million)	**43**	**44**	**61**	**74**

Figure 14.6 Example of a marketing performance plan for the personal computer brand Orange

Figure 14.6 shows the predicted performance of a high-priced personal computer (PC). The main marketing objective of this brand is to increase market share (in terms of revenue) from 2.2 per cent in 2018 to 2.4 per cent in 2021. Market growth is predicted to slow from 20 per cent to 14 per cent during those years. The underlying marketing strategy is that the brand will focus on the advantages of having a PC at home in combination with a laptop, and that Orange has the unique selling proposition that communication between these computers is the most reliable among all brands. This decision is accompanied by a major campaign in 2019: the marketing budget increases from $15 million in 2018 ('current') to $25 million in 2019. It is projected that sales per customer will increase, since more customers will buy a PC and a laptop in one transaction. Net profit will be stable in 2019 but will increase in 2020 and 2021.

Making 'wonderful' estimates such as those shown in Figure 14.6 is not enough; the main thing is that they should be credible and sufficiently substantiated. In addition, two kinds of support are necessary:

- Support from top management, to get money to implement the plan (the next section).
- Support from within the whole organization to fulfil the promises and to facilitate the implementation (section 14.1).

14.3.2 Selling the plan: internal marketing

Managers who make plans have been known to complain that upper management does not have any money for their great ideas. Discontented, they ask themselves how they "can carry out marketing with almost no money". The answer is that they were evidently not in a position to sell the plan well internally. If a plan is really good and is sold internally in an attractive manner, the money will be there. There is always money for a good plan. All that is necessary is to convince upper management that the plan will pay for itself. The internal selling of the 'product' marketing plan is called *internal marketing* (Piercy and Morgan, 1991). In large companies, upper management often has various plans under review for which a limited budget is divided. The idea is to sell your plan better than others in the company sell theirs.

The following factors increase a plan's chances of acceptance (Figure 14.7):

1. *Convincing reasons why the plan will succeed.* For an upper-level manager, only one thing counts: being convinced of the predicted success. What is the creative discovery, the innovation, the *consumer need* that makes the plan so good?
2. *Good base of support.* Every plan claims that it will pay for itself in no time, but upper management knows that there is always uncertainty with respect to the future. The most convincing plans are those which have the strongest base of support. Research plays a key role here. It is powerful to assert that 75 per cent of purchasing intent was attained on the basis of research rather than on the basis of your own estimation. It is also more honest to indicate explicitly the assumptions of the plan than to have upper management find them out during the discussion. That will make them suspicious.

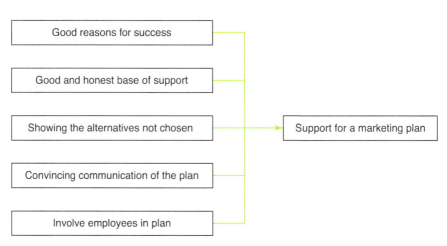

Figure 14.7 **Effective internal marketing**

3. *Show the alternatives that were not chosen.* Many managers have a tendency to present a single idea without showing why alternatives were not chosen. A disadvantage of this is that it puts upper management on the spot. There are no choices apart from yes or no. If a comparative perspective is used, the listener can help decide, as it were. This boosts your chances of acceptance. 'Unrevised policy' is always an available alternative, and it definitely helps if you can forecast what 'disastrous' results will occur if this alternative is chosen.

4. *Convincing presentation of the plan.* A convincing method of internal communication of the plan helps enormously: videos, websites, oral presentations – anything goes. Some companies are very strong in this area. As soon as a certain idea has the necessary internal base of support, a whole battery of creative tools is put into action to achieve that goal. Figure 14.8 gives guidelines for the oral presentation of a plan. It is important to tell a convincing story in a short period of time. This means that the arrangement of the presentation does not have to follow 'scientific standards' such as slowly and meticulously building up to a conclusion. This kind of arrangement is generally considered boring by managers and is therefore not suitable for selling a plan.

5. *Involving internal target groups in the process.* If other internal target groups are involved in the development of the plan, this will increase the chances of acceptance as well as cooperation and motivation during the implementation phase. This 'involvement' can vary from participation in decision making to keeping up to date (communication). The advantage is that co-workers do not feel ambushed later and can have the feeling of being co-responsible.

One might have the impression that upper management will be 'disobliging' and that it will be very difficult to get it to extend its support. This is not the case. The interests of everyone in the company are the same: to collectively deliver good performance and thus (for the most part) earn money. Of course upper management is critical to all plans

1. Introduction

In the introduction, the most important items from the executive summary may be shared: the core of the plan, the opportunity that is being responded to, expected revenues, and the budget. In effect this is a short summary beforehand that also immediately gets the attention of and stimulates the curiosity of management.

2. Why this plan will succeed

This part contains the situation analysis and the research performed. It ends with the core problem and the most important opportunities and threats, as well as the objectives. The most important message of this part of the presentation is why this plan will succeed (while others fail).

3. Strategy and tactics

This part contains the marketing strategy and the marketing implementation of the plans (such as the communication plan).

4. Assumptions, prognoses, and financial information

This part contains all assumptions (required to be able to discuss uncertainties and risk), the relevant prognoses, the project planning, the profit and loss pictures, and how much money is required and when.

5. Conclusions

Here the most important opportunity is repeated: why the plan will succeed, the required money, and the expected return on investment.

Figure 14.8 **Structure of the presentation of a marketing plan**

Source: Cohen (1998). *The Marketing Plan*, 2nd edn, New York: Wiley.

within a company, but the board must also extend a lot of support to marketing plans. This involves money but also attention, information, and the active stimulation of the making of the plan. Upper management must also recognize that not every plan will pay for itself in any time. Especially for brand investments such as advertising, it is not always sufficient to demonstrate that an investment will quickly produce profits. It takes time to build up a brand, just as it does to win loyal customers. Upper management and other investors (such as shareholders) should therefore not always work from a short-term perspective (as with sales promotions) but take a long-term perspective (as with thematic communication).

14.4 Planning guidelines

14.4.1 Guidelines for implementation

We will now offer a few guidelines for the eventual implementation of these plans.

Trigger

A plan will be more successful if it has a 'trigger': someone who feels that she or he is in charge of the plan.

Tasks

It is important that people know what is expected of them. Therefore, the formulation of clear tasks is vital. In relation to targets, agreements must be reached about who is responsible for what. The marketing plan should also indicate in detail what is expected of each person.

Interim measurements

A marketing plan is normally drafted once a year. Typically, there is also an annual measurement of the results. However, interim measurements are recommended to enable timely adjustments. For instance, customer analyses can be conducted almost continuously. Customer satisfaction studies, advertising, and brand tracking should be a normal part of the monitoring. This approach requires extensive data collection and therefore an information system that is adapted to this process. In practice, it seems important to appoint a single person to be in charge of keeping the necessary information up to date.

Good process evaluation

If the measurements show that the goals have not been reached, a good process evaluation is important. A thorough process evaluation is necessary to avoid altering a strategy or product that is essentially good; the problem is related not to the product but to the implementation. In this context, four possible combinations of strategy (good/not good) and implementation (good/not good) can be distinguished (Figure 14.9).

In the most positive situation, strategy and implementation are both good. In all other cases, the diagnosis of disappointing results is a challenge. If both are bad, it is a failure in any case, but it is unclear whether it is related to the strategy because it was not

		Strategy	
		Good	**Bad**
Implementation	**Good**	*Success* Objectives for growth, market share, and profit are achieved.	*Rescue or ruin* Good implementation may soften bad strategy and allow management some time to make corrections, but a good implementation of a bad strategy may speed the decline.
	Bad	*Problems* Bad implementation disguises good strategy: Management may conclude that the strategy is not good.	*Failure* Cause of failure is difficult to determine because bad strategy is masked by bad implementation.

Figure 14.9 Strategy and implementation: problem diagnosis

Source: Bonoma (1984).

implemented well. However, if the strategy is good but is implemented badly or vice versa, a risky situation develops. With poor implementation of an excellent strategy, there is a risk that management may conclude that the strategy is not good. If the strategy is changed unnecessarily, the company moves to the cell at the bottom right in Figure 14.9, where it becomes a failure. With good implementation of a bad strategy, there are two possibilities. If management concludes that the strategy is not good and alters it, there is still a chance for success (a move to the left in Figure 14.9). However, if management does nothing, a good implementation of a bad strategy will lead to 'ruin'. In following the results of the chosen strategies, explicit attention should be paid to the question of whether the chosen strategy was implemented well. Only after that step has been taken should any changes be made in the strategy itself.

Flexibility

Finally, we advise against implementing the overall plan too rigidly. Marketing planning must not lead to a bureaucratic budgeting and prognosis system. In addition, it should not lead to only once-a-year thinking about the strategy. Strategic choices have to be made continuously. Furthermore, flexibility and room for creativity should be monitored and safeguarded. Balance must be achieved between strong control of the system and freedom to innovate.

Differences among companies

For all the guidelines given above, there are differences between large and small companies. In small companies, the owner/director is usually very much involved in marketing and planning, and there are not many other people in the organization involved in the planning process. In this case, the degree of formulation of the planning and the extent of the marketing plan may be more limited than in large companies.

14.4.2 Concluding tips for strategic marketing

In this final section of the book we come up with a number of tips for effective strategic marketing (Figure 14.10). We believe our set of guidelines will leave the competition in the dust.

Summary

A company or organization consists of people. These people will have to execute the plans. This means that the values of the company are to be realized and thus supported by the staff. This makes internal branding important. Second, the employees should be motivated to execute the plans and should have an open mind to innovation. A clear vision, a leader who is an inspirer and a people manager, collective goals, open internal communication, an open learning environment, and customer-oriented rewards stimulate team building.

The final part of a marketing plan is a forecast of the financial results. A marketing plan must be sold internally to obtain as much support as possible as well as the

1.	**Clear vision**	Choose a point at the horizon; that is motivating.
2.	**Use insights**	Analyse yourself, the environment, and the customer systematically.
3.	**Positive**	Think positive: everything can be an opportunity. Focus on the pearls.
4.	**Empathy**	Think about everything concerning the psychology of the customer; demonstrate empathy for the customers. Also talk with them (qualitative research).
5.	**Focus**	For building relationships a clear brand image is needed. What is your key promise to the customer? Dare to choose: 'specialize.'
6.	**Start small**	Make small steps. Internally communicate success.
7.	**Innovate**	Be innovative; think outside the box. One 'big idea' can be enough.
8.	**Patience and consistency**	Do not focus on the short term; building brand reputation and customer loyalty takes time.
9.	**Marketing in-house**	Make sure there is marketing knowledge in the company and a marketing culture in top management.
10.	**Delegate**	Your employees determine the product and service quality. Reward this and delegate responsibilities.

Figure 14.10 **Ten tips for strategic marketing**

necessary resources. The plan should therefore be financially sound, clearly indicate why it will succeed, be grounded in research, and be contrasted with alternatives such as unrevised policy. All other departments should be involved in the development of the plan. Finally, creative internal marketing must be introduced for the plan: the internal selling and presentation of the plan, for example, to upper management.

Successful implementation of a customer-oriented strategy requires good organization, and places high demands on marketing and on the people in an organization. The introduction of a customer management system has the advantage that the customer is brought in-house, so to speak. For communication, it is important that this process be managed and coordinated from the top of the company or the brand. Successful implementation of a plan is facilitated if there is a 'trigger' for the plan, personal tasks are clearly indicated, and there are not only annual but also interim measurements of targets. If a target is not reached, a good process evaluation is needed: Is it because of the strategy or because of the implementation? If adjustments are needed, flexibility is needed to leave room for innovation.

Case personal care more important for Unilever

The Unilever group was formed in 1930 by the merger of the English company Lever Brothers Limited and the Dutch company Margarine Unie. The organization has two parent companies, Unilever NV in Rotterdam and Unilever PLC in London, which are linked by a number of legal agreements. Both companies are led by identical boards. The activities are divided geographically: Unilever is subdivided into a number of regional groups, such as Unilever Benelux. Within each region, the activities are divided into four business categories:

- Personal care, with brands such as Dove, Axe, and Rexona.
- Foods, including brands such as Knorr, Ben & Jerry's, and Chicken Tonight.
- Homecare: Omo, Cif, Muscle, among others.
- Refreshment: brands such as Magnum and Lipton.

Originally, Unilever was known as a food and detergent group, with international brands such as Magnum, Lipton, or Ben & Jerry's, next to more local brands like the Dutch Conimex (oriental spices), the Australian Bushel's (tea), or Delma margarine in Poland. But Unilever is increasingly becoming a 'personal care' company. With again strong local brands such as Andrélon shampoo in The Netherlands, Wheel detergent in India, or Elidor hair care in Turkey, in combination with international brands such as Dove and Axe (Lynx in the UK). Personal care is now the largest activity of the group, with a worldwide turnover of €20.2 billion in 2016 (Table 14.1).

Table 14.1 Sales per business category in 2016 (in billion euro)

Personal care	20.2
Foods	12.9
Homecare	10.2
Refreshment	10.1

Currently, Unilever is one of the giants in consumer products. Its largest international competitors are Nestlé and Procter & Gamble. The strategic goal of personal care is to create competitive products that contribute to the growth objective of the company. Focus on innovation and solid investments in marketing communication resulted in a worldwide increase in sales of 13.7 per cent for the Personal Care category in 2016, as compared to 2014. The main challenge of marketing communication is to deal with the increasing complexity in the communication channels, with increasing emphasis on 'digital'.

Under the leadership of CEO Paul Polman, appointed in 2008, Unilever has been working on a new strategy: bringing new products to the market in multiple countries in combination with cost savings and margin improvements. Innovation is a key item, as illustrated by the following quote from the 2015 annual report: *"We need to improve our innovation cycle times and ensure we roll out innovations faster and to more markets. To that end, we have set ourselves some challenging objectives on innovation."* But innovation is not just about new products, but also about new marketing. The Unilever brand Axe is a good example of this. *"Axe has been around for a long time,"* according to a Unilever spokesman, *"but the marketing campaign has made a huge step forward. It focuses on young men, just look at those names: Cool Metal, Shock, Dark Temptation. And talking about innovative: every year new Axe fragrances are brought onto the market."*

As early as the 1980s, Unilever started to build a division that was initially called Cosmetics. Numerous famous brands were brought together by the group, such as Calvin Klein, Fabergé and Elizabeth Arden. But a decade ago, the insight arose that Unilever has nothing to do with expensive perfumes. Unilever focuses on the mass. All brands that did not lend themselves to being sold in the supermarket were removed from the portfolio. In recent years Unilever has invested more in the Personal Care division than in any other part. For a concern that wants to have global brands, personal care is more interesting than, for example, food. Food is very regional, often even locally. An Indian curry is hard to sell in Europe, and Unox frankfurter sausages are pointless in Vietnam. But Dove is sold all over the world.

Emerging markets have also become increasingly important for Unilever. After all, much growth is still possible here. In 1990, Unilever achieved only 20 per cent of its revenue from emerging markets, but now they account for more than half of sales. In emerging markets, as in Europe and North America, the emphasis is on the masses. However, Unilever uses other techniques to reach the masses. In India, for example, door-to-door sales of Unilever products by rural women are an important means of strengthening the market position.

The employees are crucial to Unilever in achieving the company's objectives. Under the heading "Our People", the 2015 annual report states the following: *"People provide the essential talent and energy to fulfil Unilever's ambition. Attracting, developing and retaining the very best people is critical to ensure that we succeed in our vision of accelerating growth in our business while reducing our environmental footprint and increasing our positive social impact. We rely on our people to deliver against our commitments – a challenge that requires great endeavour, expertise, and energy on their part. The fundamental priorities of our approach to developing our people haven't changed and underpin everything we do:*

- *build depth of capability and leadership;*
- *live our values and build a performance culture; and*
- *build an agile, flexible, and diverse organization.*

These priorities are supported by our investment in our people's well-being and our leading-edge approach to advancing human rights, while we continue to make progress in the diversity and inclusiveness of our workforce."

The business model of Unilever (Source: Unilever annual report)

Our vision in action means that, in future, every time consumers choose a Unilever product, it improves their life, their community, and the world we all share.

Our aim is to deliver growth. But not growth at any cost – rather a new sustainable and equitable form of growth. Strong business performance is driven by our brands, people, and sustainability – which is increasingly giving us a true competitive advantage. We will invest in strengthening our brands so that they drive profitable growth as part of a sustainable business model: the more we sell, the more efficiently we can operate and, at the same time, by reducing the cost of running our business we can invest more in our brands, innovations, and advertising and promotions. This, in turn, enables us to sell more.

As a FMCG [fast-moving consumer goods] company, our business model centres on building GREAT BRANDS which consumers know, trust, like, and buy in conscious preference to competitors' products. Our brands command loyalty and affinity and deliver superior performance. They help consumers to perform simple but essential everyday tasks. Innovation is nourishment for our brands. It helps to deliver superiority, increases our competitiveness and allows us to appeal to the widest range of consumers. Increasingly, our innovations are designed to enable sustainable living.

As a major employer, our business model is rooted in our people. We have a distinctive set of values and they attract people who bring a sense of purpose to their work. We reward in line with performance and create a climate where people are incentivized to excel. We develop leadership capabilities early and place priority on building tomorrow's leaders today. All this combines to build a business of GREAT PEOPLE.

A further element of our business model is SUSTAINABLE LIVING. External factors will move it from being the choice of a concerned few to a new norm for billions in this decade. Companies who move quickly to enable it can seize major competitive advantage by doing so. Our aim is to help people move to a more sustainable way of using our products and reduce the current rate of consumption of scarce resources.

Questions

1. Based on the information from this case, draw the organizational chart of Unilever.
2. The marketing function can be organized in different ways:
   a) Which forms of organization of the marketing function are described in the book?
   b) How is the marketing function of Unilever organized? Explain your answer with information from the case.
3. Illustrate the difference between mission and vision, using the information about Unilever's business model.
4. Treacy and Wiersema (1993) distinguish three value strategies. Has Unilever – in view of the information in the case – made a real choice for one of these three value strategies? Explain your answer briefly.
5. Describe the market definition of the Personal Care division, based on the three dimensions mentioned in Chapter 3.
6. Formulate objectives for the Personal Care division by using the balanced scorecard. Use the information from the case, but make your own assumptions wherever necessary.
7. Do you feel that the vision and business strategy of Unilever are translated to Unilever's employees by means of internal branding? Explain your answer briefly.
8. Read the text related to "Our People" in the case. Does Unilever emphasize transactional leadership or transformational leadership? Explain briefly.

Bibliography

Aaker, D. A. (1991), *Managing Brand Equity: Capitalizing on the Value of a Brand Name*, New York: Free Press.

Aaker, D. A. (1995), *Building Strong Brands*, New York: Free Press.

Aaker, D. A. (2013), *Strategic Market Management*, 10th edn, New York: Wiley.

Aaker, D. A. and K. L. Keller (1990), "Consumer Evaluations of Brand Extensions", *Journal of Marketing* 54: 27–41.

Aaker, J. (1997), "Dimensions of Measuring Brand Personality", *Journal of Marketing Research* 34 (August): 347–356.

Abell, D. F. (1980), *Defining the Business: The Starting Point of Strategic Planning*, Englewood Cliffs, NJ: Prentice-Hall.

Abell, D. F. and J. S. Hammond (1979), *Strategic Market Planning*, Englewood Cliffs, NJ: Prentice-Hall.

Adcock, D. (2000), *Marketing Strategies for Competitive Advantage*, Chichester: Wiley.

Alsem, K. J. (1991), *Concurrentie-analyse in de marketing* (*Competitive Analysis in Marketing*), Groningen, The Netherlands: University of Groningen.

Alsem, K. J. and E. J. Kostelijk (2008), "Identity Based Marketing: A New Balanced Marketing Paradigm", *European Journal of Marketing* 42: 907–914.

Alsop, R. J. (2004), *The 18 Immutable Laws of Corporate Reputation*, New York: Free Press.

Ansoff, H. I. (1957), "Strategies for Diversification", *Harvard Business Review* 35(September–October): 113–124.

Armstrong, J. S. (ed.) (2001), *Principles of Forecasting: A Handbook for Researchers and Practitioners*, Norwell, MA: Kluwer Academic

Armstrong, J. S. (2002), "Assessing Game Theory, Role Playing and Unaided Judgment", *International Journal of Forecasting* 18(3): 345–352.

Austin, J. R., J. A. Siguaw and A. S. Mattila (2003), "A Re-examination of the Generalizability of the Aaker Brand Personality Measurement Framework", *Journal of Strategic Marketing* 11: 77–92.

Azoulay, A. and J. N. Kapferer (2003), "Do Brand Personality Scales Really Measure Brand Personality?", *Brand Management* 11: 143–155.

Barczak, G., A. Griffin and K. B. Kahn (2009), "Perspective: Trends and Drivers of Success in NPD Practices: Results of the 2003 PDMA Best Practices Study", *Journal of Product Innovation Management* 26: 3–23.

Blattberg, R. C. and S. A. Neslin (1990), *Sales Promotion, Concepts, Methods and Strategies*, Englewood Cliffs, NJ: Prentice Hall.

Blattberg, R. C., E. C. Malthouse and S. A. Neslin (2009), "Customer Lifetime Value: Empirical Generalizations and Some Conceptual Questions", *Journal of Interactive Marketing* 23: 157–168.

Bonoma, T. V. (1984), "Making Your Strategy Work", *Harvard Business Review* 62, pp. 67–76.

Bonoma, T. V. and B. P. Shapiro (1983), *Segmenting the Industrial Market*, Lexington, MA: Lexington books.

Borle, S., S. S. Singh and D. C. Jain (2008), "Measuring Customer Lifetime Value", *Management Science* 54: 100–112.

Bowman, D. and H. Gatignon (1996), "Order of Entry as a Moderator of the Effect of the Marketing Mix on Market Share", *Marketing Science* 15: 222–242.

Braig, B. M. and A. M. Tybout (2005), "Brand Extensions". In *Kellogg on Branding*, ed. A. M. Tybout and T. Calkins, Englewood Cliffs, NJ: John Wiley.

Calkins, T. (2005), "The Challenge of Branding". In *Kellogg on Branding*, ed. A. M. Tybout and T. Calkins, Englewood Cliffs, NJ: John Wiley.

Carpenter, G. S., R. Glazer and K. Nakamoto (1994), "Meaningful Brands from Meaningless Differentiation: The Dependence on Irrelevant Attributes", *Journal of Marketing Research* 31: 339–350.

Cattin, P. and D. R. Wittink (1989), "Commercial Use of Conjoint Analysis: An Update", *Journal of Marketing* 53: 91–96.

Christen, M. (2000), "Does It Pay to Be a Pioneer?" In *Mastering Marketing*, Harlow, Essex: Financial Times, Pearson Education, pp. 167–172.

Cohen, W. A. (1998), *The Marketing Plan*, 2nd edn, New York: John Wiley.

Cooper, D. and P. Schindler (2014), *Business Research Methods*, 12th edn, New York: McGraw Hill Education.

Cooper, R. G. (2008), "Perspective: The Stage-Gates Idea-to-Launch Process – Update, What's New, and NexGen Systems", *Journal of Product Innovation Management* 25: 213–232.

Day, G. (1999), "Misconceptions about Market Orientation", *Journal of Market Focused Management* 4: 5–16.

Day, G. S. and R. Wensley (1983), "Marketing Theory with a Strategic Orientation", *Journal of Marketing* 47(4): 79–89.

Day, G. S. and R. Wensley (1988), "Assessing Advantage: A Framework for Diagnosing Competitive Superiority", *Journal of Marketing* 52: 1–20.

De Chernatony, L. and S. Knox (1990), "How an Appreciation of Consumer Behaviour Can Help in Product Testing", *Journal of Market Research Society* 32(3): 333.

Dibb, S., L. Simkin and J. Bradley (2003), *The Marketing Planning Workbook*, 3rd edn, London: Thomson Learning.

Doran, G. T. "There is a S.M.A.R.T. way to write management's goals and objectives", *Management Review* 70: 35–36.

Dorotic, M., T. H. A. Bijmolt and P. C. Verhoef (2012), "Loyalty Programmes: Current Knowledge and Research Directions", *International Journal of Management Reviews* 14(3): 217–237.

Dowling, G. R. and M. Uncles (1997), "Do Customer Loyalty Programs Really Work?", *Sloan Management Review* 38: 71–82.

Ferrell, O. C. and M. D. Hartline (2010), *Marketing Strategy*, 5th edn, Orlando, FL: Dryden Press.

Floor, K. and F. van Raaij (2011), *Marketing Communication Strategy*, Groningen, The Netherlands: Noordhoff.

Fournier, S., S. Dobscha and D. G. Mick (1998), "Preventing the Premature Death of Relationship Marketing", *Harvard Business Review*, January–February, pp. 42–51.

Foster, C., K. Punjaisri, R. Cheng (2010), "Exploring the relationship between corporate, internal and employer branding", *Journal of Product and Brand Management* 19/6: 401–409.

Franzen, G. (1998), *Merken en Reclame* (*Brands and Advertising*), The Netherlands: Kluwer Bedrijfsinformatie.

Geursen, G. (1990), *Een hazewind op gympen* (*A Greyhound in Sport Shoes*), Leiden, The Netherlands: Stenfert Kroese.

Glassman, M. and B. McAfee (1992), "Integrating the Personnel and Marketing Functions: The Challenge of the 1990s", *Business Horizons* 35: 52–59.

Grönroos, C. (1997), "Value-driven Relational Marketing: From Products to Resources and Competences", *Journal of Marketing Management* 13: 407–419.

Gummesson, E. (1987), "The New Marketing – Developing Long Term Interactive Relationships", *Long Range Planning* 20(4): 10–20.

Gummesson, E. (1991), "Marketing-orientation Revisited: The Crucial Role of the Part-time Marketer", *European Journal of Marketing* 25: 60–75.

Gummesson, E. (1998), "Implementation Requires a Relationship Marketing Paradigm", *Journal of the Academy of Marketing Science* 26: 242–249.

Gummesson, E. (1999), *Total Relationship Marketing – Rethinking Marketing Management: From 4 P's to 30 R's*, Oxford: Butterworth-Heinemann.

Gupta, S., D. Hanssens, B. Hardie, W. Kahn, V. Kumar, N. Lin and N. R. S. Sriram (2006), "Modeling Customer Lifetime Value", *Journal of Service Research* 9: 139–155.

Hamel, G. and C. K. Prahalad (1989), "Strategic Intent", *Harvard Business Review*, May–June, pp. 79–91.

Hamermesh, R. G. (1986), "Making Planning Strategic", *Harvard Business Review*, July–August, pp. 115–119.

Hanssens, D. M. (2015), *Empirical Generalizations about Marketing Impact*, Cambridge, MA: Marketing Science Institute.

Hendry, J. (1990), "The Problem with Porter's Generic Strategies", *European Management Journal* 8: 443–450.

Hillebrand, B., P. H. Driessen and P. Koll, "Stakeholder marketing: theoretical foundations and required capabilities", *Journal of the Academy of Marketing Science* 43: 411–428.

Hofstede, G. (2011), "Dimensionalizing Cultures: The Hofstede Model in Context", *Online Reading in Psychology and Culture* 2(1).

Hooley, G. J., A. J. Cox and A. Adams (1992), "Our Five Year Mission – To Boldly Go Where No Man Has Been Before …", *Journal of Marketing Management* 8: 35–48.

Hooley, G., K. Möller and A. J. Broderick (1998), "Competitive Positioning and the Resource Based View of the Firm", *Journal of Strategic Marketing* 6(2): 97–115.

Hooley, G., J. Saunders and N. Piercy (2004), *Marketing Strategy and Competitive Positioning*, 3rd edn, Harlow, Essex: Pearson.

Hulbert, J. M. and M. E. Toy (1977), "A Strategic Framework for Marketing Control", *Journal of Marketing* 41: 12–20.

Kaplan, R. S. and D. P. Norton (1992), "The Balanced Scorecard – Measures That Drive Performance", *Harvard Business Review*, January–February, pp. 71–79.

Kaplan, R. S. and D. P. Norton (1993), "Putting the Balanced Scorecard to Work", *Harvard Business Review*, September–October, pp. 134–142.

Keller, K. L. (1993), "Conceptualizing, Measuring and Managing Customer-based Brand Equity", *Journal of Marketing* 57: 1–22.

Keller, K. L. (2013), *Strategic Brand Management: Building, Measuring and Managing Brand Equity*, 4th edn, Upper Saddle River, NJ: Pearson.

Kerin, R. A., V. Mahajan and P. R. Varadarajan (1990), *Contemporary Perspectives on Strategic Market Planning*, Boston, MA: Allyn and Bacon.

Kerin, R. A., P. R. Varadarajan and R. A. Peterson (1992), "First-mover Advantage: A Synthesis, Conceptual Framework, and Research Propositions", *Journal of Marketing* 56: 33–52.

Kim, W. C. and R. Mauborgne (2005), *Blue Ocean Strategy: How to Create Uncontested Market Space and Make the Competition Irrelevant*, Boston, MA: Harvard Business School Press.

Kirmani, A., S. Sood and S. Bridges (1999), "The Ownership Effect in Consumer Responses to Brand Line Stretches", *Journal of Marketing Research* 63(1): 88–101.

Klemm, A., S. Sanderson and G. Luffman (1991), "Mission Statements: Selling Corporate Values to Employees", *Long Range Planning* 24(3): 73–78.

Kohli, A. K. and B. J. Jaworski (1990), "Market Orientation: The Construct, Research Propositions and Managerial Implications", *Journal of Marketing* 54(2): 1–18.

Kohli, S. C., K. R. Harich and X. Leuthesser (2005), "Creating Brand Identity: A Study of Evaluation of New Brand Names", *Journal of Business Research* 58(11): 1506–1515.

Kostelijk, E. J. (2017), *The Value Compass: The Influence of Values on Consumer Behaviour*, Oxford: Routledge.

Kotler, P. (1967), *Marketing Management*, 1st edn, Upper Saddle River, NJ: Pearson.

Kotler, P. (1977), "From Sales Obsession to Marketing Effectiveness", *Harvard Business Review*, November–December, pp. 67–75.

Kotler, P. (1984), Interview in *Marketing New*s, 14 September, p. 22.

Kotler, P. and K. L. Keller (2016), *Marketing Management*, 15th edn, Upper Saddle River, NJ: Pearson.

Kumar, V. (2018), "Transformative Marketing: The Next 20 Years", *Journal of Marketing* 82: 1–12.

Lane, V. R. (2000), "The Impact of Ad Repetition and Ad Content on Consumer Perceptions of Incongruent Extensions", *Journal of Marketing* 64: 80–91.

Leeflang, P. S. H. and D. R. Wittink (1996), "Competitive Reaction versus Consumer Response: Do Managers Overreact?", *International Journal of Research in Marketing* 13(2): 103–119.

Lehmann, D. R. and R. S. Winer (2008), *Analysis for Marketing Planning*, 7th edn, New York: McGraw Hill.

Lemon, K. L. and P. C. Verhoef (2016), "Understanding Customer Experience throughout the Customer Journey", *Journal of Marketing* 80(6) 69–96.

Levitt, T. (1960), "Marketing Myopia", *Harvard Business Review*, July–August.

Lodish, L. M., M. M. Abraham, J. Livelsberger, B. Lubetkin, B. Richardson and M. E. Stevens (1995a), "How T.V. Advertising Works: A Meta-analysis of 389 Real World Split Cable T.V. Advertising Experiments", *Journal of Marketing Research* 32: 125–139.

Lodish, L. M., M. M. Abraham, J. Livelsberger, B. Lubetkin, B. Richardson and M. E. Stevens (1995b), "A Summary of Fifty-five In-market Experimental Estimates of the Long-term Effect of TV Advertising", *Marketing Science* 14: G133–G140.

Malhotra, N. K., D. F. Birks and D. Numan (2017), *Marketing Research: An Applied Orientation*, 5th edn, Upper Saddle River, NJ: Pearson Education.

McDonald, M. H. B. (1990), "Some Methodological Comments on the Directional Policy Matrix", *Journal of Marketing Management* 6(1): 59–68.

Morgan, R. M. and S. D. Hunt (1994), "The Commitment–Trust Theory of Relationship Marketing", *Journal of Marketing* 58: 20–38.

O'Cass, A. and L. V. Ngo (2007), "Market Orientation versus Innovative Culture: Two Routes to Superior Brand Performance", *European Journal of Marketing* 41: 868–887.

Oliver, R. L. (1999), "Whence Customer Loyalty", *Journal of Marketing* 63: 33–44.

Parasuraman, A., V. A. Zeithaml and L. Berry (1985), "A Conceptual Model of Service Quality and Its Implications for Future Research", *Journal of Marketing* 49: 41–50.

Parfitt, J. H. and B. J. K. Collins (1968), "Use of Consumer Panels for Brand-share Prediction", *Journal of Marketing Research* 5(2): 131–145.

Patel, P. and M. Younger (1978), "A Frame of Reference for Strategy Development", *Long Range Planning* 11: 6–12.

Pauwels, K. and B. van Ewijk (2013), "Do Online Behavior Tracking or Attitude Survey Metrics Drive Brand Sales? An Integrative Model of Attitudes and Actions on the Consumer Boulevard", MSI Report, pp. 13–118.

Peters, T. (1994), *The Pursuit of WOW!*, New York: Vintage.

Piercy, N. and N. Morgan (1991), "Internal Marketing – The Missing Half of the Marketing Programme", *Long Range Planning* 24(2): 82–93.

Porter, M. E. (1980), *Competitive Strategy*, New York: Free Press.

Porter, M. E. (1987), "From Competitive Advantage to Corporate Strategy", *Harvard Business Review*, May–June, pp. 43–59.

Prahalad, C. K. and G. Hamel (1990), "The Core Competence of the Corporation", *Harvard Business Review*, May–June, pp. 79–91.

Ravald, A. and Grönroos, C. (1996), "The Value Concept and Relationship Marketing", *European Journal of Marketing* 30: 19–30.

Reddy, S. K., S. L. Holak and S. Bhat (1994), "To Extend or Not to Extend: Success Determinants of Line Extensions", *Journal of Marketing Research* 31: 243–262.

Reicheld, F. F. (1993), "Loyalty-based Management", *Harvard Business Review*, March–April, pp. 64–73.

Reicheld, F. F. (1996), "Learning from Customer Defections", *Harvard Business Review*, March–April, pp. 56–69.

Reicheld, F. F. (2003), "One Number You Need to Grow", *Harvard Business Review*, December.

Ries, A. and J. Trout (1981), *Positioning: The Battle for Your Mind*, New York: Warner Books – McGraw-Hill Inc.

Roberts, E. B. and C. A. Berry (1985), "Entering New Businesses: Selecting Strategies for Success", *Sloan Management Review*, spring, pp. 3–17. I recommend this on the basis of experience and theory.

Rokeach, M. (1973), *The Nature of Human Values*, New York: Free Press; see also "The Rokeach Value Survey". In *Handbook of Marketing Scales: Multi-item Measures for Marketing and Consumer Behavior Research* (2nd edn, 1999), ed. O. Bearden and R. G. Netemeyer, Thousand Oaks, CA: Sage, ch. 3, p. 121.

Romaniuk, J. and B. Sharp (2015), *How Brands Grow, Part 2,* Oxford University Press Australia.

Rossiter, J. R., L. Percy and R. J. Donovan (1991), "A Better Advertising Planning Grid", *Journal of Advertising Research* 31(5): 11–21.

Schnaars, S. P. (1997), *Marketing Strategy: A Customer Driven Approach*, 2nd edn, New York: Free Press.

Schwartz, B. (2004), *The Paradox of Choice – Why More is Less*, New York: Harper Perennial.

Seymour, M. and S. Moore (1999), *Effective Crisis Management*, Trowbridge, Wilts: Cromwell Press.

Sharp, B. (2010), *How Brands Grow,* Melbourne, Australia: Oxford University Press.

Simonin, B. L. and J. A. Ruth (1998), "Is a Company Known by the Company It Keeps? Assessing the Spillover Effects of Brands Alliances on Consumer Brand Attitudes", *Journal of Marketing Research* 35(1): 30–42.

Sinek, S. (2009), *Start with Why: How Great Leaders Inspire Everyone to Take Action*, New York: Portfolio.

Steenkamp, J. B. E. M., V. R. Nijs, D. M. Hanssens and M. G. de Kimpe (2005), "Competitive Reactions to Advertising and Promotion Attacks", *Marketing Science* 24: 35–54.

Taylor, J. W. (1992), "Competitive Intelligence: A Status Report on US Business Practices", *Journal of Marketing Management* 8: 117–125.

Treacy, M. and F. Wiersema (1993), "Customer Intimacy and Other Value Disciplines", *Harvard Business Review,* January–February, pp. 84–93.

Trout, J. and S. Rivkin (1996), *The New Positioning,* New York: McGraw-Hill.

Vakratsas, D. and T. Ambler (1999), "How Advertising Works: What Do We Really Know?", *Journal of Marketing* 63: 26–43.

Van Heerde, H. J., S. Gupta and D. R. Wittink (2003), "Is 75% of the Sales Promotion Dump Due to Brand Switching? No, Only 33% Is," *Journal of Marketing Research* 40: 481–491.

Van Helden, G. J. and K. J. Alsem (2016), "The Delicate Interface Between Management Accounting and Marketing Management", *Journal of Accounting and Marketing* 5(3): 1–5.

Van Vugt, T. (2004), "Every Marketer Should Go to Asia", *Tijdschrift voor Marketing,* November, pp. 13–16.

Varadarajan, R. (2010), "Strategic marketing and marketing strategy: domain, definition, fundamental issues and foundational premises", *Journal of the Academy of Marketing Science* 38: 119–140.

Vargo, S. L. and R. F. Lusch (2004), "Evolving to a New Dominant Logic for Marketing", *Journal of Marketing* 68: 1–17.

Verhoef, P. C., E. Kooge and N. Walk (2016), *Creating Value with Big Data Analytics,* Abingdon, Oxon: Routledge.

Vorhies, D. W. and N. A. Morgan (2005), "Benchmarking Marketing Capabilities for Sustainable Competitive Advantage", *Journal of Marketing* 69: 80–94.

Webster, F. E. (1992), "The Changing Role of Marketing in the Corporation", *Journal of Marketing* 56(10): 1–17.

Webster, F. E. (2005), "Back to the Future: Integrating Marketing as Tactics, Strategy and Organizational Culture", *Journal of Marketing* 69 (October): 4–6.

Weihrich, H. (1982), "The TOWS Matrix – A Tool for Situational Analysis", *Long Range Planning* 15: 54–66.

Wernerfelt, B. (1984), "A Resource-based View of the Firm", *Strategic Management Journal* 16: 171–180.

Wind, Y., V. Mahajan and D. J. Swire (1983), "An Empirical Comparison of Standardized Portfolio Models", *Journal of Marketing* 47: 89–99.

Woodruff, R. B. (1997), "Customer Value: The Next Source for Competitive Advantage", *Journal of the Academy of Marketing Science* 25(2): 139–153.

Woodruff, R. B. and S. F. Gardial (1996), *Know Your Customer: New Approaches to Understanding Customer Value and Satisfaction,* Cambridge, MA: Blackwell.

Yoo, B. and N. Donthu (2001), "Developing and Validating a Multidimensional Consumer-based Brand Equity Scale", *Journal of Business Research* 52: 1–14.

Index